MW01257007

Being Muslim in Central Asia

Eurasian Studies Library

HISTORY, SOCIETIES & CULTURES IN EURASIA

VOLUME 9

The titles published in this series are listed at *brill.com/esl*

Being Muslim in Central Asia

Practices, Politics, and Identities

Edited by

Marlene Laruelle

BRILL

LEIDEN | BOSTON

Cover illustration: Front: Custodian of the Ayshah Bibi shrine near Taraz, Kazakhstan (1999). PHOTO ©
MARLENE LARUELLE.

Library of Congress Cataloging-in-Publication Data

Names: Laruelle, Marlene, editor.
Title: Being Muslim in central Asia : practices, politics, and identities /
  edited by Marlene Laruelle.
Description: Leiden ; Boston : Brill, 2018. | Series: Eurasian studies
  library, ISSN 1877-9484 ; VOLUME 9 | Includes bibliographical references
  and index.
Identifiers: LCCN 2017043608 (print) | LCCN 2017046851 (ebook) | ISBN
  9789004357242 (E-book) | ISBN 9789004306806 (hardback : alk. paper)
Subjects: LCSH: Muslims--Asia, Central. | Islam--Asia, Central.
Classification: LCC BP63.A34 (ebook) | LCC BP63.A34 B45 2018 (print) | DDC
  305.6/970958--dc23
LC record available at https://lccn.loc.gov/2017043608

Typeface for the Latin, Greek, and Cyrillic scripts: "Brill". See and download: brill.com/brill-typeface.

ISSN 1877-9484
ISBN 978-90-04-30680-6 (hardback)
ISBN 978-90-04-35724-2 (e-book)

Contents

List of Figures and Tables

Figures

Tables

Notes on Contributors

The Editor

Marlene Laruelle
is an Associate Director and Research Professor at the Institute for European, Russian and Eurasian Studies (IERES), Elliott School of International Affairs, The George Washington University. Dr. Laruelle is also a Co-Director of PONARS (Program on New Approaches to Research and Security in Eurasia), Director of the Central Asia Program at IERES and a researcher at EUCAM (Europe-Central Asia Monitoring), Brussels. Dr. Laruelle received her Ph.D. in history at the National Institute of Oriental Languages and Cultures (INALCO) and her post-doctoral degree in political science at Sciences-Po in Paris.

The Contributors

Aurélie Biard
is a Post-doctoral Fellow at the Labex TEPSIS at the School for Advanced Studies in the Social Sciences (EHESS) in Paris and an associated researcher at the Centre for Turkish, Ottoman, Balkan, and Central Asian Studies (CETOBaC, CNRS). Her research examines the impacts of present-day reconversion to Islam among post-Soviet youths, on community re-building and social integration. As part of the CERIA Initiative she is in charge of the research axis "'Bourgeois' Islam, Prosperity Theology and Ethics in Muslim Eurasia." Her main publications include "The Religious Factor in the Reifications of 'Neo-ethnic' Identities in Kyrgyzstan," in *Nationalities Papers* and "Islam, Ethno-Nationalism, and Transnational Faith Community in Kyrgyzstan," in *Religions, Nations, and Transnationalism in Multiple Modernities*.

Tim Epkenhans
is professor for Islamic Studies at the University of Freiburg (Germany). Tim studied Islamic Studies and History at the Universities of Münster, Cairo, Tehran and Bamberg, where he completed his PhD on early Iranian Modernism in 2002. Between 2002 and 2009, he worked for the German Ministry of Foreign Affairs at the Embassy in Dushanbe and as the director of the OSCE Academy in Bishkek. Tim's research is currently focused on late Soviet and post-Soviet Central Asia, especially the relationship between state, society and religion (Islam). Among his recent publications are *The Origins of the Civil War in Tajikistan: Nationalism, Islamism, and Violent Conflict in Post-Soviet Space* (Lexington, 2016).

Nurgul Esenamanova

Acting Associate Professor, Department of Philosophy and Social and Humanitarian Sciences, Kyrgyz Law Academy. Nurgul has extensive research experience in the sphere of religion, religious policy and various Islamic groups in Kyrgyzstan. Her latest research is on people imprisoned on the extremism charges.

Azamat Junisbai

is an Associate Professor of Sociology at Pitzer College. A native of Kazakhstan, he got his Ph.D. in Sociology from Indiana University in 2009. His interests include social stratification, welfare state attitudes, and public opinion about political modernization in post-communist societies. Dr. Junisbai's research has received generous support from a wide range of sources, including the National Science Foundation (NSF), Social Science Research Council (SSRC), and the National Council for Eurasian and East European Research (NCEEER). His work appeared in *Research in Social Stratification and Mobility, Social Forces, Poetics, Europe-Asia Studies, Central Asian Affairs,* and *Demokratizatsiya: The Journal of Post-Soviet Democratization.*

Barbara Junisbai

is assistant professor of Organizational Studies at Pitzer College, a member of The Claremont Consortium, in the greater Los Angeles metropolitan area. Prior to her appointment, Barbara served as Pitzer's Assistant Dean of Faculty and then as assistant professor of Political Science and International Relations at Nazarbayev University in Astana, Kazakhstan. She holds a Ph.D. from Indiana University. Her work on post-Soviet politics and society has appeared in *Perspectives on Politics, Europe-Asia Studies,* and *Central Asian Affairs,* among others.

Marintha Miles

is currently a PhD student in Cultural Studies at George Mason University. Her research explores the political intersections between migration, transnationalism, economics, gender, and religion in Tajikistan. She has periodically lived in Tajikistan, and worked and researched in the country since 2011. She previously received a MA in Anthropology at The George Washington University, and a BA in International Studies from California State University.

Emil Nasritdinov

is an Associate Professor in the Anthropology Department of American University of Central Asia, Bishkek, Kyrgyzstan. He has first-hand research experience in Kyrgyzstan and in the broader Central Asian region and Russia in the fields of migration, urban planning, international development, Islam, urban life and youth cultures. Being an anthropologist and an urban planner, he approaches his teaching and research from a variety of angles. Multi-disciplinary approach helps him to reconstruct the inherent complexity of the region.

Shahnoza Nozimova
is a Ph.D. Candidate in Political Science at George Mason University's Schar School of Policy and Government. Her research explores state and society relations in Tajikistan with a particular emphasis on women, Islam and nation-building. She was a recipient of the prestigious Doctoral fellowship from the Open Society Foundations. She has received MA in Politics and Security from the OSCE Academy in Bishkek. Previously, Shahnoza has taught at the American University of Central Asia and worked with various international organizations in Tajikistan.

Yaacov Ro'i
is professor of history emeritus at Tel Aviv University, where he served inter-mittently as director of the Center for Russian and East European Studies/the Cummings Center. He was visiting professor at Georgetown University (1977-8 and 1989-90) and visiting fellow at St. Antony's College, Oxford (1995-6). He has published books and articles on Soviet and post-Soviet Islam, Soviet Central Asia, Soviet Middle East policy and Soviet Jewry. His works include *Islam in the Soviet Union from World War II to Gorbachev* (London/New York: Christopher Hurst/Columbia University Press, 2000); *Islam in the CIS: A Threat to Stability?* (London/Washington, Royal Institute of International Affairs/Brookings Institution, 2001); and edited *The USSR and the Muslim World* (London: George Allen Unwin, 1984); *Muslim Eurasia: Conflicting Legacies* (London: Frank Cass, 1995); and *Democracy and Pluralism in Muslim Eurasia* (London: Frank Cass, 2004).

Wendell Schwab
is the Coordinator of the Bachelor of Philosophy Program and a Senior Academic Adviser at Pennsylvania State University. He studies Islamic media and Islamic traditions of learning in Kazakhstan. His work has appeared in journals such as *Central Asian Affairs, Central Asian Survey, Anthropology of East Europe Review,* and *Contemporary Islam.*

Manja Stephan-Emmrich
is a junior professor of Islam in Asian and African Societies at the Institute for Asian and African Studies, Humboldt-Universität zu Berlin. Besides, she is a

Principal Investigator at the Berlin Graduate School Muslim Cultures and Societies. She holds a Ph.D. in Social and Cultural Anthropology from Max Planck Institute for Social Anthropology and Martin-Luther Universität in Halle/Wittenberg, was recently a fellow at IGK Work and Human Lifecycle in Global History at Humboldt-Universität zu Berlin, and a visiting scholar at the Research network Reconfigurations: History, Memory and Transformation Processes in the Middle East and North Africa at the Philipps-Universität Marburg. She has published on Islamic education, Muslim youth, urban religion, Gulf migration and transnational Islam in Central Asia. Currently, she is completing a book manuscript on entangled religious and economic ties between Central Asia and the Middle East titled *Situating Muslim mobilities: knowledge, work, and piety in the Tajik Dubai business sector.*

Rano Turaeva

(author name Turaeva) is an associated researcher at Max Planck Institute for Social Anthropology in Halle Saale in Germany. She is currently working on the project 'The role of Mosques in integration of migrants in Russia' and has been writing on the topics of migration, entrepreneurship, informal economies, gender, border studies, identity and inter-ethnic relations. She published in such journals as *Central Asian Survey, Inner Asia, Communist and post-Communist studies, Anthropology of Middle East.* Her book based on her PhD thesis is out with Routledge in 2016 under the title *Migration and Identity: The Uzbek Experience.*

Alon Wainer

holds an MA degree in Russian and Soviet History from Tel Aviv University in Israel. He is currently a Ph.D. student at Tel Aviv University and is working on his thesis, "The rise of Uzbek and Kyrgyz Nationalism during the Khrushchev's Era". For the past 17 years Alon has constantly traveled to post-Soviet Central Asia, to Uzbekistan and Kyrgyzstan in particular. He has closely followed the process of national identity building in these countries and his close ties to locals grant him an insider's view of these processes. Alon is fluent in Russian and has working skills in Uzbek. Over the years since the new states' independence he has carried out research in archives in both Uzbekistan and Kyrgyzstan, has participated in field research and performed numerous interviews with locals.

Alexander Wolters

is Director of the OSCE Academy in Bishkek. In the past years he has been teaching as DAAD Visiting Professor at the Academy and the American

University of Central Asia. He has worked in Kyrgyzstan and the wider region of Central Asia for more than 10 years. Following a study year in Tambov, Russia, he did his MA in Cultural Sciences at the European University Viadrina in Frankfurt (Oder), Germany, where he also completed his Ph.D. in political sociology in 2012. In his work he focuses on the evolution of the political system in Kyrgyzstan following the turbulent times in the republic after 2005. Other research interests are the transformation of state/society relations in Central Asia, the role of public opinion as well as the nexus of religion, education, and the political. He has published his work in various journals, including *Osteuropa* and *Central Asian Affairs*.

Galina M. Yemelianova

is Associate Professor of Eurasian Studies at the Centre of Russian, European and Eurasian Studies at the University of Birmingham, UK. She is Co-Editor of *Caucasus Survey,* a Member of the National Advisory Board of *Europe-Asia Studies* (both by Routledge) and a Member of the Editorial Board of *Oriens* (by Nauka, Moscow). Her research interests encompass history, culture and politics in the Middle East and Muslim Eurasia and, particularly, the relationship between Islam, national identity and statehood in Central Asia, the Caucasus and the Volga region. Her numerous publications include *Central Asia: An Introduction* (Edinburgh University Press, 2018, forthcoming); *Many Faces of the Caucasus* (co-ed., Routledge, 2014); *Radical Islam in the former Soviet Union* (ed., Routledge, 2010); *Islam in post-Soviet Russia: Private and Public Faces* (co-ed., Routledge, 2003), *Russia and Islam: A Historical Survey* (Palgrave, 2002); and *Yemen during the Period of the First Ottoman Conquest, 1538-1635* (Nauka, 1988).

Baurzhan Zhussupov

MS, has been Biostatistics Department Chair at the Kazakh National Medical University. He held several positions at the Republican Center for Study of Public Opinion in Almaty, Kazakhstan. He worked at the Global Health Research Center of Central Asia, US CDC Central Asian office, AIDS Foundation East-West. Over the past 25 years, he has designed and implemented sociological and epidemiological studies in Kazakhstan.

Introduction

Marlene Laruelle

This edited volume results from the Central Eurasia–Religion in International Affairs (CERIA) Initiative, hosted at The George Washington University's Central Asia Program. The CERIA Initiative aims to promote state-of-the-art research on religion in contemporary Central Asia, understanding religion as a "societal shaper" – a roadmap for navigating quickly changing social and cultural values. Religion is not a given but a construct that appears alongside other aspects of life. It can thus take on multiple colors and identities, from a purely transcendental faith in God to a cauldron of ideological ferment for political ideology, via diverse culture-, community-, and history-based phenomena that help people situate themselves in the world and define what makes sense for them.

Since the end of the 1990s, with the Taliban's seizure of power in Afghanistan, and even more so since the terrorist attacks of 9/11 and the subsequent "war on terror," the policy narrative on the role of Islam in Central Asia has been shaped by a sense of danger, with analysis of religion often seen as an offshoot of security studies. Paradoxically, the Western policy community and the Central Asian regimes share similar misperceptions of Islam. They tend, though to differing extents, to conflate Islamic practices, political Islam, and paths to violence, providing security-oriented explanations of local political and social changes. The new, post-Soviet expressions of religiosity are over-interpreted as signaling "risks of radicalization." With every emergence of a new Islamist movement, from the Islamic Movement of Uzbekistan in the 1990s to al-Qaeda in the 2000s and the Islamic State in the 2010s, the global policy community has expressed concerns about the "radicalization" of Islam in Central Asia. These skewed interpretations have damaged the image of Islam in general and its appropriate place in the societies of Central Asia. There is, for instance, a striking contrast between the positive image of Buddhism in the revival of political activism in Tibet, thanks in large part to the media visibility of the Dalai Lama, and similar trends among Uyghurs in Xinjiang, which tend to be viewed negatively because Uyghur claims are associated with an Islamic identity.

However, the so-called "re-Islamization" of Central Asian societies since the collapse of the USSR has very little to do with anything political. It is, above all, an apolitical re-traditionalization marked by calls for more conservative mores and stricter gender segregation; and demands for observance of (some) Islamic rites by younger generations. This re-traditionalization aims to reconsolidate the social fabric at a time of massive upheaval and to construct new individual identities in harmony with the times but respectful of what is understood as national belonging. The local traditions of submission to the authorities, of respect for long-standing hierarchies, of assimilating religion into the community, whether national or local, are now competing with imported models in which Islam is lived as a more universal religion, less subordinated to the national or local, more confrontational and more individualist. Other, albeit smaller, trends are also visible: in Kyrgyzstan and Kazakhstan, some of the younger generations call for a kind of Islamo-nationalist ideology; globalized networks of believers work with foreign proselytizing groups such as the Tablighi Jama'at to reach out to a new community of believers; merchant groups and small entrepreneurs instrumentalize Islam to legitimize their economic success and to develop informal networks of solidarity through Islamic charities. Growing segments of the Kyrgyz and Tajik populations invoke Islam, sometimes Shari'a, to demand more social justice, less corruption, and "compensation" from states failing to deliver basic public services and security.

The field of studying Islam—the study of other religions, i.e. Christianity, focuses almost exclusively on conversion and proselytizing—has evolved dramatically since the collapse of the Soviet Union. In the 1990s, Western Sovietologists working on religion, heirs of Alexandre Bennigsen (1913–1988), found themselves challenged by scholars from Middle Eastern studies, who claimed that their knowledge of Islamic societies provided a better calibrated tool to approach the new Central Asia. Nonetheless, this new school faced difficulties in integrating the Soviet legacy and longer historical continuities in its analytical toolbox and indirectly reinforced the misreading that Central Asia was on the path to becoming a second Afghanistan or Pakistan. In the 2000s, a new generation of scholars emerged, with a more intimate knowledge of the region—often specializing in only one country—and of local languages. This new generation combined its area expertise with ongoing theoretical discussions in the social sciences and humanities with greater comparative skills than before. Academic disciplines such as cultural anthropology have deepened our knowledge of Islam to the micro-level of community, family, and gender relations, offering a more complex picture in which religion is one among many elements of everyday life impacted by macro-level political and socioeconomic changes.

Thanks to this new generation of scholars, our understanding of Islam and what it means in contemporary Central Asia has dramatically evolved and increased in complexity. The question of the "revival" of Islam has been transformed by a better understanding of the intricacies of Muslim practices during

Soviet times and the revelation of Islamic plural debates and theological conflicts inside the Spiritual Board of Muslims of Central Asia and Kazakhstan (SADUM). It also evolved by ending the simplistic division between "foreign influences" coming from abroad and domestic situations on the ground: Central Asian Islam is today a largely globalized phenomenon, with multilayered interactions that blur the boundaries between "home" and "abroad" and create transnational identities in tune with the rest of the Islamic *Ummah*. In terms of external influences, Turkey's preeminence in the early 1990s has been eclipsed by the Gulf countries, particularly the Emirates and Dubai, which are seen as the embodiment of a successful Muslim modernity, and by proselytizing groups such as Tablighi Jama'at coming from the South Asian subcontinent. Like any community, Central Asian Muslims are shaped by the multiple, contradictory definitions of what is "their own," national and traditional, and what is "other," foreign and new, especially in relation to everything that can be labelled as Arab.

One driver for new research has been to conceptualize that the central issue is not how external observers typologize the way Central Asians express their "Muslimness," but the fact that the fight to define the "right Islam" is a struggle going on *inside* the Muslim communities themselves. Some call for a Soviet-style Islam that would keep the public space secular and confine Islam to being merely one part of national traditions and identities; others call for Islam to be an individual practice carried out by each citizen according to their own conscience. Still others hope for a more normative Islam that prescribes individual manners and collective practices. Competing narratives, references and practices have therefore become the new normal for Central Asian societies. Some defend the Hanafi school against "intrusions" of Hanbali rituals; others debate the content of Salafism, Wahhabism, Deobandism, so-called radical Islam or unaffiliated Internet preachers; others discuss the Islamic legitimacy of pilgrims to local shrines and traditional medicine. The spectrum of Islamic practice is broad, stretching from Muslim "born-agains" to private entrepreneurs who capitalize on their "Muslimness" to justify their economic success in the name of an Islamic theology of prosperity. Across the region as a whole, several elements signal the structuring of Islam as a central reference for individual and collective identities: calls for teaching religion in the school system, rapid increases in the number of people fasting during Ramadan, and a rise in the number of people participating in *zakat* – giving alms to the poor and needy. References to Shari'a as religious orthodoxy, largely absent from Central Asian traditions, have become visible in Tajikistan and Kyrgyzstan. Central Asian Islamic communities are now deeply plural.

In post-Soviet Central Asia, the relationship between Islam and the state has often had a schizophrenic character: Islam has been glorified as a religion of the nation, local pilgrimage sites have been valorized, and the great national figures linked to Sufism have been celebrated, but at the same time religious practices have been monitored, sermons in the mosques are increasingly controlled, religious education is highly restricted, and interactions with the rest of the *Ummah* are looked upon with suspicion. However, the interaction between state and society emerges as much more complex than the black-and-white narrative of advocacy groups criticizing the lack of religious freedom in the region and the repressive practices of the state structures toward religion.

First, a large segment of Central Asian societies supports the securitization approach to Islam that is advanced by the state, a trend reinforced by the scary story of young people "lost" to jihad in Syria. Second, the Spiritual Boards and Council for Religious Affairs play an ambiguous role in "normalizing" what to accept and what to reject in Islamic practices and discourses. Third, some political elites, especially economic elites, are attracted by a new Islamic identity inspired by Dubai, and security service officers are often very respectful of religious leaders and of their authority. All these trends confirm, if such confirmation is needed, that the state secularism inherited from the Soviet regime is progressively eroding in the face of multiple ways to display "Muslimness." As everywhere in the world, social tensions within Muslim communities and in their interaction with non-Muslims give a large room to debates about how women dress, because the topic embodies issues of purity, morality, self-respect, and the call for a more control over a rapidly evolving society.

In the first part of the volume, we discuss what it means to be a Muslim in today's Central Asia by looking at both historical and sociological features. In Chapter 1, Galina Yemelianova argues that, throughout history, Central Asians developed a particular form of Islam that presented a productive and fluid synergy between Islam per se, their tribal legal and customary norms, and Tengrian and Zoroastrian beliefs and practices. It is characterized by a high level of doctrinal and functional adaptability to shifting political and cultural environments, the prevalence of Sufism (mystical Islam), and oral, rather than book-based, Islamic tradition. A common Eurasian space and lengthy shared political history of Central Asians and other peoples of Muslim Eurasia account for considerable similarities in their Islamic trajectories.

In Chapter 2, Barbara Junisbai, Azamat Junisbai, and Baurzhan Zhussupov investigate the rising religiosity and orthodoxy among Central Asian Muslims, drawing on two waves of public opinion surveys conducted in Kazakhstan and Kyrgyzstan in 2007 and 2012. They confirm that a religious revival is underway; however, cross-national variations remain important: religious practice, as measured by daily prayer and weekly mosque attendance, is up in Kyrgyzstan, but has fallen in Kazakhstan. They attribute these differences to political context, both in terms of cross-national political variation and regional differences within each country. In Chapter 3, Yaacov Ro'i and Alon Wainer focus on Uzbekistan and Uzbek identity and its relationship to Islam by looking at some 200 interviews with Uzbek students. While almost everyone considers himself or herself a Muslim, the vast majority perceive themselves, above all, as citizens of Uzbekistan. Moreover, their Islam is not reflected primarily in Islamic practice but rather in a somewhat nebulous Islamic traditionalism. In the international arena, young Uzbeks tend to prefer Muslim over non-Muslim peoples and communities, but not necessarily as destinations for labor migration.

The second part of the volume is devoted to Islam, politics and the state. Tim Epkenhans begins by analyzing the evolution of the Islamic Renaissance Party of Tajikistan (IRPT), the only Islamic party recognized in Central Asia (until it was banned in 2015, when the Tajik authorities abandoned the principles of the 1997 General Peace Accord, which had ended the country's civil war). Since then, the IRPT has distinguished itself as a credible oppositional political party committed to democratic principles and with an almost imperceptible religious agenda. By shifting the IRPT's attention to issues of democratization and socioeconomic development, its chairman, Muhiddin Kabirī, opened the IRPT to a younger electorate, although continuous defamation campaigns and government persecution have worn down the IRPT's activists and its electorate.

Chapter 5, by Aurélie Biard, delves into the political uses of Islam in the Kyrgyzstani Fergana Valley, through case studies of the main Kyrgyzstani Uzbek theologians based in the city of Karu-Suu, who appear to be core actors in re-Islamization and propagators of Saudi-style Salafi Islam. She argues that religious debates and postures concerning the relationship to secular power are inscribed in patronage and personal clientelist networks, as well as local power struggles. She states that we are now witnessing the reactivation of a religious utopia that challenges the existing political and financial order through local rhetoric about establishing an idealized caliphate, conveying a message not only of social justice but also of economic transparency and free trade.

In Chapter 6, Alexander Wolters examines another way in which the Central Asian states have instrumentalized Islam—namely, Islamic finance. Rather a recent phenomenon in the region, it was only with the beginning of the global financial crisis in 2007 that the cooperation between the states and the Islamic Development Bank resulted in domestic initiatives to establish forms of Islamic banking. Wolters sees a correlation between the subsequent development of such initiatives and the unfolding political crises. Specifically, the Central Asian states were eager to connect to available streams of Islamic investment capital in the early stages of the international financial crisis, but their commitment to further adapt declined when they entered periods of political crisis that forced them to reorder their reform priorities.

The third part of the volume explores the changing role of Islam in terms of societal and cultural values. Wendell Schwab looks at Asyl Arna, the most popular Islamic television channel and dominant Islamic media company in Kazakhstan. He examines how images on the social media pages of Asyl Arna create a way of understanding and engaging in contemporary Islamic life. The visual culture of Asyl Arna's social media promotes Islam as an achievable part of a middle-class lifestyle that can provide simple rules for a pious, economically successful life and a connection to the holy life through the Qur'an. Manja Stephan-Emmrich follows this search by investigating Muslim self-fashioning, migration, and (be-)longing in the Tajik–Dubai business. She analyzes how young, well-educated, and multilingual Tajiks involved in Dubai's various business fields create, shape, and draw on a sense of cosmopolitanism to convert their uncertain status as "Tajik migrants" into that of economically autonomous "Muslim businessmen." Pointing to the mutual conditionality of longing and belonging in migrant cosmopolitanism, she offers a nuanced picture of everyday life in Dubai that goes beyond the "spectacularity" of the city, challenging the prevailing representation of Tajik Muslims' engagement in transnational Islam as a security matter only. And in Chapter 9, Rano Turaeva explores the space of informal economies, focusing on transnational entrepreneurs between Central Asia and Russia. These male and female entrepreneurs live mobile economic lives in which Islam plays a central role in regulating informal economies. Islamic belonging has progressively become a stronger marker of identity than ethnicity among Central Asian migrants in Russia, and mosque communities have grown in influence as places to socialize.

The last section of the volume investigates female attire as a public debate. Emil Nasritdinov and Nurgul Esenamanova explore how the growing community of practicing Muslims asserts the right to be in the city, live according to its religious ideals, and create Islamic urban spaces. Such claims do not remain uncontested and, because religious identity has a strong visual manifestation, religious claims—especially female attire—become the subject of strong public debate. This contestation overlaps with socially constructed gender hierarchies—religious/secular claims over the urban space turn into men's claims over women, with both sides (religious and secular) claiming to know what women should wear.

Shahnoza Nozimova pursues the discussion by studying how Islamic veiling has occupied center stage in the public debate in Tajikistan. State officials and institutions view it as alien, while proponents argue that it is a religious obligation to be fulfilled by every pious woman, especially when outside of her home. She demonstrates that, as women experience increased pressure to seek employment outside of the home, there appears to be a need to construct new, socially acceptable mechanisms to conform to patriarchy and to protect female purity and honor: hijab and (pious) Islamic identity can potentially offer both. Still analyzing Tajikistan, Marintha Miles explores why women adopt hijab and other conservative head coverings as they seek identity and belonging in an evolving society, in the face of an incumbent regime that views the veiled Muslim woman as a threat to national identity.

This volume would not have been possible without the generous support of the Henry Luce Foundation and the work done by Sebastien Peyrouse in contacting authors and collecting first drafts of the papers for their publication in *Central Asian Affairs*.

PART 1

What Does It Mean to Be a Muslim in Today's Central Asia?

∴

CHAPTER 1

How 'Muslim' are Central Asian Muslims?
A Historical and Comparative Enquiry

Galina Yemelianova

Central Asia[1]—defined here as the post-Soviet republics of Uzbekistan, Tajikistan, Kazakhstan, Kyrgyzstan, and Turkmenistan—remains rather poorly known and understood in the West. At the policy level, the region has received attention for its abundant energy resources, especially on the territory of Kazakhstan and Turkmenistan, and its precarious neighborhood with war-stricken Afghanistan and unpredictable Shi'a Iran. In cultural terms, Central Asian states have been largely perceived as part of the Muslim world, comparable to Afghanistan, Pakistan, and other "stans" in terms of their economic development, social order, ethno-linguistics, and the Islamic religiosity of its population. Such a narrow and functional approach to Central Asia among Western policymakers, nongovernmental organizations (NGOs), and journalists has been complemented by the relative thinness and patchiness of the region's scholarly coverage. Thus, English-language Central Asian studies have primarily focused on contemporary issues, especially related to regime transition, energy politics and security, drug trafficking, and the so-called Islamic revival and Islamic radicalization.

The insufficient Western academic understanding of Central Asia, particularly the role of Islam, has been due to a number of factors. One has been the domination of regional studies in general, and Central Asian studies in

---

1   Here the term "Central Asia" is used in the narrow sense, referring to the five post-Soviet states of Uzbekistan, Kazakhstan, Kyrgyzstan, Turkmenistan, and Tajikistan. In the broader sense, the term "Central Asia" refers to a wider region, which in different historical periods also included present-day Afghanistan, northwestern Pakistan, northern Iran, southern Caucasus, northern Turkey, northern India, northwestern China, Tibet, Inner and Outer Mongolia, and eastern Russia. In some studies, the region is also referred to as Inner Asia or Central Eurasia. See, for example, N. Di Cosmo (ed.), *The Cambridge History of Inner Asia: The Chinggisid Age* (Cambridge: Cambridge University Press, 2009); P.B. Golden, *Central Asia in World History* (Oxford: Oxford University Press, 2011); K.A. Erturk (ed.), *Rethinking Central Asia: Non-Eurocentric Studies in History, Social Structure, and Identity* (Reading, UK: Ithaca Press, 1999), 1–8; D. Sinor, *Inner Asia: History, Civilization, Languages: A Syllabus* (Bloomington: Indiana University Press, 1969); S. Soucek, *A History of Inner Asia* (Cambridge: Cambridge University Press, 2000).

© KONINKLIJKE BRILL NV, LEIDEN, 2018 | DOI 10.1163/9789004357242_003

particular, by social and political scientists who favor theoretical robustness over "messy" empirics, an approach that tends to dissect selective and often policy-driven phenomena by means of established and intrinsically Eurocentric theoretical models and paradigms.[2] Accordingly, they largely employ deductive, quantitative research methods and rely extensively on secondary, rather than primary, sources in English and, to a lesser extent, in Russian. This is not to say that there have been no in-depth and primary-source-based studies on Islam in Central Asia by a relatively small number of Islamic studies scholars, historians, anthropologists, ethnographers, and sociologists.[3] However, those have often had a narrow geographical, temporal, or thematic focus that obscured the wider picture.

A second reason has been the post-Cold War influx into Central Asian studies of ex-Sovietologists and Kremlinologists and their disciples, who consciously or unconsciously continue to view the Central Asian region and its constituent states as objects of powerful external political and religious impulses, rather

---

2   This, and other assessments related to the state of Central Asian and other regional studies in the West, is evidently subjective but based on the author's experience of over two decades within Western academia.

3   See, for example, Y.E. Bregel, *Historical Atlas of Central Asia* (Leiden: Brill, 2003); K. Collins, *Clan Politics and Regime Transition in Central Asia* (Cambridge: Cambridge University Press, 2006); R.D. Crews, *For Prophet and Tsar: Islam and Empire in Russia and Central Asia* (Cambridge, MA: Harvard University Press, 2006); H. Carrere d'Encausse, *Islam and the Russian Empire: Reform and Revolution in Central Asia* (London: I.B. Tauris, 2009); D. DeWeese, *Studies of Sufism in Central Asia* (Farnham, UK: Ashgate, 2012); P.G. Geiss, *Pre-Tsarist and Tsarist Central Asia: Communal Commitment and Political Order in Change* (London: Routledge, 2003); A. Khalid, *Islam after Communism: Religion and Politics in Central Asia* (Berkeley: University of California Press, 2007); A. Von Kugelgen, *Legitimizatsiia sredneaziatskoi dinastii Mangytov v proizvedeniiakh ikh istorikov (XVIII–XIX vv.)* (Almaty: Dayk-Press, 2004); M. Louw, *Everyday Islam in Post-Soviet Central Asia* (London: Routledge, 2008); S. Peyrouse, *Turkmenistan: Strategies of Power, Dilemmas of Development* (Armonk, NY: M.E. Sharpe, 2012); B.G. Privratsky, *Muslim Turkistan: Kazak Religion and Collective Memory* (Richmond, UK: Curzon Press, 2001); M. Reeves, *Border Work: Spatial Lives of the State in Rural Central Asia* (Ithaca, NY: Cornell University Press, 2014); J. Meyer, *Turks across Empires: Marketing Muslim Identities in the Russian-Ottoman Borderlands, 1856–1956* (Oxford: Oxford University Press, 2014); M. Reeves, "The Time of the Border: Contingency, Conflict, and Popular Statism at the Kyrgyzstan–Uzbekistan Border," in M. Reeves, J. Rasanayagam, and J. Beyer (eds), *Ethnographies of the State in Central Asia* (Bloomington: Indiana University Press, 2014), 198–221; K. Satoru, "Sunni-Shi'i Relations in the Russian Protectorate of Bukhara, as Perceived by the Local 'Ulama'," in U. Tomohiko (ed.), *Asiatic Russia: Imperial Power in Regional and International Contexts* (New York: Routledge, 2012), 189–215.

than self-defined and self-contained entities with unique characteristics and dynamics.

A third reason has been the general decline of funding for interdisciplinary area studies (despite the rhetorical trumpeting of inter- and multi-disciplinarianism), leading to a reduction in the number of Western scholars fluent enough in Central Asian and other languages of the various peoples of the ex-USSR to conduct in-depth empirical research in the region. The arrival in Western universities of a notable number of students from Central Asia has not significantly altered this trend due to their largely uncritical acceptance of Eurocentric political/social science theoretical models.

Finally, there is the practical, logistical, and political difficulties, bordering on impossibility, of conducting both historical and contemporary empirical research on Islam in present-day Central Asia—especially in Turkmenistan and Uzbekistan but increasingly in Tajikistan and Kazakhstan—due to the authorities' tight control over the religious sphere and the local people's apprehension about any form of engagement in externally funded research on Islam-related topics.

These four epistemological difficulties and inadequacies have contributed to the emergence and recycling of a series of problematic perceptions and expectations regarding the social, political, and religious development of Central Asia. Thus, in the early 1990s it was expected that the region would succumb to the political, economic, and religious influence of its main Muslim neighbors (Turkey, Iran, and Afghanistan).[4] Later on, as the Taliban emerged in neighboring Afghanistan, the region was expected to succumb to radical Islam, including *jihadism*.[5] In the second decade of the 2000s, some observers predicted that the region would join the "Arab Spring" uprising and undergo violent regime change.[6]

---

4   See, for example, S.T. Hunter, "Iran, Central Asia, and the Opening of the Islamic Iron Curtain," in R. Sagdeev and S. Eisenhower (eds), *Islam and Central Asia: An Enduring Legacy or an Evolving Threat?* (Washington, D.C.: Center for Political and Strategic Studies, 2000), 171–191; A. Rashid, "Islam in Central Asia: Afghanistan and Pakistan," in Sagdeev and Eisenhower, *Islam and Central Asia*, 213–236; M.H. Yavuz, "Turkish Identity Politics and Central Asia," in Sagdeev and Eisenhower, *Islam and Central Asia*, 193–211.

5   See, for example, E. Karagiannis, *Political Islam in Central Asia: The Challenge of Hizb ut-Tahrir* (London: Routledge, 2010); A. Rashid, *Jihad: The Rise of Militant Islam in Central Asia* (New Haven, CT: Yale University Press, 2002).

6   See, for example, A. Schmidtz and A. Wolters, "Political Protest in Central Asia: Potentials and Dynamics," *SWP Research Paper No. 7* (Berlin, German Institute for International and Security Affairs, 2012), <https://www.swp-berlin.org/fileadmin/contents/products/research_pa

This chapter attempts to counter the prevailing compartmentalization of various cultural and socio-political phenomena of Central Asia through an integrated, interdisciplinary framework. It treats Central Asia as a historically and culturally self-sufficient region with intrinsic characteristics and dynamics. At the same time, it locates Central Asia within the spatial and cultural Eurasian context[7] and assesses the legacy of the Soviet transformation for its relations with some other parts of the post-Soviet space and the Middle East. It argues that historically, the culture and identities of various peoples of Central Asia have been shaped by four major influences. One is associated with the ancient Sogdians, who, long before the arrival of Islam in Central Asia, created a distinctive Central Asian cultural blueprint that has persisted throughout history. The second relates to the lengthy domination of Central Asia and wider Eurasia by Turco-Mongol nomads. The third relates to the arrival of Islam in Central Asia in the seventh century AD and the region's subsequent Persianized Islamization. The fourth is linked to the late nineteenth century Russian conquest, followed by Sovietization in the twentieth century. Since the disintegration of the USSR in 1991, the Islamic dynamic in Central Asia has been marginally affected by the partial re-integration of the region within the wider Muslim world and the advancing globalization and digitalization of Islam.

The Silk Road and the Sogdians

The Sogdians were an eastern Iranian people who originated from Sogdiana, an urbanized and highly developed state, which in the ancient period and the Middle Ages existed on the territory corresponding to the Samarqand- and Bukhara-centered regions of modern Uzbekistan and the Sughd region of modern Tajikistan. Later on, the Arabs named this region *Mawarannahr* ("what

---

pers/2012_RP07_smz_wolters.pdf>; "Governments Move to Thwart 'Arab Spring' in Central Asia," *Eurasianet*, April 28, 2011, <http://www.eurasianet.org/node/63386>.

7   Here, the term "Eurasia" is used to denote a socio-cultural area, rather than the much wider geographic region of Eurasia. It also differs from Russia-centered concepts of Eurasia and Eurasian ideology pioneered in the 1920s by Nikolai Trubetskoi and other Russian émigré intellectuals and re-appropriated and instrumentalized by post-Soviet Russian and Kazakhstani political elites. See more on ideological Eurasianism in M. Laruelle, *Russian Eurasianism: An Ideology of Empire* (Baltimore, MD: Johns Hopkins University Press, 2008); M. Bassin, S. Glebov, and M. Laruelle (eds) *Between Europe and Asia: The Origins, Theories, and Legacies of Russian Eurasianism* (Pittsburgh, PA: University of Pittsburgh Press, 2015); M. Bassin, *The Gumilev Mystique: Biopolitics, Eurasianism, and the Construction of Community in Modern Russia* (Ithaca, London: Cornell University Press, 2016).

is beyond the river," i.e., the Amu Darya), while the Romans called it *Transoxania* ("land beyond Oxus"). Throughout their 1,500-year history, the Sogdians, not the Chinese, acted as the main agents for luxury goods along the Silk Road[8] connecting China to Balkh (Bactria), India, Iran, and the Byzantine and Hellenized Middle East, on one side, and to the steppes of Eurasia, on the other. The Sogdian merchants were genuine "middle men" who introduced Central Asia to a diversity of music, cuisine, religions and belief systems, including Manichaeism, Zoroastrianism, Buddhism, and Christianity. They also facilitated the exchange and transfer of practical and scientific knowledge and administrative skills.[9]

In the sixth century AD, the Sogdians introduced Turkic nomads of the steppes to their first alphabet, as well as their administrative system.[10] In the eighth century AD they brought paper production technology to the Middle East, and subsequently to Europe, by optimizing the paper-making process that they had learned from Chinese prisoners, who were brought to Samarqand in the wake of the Chinese Tan Dynasty's defeat by the Arab Abbasid Caliphate in 751 AD in Talas (in modern Kyrgyzstan). Sogdian paper-making skills created the basis for the world's largest library of the Middle Ages—*Bayt al-Hikma/Dar al-Hikma* (House of Wisdom)—in Baghdad.[11] Thus, through centuries of multi-vector trade, as well as other economic and cultural activities, the Sogdians laid the foundation for the culture of religious and ethnic pluralism and adaptability to rapidly changing political environments.

The Sogdian cultural input formed the cornerstone of Central Asian identity, which persisted long after the demise of Sogdiana in the eighth century AD

---

8 It is worth noting that contemporary geopolitical economic projects of the Silk Road, known as the China-driven "New Silk Road Economic Belt" and the US-centered "New Silk Road" differ significantly from their historical predecessor in terms of geography and major actors and treat Central Asia as an object or a transit territory. See more in C. Devonshire-Ellis, *The Great Eurasian Game and the String of Pearls* (Hong Kong: Asia Briefing, 2015); M. Laruelle, "US New Silk Road," *Eurasian Geography and Economics,* 56, no. 4 (2015): 360–375; S. Peyrouse and G. Raballand, "The New Silk Road Initiative's Questionable Economic Rationality," *Eurasian Geography and Economics,* 56, no. 4 (2015): 405–420.

9 For more on the role of the Sogdians in the Silk Road, see E. de la Vaissiere, "Sogdian Trade," *Encyclopaedia Iranica*, online edition (New York, 2004), <http://www.iranicaonline. org/articles/sogdian-trade>; N. Nurulla-Hodjaeva, "'Tantsuiushchie' kuptsi vne imperii na shelkovom puti," *Vestnik MGIMO-Universiteta*, 1, no. 52 (2017): 119–139.

10 E. de la Vaissiere, "Sogdiana iii," *Encyclopaedia Iranica*, online edition (New York, 2011), 15, <http://www.iranicaonline.org/articles/sogdiana-iii-history and archeology>.

11 N. Nurulla-Hodjaeva, *Odin iz fragmentov istorii znaniia: dom mudrosti Abbasidov i o chernilakh v reke Tigr*, 2016, <http://www.mgl.ru/www/library/177/The_Abbasids.html>.

in the face of the Abbasid advance and the drastic changes in the Chinese imperial economy, which were triggered by the An Lu-shan rebellion in China in 755 AD.[12] In the ninth and tenth centuries most Sogdians, as well as the Khorezmians, Baktrians, and some other of Central Asia's sedentary people who spoke eastern Iranian dialects, were included within the Persian-dominated part of the Abbasid Caliphate and subsequently became culturally and linguistically Persianized (i.e., switched from an eastern Iranian to a western Iranian language).[13]

The Sogdian legacy shaped the political culture of the Islamized Samanids who in 819–999 AD created their state in Mawarannahr, which also encompassed the territories of present-day Turkmenistan, Afghanistan, and Pakistan. The Samanid state soon acquired de facto independence from its Abbasid suzerains in Baghdad. Thus, while the Samanid ruling elite was Persian-speaking and affiliated with Sunni Islam, their subjects included sedentary and nomadic peoples of Persian, Turkic, and other ethnic origins, who adhered to Sunni or Shi'a Islam, as well as Zoroastrianism, Buddhism, and Christianity. The Samanids, like their Sogdian predecessors, encouraged the development of sciences and arts and their capital cities of Samarqand (819–892 AD) and Bukhara (892–999 AD) rivaled Baghdad in terms of their advances in philosophy, science, art, and Islamic theology. They produced such great thinkers of the Middle Ages as Rudaki (858–941), Al-Farabi (872–950), Ferdowsi (940–1020), Al-Biruni (973–1048), and Ibn Sina (Avicenna, 980–1037), who made major contributions to the development of medicine, pharmacology, geography, astronomy, physics, mathematics, political philosophy and Islamic theology. A powerful reminder of the historical role of the Sogdians and Samanids has been the incorporation of the Samanid lineage into the nation-building project of post-Soviet Tajikistan.[14]

12   During the An Lushan Rebellion, 75–63 AD, the Sogdians joined the anti-Tan forces. E.G. Pulleyblank, *The Background of the Rebellion of An Lu-Shan* (London: Oxford University Press, 1955).

13   Compared to Tajiks, Pamiris of Tajikistan's Gorno-Badakshan speak an East Iranian language. See P. Bergne, *The Birth of Tajikistan: National Identity and the Origins of the Republic* (London: I.B. Tauris, 2009), 5.

14   D. Dagiev, *Regime Transition in Central Asia: Stateness, Nationalism, and Political Change in Tajikistan and Uzbekistan* (London: Routledge, 2014), 127.

The Steppe Factor and the Turkic–Persian Fusion

Another constituent part of the Central Asian culture and identity developed as a result of over five centuries of nomadic Turco-Mongol domination.[15] In 999 AD the Samanids were defeated by the Turkic-speaking Qarakhanids, who had arrived from present-day southern Kazakhstan, Kyrgyzstan, and western Xinjiang and established the Qarakhanid Khanate (999–1211) in Mawarannahr. In the eleventh century the western part of Central Asia was conquered by the Seljuks, the Oghuz Turks who came from the Aral Sea, and became part of the vast Seljukid empire (1037–1194), which stretched from the Hindu Kush to eastern Anatolia and the Persian Gulf (1037–1194). The Seljuk linguistic imprint is present in Central Asia's Oghuz-speaking Turkmen, as well as contemporary Turks and Azerbaijanis. In the early thirteenth century, Central Asia, along with most of Eurasia, was included within the enormous multi-ethnic and multi-confessional Mongol empire (1206–1368), created by Genghiz Khan (1162–1227). In the fourteenth century the region became part of the Timurid empire (1370–1507), created by Timur (1336–1405), a Mongol chieftain who modelled himself on Genghiz Khan.

The lengthy Genghizid and Timurid domination emphasized the Eurasian dimension of Central Asia by creating considerable structural and cultural affinities between it and other Eurasian polities under extended Genghizid/Timurid control. In the political sphere, the Genghizid/Timurid legacy manifested itself in the extreme concentration of power at the center, the merger of the ruling clan with the state, and the supremacy of personal relations between a ruler and a subject over any other relations, defined by institutional, social, or ethno-national affiliation.[16] It accounted for the rulers' reliance on genealogical and kinship, rather than Islamic mechanisms to legitimize their authority and for people's acceptance of the authority of rulers, irrespective of their policies, personal qualities, and their conformity with Islamic requirements for a

---

15 Despite the centrality of the nomadic Turco-Mongol factor in the political and societal development of Muslim Central Asia, as well as some other parts of Eurasia, it has not received due credit in historical studies on the region, which were largely based on written sources emanating from representatives of town-centered sedentary culture. The latter tended to highlight their cultural and political superiority over their nomadic counterparts. N. Masanov, "Mifologizatsiia problem etnogeneza kazakhskogo naroda i kazakhskoi nomadnoi kul'tury," in N. Masanov, Z. Abylkhozhin, and I. Erofeeva, *Nauchnoe znanie i mifotvorchestvo v sovremennoi istoriografii Kazakhstana* (Almaty: Dayk-Press, 2007), 65.

16 Masanov, "Mifologizatsiia problem," 116.

good ruler.[17] It was responsible for the persistence of predominantly tribal identities among nomads and territorialized local identities among various sedentary and urbanized Central Asians. It also channeled state formation in the region along the lines of loose multi-ethnic and multi-confessional empires with ill-defined frontiers compared with the formation of the national sovereign states of France, England, Spain, and other polities in post-Westphalian Europe (1648), which had clearly defined borders. The multi-ethnic and multi-confessional composition of nomadic empires facilitated considerable inter-ethnic and inter-confessional tolerance and the relative political insignificance of religion, ethnicity, and language compared with the dichotomy between nomads and non-nomads.[18] This was quite different from the centrality of religion in contemporary Europe, which had witnessed Crusades, the Catholic Inquisition, and protracted Catholic-Protestant internecine warfare.

In the economic sphere, the Genghizid-Timurid legacy accounted for the tribute-redistributional model between the center and the periphery. The nomadic practice of individual ownership of livestock, alongside collective ownership of land and water, was translated into the extreme power of the state, embodied by the ruler, and the relative weakness of both private landowners and cities, which functioned as merchant hubs but also stood as symbols of a particular ruler's prestige. This model differed from that in contemporary Western Europe, where the economic power of states and monarchs could be, and often was, challenged by the Church, regional gentry, as well as by politically and economically strong cities, which enjoyed considerable autonomy from monarchs in the form of their representative bodies—the early precursors of civil society.[19]

In the cultural sphere the Turco-Mongol impact is evidenced in the linguistic and demographic Turkicization of most Central Asians (with the exception of Tajiks and Pamiris), while retaining the Sogdian/Samanid cultural blueprint. From the fourteenth century onward, due to the Sogdian/Samanid and nomadic Turkic synergy, the initial differences in the way of life, culture, and cuisine between the originally nomadic Turkic peoples, who spoke different Turkic languages (Turki/Chagatay, Oghuz, and Qipchak), and Persianized sedentary peoples became blurred, and many Central Asians acquired dual Turkic–Persian identities and spoke both languages. A case in point would be the

---

17   B.M. Babadjanov, *Kokandskoe khanstvo: vlast,' politika, religiia* (Tashkent: TIAS, 2010), 307.

18   Masanov, 'Mifologizatsiia problem," 95.

19   For a detailed discussion of the Genghizid legacy see G.M. Yemelianova, *Russia and Islam: A Historical Survey* (London: Palgrave, 2002), 1–5.

Turkic- and Iranian-speaking sedentary Sarts.[20] On the other hand, the sedentarization of Uzbeks and other Turkic peoples of Central Asia occurred in parallel with their cultural Persianization along Sogdian/Samanid lines. Thus, the Uzbek leaders, as well as some other Turkic rulers of the region, routinely employed Persian-dominated administrations.[21]

The Turco-Mongol and Persian Islamic cultural synthesis strengthened the distinctiveness of Central Asian Islam[22] and further distanced it from Islam in other parts of the former Abbasid domain. In this respect, the "making" of Central Asian Islam was quite different from that of other versions of regional Islam, for example, in Southeast Asia, West Africa, or even in Turkey, which were never parts of Arab Caliphates and were Islamized at much later periods. From the sixteenth century onward, Central Asian Islam acquired physical and political boundaries as a result of the consolidation of the Safavid Empire (1501–1736), the Ottoman Empire (1299–1923) and the Chinese empire, first under the Ming dynasty (1368–1644) and later under the Manchu dynasty (1644–1912), which sought the annexation of Muslim-dominated Xinjiang.[23] On the other side, many centuries of common Turkic and Genghizid tutelage interconnected the politics, economies, and cultures of the nomadic and sedentary inhabitants of Central Asia and wider Eurasia, including Russia, and therefore contributed to their better mutual awareness and understanding, their ethnic intermingling, as well as their substantial mutual borrowings in the field of language, design, cuisine, and beliefs.[24] It made for the emergence on the territory of present-day Russia of Mongolic- and Turkic- speaking populations adhering to Buddhism, Zoroastrianism, Tengrism, Shamanism, Judaism, and Islam.[25]

---

20   Dagiev, *Regime Transition,* 21.

21   Roy, *The New Central Asia,* 5-6.

22   Here the term "Central Asian Islam" is used to denote distinctive and integrated Central Asian Islamic dogmas, beliefs, and practices that have notable differences from Salafi (lit. "of ancestors") interpretations of the Islamic creed and practices, which are attributed by some Islamic scholars to the period of the first 400 years after the Prophet Muhammad.

23   The borders between Central Asia and China remained undefined until the end of the nineteenth century, when Xinjiang was finally incorporated into China. Even so, until the 1930s these boundaries remained transparent and witnessed an exodus of Kazakhs and other nomads fleeing Stalinist sedentarization, collectivization, and *golodomor* (death through hunger). See A. Abdakimov, *Istoriia Kazakhstana,* 4th ed. (Almaty: "Kazakhstan," 2003), 225.

24   Golden, *Central Asia,* 89; Yemelianova, *Russia and Islam,* 27.

25   Among Russia's Mongolian-speakers are Buryats, Kalmyks, and Tuvans, while Turkic/ Qipchak-speakers include Muslim Tatars and Bashkirs of the Volga-Urals and Karachay

The Iranian and Turco-Mongol ethno-cultural fusion also distanced Central Asia and wider Eurasia, including Russia, from Europe. Between the eleventh and fifteenth centuries—when Central Asia and most of Eurasia, including proto-Russia, were parts of the Islamized Genghizid empire—European rulers were engaged in the papally sanctioned Crusades in the Levant. In the sixteenth century, Europe's geographical and political disengagement from Muslim Asia was supplemented by the development of a racial superiority complex toward Asians, especially Muslim Turks and "Tartars," as well as Orthodox Muscovites who were perceived as being on a par with "Tartars."[26] These attitudes were conceptualized during the Renaissance and Enlightenment periods, when the foundation for the modern Western ideas of liberty, progress, human rights, and civic society was laid. These fundamental differences were reflected in their respective historical narratives. Thus, most Central Asian and Eurasian historiographies emphasized the Irano-Turkic and Mongol cultural core of various peoples of the region represented by Sogdians, Samanids in Central Asia, and Scythians[27] in Central Eurasia and various Turkic peoples across Eurasia.[28] By contrast, most European historiography anchored early European civilization in the ancient Greek and Latin heritage and treated nomads and Asians as an inferior "other."

The Islamic Factor

Arabs brought Islam to Mawarannahr in the seventh century AD when Central Asia was formally included into the Arab Caliphate. However, the pace and nature of the region's ensuing Islamization were largely determined by its inherent ethno-cultural and religious pluralism as shaped by the Sogdians. It defined such Central Asian Islamic perceptions as the believers' equal acceptance of God's revelation and an individual's capacity and will to act, as well as a largely cyclic and contemplative, rather than progressive and critical, worldview. By the end of the ninth century AD, Islam had become the official religion

---

and Balkars of the North Caucasus and Oghuz-speaking Muslim Azeris in Dagestan, as well as in the post-Soviet republic of Azerbaijan.

26 D. Schimmelpennick, *Russian Orientalism: Asia in the Russian Mind from Peter the Great to the Emigration* (New Haven, CT: Yale University Press, 2010), 2.

27 The Scythian empire existed in Central Eurasia between the ninth century BC and the first century AD.

28 V.I. Novikov, ed., *Russkaia literatura XI–XVII vv.* (Moscow: Olimp, 1998).

of the Samanids.[29] The Samanids' promotion and patronage of scholarship and the arts encouraged the development of Islamic theology in the region. Notably, two out of six authoritative compilers of *hadith*[30] among Sunni Muslims were natives of the region. They were Muhammad ibn Ismail al-Bukhari (810–870) and Abu 'Isa Muhammad al-Tirmidhi (825–892).[31]

Of particular significance to the making of Central Asian Islam was the contribution of local Islamic jurists. Among their leading representatives was the Samarqandi Hanafi[32] theologian Abu Mansur al-Maturidi (853–944) who, along with the Shafi'i theologian Abu al-Hasan al-Ash'ari (873–935) in Iraq, created the two main schools of Sunni *kalam* (Islamic scholastic theology). The *kalam* of al-Maturidi, later known as Al-Maturidiyya, developed in opposition to the Basra-based Mu'tazilite Islamic theological school, which prioritized reason and rational thought and denied the eternal nature of the Qur'an.[33] By comparison, al-Maturidiyya significantly modified the creed of Islam and Hanafite doctrine by including in them elements of both the Mu'tazilite teaching and Central Asian non-Islamic customary norms and beliefs. As a result, Al-Maturidiyya asserted the supremacy of God in man's acts alongside man's capacity and will to act and thus provided a doctrinal framework for the flexibility, adaptability, and syncretism in Hanafi-based Central Asian Islam.[34]

The combination of the Sogdian–Samanid cultural matrix and Al-Maturidiyya paved the way for a Persianized, rather than Arabized, understanding of Islam. The former drew on pre-Islamic Sassanid political, cultural, and musical traditions and prioritized Sufi (mystical) Islam. Sufis acted as the main agents of the Islamization of the Turco-Mongol nomads of the region. Furthermore, Central Asia produced some of the leading Sufi scholars and teachers in the Muslim world. Among them was, for example, the Turkic-speaking Ahmed

29   See more on the Samanids in Richard Nelson Frye (ed.) *From the Arab Invasion to the Saljuqs,* Vol. 4: *The Cambridge History of Iran* (Cambridge: Cambridge University Press, 1975), 136–161.

30   *Hadith* (pl. *Ahadith*) is an account of Prophet Muhammad's sayings or actions. It is regarded as the second, after the Qur'an, most important source of Islamic jurisprudence.

31   Khalid, *Islam after Communism*, 25.

32   Hanafism is one of the four *madhhabs* (juridical schools) within Sunni Islam. The other *madhhabs* are Hanbalism, Shafiism, and Malikism.

33   See more on Mu'tazilites in R.C. Martin, M.R. Woodward, and D.S. Atmaja, *Defenders of Reason in Islam: Mu'Tazilizm from Medieval School to Modern Symbol* (London: Oneworld Publications, 1997); Y.M. Choueiri, *Islamic Fundamentalism: The Story of Islamist Movements*, 3rd ed. (London: Continuum, 2010).

34   G.M. Yemelianova (ed.), *Radical Islam in the Former Soviet Union* (London: Routledge, 2010), 214.

Yasawi (1093–1166), the founder of the Yasawiyya *tariqa* (brotherhood), who was born in the town of Sayram, today a suburb of Shymkent in southern Kazakhstan. His followers played a central role in the proliferation of Islam among the nomads of the Kazakh steppe and in the wider Turkic world. Central Asia's prominent Persian-speaking Sufis were Jalal ad-Din Muhammad Rumi (1207–1273), a native of Balkh in present-day Afghanistan whose followers formed the *tariqa* of Mewlawiyya, and the most famous Sufi of Central Asia, Baha-ud-Din Naqshband (1318–1389), a native of Bukhara, who acquired a global following as the founder of the Naqshbandi *tariqa*.

The nomadic essence of Genghizid-Timurid ruling elites further contributed to the pluralist outlook of Central Asian Islam, which absorbed other elements of paganism, nomadic customary norms, Zoroastrian, Tengrian, and Shamanist beliefs and practices, as well as Nestorian Christianity. It also defined the supremacy of oral and ritualistic Islamic practices over scripture-based Islamic traditions. Among such Islamized, although originally pagan, customs were, for example, hanging pieces of colored fabric on trees, kissing grave headstones, and rubbing dust over one's face.[35] The nomadic heritage of many Central Asians accounted for the strong role of female Islamic authority[36] in regional Islam, which was personified by *bibiotuns/otynchas*.[37] It is also symptomatic that the major popular holiday in today's Central Asia is *Nowruz* (Festival of Spring),[38] which in terms of its popularity and the scale and length of the festivities, much exceeds the main Islamic holidays of Qurban-Bayram/Qurban-Hait ('Id al-Adha) and Uraza-Bayram/Uraza-Hait ('Id al-Fitr).

---

35   Ibid., 213.

36   This also applies to Russia's Tatars and Bashkirs where *abystays* (female Islamic authorities) enjoy a high social status. See G. Yemelianova, "Islam and Power," in H. Pilkington and G. Yemelianova (eds), *Islam in Post-Soviet Russia: Public and Private Faces* (London: RoutledgeCurzon, 2003), 74–75.

37   R. Sultanova, *From Shamanism to Sufism: Women, Islam, and Culture in Central Asia* (London: I.B. Tauris, 2014), 130.

38   *Nowruz* symbolizes, the cyclic nature of life and the contemplative world view. It is also widely celebrated among Azerbaijanis, Ossetians and Georgians in the Caucasus. See Babadjanov, *Kokandskoe khanstvo*, 640.

The Russian Factor

The rise of Christian Orthodox Russia[39] as a major Eurasian power began following Ivan the Terrible's conquest of the Muslim khanates of Kazan (1552),
Astrakhan (1556), Siberia (1582), and the splinter states of the Genghizid
Golden Horde, which ruled over proto-Russia between 1240 and 1480. In 1480
the refusal by Muscovy *kniaz'* Ivan III to continue to pay tribute to his sovereign in the Golden Horde marked the transformation of proto-Russia into
Russia *per se*. Russia's Genghizid heritage acted as a facilitator for her eastward
advance.[40] By the late eighteenth century, i.e., prior to Russia's sustained
advance into the Kazakh steppe and Central Asia, Russia conquered the last
Genghizid remnants – the Nogay and the Crimean Khanates and became
involved in the geopolitical and military rivalry with the Ottoman and Safavid
Empires. Despite this rivalry, their mutual trade, cultural borrowing, territorial
delimitation, and population exchanges were conducted on level terms. This
contrasted with the nature of Europe's engagement with Asia, which from the
fifteenth century onward had been framed in Eurocentric and civilizational
terms and accompanied by Christian missionary activism.

In the case of Russia, the introduction of some elements of civilizational
discourse in her relations with her Asian neighbors occurred much later and
was prompted by the drive by Peter the Great (1672–1725) toward Russia's symbolic Europeanization. By the eighteenth century the Russian elite had adopted
some European attitudes of civilizational superiority towards their non-
Russian and non-Christian Orthodox subjects.[41] Those attitudes became
particularly prominent in St. Petersburg's policies when it embarked on the
conquest of Central Asia in the nineteenth century. Among the drivers of
Russia's eastward expansion was her Great Game with Britain for the control
over Eastern and Central Asia.[42] Russia's Central Asian expansion received an

---

39 In 988 AD *kniaz* (prince) Vladimir chose Orthodox Christianity as the official religion of
  Rus' in order to juxtapose it with his major rivals, the Judaist Khazar Khaganate in the east
  and the Islamic Abbasid Caliphate in the south.

40 On the implications of Russia's Eurasian expansion for the ensuing development of her
  polity and society see Yemelianova, *Russia and Islam*, 1–27.

41 R. Vulpius, "The Russian Empire's Civilizing Mission in the Eighteenth Century: A Comparative Perspective," in U. Tomohiko (ed.), *Asiatic Russia: Imperial Power in Regional and
  International Contexts* (New York: Routledge, 2012), 27.

42 For a detailed analysis of the Great Game and its political and cultural implications for
  the region see P. Hopkirk, *The Great Game: The Struggle for Empire in Central Asia* (New
  York: Kodansha International, 1992); E. Sergeev, *The Great Game, 1856–1907: Russo–British
  Relations in Central and East Asia* (Baltimore, MD: John Hopkins University Press, 2013).

impetus as a result of her defeat in the Crimean War (1853–1856), which curtailed her territorial ambitions in the Middle East. In the 1860s Russia subjugated the Khanate of Kokand and transformed it into the Fergana province of Russian Turkestan, which was established in 1867 with its center in Tashkent. By comparison, St. Petersburg chose to preserve the territorial integrity of most of the Bukhara Emirate and the Khiva Khanate as Russian protectorates, which were modeled on British and French treaties with various princely states in India and North Africa, respectively.[43]

Russia's Eurocentric attitudes and policies toward and in Central Asia were largely superficial and did not override her inherent Eurasianism and appreciation of the shared historical and cultural heritage of Russia and Central Asia.[44] Even the Voltaire-influenced Catherine the Great had a profound respect for Islam as a civilizational force and chose to draw on the Ottoman *millet* system in her approach toward Russia's Muslims. In 1788 she introduced the institution of the muftiate in Orenburg to manage and control Muslim subjects, and she encouraged the Islamic proselytizing activities of Tatars among "unruly" and religiously syncretic Kazakh and Kyrgyz nomads.[45] In the longer term, Catherine the Great's Islamic policy, which combined Islam's legalization and "nationalization," cooptation, and depoliticization, became the model of the Russian state–Muslim relations.

Due to Russia's intrinsic Eurasianism, as well as her predominantly military and political (rather than social and cultural) domination over Central Asia, Central Asian Islam retained most of its key characteristics, especially among the majority of Iranian-speaking Tajiks and Turkic-speaking Sarts/Uzbeks of the Bukhara Emirate and the Khiva Khanate. The Kazakh and Kyrgyz nomads remained Muslims in a socio-cultural rather than in a religious sense and continued to associate mullahs with misfortune and disaster.[46] However, for a small fraction of the Turkestani and Bukhara Muslim elite, Russian rule, especially the medium of Russo-native schools, facilitated the development of a Central Asian version of jadidism (Islamic reformism),[47] whose leading

---

43   A. Khalid, *The Politics of Muslim Cultural Reform: Jadidism in Central Asia* (Berkeley: University of California Press, 1998), 15.

44   Schimmelpennick, *Russian Orientalism*, 239.

45   H. Mati, "Tatarskaiia kargala in Russia's Eastern Policies," in Tomohiko (ed.), *Asiatic Russia*, 37.

46   Masanov, "Mifologizatsiia problem," 121.

47   *Jadidism* was a specific Russian Islamic phenomenon. It was pioneered by the Tatar Muslim elite in the 1880s in response to Russia's modernization initiated by Alexander II (1818–1881). It had some similarities with the late nineteenth and early twentieth century Islamic reformism of Jamal ad-Din al-Afghani (1838–1897), Muhammad Abduh

proponents were Mahmud Khoja Behbudi (1874–1919), Abduqadir Shakuri (1875–1943), Sadriddin Ayni (1878–1954), Abdurauf Fitrat (1886–1938), and Munawwar Qari (1878–1931).[48]

It is also important to bear in mind that Russia's exclusively Eurasian territorial expansion and her non-involvement in the European colonization of the Muslim Middle East, driven by Britain, France, and some other European powers, accounted for the development there of divergent popular perceptions of Russia and Western Europe. They were particularly influenced by the secret Sykes–Picot Agreement (1916) between Britain and France, which divided the Ottoman Middle East according to their political and economic interests (access to oil reserves), rather than along ethno-cultural and religious lines, as well as by the British-sponsored Balfour Declaration (1917), which laid the foundation for the creation of the Jewish homeland in Palestine and, subsequently, the state of Israel.

The Soviet Factor

Although the Soviet period in the history of Central Asia has received comparatively more attention in Western scholarship,[49] it still remains to some extent a *terra incognita*. It has suffered, more than other periods in the history of the region, from a Moscow-centered perspective, which treats the Soviet Union as an empire and Central Asia as its colony.[50] This approach is responsible for a considerable misreading of Central Asia's internal and external

---

(1849–1905), Rashid Rida (1865–1935) and Mirza Malkum Khan (1833–1908), which, however, developed as a reaction to modernity emanating from outside. See more on Tatar-centred *Jadidism* in G.M. Yemelianova, "The National Identity of the Volga Tatars at the Turn of the 19th Century: Tatarism, Turkism, and Islam," *Central Asian Survey*, 16, no. 4 (1997): 543–572.

48   See more on Central Asian jadidism in Khalid, *The Politics of Muslim Cultural Reform.*

49   Among in-depth studies of some aspects of Sovietization of Central Asia are: A. Bennigsen and S.E. Wimbush, *Muslims of the Soviet Empire* (London: C. Hurst & Co., 1985); D. Brower, *Turkestan and the Fate of the Russian Empire* (London: Routledge, 2003); W. Fierman (ed.), *Soviet Central Asia: The Failed Transformation* (Boulder, CO: Westview, 1991); M. Kamp, *The New Woman in Uzbekistan: Islam, Modernity, and Unveiling Under Communism* (Seattle: University of Washington Press, 2006); Y. Ro'i, *Islam in the Soviet Union: From the Second World War to Gorbachev* (London: Hurst & Co., 2000).

50   On the critique of the Eurocentric approach towards Central Asia see, for example, A.G. Frank, "ReOrient: From Centrality of Central Asia to China's Middle Kingdom," in Korkut A. Ertürk (ed.), *Rethinking Central Asia: Non-Eurocentric Studies in History, Social Structure, and Identity* (Reading, UK: Ithaca Press, 1999), 11–38; N. Nurulla-Hodjaeva, *Odin*

dynamics,[51] which were largely congruent with the developmental trajectories identified earlier. Because of this congruence the Bolsheviks managed to secure their position in Muslim Central Asia and in other parts of the Russian empire by instrumentalizing patterns of power relations, social mobilization, and cultural awareness that had been reproduced throughout history across the whole of Eurasia, even if they framed them now in Marxist-Leninist terms.[52] They also continued with Catherine the Great's model of state-Muslim relations and even developed it further.

Nevertheless, the pluralistic and adaptable nature of Central Asian Islam ensured its survival under state atheism. It acquired different forms and became dissolved within Sovietized national cultures. For example, some *chaykhonas* (tea houses), bakeries, *doma kul'tury* (houses of culture), or other non-religious public places turned into undercover mosques with improvised *mihrabs* (a niche in the wall directed towards the Kaaba in Mecca). Muslims continued to conduct *ziiarats* (visitations) to their Sufi *mazars* (shrines), now repackaged as secular historical sites.[53]

The effects of Sovietization varied among different Central Asian Muslim communities. In the case of sedentary Tajiks and Uzbeks, the Bolshevik assault on Muslim clergy[54] and Islamic infrastructure, as well as the change of alphabet from Arabic to Latin and finally to Cyrillic that occurred between 1925 and 1943, undermined the Persianized and Sufi-centered Islamic literary tradition and forced its bearers deep underground. Its transmission was secured by the efforts of a small number of surviving *'ulama* and *ishans*, who embodied "unofficial" or "parallel" Islam.[55] They defied the Soviet authorities and

iz fragmentov istorii znaniia: dom mudrosti Abbasidov i o chernilakh v reke Tigr, 2016, <http://www.mgl.ru/www/library/177/The_Abbasids.html>.

51   See, for example, Bennigsen and Wimbush, _Muslims of the Soviet Empire_; M. Rywkin, _Moscow's Muslim Challenge_ (Armonk, NY: M.E. Sharpe, 1982).

52   The absence of such patterns in Europe arguably was one of the reasons for the failure of socialist revolutions in Germany in 1918 and Hungary in 1919.

53   S. Abashin, _Sovetskii kishlak: mezhdu kolonializmom and modernizatsiei_ (Moscow: Novoe literaturnoe obozrenie, 2015), 498–548; Z. Salmorbekova and G. Yemelianova, "Islam and Islamism in the Ferghana Valley," in G. Yemelianova (ed.), _Radical Islam in the Former Soviet Union_ (London: Routledge, 2010), 216.

54   Given that, unlike Christianity, Islam does not require an institutionalized hierarchy the chapter uses the Christian term "clergy" in relation to _'ulama_ (Islamic scholars), _qazi-qolons_ (supreme Islamic judges), _shaykhs-ul-Islam_ (supreme Islamic authorities), muftis, mullahs, shaykhs, _ishans_ (Sufi masters), and other representatives of Islamic authority for the sake of utility and simplicity only.

55   On complex relationship between representatives of "official" and "unofficial" Islam see B. Babadjanov, A. Muminov, and A. von Kugelgen, _Disputy musul'manskikh religioznykh_

"official" Islam, represented by the muftiate of Central Asia and Kazakhstan (SADUM), which was established by Stalin in 1943,[56] and continued to teach Al-Maturidi's version of Hanafi Islam in *hujras* (underground Islamic cells), which functioned across historical Mawarannahr. Their leading authority was Muhammadjon Rustamov, known as Hajjee Domla (Professor) Hindustoni (1892–1989).[57]

Sovietization was especially detrimental for the Islamic identity of nomadic Kazakhs, Kyrgyz, and Turkmen because of its organic intertwining with nomadism, which was destroyed in the 1930s as part of the wider process of sedentarization associated with Soviet land reform and collectivization.[58] Kazakh population drastically declined due to the *golodomor* (1931-33) and the Kazakh mass emigration to China, Afghanistan and other parts of the wider Eurasia. As a result, by the late 1930s the Kazakhs had become an ethno-confessional minority in their titular republic.[59] An aggravating factor was a huge influx into northern Kazakhstan of Russian and Ukrainian settlers during the 1954 Khrushchev Virgin Lands campaign. All these factors led to the transformation of tribal genealogy into the key marker of the ex-nomads' identity while weakening their Muslimness. Their oral Islamic tradition was irreversibly damaged as a result of the Bolshevik eradication of Sufis, who were the main transmitters of Islam among them, and their higher level of susceptibility, compared to sedentary Uzbeks and Tajiks, to the version of Islam promoted by the Tashkent-based SADUM.[60]

---

avtoritetov v Tsentral'noi Azii v XX veke (Almaty: Dayk-Press, 2007); D. DeWeese, "Islam and the Legacy of Sovietology: A Review Essay on Y. Ro'i's Islam in the Soviet Union," *Journal of Islamic Studies*, 13, no. 3 (2002): 298–330.

56 The other three muftiates were the Ufa-centered muftiate, which oversaw the Tatar and Bashkir Sunni Muslims of the European part of Russia; the Buynaksk-based muftiate, which dealt with the Sunni Muslims of the North Caucasus; and the Baku-centered muftiate, which administered the Shi'a and Sunni Muslims of Azerbaijan. For a detailed discussion of Soviet muftiates, see Ro'i, *Islam in the Soviet Union*.

57 Babadjanov, Muminov, and von Kugelgen, *Disputy musul'manskikh religioznykh avtoritetov*, 20.

58 Masanov, "Mifologizatsiia problem," 108; Khalid, *Islam after Communism*, 96.

59 According to the 1939 census, the Kazakhs made up 37.8 percent of the population of Kazakhstan. See *Demoskop*, November, 14–27, 2016, <http://demoscope.ru/weekly/ssp/sng_nac_39.php?reg=5>.

60 Since the 1970s SADUM was the leading Soviet muftiate and the exclusive provider of Islamic secondary and higher education through its overseeing of the *Mir-i Arab* madrasa (secondary Islamic school) in Bukhara and the Imam al-Bukhari Islamic Institute in Tashkent. It also acted as an agency of Soviet ideological and cultural influence in the Middle East and other countries of the Muslim world. D. Eickelman, "The Other

The theological position of SADUM[61] was ambiguous, however. On the one hand, its first mufti was Eshon Bobokhon ibn Abdulmajidkhon (1858–1957), a Naqshbandi[62] shaykh from Tashkent; some other senior Islamic clergy claimed their adherence to Central Asian Islamic tradition as well. On the other hand, Moscow's particular hostility toward Sufism helped strengthen the pro-*Jadidist* and pro-Salafi lobby within SADUM. This lobby was influenced by the teaching of Shami Domullo al-Tarablusi (d. 1932), who had come to Central Asia in 1919 from Lebanon via Eastern Turkestan.[63] Al-Tarablusi introduced elements of Hanbali *madhhab* in his teaching and gathered around himself a group of followers, known as *Ahl-i Hadith* (People of *Hadith*), who refuted Central Asian Islam as *bid'a* (sinful innovation) and called for the return to the Islam of Prophet Muhammad and the four righteous Caliphs. He favored the use of *ijma* (consensus), while opposing *rai* (opinion) and *qiias* (analogy) in the interpretation of *hadiths*.[64] Shami Domullo's followers included mufti Ziyovuddinkhon ibn Eshon Bobokhon (1908–1982), who succeeded his father in 1957, and members of his close circle.[65]

Overall, despite the relatively short time frame, the comprehensive Sovietization process radically transformed polities and societies in Central Asia and across the USSR. It created the political, national, institutional, ideational, and societal templates that maintain their validity a quarter of a century after the demise of the USSR. It further strengthened the Eurasian dimension of identity of Central Asians and turned them into the Central Asian type of

'Orientalist' Crisis," in D. Eickelman (ed.), *Russia's Muslim Frontiers: New Directions in Cross-Cultural Analysis* (Bloomington: Indiana University Press, 1993), 7.

61   Between 1943 and 1989 the SADUM was controlled by the Bobokhon family.

62   According to some sources, he belonged to Yasawiyya *tariqa*. See, for example, V. Naumkin, *Radical Islam in Central Asia: Between Pen and Rifle* (Lanham, MD: Rowman & Littlefield, 2005), 39.

63   Author's interview with Dr. Marat Safarov, a scholar of Eurasian Islam, Moscow, September 4, 2016.

64   Sayid ibn Muhammad al-Asali al-Tarablusi al-Shami al-Dimashqi, "Al-Djumal al-Mufida fi Sharh al-Djawhara al-Farida," in Babadjanov, Muminov, and Kugelgen, *Disputy musul'manskikh religioznykh avtoritetov,* 70.

65   SADUM's pro-Salafi leaning was reflected in the curricula of the Bukhara madrasa and Tashkent Islamic Institute, which instead of the study of *al-Maturidiyya* and other medieval commentaries on *fiqh* (Islamic jurisprudence) in Persian, focused on intensive training in Arabic, *tajwid* (the recitation of the Qur'an), *tafsir* (the explication of the Qur'an) and *hadiths* from Arabic primary sources. A. Muminov, "Fundamentalist Challenges to Local Islamic Traditions in Soviet and Post-Soviet Central Asia," in U. Tomohiko (ed.), *Empire, Islam, and Politics in Central Eurasia* (Sapporo: Hokkaido University, Slavic Research Center, 2007), 254–256; Naumkin, *Radical Islam in Central Asia,* 40–43.

Homo Sovieticus Islamicus, who largely subscribed to a secularized version of Central Asian Islam, which distanced them even more from their co-religionists in historical Eurasia, encompassing Xinjiang, Afghanistan, northern Iran and Turkey, and from Muslims in the Middle East.

The transformative and enduring impact of Sovietization on Central Asia (and, indeed, on most of post-Soviet Eurasia) suggests that the Soviet Union was a unique historical and geopolitical phenomenon that could not be conceptualized entirely along the same lines as the British, French, and other Europe-centered overseas empires. Although there were a number of features that superficially resembled those of European empires (e.g., the coercive sedentarization of the Kazakh, Kyrgyz, and Turkmen, or the cotton mono-culture in Uzbekistan) the USSR substantially differed from them in terms of its much higher investment in Central Asia, the involvement of Central Asians in the central political and economic bodies of power, its promotion of national political infrastructures and cultures, as well as the inclusion of Central Asians in the nation-wide comprehensive and free secondary and higher education and health care. These major differences shed some light on why, unlike the British, French, or Portuguese empires, which fell apart as a result of sometimes lengthy and often bloody national-liberation movements in their colonies (e.g., India, 1757–1947; Algeria, 1954–1962; Kenya, 1952–1960; South Yemen, 1963–1967; Mozambique, 1964–1974; and Angola, 1956–1975), none of the five Central Asian republics—their leaders and their citizens—sought independence even while the USSR was disintegrating around them.[66]

---

66   Thus, publicly at the nation-wide referendum on the preservation of the USSR as a "reformed federation of equal and sovereign states" in March 1991, Kazakhstan voted 94 percent in favor of the preservation of the USSR; Kyrgyzstan 96.4 percent in favor; Uzbekistan 93.7 percent in favor; Tajikistan 95.2 percent in favor and Turkmenistan 97 percent in favor (see "Ob Itogakh Referenduma SSSR 17 March 1991 (Iz Soobshcheniia Tsentral'noi Komissii o Referendume SSSR)," *Izvestiia,* March 27, 1991. Those results were largely congruent with the pro-Union position of the vast majority of ordinary Central Asians compared with their elites. (Based on the author's research findings within the Nuffield Foundation (UK) funded project on "Islamic Radicalism in Uzbekistan, Tajikistan and Kyrgyzstan, 2002–2005, and within the British Council-funded INSPIRE project on "Innovative Research and Teaching through the Academic Partnership" between the University of Birmingham (UK) and the Kazakh-British Technical University (Kazakhstan), 2010–2013).

Independence and Globalization

The sudden dissolution of the Soviet Union in 1991 presented the elites of the five Central Asian republics with a difficult dilemma. They had to preserve social and political order and to create nation-states within fixed borders that had been imposed from above and that often cut across homogeneous ethnic communities. More importantly, at least for them, in order to stay in power they needed to generate a new legitimizing ideology that would replace the supra-national Communist and Soviet ideology.

Remarkably, four out of the five Central Asian leaders managed to achieve this, though with different degrees of success. Thus, Communist Party First Secretaries Islam Karimov (1938–2016), Nursultan Nazarbayev (b. 1940), Kakhar Mahkamov, (1932–2016), and Saparmurat Niyazov (1940–2006) maintained their supremacy by repackaging themselves as the presidents of Uzbekistan, Kazakhstan, Tajikistan, and Turkmenistan, respectively, and leaders of ruling parties that were created overnight. They rhetorically denounced the Soviet past, while in fact preserving the Sovietized version of the Eurasian political and economic model. Niyazov went even further, appointing himself as "Turkmenbashi" (leader of the Turkmen), president for life in 1999, and in 2002 as a de facto prophet who had received God's latest revelation in the form of *Ruhmana* (*The Book of the Soul*), while simultaneously drastically reducing the role of the legislative and judicial powers.[67]

At the same time, Absamat Masaliev (1933–2004), the Communist Party's first secretary in Kyrgyzstan, was ousted from office by Askar Akayev (b. 1944), a non-*apparatchik* and former president of the Academy of Sciences of Kyrgyzstan who aspired to break away from Soviet/Eurasian authoritarianism in favor of Western liberalism, to advance the development of civil society and civic, rather than ethnicity-based, citizenship. This political experiment was short-lived, however. In 2005 President Akayev was ousted from office amid the "Tulip Revolution," which was triggered by widespread popular anger over his failed economic and political program.[68] His successor, Kurmanbek Bakiyev (b. 1947), was equally unsuccessful in reversing the country's spiralling decline and its becoming a de facto failed state on the brink of political disintegration. Since 2011 Kyrgyzstan has been ruled by President Almazbek Atambayev (b.1956) who has steadily steered its development from the "democratic transition'" toward a more familiar Eurasian economic and political path, an

---

67   Peyrouse, *Turkmenistan*, 72, 82, 93.

68   Following the "Tulip Revolution" in 2005 President Askar Akayev fled to Moscow, where
       he resumed his academic career as professor of mathematics at Moscow State University.

approach that received a further boost as a result of Kyrgyzstan's joining of the Eurasian Economic Union (EEU) in 2015.[69] Across the region, the vertical executive-power structures have been safeguarded, as in the Soviet time, by powerful national security forces, successors of the KGB, that have ignored the new states' proclaimed adherence to people's sovereignty, separation of powers, and government accountability.[70] Such structural political continuity has been accompanied by a radical change in the ideological discourse from supranational Soviet nationhood to de facto primordial ethno-nationalism of the titular ethnic group, which has been camouflaged by the constitutionally endorsed principles of civic nationalism. Epistemologically, this discourse, however, has been informed by Yulian Bromley's theory of *etnos*.[71] Specifically, the post-Soviet Central Asian leaders have mobilized archaeologists, historians, and ethnographers to provide "academic historical evidence" for their "legitimate" claims to their post-Soviet territories and have imposed political, administrative, and informational barriers between ethnically and religiously closely related peoples of historical Mawarannahr.

The five new historical narratives have clashed over national "ownership" of major political and cultural figures of the past. Thus, both the Kazakhstan and Uzbekistan leaderships have asserted the Genghizid roots of their respective nations with the Uzbekistani elite emphasizing their Timurid, rather that Shaybanid Uzbek, origins.[72] Similarly, the Tajikistan leadership (since 1992 under Emomali Rahmon, b. 1952) asserted the Sogdian/Samanid origins of

---

69   Following the "Tulip Revolution" in 2005 President Askar Akayev was ousted from office and fled to Moscow, where he reverted to his academic career as professor of mathematics at Moscow State University.

70   For more on the post-Soviet transition in Central Asia, see S. Cummings, *Understanding Central Asia: Politics and Contested Transformations* (London: Routledge, 2012); M.B. Olcott, *Kazakhstan: Unfulfilled Promise* (Washington, D.C.: Carnegie Endowment for Peace, 2002); P.J. Luong, *Institutional Change and Political Continuity in Post-Soviet Central Asia: Power, Perceptions, and Pacts* (New York: Cambridge University Press, 2012).

71   Academician Yulian Bromley (1921–1990), the leading Soviet ethnologist, founded the Soviet theory of ethnicity and nationalism, which emphasized ethnic, rather than civic, consciousness as the core element of nation-building. Y.V. Bromley, *Ocherki teorii etnosa* (Moscow: LKU, 2008).

72   Between the fourteenth and sixteenth centuries, the nomadic Shaybanid Turco-Mongol Persianized empire existed on the territory of present-day Central Asia and parts of Afghanistan and Iran. Shaybanids were the first to assume the name of Uzbeks after Uzbeg Khan (128–341), the longest reigning khan of the Golden Horde. In the 1460s the Shaybanid empire split into two parts as a result of the rebellion of Janybek Khan (d. 1480) against Abu Khayr Khan (141–468). See, Soucek, *A History of Inner Asia*, 14–61; Masanov, "Mifologizatsiia problem," 98–100.

present-day Tajiks.[73] The Kyrgyz elite has chosen heroes of the sixteenth-century Kyrgyz epic *Manas* as their ethnic forebears,[74] while the Turkmen elite opted for the heroes of the early seventeenth-century epic *Koroghlu*.[75] It is significant that all post-Soviet Central Asian political elites have derived their historical legitimacy from their pre-Islamic or semi-Islamic nomadic, or urbanized ancestors, rather than from major Islamic figures associated with the region's Islamicization by Arabs in the seventh century AD and its subsequent inclusion within Arab Islamic Caliphates, centered in Medina (632–662), Damascus (661–750), and Baghdad (750–1258). By contrast, famous Central Asian Islamic thinkers (e.g., Al-Bukhari, Al-Farabi) and great Sufi teachers (e.g., Khoja Ahmed Yasawi and Baha-ud-Din Naqshband) have been turned into cultural, rather than Islamic, national symbols.[76]

In general, both the post-Soviet Central Asian elites and the wider public have had an unhappy relationship with Islam. On the surface, it appears that all the Central Asian republics, like other post-Soviet Muslim-majority regions, have experienced an Islamic revival that was triggered by the end of official atheism and the restoration of links with the wider Islamic world. Islamic symbols have been integrated in the five nationalizing discourses to ensure a cultural break from historically Orthodox Christian Russia. The republics witnessed an unprecedented Islamic building boom, resulting in the emergence of many hundreds of mosques, madrasas, as well as Islamic and Islamo-nationalist political parties and social organizations. In the first years of independence Central Asian parliaments, except in Turkmenistan, adopted new, liberal religious laws that provided a framework for various Islam-related activities, including a surge in the number of *hajjees* (pilgrims) to Mecca and Medina. They also welcomed the activities of foreign Islamic funds, preachers, and teachers from Saudi Arabia, the Gulf States, Egypt, Turkey, and other Muslim countries. The leaders of the republics endorsed the formation of national muftiates that split from the Soviet-era, Tashkent-based SADUM and secured membership of their respective states in the Organization of Islamic Cooperation (OIC).[77]

---

73   Dagiev, *Regime Transition*, 72.

74   Sultanova, *From Shamanism to Sufism,* 22.

75   Peyrouse, *Turkmenistan*, 59.

76   G.M. Yemelianova, "Islam, National Identity, and Politics in Contemporary Kazakhstan," *Asian Ethnicity* 15, no. 3 (2014): 292.

77   See more on Islamic trajectories in post-Soviet Central Asia in R. Sagdeev and S. Eisenhower (eds), *Islam and Central Asia: An Enduring Legacy or an Evolving Threat?* (Center for Political and Strategic Studies, Washington, D.C., 2000); Naumkin, *Radical Islam;* Khalid, *Islam after Communism*, and Yemelianova, *Radical Islam*.

It could be argued, however, that the Islamic revival has been more symbolic than substantive. In practice, and especially from the mid-1990s onward, official policies toward Islam and Muslims have resembled the imperial Russian/Soviet approach outlined earlier.[78] The geographical closeness of Central Asia to Taliban-infiltrated Afghanistan has been behind the particularly tough state crackdown on political Islam and other forms of "unofficial Islam." Among the main government targets have been members and sympathizers of the Islamic Renaissance Party of Tajikistan (IRPT), the Islamic Movement of Uzbekistan (IMU) and its successor the Islamic Movement of Turkestan (IMT), Hizb ut-Tahrir al-Islamii (Party of Islamic Liberation, HT), the Jund al-Khalifat (Soldiers of Caliphate, JK), and the Islamic State of Iraq and Syria (ISIS), which were banned in all five republics.[79] At the societal level, Central Asian Muslims have largely remained aloof from the global jihadist mobilization message and maintained their allegiance to the Soviet-era principle of secularism, intertwined with Central Asian Islam, important features of which have been disengagement from politics, the merger with Genghizid *adats* (customary norms), Zoroastrian and Tengrian beliefs and rituals, and strong oral Sufi and musical traditions infused with shamanism.[80] This resil-

---

78 This is confirmed by the author's comparative analysis of Islamic trajectories in post-Soviet Islamic space. See Yemelianova, *Radical Islam*.

79 For more on these organizations, see in Karagiannis, *Political Islam in Central Asia*; Naumkin, *Radical Islam in Central Asia*; Rashid, *Jihad*; N. Tucker, "Public and State Responses to ISIS Messaging: Tajikistan," *Central Asia Program Paper No. 11* (Washington, D.C.: George Washington University, 2016); E. Karin, *The Soldiers of the Caliphate: The Anatomy of a Terrorist Group* (Astana: KazISS, 2016).

80 This conclusion is based on my field-work findings in Uzbekistan, Kazakhstan and Kyrgyzstan in the period between 1999 and 2014, as well as findings of other scholars who conducted empirical research in the region, including: J. Heathershaw and D. Montgomery, *The Myth of Post-Soviet Muslim Radicalization in the Central Asian Republics* (London: Chatham House, 2014); J. Rasanayagam, *Islam in Post-Soviet Uzbekistan: The Morality of Experience* (Cambridge: Cambridge University Press, 2011); A. Khamidov, "The Lessons of the 'Nookat Events': Central Government, Local Officials and Religious Protests in Kyrgyzstan," *Central Asian Survey*, 32, no. 2 (2013): 148–160; Louw, *Everyday Islam*; David W. Montgomery, *The Transmission of Religious and Cultural Knowledge and Potentiality in Practice: An Anthropology of Social Navigation in the Kyrgyz Republic*. Ph.D. Dissertation. Boston University (Ann Arbor MI: ProQuest Information and Learning Company, 2007); Salmorbekova and Yemelianova, "Islam and Islamism in the Ferghana Valley," in Yemelianova, *Radical Islam*, 211–243.

ience of Central Asian Islam has been under-emphasized because Western scholarship and media have focused on Central Asian Islamists.[81]

However, Central Asia has not been entirely immune to Islamic radicalism, as evidenced by IRPT, IMU, IMT, HT, JK, and the ISIS *Khorasan Vilayet* (Khorasan Province), which number between several hundred and a few thousand members.[82] There have been a few Islamist enclaves in the Fergana Valley, as well as in western Kazakhstan. However, the factors of Islamic radicalization, as well as the mobilizing narratives that have been employed there, have differed significantly from those in both the Middle East and the West. They have been determined primarily by domestic issues, such as economic hardship, lack of opportunities, the pervasive corruption of local authorities, and the heavy-handedness of the police and security services. My findings have also revealed that most local Islamists and their sympathizers were not seriously concerned with major radicalizing issues among Muslims in the Middle East and the West, such as the Western policies in the Middle East, Western support for Israel against the Palestinians, the perceived cultural offense and discrimination related to Islamic dress, or the mocking/caricaturing of the Prophet Muhammad in the media, art exhibitions, and theatre.[83] This is not to say that no Central Asian jihadists have embraced the global jihadist message. However, their number has been limited. Some of them were trained in the Afghanistan–Pakistan border zone by jihadist instructors, many of whom originated from Muslim communities in Europe, while some others had a predominantly virtual existence.[84]

---

81   For a critique of the Western academic preoccupation with Islamic radicalism and jihadism in Central Asia see Heathershaw and Montgomery, *The Myth of Post-Soviet Muslim Radicalization.*

82   According to the data collected by the Commission on Security and Cooperation in Europe, in 2015 among ISIS fighters there were 500 Uzbeks, 360 Turkmen, 250 Kazakhs and 100 Kyrgyz. "Hearing Before the Commission on Security and Cooperation in Europe, June 10, 2015," 114th Congress, <http://ceriainitiative.org/likepomeps/wp-content/uploads/2015/09/Wanted-Foreign-Fighters-The-Escalating-Threat-of-ISIL-in-Asia.pdf>. Other sources suggest that in 2015 the total number of Central Asian ISIS fighters was around 4,000. See A. Malashenko, "Rossiia i Islamskoie Gosudarstvo," paper presented at the conference "Islam in Russia." Cambridge, MA, Harvard University, Davis Center of Russian and Eurasian Studies, October 1–16, 2015.

83   Yemelianova, *Radical Islam,* 239–240.

84   Among the latter were, for example, members of so called the *Kazakh Islamic Jihad,* the *Jaysh al-Mahdi* (Army of Mahdi), *Jamaat Ansarullah* (Community of Supporters of Allah), *Imam Bukhari Jamaat* (Community of Imam Bukhari), *Sabiri Jamaat* (Sabiri Community). See Karin, *The Soldiers of the Caliphate,* 84, 133,142,153.

Thus, in relative terms, the number of Central Asians fighting within ISIS has been much lower than the number of European jihadists. Thus, out of around 25,000 foreign ISIS fighters, Central Asian jihadists constitute only a tiny minority of the total Muslim population. Even if we accept the highest possible estimate of around 4,000 Central Asian jihadists fighting in Syria and Iraq, this will make up around 0.006 percent of the total population of Muslim Central Asia of 66 million.[85] This is incomparably lower than the number of Western European jihadists who joined ISIS. For example, Belgium-born ISIS fighters constitute around 0.9 percent of the total Muslim population of Belgium of 672,000; ISIS fighters coming from Sweden constitute 0.06 percent of the total Muslim population of Sweden of 500,000; French-born ISIS fighters make up 0.03 percent of the total Muslim population of France of 4.5 million; and UK-born jihadists also constitute 0.03 percent of the total UK Muslim population of 2.7 million.[86] Also, many Central Asian ISIS fighters, with the exception of Kazakhs,[87] came not from Central Asia per se, but from Central Asian immigrant communities in non-Muslim regions. The cases in point are some Uzbek, Tajik, and other Central Asian labor migrants in the Russian-majority Urals[88] who became radicalized as a result of their socio-cultural segregation and discrimination, which was not dissimilar to that among various Muslim migrants in the West.

---

85   For comparison, the number of Russia's Muslims (mainly of Caucasian and Tatar origins) fighting for ISIS is estimated to be between 4,000 and 7,000 out of a total Muslim population of around 20 million; the number of Azerbaijani jihadists is around 500 out of a total Muslim population of 9 million and the number of Georgia's jihadists (mainly Chechens from the Pankisi Gorge) is around 400 out of a total Muslim population of 300,000. See N. Burchuladze, "The ISIS 'Skype Warriors' of Pankisi Gorge," *Georgian Journal*, June 25–July 1, 2015, <http://www.georgianjournal.ge/military/30808-the-isis-skype-warriors-of-pankisi-gorge.html>; A. Yarlykapov, "Islamskoe gosudarstvo stroit v Rossii podpol'e," *Pravda*, May 27, 2015, <http://www.pravda.ru/news/expert/27-05-2015/1261474-yarlikapov-0/>.

86   "Number of Fighters per Capita,"*Radio Liberty*, July 6, 2016, <http://www.rferl.org/content infographics/foreign-fighters-syria-iraq-is-isis-isil-infographic/26584940.html>.

87   T. Wyke and D. Boyle, "ISIS Release Shocking New Video of Child Soldiers from Kazakhstan," *Daily Mail Online*, November 22, 2014, <http://www.dailymail.co.uk/news/article-2845531/ISIS-release-shocking-new-video-child-soldiers-Kazakhstan-trained-AK47s.html>; Karin, *The Soldiers of the Caliphate*.

88   On Islamic radicalization of Central Asian labor migrants in the Urals, see A. Malashenko and A. Starostin, *Islam na sovremennom Urale* (Moscow: Carnegie Center, April 2015).

Conclusion

Central Asian Islam was shaped by the Sogdian, Samanid, Genghizid, and Al-Muturidiyya cultural and Islamic influences. It has been characterized by a high content from the Sufi tradition, its intertwining with pre-Islamic Shamanist, Zoroastrian, and Tengrian beliefs, and Islamized Genghizid rituals and *adats,* as well as by its apolitical, flexible, and adaptable nature. For this reason, compared to Islam in the Islamic heartland with its centers in Mecca, Medina, Damascus, and Baghdad, it has not played the key role in the legitimization of political authority of Central Asian rulers, who prioritized genealogy over Islamic law, and it has only rarely served as a mobilizing political ideology (for example, as in the Basmachi movement in the 1920s and 1930s) in Central Asians' numerous conflicts with external invaders.

The shared Genghizid legacy facilitated the governance of Central Asia by imperial and Bolshevik Russia and enabled Moscow to adapt Catherine the Great's model of state-Muslim relations to Central Asia. It included the promotion of state-sponsored apolitical "official" Islam, the suppression of any other forms of "unofficial" Islam, and the segregation of local Muslims from their co-religionists abroad. This model maintained its centrality after the dissolution of the USSR, although "official" Islam has been widely rebranded as "traditional" Islam, and "unofficial" Islam as "non-traditional" Islam. Since the late 1990s, and especially in the wake of the 9/11 terrorist attacks, the Central Asian official discourse on "non-traditional" Islam has been securitized and criminalized along the same lines as the Russian official discourse, which arguably has been of considerable influence across Muslim Eurasia.

Central Asian Islam has largely retained its disengagement from Islamist trajectories in both the Middle East and the West, though its historical disengagement from politics has been increasingly challenged by the continuing socioeconomic hardships and political repression within particular Central Asian republics, as well as by the greater digital exposure of young Central Asians to Islamic messages emanating from outside the region. These messages have especially resonated among Uzbek and Tajik labor migrants in Russia and other non Muslim-majority countries, as well as Kazakhs and Kyrgyz within their respective republics whose Islamic identity was destroyed, or at least severely undermined, by their Soviet sedentarization. This also explains a larger number of conversions among them to Protestantism (Pentecostalism, Evangelical Christianity, Baptism, Methodism, etc.), compared to that among the Uzbeks and Tajiks.[89] In the long term, the perpetuation

---

89   The authors' findings within the above-mentioned Nuffield Foundation (UK)-funded
      research project on "Islamic Radicalism in Uzbekistan, Tajikistan and Kyrgyzstan,"

of distinctive Central Asian Islam will be determined by the ability of Central Asian political elites to ensure the viable social, economic, and political development of their respective countries, to overcome nationalist isolationism, and to restore full-fledged societal and political interaction across Central Asia and the wider post-Genghizid Eurasia. As for scholarship, an adequate understanding of contemporary Central Asian Islam and Muslims must be informed by an approach that avoids mono-theoretical compartmentalization and recognizes the significance of their historical, theological, and Eurasian context.

2002–2005, and the British Council-funded INSPIRE project on "Innovative Research and Teaching through the Academic Partnership" between the University of Birmingham (UK) and the Kazakh-British Technical University (Kazakhstan), 2010–2013); G.E. Shlymova (ed.), *Protestantizm: istoriia, napravleniia i kazakhstanskie realii* (Astana: RGU, 2012), 44.

Two Countries, Five Years: Islam in Kazakhstan and Kyrgyzstan Through the Lens of Public Opinion Surveys

Barbara Junisbai, Azamat Junisbai, and Baurzhan Zhussupov

At least since the 1990s, policymakers and scholars have been tracking the growing salience and practice of Islam in Central Asia.[1] The region's governments and policymakers, as well as their Western counterparts, are primarily concerned about the implications of religious revival, particularly the political implications.[2] For example, how can (and is) Islam be(ing) used to undermine or promote political stability?[3] How does Islam challenge or bolster regime legitimacy and durability?[4] And what aspects of Islam should be excluded from or incorporated into the official nation-building project?[5] Scholars share these interests, with a prominent strand of research investigating the interplay between regime politics and religiosity.[6] Still other studies of Islam in Central

1 S. Akiner, "The Politicisation of Islam in Postsoviet Central Asia," *Religion, State, and Society,* 3, no. 2 (2003): 97–122.

2 M. Karim, "Globalization and Post-Soviet Revival of Islam in Central Asia and the Caucasus," *Journal of Muslim Minority Affairs*, 25, no. 3 (2010): 439–448; International Crisis Group, "Is Radical Islam Inevitable in Central Asia?" (2003).

3 E. McGlinchey, "Islamic Revivalism and State Failure in Kyrgyzstan," *Problems of Post-Communism*, 56, no. 3 (2009): 16–28.

4 M.Y. Omelicheva, "Islam in Kazakhstan: A Survey of Contemporary Trends and Sources of Securitization," *Central Asian Survey*, 30, no. 2 (2011): 243–256; G. Tazmini, "The Islamic Revival in Central Asia: A Potent Force or a Misconception?", *Central Asian Survey,* 20, no. 1 (2001): 63–83.

5 T.J. Gunn, "Shaping an Islamic Identity: Religion, Islamism, and the State in Central Asia," *Sociology of Religion*, 64, no. 3 (2003): 389–410; C. Hann and M. Pelkmans, "Realigning Religion and Power in Central Asia: Islam, Nation-State and (Post)Socialism," *Europe-Asia Studies*, 61, no. 9 (2009): 1517–41; S. Peyrouse, "Islam in Central Asia: National Specificities and Post-Soviet Globalisation," *Religion, State and Society*, 35, no. 3 (2007): 245–260; G.M. Yemelianova, "Islam, National Identity, and Politics in Contemporary Kazakhstan," *Asian Ethnicity*, 15, no. 3 (2016): 286–301.

6 Akiner, "The Politicisation of Islam in Postsoviet Central Asia"; K. Collins and E. Owen, "Islamic Religiosity and Regime Preferences: Explaining Support for Democracy and Political Islam in Central Asia and the Caucasus," *Political Research Quarterly*, 20, no. 10 (2012): 1–19;

© KONINKLIJKE BRILL NV, LEIDEN, 2018 | DOI 10.1163/9789004357242_004

Asia eschew a narrowly political lens or challenge assumptions that Islam is necessarily political in nature, examining instead how Central Asians make sense of and engage in everyday Islamic praxis on the spiritual, communal, social, and personal levels.[7]

Most of the research in both of these veins—the role of Islam in political and nonpolitical life—take a qualitative approach, draw on secondary sources, and/or are meta-projects that extrapolate from existing work. Commonly used methods include focus groups, participant observation, and in-depth case studies at the subnational level, with specific cities, neighborhoods, and places of worship as the sites of investigation. With the exception of Collins and Owens and McGlinchey, and the partial exception of Ro'i and Wainer, research on the topic that draws on large-n public opinion data from the region is rare.[8]

While localized studies are invaluable in revealing meanings and the making of meaning in a given setting, there are also limitations. In particular, we

---

E. Karagiannis, "Political Islam and Social Movement Theory: The Case of Hizb ut-Tahrir in Kyrgyzstan," *Religion, State, and Society*, 33, no. 2 (2005): 137–150; Karim, "Globalization and Post-Soviet Revival of Islam"; Adeeb Khalid, *Islam after Communism: Religion and Politics in Central Asia* (Berkeley, CA: University of California Press, 2007); Hann and Pelkmans, "Realigning Religion and Power in Central Asia"; McGlinchey, "Islamic Revivalism and State Failure in Kyrgyzstan"; R. Zanca, "Believing in God at Your Own Risk: Religion and Terrorism in Uzbekistan," *Religion, State, and Society*, 33, no. 1 (2005): 71–82.

7   S. Abashin, "The Logic of Islamic Practice: a Religious Conflict in Central Asia," *Central Asian Survey*, 25, no. 3 (2006): 267–286; Pawel Jessa, "Aq Jol Soul Healers: Religious Pluralism and a Contemporary Muslim Movement in Kazakhstan," *Central Asian Survey*, 25, no. 3 (2006): 359–371; F. Heyat, "Re-Islamization in Kyrgyzstan: Gender, New Poverty and the Moral Dimension," *Central Asian Survey*, 23, nos. 3–4 (2004): 275–287; A. Khalid, "A Secular Islam: Nation, State, and Religion in Uzbekistan," *International Journal of Middle East Studies*, 35, no. 4 (2003): 573–598; M.E. Louw, *Everyday Islam in Post-Soviet Central Asia* (New York: Routledge, 2007); D.W. Montgomery, "Namaz, Wishing Trees, and Vodka: The Diversity of Everyday Religious Life in Central Asia," in J. Sahadeo and R. Zanca (eds), *Everyday Life in Central Asia: Past and Present* (Bloomington: Indiana University Press, 2007), 355–370; S.R. Roberts, "Everyday Negotiations of Islam in Central Asia: Practicing Religion in the Uyghur Neighborhood of Zarya Vostoka in Almaty, Kazakhstan," in J. Sahadeo and R. Zanca (eds), *Everyday Life in Central Asia: Past and Present* (Bloomington: Indiana University Press, 2007), 339–354; Y. Ro'i and A. Wainer, "Muslim Identity and Islamic Practice in Post-Soviet Central Asia," *Central Asian Survey*, 28, no. 3 (2007): 303–322; M. Stephan-Emmrich and A. Mirzoev, "The Manufacturing of Islamic Lifestyles in Tajikistan through the Prism of Dushanbe's Bazaars," *Central Asian Survey*, 35, no. 2 (2016): 157–177; Tazmini, "The Islamic Revival in Central Asia."

8   See Collins and Owen ("Islamic Religiosity and Regime Preferences"), McGlinchey ("Islamic Revivalism and State Failure in Kyrgyzstan"), and the partial exception of Ro'i and Wainer, "Muslim Identity and Islamic Practice."

know little about how Central Asians *across society as a whole* practice religion in their everyday lives or understand Islam's implications for conducting and organizing politics. We also know little about how and to what extent societal groups differ from one another in their practice of Islam or what factors affect how individuals interpret Islam's political role. Finally, given that existing small-n and large(r)-n data are almost always taken at a single point, we lack a firm sense of how views and practices have evolved over time and in which direction(s).

To address these gaps in our knowledge, we present the results of two rounds of nationally representative surveys, spaced five years apart, in Kazakhstan and Kyrgyzstan. Our study sheds light on patterns of religious identification, attendance of religious services, daily prayer, belief in the afterlife, and support for *shari'a* among members of Muslim ethnic groups[9] in these two countries. Importantly, our data allow us to compare changes that have taken place between 2007, when the surveys were first launched, and 2012, when we conducted the second wave.

We see our work as complementing and building upon prior research, while also providing a useful bird's eye view that allows us to perceive broader trends, both within and between these two societies. Our data confirm that a religious revival is indeed taking place among the two countries' Muslim populations, with almost 100 percent self-identification with Islam. Another indicator of religion's growing salience—belief in life after death, heaven, and hell—increased sharply in Kazakhstan by 2012, but still remained much lower than in Kyrgyzstan, where levels were relatively unchanged over the five-year period. Finally, religious orthodoxy, as measured by support for *shari'a*-based law, increased significantly in both countries in the five-year period. Combined, these developments suggest a growing acceptance of religious values, as well as political preferences that reflect religious values.

At the same time, how individuals practice Islam differed markedly between the two countries. In Kyrgyzstan weekly attendance of religious services more than doubled (112 percent increase), and those engaging in daily prayer grew by 62 percent. We observe the opposite trend in Kazakhstan, where the share of people praying daily and attending mosque weekly declined. Given abiding interest in Central Asia's Islamic revival, we unpack the factors associated with greater religiosity. Who is more likely to attend weekly religious services and pray daily? Who is more likely to support the implementation of *shari'a* law? To answer these questions, we run three regression models, where the outcomes of interest are religious practice and religious orthodoxy.

---

9 We provide a definition "Muslim ethnic groups" in the results section.

The chapter proceeds as follows. First, we derive predictions from the extant literature on Islam in Central Asia and test these against data from the 2007 and 2012 surveys. Next, we briefly explain the research design behind the surveys and how we collected our data. We then document changes in religious practice, religious beliefs, and support for shari'a in Kazakhstan and Kyrgyzstan over the five-year period. After describing these changes we run a series of regressions that help adjudicate between competing explanations behind what is driving the revival in Islamic practice and Islamic orthodoxy. We conclude by raising questions for future research on the implications of the evolving religiosity for the political and social environments in these two societies.

Religiosity Among Ethnic Muslims in Central Asia: The Current State of Knowledge

A growing body of research on Islam in Central Asia examines the delicate interplay between politics, nation-building, and identity formation, on the one hand, and the evolving practice of Islam, on the other.[10] Some studies use participant observation, focus groups, and in-depth interviews to provide embedded accounts of everyday religious practices among post-Soviet Central Asians.[11] Yet others focus on the threat of radical Islam in the region[12] and the role of non-indigenous religious movements on Islamic practice.[13] Based on prior empirical investigations, the following five statements represent what

---

10   e.g., Akiner, "The Politicisation of Islam in Post-Soviet Central Asia"; Hann and Pelkmans, "Realigning Religion and Power in Central Asia"; S. Spehr and N. Kassanova, "Kazakhstan: Constructing Identity in a Post-Soviet Society," *Asian Ethnicity*, 13, no. 2 (2012): 135–151; Yemelianova, "Islam, National Identity, and Politics in Contemporary Kazakhstan."

11   e.g. Montgomery, "Namaz, Wishing Trees, and Vodka"; Roberts, "Everyday Negotiations of Islam in Central Asia."

12   e.g., Karagiannis, "Political Islam and Social Movement Theory"; V. Naumkin, *Radical Islam in Central Asia* (Lanham, MD: Rowman and Littlefield Publishers, 2005); M.Y. Omelicheva, "The Ethnic Dimension of Religious Extremism and Terrorism in Central Asia," *International Political Science Review*, 31, no. 2 (2010): 167–186; Yemelianova, "Islam, National Identity, and Politics in Contemporary Kazakhstan"; Zanca, "Believing in God at Your Own Risk."

13   e.g., A. Muminov, "Fundamentalist Challenges to Local Islamic Traditions in Soviet and Post-Soviet Central Asia," in U. Tomohiko (ed.), *Empire, Islam, and Politics in Central Eurasia* (Sapporo, Japan: Slavic Research Center, 2007), 249–262.

scholars have uncovered about modern-day religiosity among Central Asian Muslims:

1. Being Muslim is a key part of Central Asian identity, and Muslimness is expressed in a variety of ways and through diverse practices.[14]

2. Revival in Islamic practice is a localized response to ineffective government, in which the state is unable to fulfill its basic social and economic responsibilities to an impoverished citizenry.[15] Islam serves as an important source of stability and survival.[16]

3. Over time there has been an increase in Central Asian religious orthodoxy and Islamic militancy.[17] This increase is driven by government control over and crackdown on religious practice.[18] Alternatively, support for fundamentalism remains limited to a minority and is unlikely to grow precisely because government repression and control are strong.[19]

4. Support for Islamic orthodoxy is stronger among ethnic minorities than among titular ethnic groups (i.e., Kazakhs in Kazakhstan and Kyrgyz in Kyrgyzstan). This dynamic is due to increased ethnic tensions or perceived discrimination against non-titulars[20] and exclusionary policies.[21] Alternatively, there is no difference in support for extremist ideologies between members of ethnic minorities and the titular ethnic group.[22]

5. Greater religiosity can be associated with lowered support for political tolerance, pluralism, and liberal democracy; in addition, individuals who are more religious are less likely to support secular forms of government and more likely to support the idea that Muslims should live in a

---

14   Jessa, "Aq Jol Soul Healers"; Heyat, "Re-Islamization in Kyrgyzstan"; Khalid, *Islam after Communism*; Omelicheva, "Islam in Kazakhstan"; Ro'i and Wainer, "Muslim Identity and Islamic Practice."

15   Heyat, "Re-Islamization in Kyrgyzstan"; McGlinchey, "Islamic Revivalism and State Failure in Kyrgyzstan."

16   Heyat, "Re-Islamization in Kyrgyzstan"; Jessa, "Aq Jol Soul Healers"; McGlinchey, "Islamic Revivalism and State Failure in Kyrgyzstan"; Montgomery, "Namaz, Wishing Trees, and Vodka"; Ro'i and Wainer, "Muslim Identity and Islamic Practice."

17   Omelicheva, "The Ethnic Dimension of Religious Extremism and Terrorism in Central Asia."

18   Ibid.; Zanca, "Believing in God at Your Own Risk."

19   Akiner, "The Politicisation of Islam in Post-Soviet Central Asia."

20   Abashin, "The Logic of Islamic Practice."

21   Omelicheva, "The Ethnic Dimension of Religious Extremism and Terrorism in Central Asia."

22   Montgomery, "Namaz, Wishing Trees, and Vodka"; Roberts, "Everyday Negotiations of Islam in Central Asia."

caliphate.[23] Alternatively, there is no clear or consistent relationship between religiosity and regime preference.[24]

At this point, we would like to offer some observations about the above statements. In the first four, religious identity and religious views are conceived of as the outcome of interest. That is, forms of religiosity are framed as outcomes to be unpacked and understood. Furthermore, statements 2, 3, and 4 offer specific causal arguments for Central Asian religious revival and support for orthodoxy, resulting from other economic, political, and societal factors. The fifth statement represents a shift in focus. Here, religiosity is viewed as an important factor that influences individual political preferences, including preferences about regime type. Religiosity affects or is bundled with other political values; the focus thus moves from understanding the determinants of (or causes behind) religiosity to interpreting its political implications.

One way of engaging with these statements is to view them not only as the outlines of what is known about religiosity among Central Asian Muslims, but to see them as a series of explanations for and expectations about how religiosity plays out. In some ways, explanations and expectations appear to coalesce, while in other ways they contradict one another. Our nationally representative, comparative public opinion data from Kazakhstan and Kyrgyzstan in 2007 and 2012 can help sift through these at times competing arguments. Where do our data support and enhance the findings and hypotheses drawn from prior studies? Just as important, where do they diverge or suggest a different interpretation? This is the task to which we now turn. Before comparing the results of our data analysis with previous findings, however, we first describe our research design and the collection of survey data.

Research Design and Data Collection

Despite a growing body of research and ongoing interest in the subject, our grasp of how Islam, religiosity, and their effect on political views have evolved among the general public is surprisingly limited. This study is unique in that it provides nationally representative data from two periods in time in two

---

23   Collins and Owen, "Islamic Religiosity and Regime Preferences"; Karagannis, "Political Islam and Social Movement Theory."

24   Collins and Owen, "Islamic Religiosity and Regime Preferences"; Khalid, "A Secular Islam"; Roberts, "Everyday Negotiations of Islam in Central Asia"; Montgomery, "Namaz, Wishing Trees, and Vodka"; Tazmini, "The Islamic Revival in Central Asia."

different countries. One of the very few survey-based studies of religiosity in Central Asia was carried out by Ro'i and Wainer in 2006.[25] They conducted 697 structured interviews in Kazakhstan, Kyrgyzstan, Tajikistan, and Uzbekistan, and most participants were selected using the snowball method. Surveys conducted in Azerbaijan and Kyrgyzstan by Collins and Owens are also from 2006.[26] Overall, the lack of more recent nationally representative public opinion data is striking.[27]

Our surveys were designed to produce an internationally comparative dataset. The questionnaire covers a broad range of socio-political and economic topics; in addition to our interest in religious practice, we incorporated other sets of questions that reflect theoretical and empirical debates in sociology, political science, and area studies. These include questions that tap into citizens' media consumption, political attitudes, perceptions of social and economic inequality, ideas about the role of government in the economy, trust in institutions, and inter-generational social mobility. All questions were drawn from well-established surveys, including the International Social Justice Project (ISJP), the International Social Survey Program (ISSP), the World Values Survey, and Afrobarometer. The use of pre-tested and commonly used questions was an intentional component of the study's design, as it both helps ensure reliable and valid measurement and enables theoretically intriguing comparisons of data collected in Central Asia to that collected elsewhere.[28] We recognize that surveys geared toward generalizability risk overlooking context-specific understandings and assume that respondents share interpretations of certain definitions and concepts that may in fact be quite different. Yet, we are confident that these risks are offset by the advantages of survey research, especially since our work takes place within a research context that is primarily qualitative, with numerous studies that do an excellent job of uncovering meaning at the individual and local levels.

In 2007, our research team completed 1,099 interviews in Kazakhstan and 1,000 in Kyrgyzstan. In 2012, additional funding permitted us to increase the sample size, and 1,500 interviews completed in each country. The 2007 response rates in Kyrgyzstan and Kazakhstan were 94 percent and 76 percent,

---

25   Ro'i and Wainer, "Muslim Identity and Islamic Practice."
26   Collins and Owens, "Islamic Religiosity and Regime Preferences."
27   As cited in Ro'i and Wainer ("Muslim Identity and Islamic Practice"), in the early 1990s there were several studies of public opinion in Kazakhstan and Uzbekistan that included questions dealing with religiosity.
28   Details of the research design and respondent selection are available from the authors upon request.

respectively; in 2012 the Kazakhstan portion of the study equaled 60.1 percent, while the response rate for the Kyrgyzstan portion was 89.6 percent. According to the research organizations that carried out the surveys, these response rates are typical. Lowered response rates in Kazakhstan are commonly attributed to growing weariness with survey researchers brought about by the recent proliferation of marketing studies. In Kyrgyzstan, fewer public opinion studies take place due to a weak economy and, as a consequence, people are "unspoiled" by attention from researchers. There was some difficulty in accessing wealthy households, but this problem is endemic to survey research, as it is nearly impossible to survey the most well off in any society.[29]

Results from the 2007 and 2012 Surveys

For the purposes of the present analysis, we restrict our data to include only responses from ethnic groups that are considered traditionally Muslim. Although our surveys were administered to people from various faiths and life experiences, including both Muslims and non-Muslims, here we exclude responses from non-Muslim ethnicities (e.g., Russian, Ukrainian, Korean, etc.). We use the term "ethnic Muslim" to describe members of ethnic groups that converted to Islam prior to Soviet rule and "where Islam (has) constituted a central component of the national culture."[30] Among our survey respondents, Muslims include Kazakhs, Kyrgyz, Uzbeks, Tatars, Uyghurs, and other ethnicities, for a total of nearly 30 different groups.[31] Note that the question of religious self-identification is separate from belonging to a Muslim ethnic group, as some respondents who are ethnically Muslim self-identify as Muslim while others do not. In our 2007 sample, there were 606 ethnic Muslims in Kazakhstan and 912 in Kyrgyzstan. The number of ethnic Muslims in the 2012 sample equaled 912 in Kazakhstan and 1,383 in Kyrgyzstan.

In this section, we report on indicators of religious practice based on data from both waves of surveys. We are interested in uncovering empirical similarities and differences between Kazakhstan and Kyrgyzstan and especially any trends or divergence that have occurred from 2007 to 2012. Wherever possible,

---

29 For an impressive exception to this rule in the US context, see B. Page, L. Bartels, and J. Seawright, "Democracy and the Policy Preferences of Wealthy Americans," *Perspectives on Politics*, 11, no. 1 (2013): 51–73.

30 R'oi and Wainer, "Muslim Identity and Islamic Practice," 306.

31 A full list of the ethnic Muslim groups included among our respondents is available from the authors upon request.

we relate our findings to those derived from prior studies. Following our discussion of the trends in evidence, we make an effort at causal inference and run a series of regression analyses. We test whether the determinants of religious practice (measured by weekly attendance at religious services and daily prayer outside of religious services) as described in the existing literature hold true among the general population of ethnic Muslims in Kazakhstan and Kyrgyzstan. Next, to get at the question of religious orthodoxy, we use regression analysis to uncover the factors impacting the level of support for shari'a law.

Muslim Identity and Religious Practice

As noted, prior studies highlight the growing importance of Islam in Central Asian identity; in fact, there is broad consensus that a revival in Islamic practice is currently taking place.[32] Our data, presented in Table 2.1, generally bear these findings out. If we look at religious self-identification, for example, by 2012 nearly 95 percent of ethnic Muslims in both countries described themselves as Muslim. This high rate clearly confirms the strong salience of Muslim self-identification across the two societies.

TABLE 2.1   *Trends in religiosity by country, 2007 and 2012*

Percentage of respondents who:	Kazakhstan		Kyrgyzstan	
	2007 (n=606)	2012 (n=912)	2007 (n=839)	2012 (n=1,383)
Self identify as Muslim	79.87	93.53	97.50	94.79
Express belief in life after death	36.30	51.54	71.39	66.67
Express belief in hell	41.58	57.24	72.59	73.10
Express belief in heaven	43.73	60.64	72.94	78.45
Attend religious services at least once a week	15.51	12.72	15.38	32.61
Pray to God daily outside of religious services	22.94	18.20	35.76	57.99
Belief that it is very important that "good government should implement only Shari'a law"	5.45	13.04	7.15	10.34

---

32   Omelicheva, "Islam in Kazakhstan"; Ro'i and Wainer, "Muslim Identity and Islamic Practice."

At the same time, the data reveal interesting cross-national variation. Just five years prior, in 2007, less than 80 percent of ethnic Muslim respondents in Kazakhstan identified themselves as Muslim. To compare, in Kyrgyzstan this number exceeded 97 percent. Our data suggest that the revival described in prior studies began sooner in Kyrgyzstan than in Kazakhstan. It may also be that the salience of Muslim identity was higher in Kyrgyzstan to begin with. In either case, by the early 2010s this gap was closed, and religious identification among Kazakhstani ethnic Muslims is now on par with their counterparts in Kyrgyzstan. It appears that self-identifying as Muslim is now the norm among the vast majority of both countries' ethnic Muslims.

Other differences emerge in the data. We can divide these into two broad categories: religious beliefs and religious practice. As an indicator of religious beliefs, we asked respondents if they believed in heaven, hell, and the afterlife.[33] In 2007 those reporting belief in life after death, heaven, and hell were much lower in Kazakhstan than in Kyrgyzstan. By 2012, belief in the afterlife increased sharply in Kazakhstan, but still fell well short of the degree of belief observed in Kyrgyzstan. In Kyrgyzstan, those expressing belief in heaven, hell, and the afterlife hovered between 67 and 78 percent, while only half to three-fifths of Kazakhstani respondents shared these beliefs. Although a religious revival in terms of self-identification with Islam is taking place in the two societies, other aspects—such as internalization of certain religious beliefs—are less clear-cut. By looking at beliefs, then, we are presented with a more nuanced comparative picture.

Further cross-national distinctions surface when we look at religious practice. In 2007 the two countries had essentially identical percentages of respondents who attended religious services on a weekly basis (around 15 percent). Yet, by 2012 they diverged sharply. Based on survey responses, weekly attendance more than doubled in Kyrgyzstan to 33 percent, and the percentage of people engaging in daily prayer outside of religious services grew sharply, from 36 to 56 percent. Interestingly, we observe no comparable increase in Kazakhstan. Although our data generally support previous studies that show that most Muslims in Kyrgyzstan, as well as in Kazakhstan, "do not attend

---

33   We used this question to be as applicable to as many respondents as possible. As noted, respondents represent a variety of religious faiths; thus we decided to use questions that would apply irrespective of their particular religion. In future iterations we intend to include additional questions that get at the beliefs that actually distinguish Muslims (in the eyes of Muslims) from believers of other faiths. We thank one of our anonymous reviewers for this suggestion.

mosque, even occasionally,"[34] the data also suggest alternate—and perhaps opposing—patterns. In Kyrgyzstan, the trend seems to be toward greater participation in religious practice over time. In Kazakhstan, on the other hand, the trend is either maintenance of low levels of participation or even a slight decline in participation.

These findings about religious beliefs and religious practices coincide for the most part with prior studies. Despite strong self-identification with Islam, within Central Asia religious beliefs and practices are indeed diverse.[35] We show, moreover, that religious diversity *between* countries is as important to consider as that within a particular group or community. Although one-third of Kyrgyzstani Muslims state that they attend mosque weekly, and more than half report engaging in daily prayer, less than 20 percent of Kazakhstani Muslims state that they do so. Rather than greater religious participation over the years, it appears that Kazakhstani Muslims are less likely to participate as time passes.

Finally, we asked a question about shari'a law, which has been used in prior studies as a proxy for religious orthodoxy.[36] Support for shari'a can also serve as a measure of political preferences, and this is important because some studies show a link between religious values and political values.[37] While a minority view, the opinion that "good government should implement only shari'a law" is on the rise. In Kazakhstan those who felt that it was "very important" for good government to adopt laws in line with shari'a more than doubled from 2007 (5.45 percent) to 2012 (13.04 percent). Kyrgyzstan has also seen an increase in this category. However, the increase, from seven to ten percent, was less dramatic.

Curiously, Kazakhstan, despite having lower levels of daily prayer and weekly religious service attendance, had surpassed Kyrgyzstan in the share of

---

34   C. Chotaeva, "The Ethnic and Religious Situation in Kyrgyzstan," *Central Asia and the Caucasus*, 33, no. 3 (2005): 70; as referenced by R'oi and Wainer, "Muslim Identity and Islamic Practice."

35   Jessa, "Aq Jol Soul Healers"; Heyat, "Re-Islamization in Kyrgyzstan"; Khalid, *Islam after Communism*; Omelicheva, "Islam in Kazakhstan"; Ro'i and Wainer, "Muslim Identity and Islamic Practice."

36   N.J. Davis and R.V. Robinson, "The Egalitarian Face of Islamic Orthodoxy: Support for Islamic Law and Economic Justice in Seven Muslim-Majority Nations," *American Sociological Review*, 71, no. 2 (2006): 167–190; A. Junisbai, "Understanding Economic Justice Attitudes in Two Countries: Kazakhstan and Kyrgyzstan," *Social Forces*, 88, no. 4 (2010): 1677–1702.

37   Collins and Owen, "Islamic Religiosity and Regime Preferences"; Davis and Robinson, "The Egalitarian Face of Islamic Orthodoxy."

the strongest supporters of shariʾa by 2012. One way to explain this difference is to refer back to insights from Omelicheva and Zanca, who argue that government repression and crackdowns on religious practice have generated greater support for what has been described as radical or fundamentalist Islam.[38] Comparatively, officials in Kazakhstan exert much greater control over religious expression than in Kyrgyzstan. It is worth asking if more rigorous efforts to control religious practice in Kazakhstan produced the unexpected surge in religious orthodoxy there. It could be that government control and monitoring of religious activity have dampened certain forms of religious practice, such as weekly mosque attendance and daily prayer, while encouraging alternative forms—or forms that challenge the political status quo. Indeed, if we follow the line of argument by Omelicheva and Zanca, Kazakhstani government policies toward Islam may be exacerbating, rather than curbing, religious orthodoxy—and this may be a societal and individual-level response to government efforts to clamp down on religion. We revisit and expand upon our political interpretation of support for shariʾa in the next section.

Weekly Religious Services and Daily Prayer
We now consider what individual-level factors account for the variation we find in religious practice and religious orthodoxy in Kazakhstan and Kyrgyzstan. To do so, in this and the next sub-section we engage with some of the causal arguments that have been offered about what accounts for the growing salience of Islam in Central Asia. To get at religious practice we first raise the question, What characteristics are associated with greater proclivity toward weekly mosque attendance and daily prayer? To get at orthodoxy we then ask, What distinguishes those who strongly support the implementation of shariʾa law?

According to prior studies, the revival in Islamic praxis is associated with and affected by a number of factors. Poverty, minority (non-titular) ethnic status, and government ineffectiveness (or the government's inability to fulfill its social and economic obligations) have all been cited as causes.[39] We test these explanations by running two separate logistic regression models in which the outcome of interest is religious practice in the form of (a) attending mosque weekly and (b) praying daily.

---

38   Omelicheva, "The Ethnic Dimension of Religious Extremism and Terrorism in Central
      Asia"; Zanca, "Believing in God at Your Own Risk."
39   Heyat, "Re-Islamization in Kyrgyzstan"; McGlinchey, "Islamic Revivalism and State Failure
      in Kyrgyzstan"; Omelicheva, "The Ethnic Dimension of Religious Extremism and Terror-
      ism in Central Asia."

TABLE 2.2   *Explanatory factors/independent variables included in regression models*

Variables	Definition
Male	= 1 if respondent is male; otherwise = 0
Age	= respondent's full years of age
Rural	= 1 if respondent resides in a rural area; otherwise = 0
University	= 1 if respondent has a Bachelor's degree or higher
Household income	= respondent's monthly household income, standardized
Opinion about income differences	= degree of agreement with the following statement: "Current differences in income in COUNTRY are too large"
Perceived fairness of economic system	= scale computed as mean value of respondents' degree of agreement with the following statements: (1) In COUNTRY people get rewarded for their intelligence and skill. (2) In COUNTRY people get rewarded for their effort. (3) In COUNTRY people get what they need. (4) In COUNTRY people have equal opportunities to get ahead. Answers ranged from strongly disagree (1) to strongly agree (5) with a higher score corresponding with the view of society's economic system as legitimate.
Ethnic minority	= 1 if respondent belongs to non-titular ethnic group; otherwise = 0
North Kazakhstan (south Kazakhstan = reference)	= 1 if respondent resides in Akmola, Kostanai, Pavlodar or North Kazakhstan *oblasts*
East Kazakhstan	= 1 if respondent resides in East Kazakhstan *oblast*
West Kazakhstan	= 1 if respondent resides in Aktobe, Atyrau, Mangystau or West Kazakhstan *oblasts*
Central Kazakhstan	= 1 if respondent resides in Karaganda *oblast*
Astana	= 1, if respondent resides in the city of Astana; otherwise = 0
Almaty	= 1, if respondent resides in the city of Almaty; otherwise = 0
North Kyrgyzstan (south Kyrgyzstan = reference)	= 1 if respondent resides in Chui, Naryn, Issyk-Kul, or Talas *oblasts*
Bishkek	= 1, if respondent resides in the city of Bishkek; otherwise = 0
Osh	= 1, if respondent resides in the city of Osh; otherwise = 0

Before we report the results of the two regressions, we first briefly describe the variables that we included as potential explanatory factors (see Table 2.2). To account for poverty, we use household income.[40] To account for perceptions of government ineffectiveness, we include two attitudinal measures: whether or not respondents perceive differences in income in their country to be too great and whether they perceive the current economic system to be fair. Third, to see if there are differences between the titular ethnicity and minority ethnic groups, we include respondents' self-reported ethnicity and categorize these as either minority or titular ethnicity. We also control for demographic factors like sex, age, rural versus urban residence, and educational attainment, given that such characteristics have been found to affect individual behaviors and attitudes more generally.

For ease of interpretation, we report only the direction of the relationship—no relationship, positive relationship, or negative relationship—rather than provide numerical output from the regression.[41] The number 0 (zero) indicates that there is no statistically significant relationship between the listed variable and the particular form of religious practice. In other words, an individual exhibiting the characteristic in column 1 is no more likely than others to attend weekly religious services or pray daily. The + (plus) sign means that there is a positive relationship between that characteristic and religious practice. The − (minus) sign means that there is a negative or inverse relationship between a particular characteristic and religious practice.

Referring to the results in Tables 2.3 and 2.4, we find a number of commonalities between the countries in both years. Men are more likely than women to attend mosque on a weekly basis. Women, on the other hand, are more likely than men to pray daily outside of religious services. Like women, older individuals are more likely to engage in daily prayer. Yet, while older individuals were more likely to attend mosque weekly in 2007, they were no more likely than other age groups to do so in 2012.

We observe other non-differences between groups that are worth drawing attention to. One might hypothesize that those with university education are less likely to engage in religious practice, as additional education is generally

---

40   There are alternative indicators of poverty, some of which ask respondents to include informal sources of income. Here, we followed standard practice in sociology and political science and include household income. In future iterations of our survey, we may include alternative measures.

41   Please contact the authors for the regression output.

TABLE 2.3   *Determinants of weekly religious services by country, 2007 and 2012*

	Kazakhstan		Kyrgyzstan	
	2007	**2012**	**2007**	**2012**
Demographic characteristics (control variables)				
Male vs female	+	+	+	+
Age	+	o	+	o
Rural vs urban	+	o	−	o
University degree	o	o	o	o
Poverty				
Household income	o	o	o	o
Perceived fairness of economic system				
Income differences in the country are too large	o	o	−	o
Perceived economic system legitimacy	o	+	o	o
Ethnic group differences				
Minority vs titular ethnicity	+	o	+	o

TABLE 2.4   *Determinants of daily prayer by country, 2007 and 2012*

	Kazakhstan		Kyrgyzstan	
	2007	**2012**	**2007**	**2012**
Demographic characteristics (control variables)				
Male vs female	−	−	−	−
Age	+	+	+	+
Rural vs urban	o	o	o	o
University degree	o	o	o	−
Poverty				
Household income	o	o	o	+
Perceived fairness of economic system				
Income differences in the country are too large	o	o	o	o
Economic system legitimacy	o	+	o	+
Ethnic group differences				
Minority Muslim vs titular ethnicity	o	+	+	+

associated with greater secularism.[42] One might also speculate that those living in rural areas are more likely to pray and attend mosque than city dwellers, given that urbanization is similarly associated with secularism. Alternatively, one might argue that certain populations of urban dwellers are more likely to exhibit religiosity; this could be due to alienation and less social embededness or due to greater access to religious education.[43] In the case of both possibilities, the regression results reveal no group differences, either by educational attainment or rural residence. University graduates are no more or less likely than others to attend mosque in either country. Moreover, with the exception of Kyrgyzstan in 2012, those with higher education pray at similar levels as those with less education. Only in Kyrgyzstan during the second wave of surveys do we observe a statistically significant difference between the well educated and other groups, and the effect is in the direction predicted: Those with higher education are less likely to engage in daily prayer.

Turning to rural versus urban residency, the data show that those who live in villages are no more likely than others to pray daily. Again, this finding applies to Kazakhstan and Kyrgyzstan in both years. Nor are the two countries' rural residents consistently more likely to regularly visit the mosque. In 2007 villagers were more likely than others to attend weekly religious services in Kazakhstan, but less likely to do so in Kyrgyzstan. By 2012 these differences were no longer observable. Those living in urban areas were just as likely as their rural counterparts to attend mosque once a week.

Non-differences extend to poverty, as well. Research suggests that poverty is associated with an increase in religious practice, as people and communities in need turn to Islam as a source of stability and survival.[44] Our data tell a somewhat different story. Those living in poorer households are no more or less likely than other income groups to attend weekly religious services. This finding holds true in Kazakhstan and Kyrgyzstan and in both of the years that the surveys were administered. In Kazakhstan, furthermore, we find that those residing in families with lower incomes are no more likely to pray daily, just as the poor in Kazakhstan are no more likely than those from higher socioeconomic groups to attend mosque weekly. Interestingly, in Kyrgyzstan in 2012 those from wealthier families were *more* likely, rather than less likely, to pray

42   R. Inglehart and C. Welzel, *Modernization, Cultural Change, and Democracy: The Human Development Sequence* (New York: Cambridge University Press, 2005).

43   We would like to thank our peer reviewers for pointing this alternative out to us.

44   Heyat, "Re-Islamization in Kyrgyzstan"; Jessa, "Aq Jol Soul Healers"; McGlinchey, "Islamic Revivalism and State Failure in Kyrgyzstan"; Montgomery, "Namaz, Wishing Trees, and Vodka"; Ro'i and Wainer, "Muslim Identity and Islamic Practice."

daily. Collectively, these findings suggest that there is either no relationship between poverty and religious practice at the individual level or that the relationship is at times inconsistent with predictions drawn from the literature.

We now turn from poverty as a determinant of increased religious practice to perceptions of economic fairness. Some scholars connect the revival and increase in religious practice to government ineffectiveness.[45] When the government cannot ensure a basic level of social support and promote conditions for the economy to flourish, poverty spreads and individuals and communities turn to religious institutions and religious practice for support. Our results partially conform to expectations that government ineffectiveness is associated with an increase in religious practice.

As a proxy for government ineffectiveness, we include two variables: opinion about income differences in the country and an index of economic system fairness. We recognize that these are imperfect measures, but also argue that they represent a reasonable initial attempt at operationalizing how individuals perceive the degree to which government is carrying out its social and economic responsibilities. Studies linking government performance to religious practice at the individual level suggest that failure to address poverty and, relatedly, inequality indicates government ineffectiveness. In the same spirit, individual perceptions of how (un)equal society is and how (un)fair the economic system is both tap into the degree to which government is seen as effective or ineffective in fulfilling its role in promoting collective well-being.

Based on the regression results, for the most part individual perceptions of the economic system have no bearing on religious practice in either country. Those who feel that their country is characterized by too much income inequality are no more likely to pray than others, and this non-difference is found in Kazakhstan as well as in Kyrgyzstan during both waves of our survey. Those who believe that income differences in the country are too great are similarly no more likely to attend mosque weekly—with the exception of Kyrgyzstan in 2007.

The second variable measuring perceptions of system fairness, however, yields unexpected results. Those who believe that the economic system is fairer were more likely to pray daily in both Kazakhstan and Kyrgyzstan in the 2012 sample. They were also are more likely to attend weekly religious services in Kazakhstan in 2012. Put otherwise, those who are vested in the current economic system and believe it to be legitimate appear to be more likely to engage in religious practice. This finding is in line with McGlinchey, who argues that

---

45   Heyat, "Re-Islamization in Kyrgyzstan"; McGlinchey, "Islamic Revivalism and State Failure in Kyrgyzstan."

participation in religious worship may enhance political and social stability, rather than represent challenges to it.[46] On the other hand, the fact that those who are more critical of the status quo were less likely to pray and attend mosque in Kazakhstan in 2012 could be troubling for stability there. For example, lower levels of participation in weekly services by those who are dissatisfied with the current economic system may indicate disengagement from publicly acceptable and mainstream religious practice.

Finally, the data reveal that ethnic minorities in Kyrgyzstan and Kazakhstan are indeed different from members of the titular ethnicity in terms of religious practice. Non-titular Muslims are more likely to attend weekly services in both countries (in the 2007 data) and consistently more likely to pray daily (with the exception of Kazakhstan in 2007). While the question of religious practice differs from the question of support for orthodoxy, our results lean toward supporting Omelicheva's prediction that minorities in Central Asia are qualitatively different in their expression of religiosity than the dominant ethnic group.[47] Yet, it is not clear if this means that minorities are more likely to hold views that might undermine social and political stability, as has been proposed in other studies. We return to the connection between ethnic minorities and religious orthodoxy below.

In these two regression models, we found only a few characteristics to be closely associated with heightened religious practice. These include differences by sex and ethnic group. Other often-cited factors at the individual level, such as poverty and rural residence, have no significant effect, signaling that engagement in religious praxis, as operationalized in our study, is evenly distributed across social groups. There is no defined individual or social profile that makes some more likely to engage in practices associated with greater religiosity or religious revival. At the same time, at least in Kazakhstan, more optimistic assessments of economic system fairness tend to be associated with religious participation. Our findings for Kazakhstan diverge from expectations that the rise in religious practice is driven by perceptions of government ineffectiveness; instead, we find that positive perceptions generate greater participation.

Support for Sharīʿa

We now turn to the final question animating our study: What characteristics are associated with greater support for Islamic orthodoxy? We raise this

---

46   McGlinchey, "Islamic Revivalism and State Failure in Kyrgyzstan."

47   Omelicheva, "The Ethnic Dimension of Religious Extremism and Terrorism in Central Asia."

question to engage with research that reports a growth in what has been described as "fundamentalist" or "radical" views among Central Asian Muslims and/or greater support for groups espousing these views.[48] Perceived importance of shari'a as the basis of law provides one measure of orthodoxy. We follow Davis and Robinson[49] by asking respondents to assess the importance of shari'a for good governance. Those who feel that shari'a should be the basis of the country's legal foundation are considered to be more religiously orthodox.

Recall that in the latest wave of surveys 13 percent of respondents in Kazakhstan and ten percent in Kyrgyzstan considered the implementation of Islamic law to be very important. If we look at the opposite end of the spectrum, to those who consider shari'a to be completely unimportant to good governance, we witness a concomitant decline. In 2007 around 21 percent of Kazakhstani ethnic Muslims and around 17 percent of Kyrgyzstani ethnic Muslims fell in this category. In 2012, however, these figures were 17 percent and 10 percent, respectively. The decline in Kyrgyzstan is especially striking, with a seven-percentage point drop. These trends—more of those who find shari'a to be very important and fewer of those who find to it be not important—align with extant scholarship that describes growth in religious orthodoxy in the region in recent years.

To determine what factors are associated with religious orthodoxy, we run an ordered logistic regression model. The results are summarized in Table 2.5.[50] The variables listed in column 1 include the usual demographic controls (sex, age, and education), plus the factors that prior studies argue are causally important: poverty, perceptions of economic system fairness, and ethnic minority status. We augment this list with geographic or place-specific divisions within each country, hypothesizing that location and context matter in forming individual preferences. For example, we expect rural residents and those living in the South to be more religiously orthodox than others, whereas those living in capital cities should be more likely to subscribe to liberal or secular values. Again, the alternative could also be true—compared with rural residents, urbanites could have access to religious education that might encourage greater orthodoxy.

---

48   Abashin, "The Logic of Islamic Practice"; Omelicheva, "The Ethnic Dimension of Religious Extremism and Terrorism in Central Asia."
49   Davis and Robinson, "The Egalitarian Face of Islamic Orthodoxy."
50   The results presented in Table 2.5 can be read in the same manner as the output presented in Tables 3 and 4. The level of statistical significance for + and − is at the 0.05 level or higher.

TABLE 2.5   *Determinants of support for Shari'a law by country, 2007 and 2012*

	Kazakhstan		Kyrgyzstan	
	2007	2012	2007	2012
Demographic characteristics (control variables)				
Male vs female	O	O	O	O
Age	O	O	O	O
University degree	O	–	O	O
Poverty				
Household income	O	–	O	O
Perceived economic system fairness				
Income differences in country too large	O	O	+	+
Economic system legitimacy	O	+	O	O
Ethnic group differences				
Minority Muslim vs titular ethnicity	O	O	O	–
Contextual/place-based differences				
Rural v urban	+	O	+	O
North KZ	–	O	NA	NA
East KZ	–	–	NA	NA
West KZ	–	O	NA	NA
Central KZ	–	+	NA	NA
Astana	O	O	NA	NA
Almaty City	+	+	NA	NA
North KG (south = reference category)	NA	NA	–	–
Bishkek	NA	NA	O	O
Osh City	NA	NA	+	O

Beginning with non-differences, we find a number of similar trends in the two countries. Individual support for shari'a is evenly distributed across society, irrespective of economic status, age, sex, or educational attainment. This suggests that the appeal of shari'a may be growing not only among more vulnerable populations, but felt broadly among diverse social groups. In other words, the tendency toward orthodoxy is not restricted to people from less privileged socioeconomic backgrounds. Being part of the middle class, with access to higher education and higher household income, is not necessarily a deterrent against politically tinged views that Central Asian governments find threatening.

Neither are ethnic minorities generally more likely to support orthodoxy than members of the titular nationality. Only in 2007 in Kyrgyzstan do non-titulars hold significantly different views of the importance of shari'a. Crucially, they are less—not more—likely to express support for shari'a. This finding diverges from that of Omelicheva, who argues that ethnic minorities in Central Asia are more likely to support radicalism and radical religious groups.[51] Although the question we posed is not identical to that posed by Omelicheva, we argue that both formulations tap into support for orthodoxy, albeit in different ways.

Juxtaposed against the above non-differences are the effects of a number of contextual or place-based factors. In both Kazakhstan and Kyrgyzstan area of residence has a strong effect on individual tendencies to hold more orthodox views. Unsurprisingly, those who live in the South are far more likely to express support for shari'a law than those residing elsewhere. Yet, there are exceptions to this pattern in Kazakhstan. In 2012, there was no significant difference in orthodoxy between southern and western residents or between southern and northern residents. Both the West and the South are considered more conservative than other parts of the country, so the non-difference between them makes intuitive sense. The North and South, however, are usually considered very different, with greater Russian influence and russification in the north. It is therefore surprising that for one of the survey years there was no statistically significant difference in the probability of supporting shari'a in the South as compared to the North.

As is the case with residing in the South, living in the main southern cities, Almaty, Kazakhstan, (in 2007 and 2012) and Osh, Kyrgyzstan (in 2007), had a strong positive effect. Residents in these two cities were more likely than others to believe in the importance of shari'a in the formulation and implementation of laws. Today both cities are considered centers of southern culture and commerce, although Almaty (as the former capital of Kazakhstan and the Kazakh Soviet Socialist Republic before it) was highly russified during the Soviet period. To account for stronger preferences for orthodoxy in these two cities, we interpret support for shari'a through a political lens. As Davis and Robinson argue, support for shari'a not only represents a set of religious values, but is also inherently political in nature.[52]

Building on this logic, we argue that greater support for shari'a in Almaty and Osh coincides with these two cities' status as historically sympathetic to

51   Omelicheva, "The Ethnic Dimension of Religious Extremism and Terrorism in Central Asia."

52   Davis and Robinson, "The Egalitarian Face of Islamic Orthodoxy."

opposition movements, parties, and politicians. Almaty is known as the city where the ruling presidential party consistently receives the lowest electoral support. Osh, similarly, is well known as a bastion of pro-opposition and anti-regime sentiment, and this was true especially during the Akayev presidency. Finally, both cities are known for having more developed civic institutions and greater civic and political activism as compared with other parts of the country.[53] We thus interpret stronger support for Islamic law in both cities as an alternative vision of politics that stands in contradistinction to the political status quo.

In contrast to the broadly similar relationships between locale and support for shari'a in Kazakhstan and Kyrgyzstan, there is one notable way in which the countries' internal dynamics differ. In Kyrgyzstan, those who feel that income differences are too large are significantly more likely to espouse orthodox views, while in Kazakhstan there is no clear relationship between perceived fairness of the economic system and support for shari'a. The two countries' divergent economic trajectories following the collapse of the Soviet Union, in particular economic decline in Kyrgyzstan and a far smaller role there for government in providing basic social services and social safety net, may account for the dissimilar dynamics at play in each country.[54]

Conclusion

In Kazakhstan and Kyrgyzstan the overwhelming majority of Muslims self-identity as such—nearly 100 percent among our 2012 sample and up from 80 percent in Kazakhstan in 2007. If we dig a bit deeper, however, we observe cross-national variation in religious beliefs and religious practice. Belief in the afterlife, heaven, and hell are more widespread among ethnic Muslims in Kyrgyzstan than in Kazakhstan, by 15 percentage points or more. Ethnic Muslims in Kyrgyzstan are also more likely to attend mosque weekly and to pray daily outside of religious services. From 2007 to 2012 those who reported attending mosque weekly grew more than two-fold and those who reported praying daily went up by 62 percent. During the same period, Kazakhstan experienced a drop in both forms of religious practice, with just under 13 percent of respondents indicating that they attend mosque weekly and 18 percent

53 K. McMann, *Economic Autonomy and Democracy: Hybrid Regimes in Russia and Kyrgyzstan* (New York: Cambridge University Press, 2006).

54 A. Junisbai, "The Determinants of Economic System Legitimacy in Kazakhstan," *Europe-Asia Studies,* 66, no. 8 (2014): 1234–52.

reporting that they pray daily. Contrasted against the backdrop of greater engagement in religious practice in Kyrgyzstan is a steep rise in expressions of religious orthodoxy in Kazakhstan. While both societies have experienced a growth among those who express strong support for shari'a, this group more than doubled in Kazakhstan (with a rise of 139 percent, as compared with 45 percent in Kyrgyzstan).

Drawing on two waves of public opinion surveys in the first decade and a half of the 2000s, we tested factors commonly cited as explanations for the increase in religiosity and orthodoxy in Central Asia. Based on our analysis, many of the "usual suspects"[55] have either no significant effect or exhibit effects that are inconsistent with, or even contradict, expectations. These include poverty, minority status, and government failure to provide basic social benefits. Instead, we propose two alternative explanations. First, building on the work of Omelicheva and Zanca, we attribute the differences in belief, practice, and orthodoxy to differences in how the regime responds to religious expression. Greater control over and repression of religiosity in Kazakhstan may be re-routing individuals toward more orthodox views there than in Kyrgyzstan, where there is greater freedom—or at least less hindrance on the part of government—to worship.

Our second explanation similarly looks beyond individual-level factors or factors at the social-group level to institutional effects. By introducing regions into the analysis, we confirm that residing in the South has a strong and positive effect on the probability that someone will hold more orthodox views. We see region as providing a socializing context through a host of institutions, from religious and social to political. Those residing in the South tend to express more orthodox views precisely because the context in which they are socialized promotes these.

At the outset we inferred five statements or hypotheses about Islam in Central Asia from the existing literature. Four of these were explanations for religious revival and descriptions of who is likely to engage in religious practice and why. The last statement, in contrast, explained the connection between religiosity and political preferences or values. Our analysis focused mainly on testing predictions about who is more likely to exhibit behaviors associated with greater religiosity. Only in our analysis of shari'a do we touch upon the political, arguing that context—regime-level, as well as regional or place-based context—affects individual behavior and preferences.

55   J. Hacker and P. Pierson, *Winner-Take-All Politics: How Washington Made the Rich Richer— and Turned Its Back on the Middle Class* (New York: Simon and Schuster, 2010).

In a future study we plan to shift focus to investigate the effects of religious praxis and orthodoxy, among other factors, on political preferences and values in Kazakhstan and Kyrgyzstan. How, if at all, do religiosity and secularism impact political values? For example, are the religiously orthodox more or less likely to view free expression and fair elections as essential? What effect, if any, does the divergence in the two societies' economic fortunes and religious praxis have on public support for democracy? Our data are uniquely suited to help shed light on these important questions.

CHAPTER 3

Uzbekness and Islam: A Survey-based Analysis of Identity in Uzbekistan

Yaacov Ro'i and Alon Wainer

Uzbekistan came into being as an independent nation-state with the break-up of the Soviet Union toward the end of 1991, retaining the boundaries of the Uzbek Soviet Socialist Republic. Unlike some of the USSR's 15 successor states, Uzbekistan – like its four Central Asian neighbors – had not had a meaningful national movement through the 1980s. The few nationalistically inclined groups and parties, such as Erk and Birlik, that surfaced in the second half of the decade had put forward nationalist platforms in an attempt to provide an alternative to the established hierarchy that ruled the Uzbek union republic. They had, however, no significant constituency and stood little chance against the well-oiled and politically experienced establishment that took over the new state framework.

Inevitably, one of the tasks of the old-new rulers was to provide the new state with an ideology or collective value system and identity that would supplant the defunct Marxist-Leninist framework.[1] This was essential in light of the much-publicized threat of an Islamist takeover such as was imminent in neighboring Afghanistan, where Islamist opposition factions had engulfed the country in civil war, and seemed at one point likely to jeopardize Tajikistan. The Uzbek SSR's Communist Party First Secretary, Islam Karimov, became independent Uzbekistan's first – and so far only – president. Early in the independence era, he encountered a single pocket of serious resistance to his rule, in Namangan in the Fergana Valley. Throughout the Soviet period, Namangan had been the main center of popular, non-institutionalized Islam and had from time to time been a major headache for the Communist regime. After a

---

[1] Upon acquiring independence, the Soviet Union's fourteen non-Russian successor states had to embark on nation-building, a process that became caught up "in a form of identity politics … designed to produce and reproduce nationally defined contours of community and to reflect nationally defined interests and values predicated on fulfilling a normative concept of statehood in which nation and statehood should be spatially congruent." G. Smith, V. Law, A. Wilson, A. Bohr, and E. Allworth, *Nation-Building in the Post-Soviet Borderlands: The Politics of National Identities* (New York: Cambridge University Press, 1998), 2.

few compromises and concessions, Karimov was able to establish control over that restive area.

Karimov, with his sharp political acumen, opted for a path that was grounded neither in Islam nor in ethnic nationalism. His credo was wholly secular, although he paid lip-service to Islam when creating a new Uzbekistani national identity. While focusing on the Uzbeks, who comprised the overwhelming majority of his citizenry, and on the Uzbek tongue, which became the state language,[2] this new identity highlighted the new state's historical heritage as the region's leading body politic, heir to the great Timurid Empire of Timurlane.[3] Indeed, Timurlane has been adopted as a – if not the – father of the Uzbek nation, "the embodiment of Uzbek national identity."[4] He is joined by other illustrious medieval scholars and writers who lived in Central Asia, not necessarily even in the territory of modern Uzbekistan, and have been similarly and anachronistically "annexed," like al-Khwarazmi, al-Farabi, and Ibn Sina (Avicenna).[5]

To ensure the success of his enterprise, Karimov suppressed the Islamic resurgence of the first half of the 1990s, closed down most of the madrasas, or seats of Islamic learning, that mushroomed in this period, as well as a large number of mosques, instituting draconic legislation on the registration of prayer-houses of all faiths. As the great majority of these prayer-houses were mosques, the Muslim faith was necessarily the most affected by these laws. Forum 18, a Norwegian-based human rights organization dedicated to promoting religious freedom and recording religious persecution in the Commonwealth of Independent States (CIS) and a number of other countries, reports periodically cases of persecution of Muslims (and adherents of other faiths) in Uzbekistan, mostly on the pretext of Islamic "extremism." At the same time, Karimov incorporated a number of Islamic customs into his new ethos; for instance, he made both Ruza Hayit (`Id al-Fitr) and the first day of Qurbon

---

2 Uzbek officially became the state language of the Uzbek SSR as of 1989; the 1995 version of the Law on the State Language further promoted its status.

3 A. Bohr, "Uzbekistan: Politics and Foreign Policy" (London: The Royal Institute of International Affairs, 1998), 20–22. See also I. Karimov, *Uzbekistan on the Threshold of the Twenty-First Century: Challenges to Stability and Progress* (New York: St. Martin's, 1997).

4 E. Paskaleva, "Ideology in Brick and Tile: Timurid Architecture of the Twenty-First Century," *Central Asian Survey*, 34, no. 4 (December 2015): 418.

5 This trend had evolved in the late Soviet period, when "Uzbeks tended to claim the entire heritage of the region as their own," contending that figures such as Abu Rayhan Berumi, Ibn Sina, Alisher Navoiy, and Mirza Ulughbek were all Uzbeks. See A. Khalid, *Islam after Communism: Religion and Politics in Central Asia* (Berkeley and Los Angeles: University of California Press: 2007), 96.

Hayit (`Id al-Adha),[6] the two main Muslim festivals, official national holidays. Adeeb Khalid has shown how even in the Soviet period, when ideologically the two concepts were mutually contradictory, being Muslim was not counterposed by Central Asians to being Soviet, but it meant something specific, "belonging to a local community. ... Islam was not a political threat to the Soviet order" but was "subordinated to the terms of public debate." It was therefore not a far-fetched transformation to "co-opt Islam, while controlling it."[7]

The present chapter evaluates how much the country's population has internalized Karimov's message and teaching. We hope to be able to gauge the overlap in Uzbekistan of what has been called "imagined" and "real" nation-building.[8] We believe that this is a legitimate exercise although we appreciate that the ways in which states – and other organizations – "classify and identify their subjects, citizens, and clients have profound consequences" for their self-understanding.[9] In summer 2015, 24 years after Uzbekistan achieved full sovereignty, we conducted a survey among just over 200 citizens in Uzbekistan's various regions to gauge the sense of citizens' self-perceptions on the collective level.

In a previous article, written in 2007 and published in 2009, we surveyed Islamic practice in the Soviet Union's five Central Asian successor states.[10] The purpose at the time was to establish which practices the region's inhabitants observed with the greatest strictness. We found that the observances that attracted them most were those that were ethnically and socially meaningful. This indicated, as we pointed out, that Central Asians tended to perceive Islam as a basic component of their collective identity even though they did not strictly observe its precepts.

By focusing on Uzbekistan, the region's most populous country with about 30 million inhabitants (including an estimated five million working abroad), and using a very different questionnaire, we hope to understand the place of

---

6   The festival, in fact, lasts three days. Id al-Fitr is a one-day occasion.

7   Khalid, *Islam after Communism*, 98, 106–107, 115, and 118.

8   R. Isaacs and A. Polese, "Between 'Imagined' and 'Real' Nation-Building: Identities and Nationhood in Post-Soviet Central Asia," *Nationalities Papers*, 43 no. 3 (May 2015): 371–372. Unfortunately, this special issue devoted to this topic does not have an article on Uzbekistan.

9   R. Brubaker, M. Loveman, and P. Stamatov, "Ethnicity as Cognition," *Theory and Society*, 33, no. 1 (2004): 35.

10   Y. Ro'i and A. Wainer, "Muslim Identity and Islamic Practice in Post-Soviet Central Asia," *Central Asian Survey*, 28, no. 3 (September 2009): 303–322.

Islam and ethnicity in the identity of its citizenry.[11] We assume that today, as a result of globalization and multi-culturalism, group identity is a very complex and composite phenomenon that allows, even presupposes, a variety of components that need not – but often do – include faith and/or ethnicity. Undoubtedly, the two frequently co-exist, yet, as has been pointed out, given "the multi-dimensional nature of social identification, the salience of particular categories varies under different contexts."[12] Islam and "Uzbekness," therefore, are not presented here as dichotomous values or identity components, but as different components of social identity that are understood both by us and our respondents as being mutually compatible. In the words of a social anthropologist, complex identities are formed that may include seemingly contradictory components. In this way, for instance, in Soviet times, people even declared themselves to be simultaneously Soviet, Muslim, and Uzbek.[13] We use the term identity in much the same way as it is described by Perry London and Alissa Hirschfeld, "a person's sense of self in relation to others, or … the sense of oneself as simultaneously an individual and a member of a social group."[14]

We also hope to reveal some of the less conformist or even non-conformist views and positions that can be found in Uzbek social networks. While in more open societies, social networks like Facebook and its Russian counterpart, *Odnoklassniki* (classmates), serve mainly a social purpose, for the younger generation in Uzbekistan, they also serve as a source for information that cannot be obtained through official channels and a forum where non-official views on such taboo topics as Islam can be expressed.[15] In the last three or four years, we have seen many posts promoting Islamic virtues such as helping people in need – i.e., the practice of *sadaqa*, charity – and praising Allah for "all the good

---

11   Our study addresses these issues only regarding residents of Uzbekistan. No study has as yet surveyed the level of ethnic and Islamic identification among the country's labor migrants.

12   B. Hierman, "Central Asian Ethnicity Compared: Evaluating the Contemporary Social Salience of Uzbek Identity in Kyrgyzstan and Tajikistan," *Europe-Asia Studies*, 67, no. 4 (June 2015): 521.

13   P. Finke, *Variations on Uzbek Identity: Strategic Choices, Cognitive Schemas, and Political Constraints in Identification Processes* (Oxford, UK: Berghahn Books, 2014), 11.

14   P. London and A. Hirschfeld, "The Psychology of Identity Formation," in D. Gordis and Y. Ben-Horin (eds), *Jewish Identity in America* (Los Angeles: Wilstein Institute, 1991), 33.

15   The Uzbek regime monitors internet traffic and does not allow access to non-censored websites and other content, including even some search terms that are blocked on Google's search engine. Therefore, social networks like "Facebook," which are harder to monitor and also provide a space for interaction between Uzbek citizens and people from other countries, have become an outlet of unofficial information.

he has bestowed upon us."[16] Facebook is also a stage for expressing Islamic solidarity, especially with the fate of the Palestinians, perhaps because this topic has no local or regional implications.

The Sample

Our sample includes 203 respondents over the age of 18; 118 of them male and 85 female. Some 167 (81.2 percent) are between 18 and 45 years old. There are 173 people (85.2 percent) defining themselves as Uzbeks, corresponding approximately to the percentage of Uzbeks in the population as a whole, 21 as Tajiks,[17] the country's second largest traditionally Muslim group, and eight as Tatars (the sole remaining respondent is a Kabardin). Citizens of Uzbekistan who are not members of a traditionally Muslim ethnic group were excluded from the sample a priori. Respondents come from different parts of the country, with over one-third (76 in all) living presently in Tashkent. Fifty-four of these Tashkentis were born elsewhere, particularly in the Ferghana Valley; residential permits, except for purposes of study, are granted almost solely to inhabitants of either the Ferghana Valley or Khorezm. Of our respondents, 47 reside currently in the city and province of Samarkand, 33 in the Fergana Valley, 24 in Khorezm Province, 20 in Bukhara, and 3 in Navoi.

Before analyzing the responses we received to our set questionnaire, it behooves us to emphasize that a rather large number of people whom we approached refused outright to respond in any way. This refusal to take part in our survey was explained as an unwillingness to answer a questionnaire that somehow related to Islam. Islam is a taboo topic that just cannot be addressed, even though prospective respondents were assured that the answers would remain anonymous. Indeed, we did not ask them their names or require any other identifying data. Be this as it may, the consequence has been that our sample was dictated to a considerable extent not by our choice or by a careful selection so as to match the country's demography, but rather by a not unexpected subjective circumstance. In 2007, we encountered similar difficulties in implementing our survey although at the time our main problem was that

---

16   Most of these posts do not originate in Uzbekistan but come from other Islamic countries; they are frequently "liked" or "shared" by Uzbek citizens.

17   At least some of those who gave their identity as Uzbek and may indeed be so registered in their documents, are in fact Tajiks who, for a variety of reasons, prefer identifying as Uzbeks.

respondents simply evaded addressing questions they perceived as unduly sensitive; nobody refused to be interviewed altogether.

There is, of course, another possible explanation for refusing to be included in the survey, namely that it was not motivated by fear of reprisal, but rather the opposite. It cannot be ruled out that those who agreed to participate believed that their views coincided more or less with those of the regime and therefore had little grounds for apprehension, whereas citizens who held differing opinions did not wish to divulge them for fear of exposing themselves. Without doubt, there are dissidents in Uzbekistan whose perception of Uzbek identity presents an alternative narrative. This was made evident by the popularity of the poems condemning the massacre in Andijan in May 2005 – "What have you done, you wretches?"; "Blood in Andijan," and "There was a massacre in Andijan."[18] Be all this as it may, those who agreed to take part in our survey were basically people who considered it safe because they knew us or our interviewers personally.

Whatever the reasoning behind balking at the idea of being interviewed, even in an anonymous survey, we have to make do with what appears feasible and are knowingly presenting findings that are based on a sample that represents neither the geographical distribution of the population nor its level of education, nor even a full spectrum of standpoints. Thus, for example, our sample has over one-half (54 percent) of respondents who have either completed academic studies or are in the process of studying at an institution of higher learning, these being by and large the people who were prepared to be interviewed.[19]

We are, of course, aware that respondents are prone to answer differently to different surveys, but this is a handicap that all surveys have to cope with, not just in autocracies, and we saw no reason to believe that our respondents were less trustworthy than those addressing survey questionnaires in other circumstances. We did, in fact, tell them that the survey was being conducted for academic research outside Uzbekistan; we were told that had they thought the

---

18   For this poetry and its significance, see S. Kendzior, "Poetry of Witness: Uzbek Identity and the Response to Andijon," *Central Asian Survey*, 26, no. 3 (September 2007): 317–334.

19   There has been no official population census in Uzbekistan since the last Soviet population census in January 1989. We are therefore unable to provide any reliable data either for the population's age distribution or its level of education. We are confident, however, that the percentage of those who are studying in institutions of higher learning or have completed such study is well under 54.

survey was intended for Uzbek academics, they would have refused to answer altogether, for fear of reprisals.[20]

The interviews were based on a set questionnaire with 22 questions addressing sundry aspects of the respondents' collective identity, in particular the measure of its Islamic component. The questionnaire was written in Russian as we were informed by Uzbek citizens is customary for sociological surveys in Uzbekistan, since Uzbek does not lend itself to many of the subtleties required for addressing some salient points. Frequently, the questions needed to be explained orally to respondents, not a few of whom had little or no knowledge of Russian. All questions provided the interviewee with a choice between two or four answers. We believe that the data furnish us with a rather good idea of how the inhabitants of Uzbekistan perceive themselves – insofar as they allow themselves to think of such issues. Wherever we found marked differences between age groups or sex, we have specified this; in other responses the differences were insignificant.

Perceived Identity

The three opening questions ask specifically about the respondent's perception of his or her identity. Almost 99 percent (200) said they are Muslims, yet just 154 (75 percent) consider themselves believers, 46 "believers to a degree," and 3 non-believers (see Figure 3.1). This is similar to a 2012 Pew Research Center survey of religious commitment throughout the Muslim world that found that in Uzbekistan 97 percent of Muslims believe in God and Muhammad – the *shahada,* the first of Islam's Five Pillars.[21])

When asked about the most important element in their collective identity (see Chart 2), 24 (11.8 percent) said Muslim;[22] 23 (11.3 percent; 21 of them Uzbeks) gave their ethnic affiliation; none opted for the third choice, their

20   For some of the problematics of survey research in Central Asia, see T. Dadabaev, "Introduction to Survey Research in Post-Soviet Central Asia," *Asian Research Trends: New Series*, no. 3 (2008): 45–69.

21   "The World's Muslims: Unity and Diversity," *Pew Forum on Religion and Public Life* (Washington D.C.: Pew Research Center, September 8, 2012), 7.

22   The Pew survey asked different questions; one of them, however, inquired whether religion was very important in their lives, to which 30 percent answered positively in Uzbekistan. This is a very low percentage compared to other "Muslim" countries, higher only than Albania (15 percent) and Kazakhstan (18 percent). In Tajikistan and Kyrgyzstan, for example, the figures were 50 percent and 49 percent respectively, *Pew Forum on Religion and Public Life*, 8.

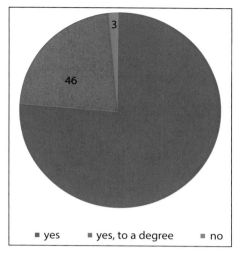

FIGURE 3.1
Do you consider yourself to be a believer?

■ yes   ■ yes, to a degree   ■ no

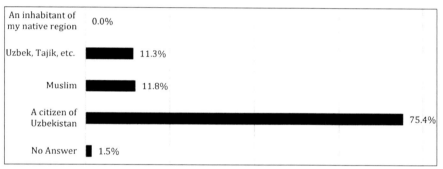

FIGURE 3.2 *What do you consider yourself in the first place?*

regional affiliation (Tashkent, Samarkand, etc.); and 153 – 75 percent – stated they are above all citizens of Uzbekistan (3 did not answer). On the face of it at least – that is, insofar as our respondents felt free to answer truthfully – this is manifestly a victory for Karimov's "nation-building" program.[23]

We were somewhat surprised that not a single respondent opted for his or her regional affiliation, since the literature has traditionally indicated the importance of localism or regionalism in Uzbek politics. One possible explanation is that a distinction needs to be drawn between the identity of the private citizen and that of the ruling elite, which has been the subject of much of the research and has tended to resort to regional affiliation as a factor or instrument of mobilization for building ruling networks. Another might be that

---

23   See Karimov, *Uzbekistan on the Threshold of the Twenty-First Century*, especially chapters
      8 and 9.

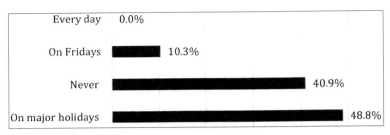

FIGURE 3.3 *How often do you attend Mosque?*

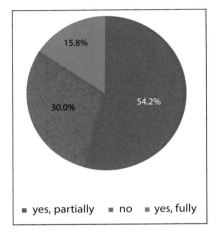

FIGURE 3.4 *Do you observe the Uraza fast?*

many of our respondents had migrated from their native region to Tashkent. Internal migration in order to receive higher education and/or find employment is becoming increasingly common among younger Uzbek citizens.[24] A third one may be of not wanting to discuss the regionalism issue with foreigners.

At least one major study of Uzbek identity, however, that appeared in 2014 seems to flatly contradict our finding, attributing major significance to regional variations, particularly in Khorezm. However, this study analyzes differences in the essence of Uzbekness in the various regions, which is a totally disparate

---

[24] One study on Uzbek youth in the 16–27 age bracket contends that a transformation of traditions and actual regional ties is taking place, especially if people live for an extended period outside their region of origin, and goes on to argue that young people in Uzbekistan are prepared to do "anything, anywhere" in order to get out of the cotton fields. D. Ziyaeva, "Changing Identities among Uzbek Youth: Transition from Regional to Socioeconomic Identities," Seattle, WA: National Bureau of Asian Research (NBR), June 2006.

perspective.[25] A second study, based admittedly on research done in 2003, like-wise stresses the importance of localism in social life in addition to "elite mobilization through localism" as "a significant determining factor in the polit-ical or professional career of elites."[26] Our findings do not refute the significance of localism, but indicate that people do not consider it the most important component of their collective identity.

Islamic Practice

The next two questions inquired about observance of two religious practices. The first asks about mosque attendance (see Figure 3.3); here we have clearly to distinguish between males and females as in most parts of Uzbekistan women do not attend mosque. Not one respondent reported going to the mosque daily, 21 – 10.3 percent – all males – go every Friday,[27] 99 – 48.8 percent attend mosque "several times a year, on major festivals," and 83 never go. Here there are meaningful differences between age groups and between men and women: while 38 percent of those aged between 18 and 25 go to the mosque several times annually, 60 percent of those above 55 do. Whereas 17.8 of the males attend mosque every Friday, 58.5 several times a year, and 23.7 never go to the mosque, the corresponding percentages for females are 35.5 percent who go to mosque on major festivals and 64.5 who do not go at all.[28] The per-centage for female attendance at the two festivals seems questionable; we were told that throughout Uzbekistan women do not attend mosque at all, except apparently in Bukhara, where in recent years the authorities – "repre-sentatives of the law enforcement bodies, clergy and mahalla (district) com-

25   Finke, *Variations on Uzbek Identity*. Moreover, Finke corroborates the main thesis of our study, namely that "The nation state ... serves as an extension of the regional focus. On a larger scale all citizens of Uzbekistan become Uzbek – both in a national as well as ethnic or cultural sense." See "Central Asian Attitudes towards Afghanistan: Perceptions of the Afghan War in Uzbekistan," in R.L. Crawfield, G. Rasuly-Paleczek (eds), *Ethnicity, Authority, and Power in Central Asia: New Games* (London and New York: Routledge, 2011), 69.
26   T. Dadabaev, "Post-Soviet Realities of Society in Uzbekistan," *Central Asian Survey*, 23, no. 2 (June 2004): 148–149.
27   The Pew finding is not meaningfully different – 9 percent (1 percent who go more than once a week and 8 percent who go every Friday): *Pew Forum on Religion and Public Life*, 130.
28   The Pew survey, however, found that 39 percent of males and 93 percent of females never attended mosque: *Pew Forum on Religion and Public Life*, 48.

mittees" – have been urging women to cease attending mosque.[29] It seems most probable that female respondents who claim that they attend mosque for festivals are referring rather to shrines and "holy places" where, indeed, according to many testimonies, women tend to visit during the festivals. Were we to have asked specifically about shrine visitation, we would presumably have scored much higher, especially as men, too, perform the *ziyarat* (visitation).[30]

The second question in this category relates to observance of the fast for Ramadan (see Figure 3.4), where we found no meaningful difference between the sexes. Thirty-two – a mere 15.8 percent – observe the fast fully,[31] 110 (54.2 percent) do so partly ("as much as I can"), and 61 (30 percent) do not observe it at all,[32] a figure that includes all those who consider themselves believers to a degree and some who consider themselves believers – without reservation.[33]

Both these questions are almost identical to questions we asked less than a decade ago. A comparison between the responses we got for Uzbekistan on the first round indicates that then some 20 percent went to mosque every Friday, and more than 30 percent never went at all. As for the fast, we see an opposite tendency with only 60 percent observing the fast.[34] We asked about Islamic practice in order to provide a framework of reference. We are well aware that for many young people Islam boils down to giving charity, heeding and respecting one's parents, and "preserving the tradition."

---

29   "Uzbekistan: Women in Bukhara Are Prohibited to Go to Mosques," *Ferghana News*, August 17, 2009, <http://enews.fergananews.com/news.php?id=1324>.

30   Our previous survey registered 70 percent of Uzbeks as visiting shrines – 60 percent of the women and 76 percent of the men.

31   Out of the 32 people who say they observe the fast fully, 30 also state that they are "believers"; the other two state that they are "believers to an extent."

32   Here again the Pew finding is rather different, but so was the question. The survey did not break down the degree of observance of the fast, asking simply whether people fasted or not. Some 50 percent said they observed the fast. We have found that people in Uzbekistan tend to say they observe the fast even if they do so partially or resort to ingenious methods of observance. For example, some of those interviewed in 2007 said they observed the fast by not drinking alcohol and refraining from going out to restaurants and bars during the Uraza. Apart from that, they ate and drank as usual.

33   Forty-four of the 62 who "do not fast on Uraza" consider themselves "believers" without reservation.

34   We have, however, to note that in the previous survey we did not distinguish between complete and partial observance. Nevertheless, it seems more than likely that those who fasted only partly will state that they observed the fast.

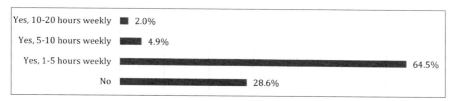

Yes, 10-20 hours weekly ■ 2.0%

Yes, 5-10 hours weekly ▬ 4.9%

Yes, 1-5 hours weekly ▬▬▬▬▬▬▬▬▬▬▬ 64.5%

No ▬▬▬▬▬ 28.6%

FIGURE 3.5 *Do you feel islamic tuition should be allowed in schools?*

Attitude to Islam within Uzbekistan

We asked three questions relating to citizens' understanding of how the state should treat Islam among the population. As noted, Islam's two major festivals have been accepted as official state holidays, on which people do not go to work and schools do not open.

The first two questions relate to the official working day. To the question, should people who read the *namaz*, that is who pray five times a day as required by Sunni Islam, be permitted to do so during working hours, nearly 90 percent (89.2) replied in the affirmative. On the other hand, when asked whether the working day should be curtailed for those who observe the fast, the Uraz, or Ramadan, just 22 respondents (10.6 percent) think it appropriate. The reasoning behind the apparent contradiction is probably purely practical: of the five daily prayers, only two fall during regular working hours, and one during the lunch break, so that enabling people to pray at work is just a question of five minutes per day, whereas shortening the workday during the month of the fast would disrupt work completely and cause a variety of complications.

The third question in this bracket addressed Islamic tuition in state schools (see Figure 5). Some 28.6 percent of respondents think there should be no teaching whatever of Islam in the official school system. At the other extreme, those who consider that a sizable part of the school curriculum should be devoted to Islamic studies comprise a negligible proportion of the population – a mere 2 percent opted for between 10 and 20 hours per week and only 4.9 percent for 5–10 hours a week. The majority of respondents – 64.5 percent – chose a middle path, namely that Islamic tuition should take up one to five hours a week of their children's education. This appears to be the one issue on which our survey found a major break with state policy, for there is no Islamic tuition whatever in any of the regular state schools – except for the handful of *madrassas* still permitted to function – so that opting even for a minimal Islamic tuition indicates a measure of dissatisfaction with the status quo.

Islamic Solidarity

Our next category moves beyond Uzbekistan's borders and discusses the way our respondents regard the issue of Islamic solidarity. We asked how they felt regarding Muslims in other countries and to what extent they identified with them as a collective.

The first question was whether the respondents were more concerned by the Muslims in countries such as Pakistan, Iran, Turkey, Egypt – than by inhabitants of countries like Germany, China and India. Here 56.6 percent answered positively, and 39.4 percent replied in the negative. There also were significant differences in the various age groups: 71 percent of those aged over 45 answered positively and 21 percent negatively. The 18–25 age group also deviated somewhat from the mean: below it among those who gave a positive reply and above those who answered negatively.

We then asked whether our respondents were more concerned by Muslims in other countries and regions of the former Soviet Union – Tajikistan, Tatarstan, Chechnya, Azerbaijan – than by that non-Muslim inhabitants of Ukraine, Belarus, and Russia. Replies corresponded to those in the previous question, with 57.6 answering positively and 37.4 negatively. Again there were meaningful digressions in the different age groups. In this instance, both the youngest and the oldest cohort were much more concentrated in the first bracket – 69 and 71 percent, respectively – and considerably under-represented in the second, 24 and 16 percent, respectively, answering negatively.

Our third question in this group asked whether respondents had ever donated money to their Muslim brethren in other countries when they were faced with a crisis or disaster. An overwhelming majority, 99.5 percent, had never given any money – some of them stated specifically that they had no money to give, so that the question was not pertinent. At the same time, we should remember that charity, *sadaqa*, is the most widely observed of Islam's practical precepts – 77 percent in our previous survey; yet, charity manifestly begins at home, where there are no end of people in dire economic straits. One single individual had given money – to Iran. Prior to receiving their comment regarding their lack of means, we asked, if they were in a position to donate money to people inhabiting zones where hostilities were occurring, would their first preference be to the civilian population of Iraq, to Russians and Ukrainians in Eastern Ukraine, or to the inhabitants of Yemen (see Chart 6). Some 40.3 percent opted for the second choice, while 56.6 percent replied "none of the above."

Indeed, the protests and government crackdown that shook Ukraine in late 2013 received considerable attention in the Uzbek media – Russia's following actions were less publicly discussed. On visits to Uzbekistan in 2014 we found widespread sympathy for the Euromaidan movement among people with whom we talked. In addition, the apparently insignificant independence movement in the Karakalpak Autonomous Republic was reportedly encouraged to assert its demands in the wake of developments in Ukraine.[35] We pressed this issue, going on to ask: if they had the money to give to people in need (see Chart 7), would their first preference be the Iraqi civilian population, the Palestinian inhabitants of the Gaza Strip, or Uzbeks inhabiting the region of Osh in neighboring Kyrgyzstan? No less than 86.7 percent said they would give their money to Uzbeks in Osh, while 11.3 percent would not give to any of these groups. The empathy felt by large sectors of the Uzbek population with their co-ethnics in Southern Kyrgyzstan – most specifically in Osh and Jalalabad – was given expression in spontaneous acts of assistance to the 100,000 or so refugees who fled to Uzbekistan following the outbreak of ethnic violence in Osh in June 2010. This help was rendered despite the very limited information in Uzbekistan's media on the topic, reportedly intended to keep Uzbek passions in check and to reduce the chances of Uzbek retaliation.[36] There are, however, online posts in support of Muslims in conflict areas. For example, we have seen posts upholding the position of the civilian Palestinian population during the military conflict with Israel in the summer of 2014. Nevertheless, these posts were not of a political nature and were relatively tame, merely identifying with the suffering of innocent civilians.[37]

Our final question touching upon Islamic solidarity asked whether states where the greater part of the population professes Islam should assist one another. Here we received an overwhelming majority of positive replies – 75.4 percent as against 24.1 percent. We refrained from using the term "Islamic countries," which in the Uzbek political and social discourse has a connotation of countries living under Shari'a law. Even though the question was as apolitical as we could make it, still nearly a quarter answered "no," probably because

---

35   "Uzbekistan Separatist Movement Threatens Ancient Culture," *The Guardian*, February 5, 2015.

36   Here, Peter Finke's findings again seem incompatible with ours. He says that Uzbek nationals living in Uzbekistan show little interest in the Uzbek diaspora, although he admits that the attitude to those living in former Soviet republics "is somewhat different." Finke, "Central Asian Attitudes," 68–69. Also see "Uzbekistan's Karimov Treads Cautiously in Response to Southern Kyrgyzstan Violence," *Eurasia Net*, June 17, 2010, <http://www.eurasianet.org/node/61333>.

37   One particularly popular post was a picture of a crying Palestinian baby with attached text reading, "You do not have to be a Muslim to identify with his suffering – you simply have to be human."

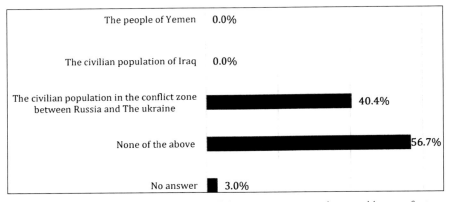

FIGURE 3.6 *If you had the means to help people living in a war zone, whom would you prefer to help?*

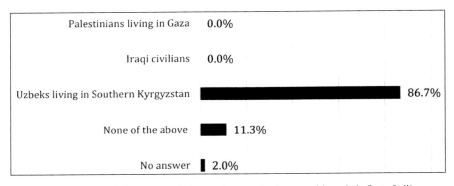

FIGURE 3.7 *If you had the means to help people in need, whom would you help first of all?*

the very implication of Islamic unity might be considered subversive. To quote one of our Uzbek friends: had the question been "should the countries of the world work together and help each other?" 100 percent of the participants would have agreed.

Religion, and Islam Specifically, under Soviet Rule

Two questions address the situation of Islam under Soviet rule. Our intention here was to touch upon something that is not directly affected by Karimov's policy, although he refrains from denouncing Soviet-era policy in any respect, and to try to indirectly measure people's empathy with Islam. We asked whether the Soviet regime repressed religious faiths and believers – 76.3 answered in the affirmative (69 percent in the 18–25 cohort who had had no direct experience of Soviet rule and 82 percent of those above 45 who had experienced Soviet rule as adults) while 23.6 percent rejected the suggestion, 31 percent in the youngest age bracket and just 18 percent in the over 45s.

Yet, when asked whether the Soviet Union had treated Islam and Muslim believers worse than other faiths and believers, the responses were very different and somewhat unexpected: 45.8 agreed, while 53.7 dismissed the idea – 63 percent of those who had not known Soviet rule and just 34 percent of the oldest cohort who, of course, had. This latter result may mean that these older Uzbeks wish to excuse themselves for not having taken up cudgels against their Soviet rulers, or perhaps it is designed to indicate that they did not identify with Islam at the time and therefore had no reason to register any protest, the implication being that they do not identify with Islam at the present, either. Timur Dadabaev provides a very insightful study of the "hybrid discourse on the concept of religion" that developed in Uzbekistan in the Soviet period and "is demonstrated by the multiple means of evaluating Soviet religious policies" among elderly citizens of post-Soviet Uzbekistan. "The public remembers policies initially shocking but eventually accepted as positive because they assisted the modernization policy," in that they liberated the women and facilitated their entry into public life and introduced modern education and general literacy.

> In the post-Soviet context, such positive memories regarding certain religious policies of the past ... shed light on the process of reevaluation and the redefinition of new boundaries of religiosity during the post-Soviet period. People's recollections thus provide useful insights ... into how they understand their past experience on the basis of their current position. In many cases, memories are an indication of the public's attitude towards their present understanding of religiosity, in which their past is the material against which their present conceptualisation of religion is tested and corrected.

In his conclusion, he writes that "differentiation in the evaluation of past policies can also be connected to the ways in which ordinary citizens adapted to ideological constraints."[38]

---

38 T. Dadabaev, "Religiosity and Soviet 'Modernisation' in Central Asia: Locating Religious Traditions and Rituals in Recollections of Anti-Religious Policies in Uzbekistan," *Religion, State, and Society*, 42, no. 4 (December 2014): 328–353. In another paper that focused on Soviet ethnic policies, Dadabaev shows that those among the indigenous population who adapted successfully to Soviet reality emerged in post-Soviet Uzbekistan as "a new group

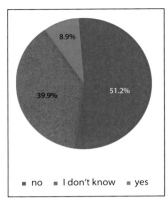

FIGURE 3.8
Do you think islam is stricter and more demanding than other religions?

no ■ I don't know ■ yes

The Nature of Islam

We also asked our respondents whether in their opinion Islam is a stricter and more demanding religion than others (see Chart 7). Here 8.9 percent replied in the affirmative – among the youngest cohort, just 4.5 agreed, while among the oldest bracket, no less than 31.5 concurred. This would seem to confirm our understanding that those above 45 were the least ready to demonstrate any Islamic identity, or actually do not identify with the Islamic way of life, although it is not clear whether we can draw conclusions from this regarding the general Uzbek population – it is possible that only those who had reservations regarding Islam were prepared to answer our questionnaire, those with what might seem an undue commitment to Islam preferring not to stick out their necks. This was the question that drew a large percentage of "Don't knows" – 39.9 percent, although just 21 percent among the oldest cohort.

We then asked whether, in the view of our respondents, non-Muslims perceived Islam as a religion that is spread by force. Approximately one-third (36.5 percent) agreed and 63 percent demurred. Yet, when asked whether they themselves accepted this postulate, a mere 14.8 percent agreed and a full 85.2 percent rejected it. The gist was clearly that those who favor using, or resort in practice to, force violate the message of Islam and one of Islam's basic values.[39]

---

of Russophile(s)." See T. Dadabaev, "Recollections of Emerging Hybrid Ethnic Identities in Soviet Central Asia: The Case of Uzbekistan," *Nationalities Papers*, 41, no. 6 (November 2013): 1026–48.

39   In informal conversations, we found that many Uzbeks think that Islam suffers from a reputation of being a violence-propagating religion due to the actions of Islamic

Moving on to a question regarding the Islamic State of Iraq and Syria (ISIS), we appreciated we were touching upon a very sensitive topic. The authorities in Tashkent had for some time been visibly anxious about a possible ISIS threat in Uzbekistan, especially since the effective termination at the end of 2014 of the International Security Assistance Force (ISAF) in Afghanistan and the announcement by the Afghan interior minister in February 2015 confirming the presence of ISIS militants in his country. In November and December 2014 arrests had been carried out of Uzbek citizens, alleged members of ISIS and the IMU (Islamic Movement of Uzbekistan, which in mid-2015 pledged allegiance to ISIS), charged with having undergone military training in Pakistan and returning home to recruit young people for ISIS. In February 2015, Tashkent's chief imam condemned ISIS on Uzbek TV, urging Uzbeks not to join its ranks and denouncing the organization as having "nothing to do with Islam." In April 2015, a Tashkent-based political analyst stated that Uzbekistan's law-enforcement bodies were undertaking several approaches to assess and counter the ISIS threat, with a special program for meeting returning Uzbek citizens.

This, then, was the backdrop against which we posed the following question: Do you think that ISIS represents Islamic values? To this, just one individual answered in the affirmative, 53.2 answered negatively (44.5 among the 18–25s and 42 percent among the over 45s). Not surprisingly, given that ISIS is an unmentionable, no less than 46.3 percent replied "Don't know" (including 55.5 percent among the youngest bracket and an almost identical 56 percent among the oldest cohort). On Facebook, however, one can see posts by Uzbek citizens addressing the topic of ISIS and fellow terrorist groups. Most posts regarding ISIS are humorous and tend to make fun of the extremist Islamic organization; yet some of them condemn its actions outright. Out of several hundred posts reviewed, we were unable to find any posts supporting ISIS.

---

extremists, who misrepresent the true values of Islam. Many Uzbeks told us that their elders taught them that violence and the use of force are banned by Islam and that hurting another human being is the worst crime one can commit.

The World Outside

The final two questions addressed the outside world.[40]

Our very last question was: If you were offered a job abroad and the pay were identical, would you prefer to work in a Muslim or a non-Muslim country? We found that a minority – 36.5 percent – would prefer to work in a Muslim country and 62.5 in a non-Muslim one. Both extreme-age cohorts were even more decisive in their preference for a non-Muslim country – 73.4 percent among the 18–25s and 74 percent among the above 45s, whereas women were more evenly split: 42.5 percent would prefer a Muslim country and 55 percent a non-Muslim one. The 62 percent who chose the non-Muslim option divided up as follows: 41 percent said outright that they have a clear preference for a secular and democratic state; to be precise, their answer was "because I (want to) live in a democratic country," thereby simultaneously renouncing the idea that Muslim countries could be democratic and echoing regime propaganda regarding Uzbekistan's democratic nature; 11 percent said that non-Muslim states treated Uzbeks well; and 10 percent vindicated their preference by saying that life in non-Muslim states was easier.

Of the 36.5 percent who preferred a Muslim state, only 10 percent gave their reasons: 5 percent said that the way of life and culture in those states were closer to their own; 4 percent opined that Muslim states respected Uzbeks more; while a mere one percent – two individuals – stated simply that they preferred the Muslim option because they themselves were Muslims. These statistics reflect well the current migration flows: the great majority of Uzbek citizens who are working abroad – their official number is somewhere between four and five million although the grapevine speaks about as many as eight million – are to be found in Russia, with some also in Ukraine, Belarus, and South Korea; a rather small minority has found employment in the United Arab Emirates, especially in Abu Dhabi and Dubai.

---

40   In fact, we posed two questions in this category, but had to disqualify one that asked whether our respondents believe that Western countries misunderstand Islam. We received very few replies, apparently because respondents did not fully comprehend the options we put to them that demanded a certain amount of sophistication. All, therefore, that we could learn on this score was that survey questionnaires have to keep to straightforward questions that require simple replies.

Conclusion

We can draw a number of conclusions from our findings. In the first place, the citizens of Uzbekistan seem to identify by and large with their President's message. Their primary identity is with Uzbekistan as a state, and a state, moreover, in which neither the titular nation's ethnic culture nor Islam receives major emphasis, although both have been partially subsumed in the country's "national" ethos. At the same time, we would like to suggest that the general acceptance of a regime that is manifestly repressive emanates in the first place from an understanding or a sense that the stability and security provided by the current authorities are infinitely preferable to the chaos they see in neighboring countries – in Tajikistan and Kyrgyzstan, not to speak of Afghanistan.

Uzbekistan's inhabitants perceive their ethnic and Islamic affiliation as givens that play an inherent role in their collective identity. They perceive themselves as Muslims and believers. Yet, when speaking of Islam, they do not mean a strictly orthodox Islam, but rather customs and traditions, almost folklore or appurtenances. These cannot be shaken off but are to be retained as symbols and their children should perhaps become acquainted with them as part of their official education. Conforming to this understanding, the Uzbek state has made the Qurbon Hayit and Ruza Hayit official national holidays, as it has the Nowruz, the traditional Persian New Year celebrated on the March equinox, which was unofficially reinstated in some parts in the latter Soviet period. Islam is basically not an issue that features in the national discourse and rarely also in the media, but is generally played down, with the notable exception of the occasional denunciation of "Islamic extremism" both in the domestic and in the international context. The population, accustomed from the Soviet period to taking its cue from what has remained essentially a heavily censured state, is inclined to go along with the menu it is offered.

The perception of the state as the primary focus of identity means, too, that citizens of Uzbekistan no longer see in their local or regional affiliation their paramount source of identity. This does not mean that they refute this affiliation, but that it maybe takes a lower place in the composition of their collective self-perception. In this connection, it is surely relevant that close to thirty percent of our respondents are internal migrants. Finally, an Islamic-grounded solidarity seems to appear threatening to Uzbek citizens who aspire basically to live in a secular and "democratic" state, namely the antithesis of a body politic dominated by Islamic norms and standards. Insofar as they sense solidarity with the world outside, their predominant orientation is toward states or nations that share a Soviet socio-cultural heritage, more than toward the rest of the *Ummah*.

PART 2

Islam, Politics, and the State

∴

CHAPTER 4

The Islamic Renaissance Party of Tajikistan: Episodes of Islamic Activism, Postconflict, Accommodation, and Political Marginalization

Tim Epkenhans

On March 2, 2015, the chairman of Tajikistan's Central Election Committee, Shermuhammad Shohiyon, announced the preliminary results of the parliamentary elections. The Islamic Renaissance Party of Tajikistan (*Hizbi nahzati islomii Tojikiston*—IRPT) had failed to clear the 5 percent threshold and therefore would not be represented in Tajikistan's Lower House (*Majlisi namoyandigon*) in the forthcoming legislative period. The audience—mostly representatives of the different political parties and Dushanbe's civil society—was silently perplexed by the historic outcome of the elections and the ultimate termination of Tajikistan's postconflict political economy that had originated in the 1997 General Peace Accord. In his initial response, the IRPT's chairman, Muhiddin Kabirī, criticized the administration of the elections but immediately confirmed the IRPT's compliance with the secular-democratic system (including the participation in elections) and therefore remained faithful to the discursive conventions of postconflict Tajikistan conjuring peace (*tinj*) and stability.[1] In contrast, Shodī Shabdolov—a veteran politician who has been chairman of the Communist Party since the tumultuous independence in 1991—drily commented:

> To whom should we complain, to the General Procurator, to the Central Election Committee, to whom? Everything is in the hands of one party and its leadership is with the President. We will not file any complaint, but the outcome of this election will not be positive. I do not know who advised the President on this issue, but a person should think about the consequences of his decisions. The campaign that happened in our country on 1 March was not an election; it was decreed (*ta'inot*).[2]

---

1 For postconflict Tajikistan see J. Heathershaw, *Tajikistan: The Politics of Peacebuilding and the Emergence of Legitimate Order* (London: Routledge, 2009).
2 The interview with Shodī Shabdolov on the Tajik service of Radio Liberty/Radio Free Europe *Radioi Ozodī* homepage (<http://www.ozodi.org/content/reaction-for-parliament-election-

Shabdolov's comments indicate the trajectories of "virtual politics" in Tajikistan and the perception that political institutions and processes are orchestrated and manipulated.[3] And although senior IRPT representatives (including Kabirī) shared a similar perception in conversations over the past years, the IRPT nonetheless consistently adheres to the informal political arrangements of postconflict Tajikistan, acknowledging the achievements of the political transition since 1997 and the legitimacy of the political system. Nonetheless, the government has consistently marginalized the IRPT since the mid-2000s and increased the pressure in recent months. The exclusion from the Lower House is far more significant for the IRPT than the loss of two seats in a rubber-stamp institution dominated by the presidential People's Democratic Party of Tajikistan. Despite the political marginalization and continuous defamation campaigns, the formal representation of the IRPT in parliament had always been a symbol of the mutual recognition of the terms of the Peace Agreement and of the exemplary character of Tajikistan's postconflict politics. This has now ended.

The political marginalization, defamation, violent assaults on individual IRPT politicians as well as their public persecution by local officials has para-lyzed the party politically and consumed its leadership's energy.[4] At the same time, the IRPT has been additionally challenged by the profound social, politi-cal, and cultural transformation of Tajik society in recent years and has only slowly adapted to these challenges: labor migration has undermined the tradi-tional social fabrics in the conservative patriarchic milieu of rural Tajikistan (where the IRPT had a large electorate); the government has reorganized the religious administration and has increased government control over religious institutions appropriating "Islam" in its official imagination of Tajik national identity; simultaneously, popular and independent religious authorities rene-gotiate Islam among a younger generation of Tajik Muslims, encouraging a "new" assertiveness in public religious practice without including the IRPT at all. As a political party with a pronounced religious agenda promoting Islamic

---

in-tajikistan/2687699o.html>). See additionally the online version of the newspaper *Faraj*: "Intikhobot: Oghozi "era"-i nav" at <http://faraj.tj/main/8498-intihobot-011710zi-era-i-nav. html>. Also see "Intikhobi ta'rikhī: Hizbi nahzati islomii Tojikiston basta shavad yo ne?", *Nigoh*, April 1, 2015.

3   For the concept of "virtual politics," see A. Wilson, *Virtual Politics: Faking Democracy in the Post-Soviet World* (New Haven, CT: Yale Univ. Press, 2005). For the application of Wilson's concepts in the context of Tajikistan, see J. Heathershaw, "The Global Performance State," in M. Reeves, J. Rasanayagam, and J. Beyer (eds), *Ethnographies of the State in Central Asia: Performing Politics* (Bloomington: Indiana University Press, 2013), 29–54.

4   Conversation with IRPT representatives in April 2015 in Dushanbe.

values, the IRPT has difficulties—beyond the hostile government politics—in responding to the changing societal environment in Tajikistan.

This chapter looks at three interrelated aspects, or episodes, of the IRPT's interaction with the wider society: First, I explore the difficult historical relationship of the IRPT with the larger religious field (in the sense of Pierre Bourdieu), in particular with the registered as well as independent *ulamo* before the outbreak of the Civil War in 1992.[5] Second, I refer to the changing government administration of religion (Islam) in Tajikistan, i.e., the proliferation of the High Council of Tajikistan's *ulamo* as the central administrative institution since 2010, further restricting the IRPT's room to maneuver. Third, I look at the changing government imagination of Tajik identity and the IRPT's response to it. These three aspects highlight the changing context of Islam and politics in Tajik society in the past decades.

Origins: The IRPT IN Tajikistan's Religious Field

Political Islamism and the proto-Islamic Revival Party[6] emerged in rural Tajikistan, in particular the Qarotegin and Vakhsh Valley, among a post-Stalin generation of men who repudiated the Soviet system and intentionally remained at the margins of Soviet society by relinquishing Soviet career patterns.[7] The group around the IRPT's founder, Abdulloh Nurī (1947–2006), developed a conservative Sunni-Hanafi religious agenda that aimed at (re-) establishing a public and normative religious practice as well as the so-

---

5   *Ulamo* is the Tajik version of the Arabic *ulamā*, the plural of *'alim*, which usually describes religious scholars in the Islamic tradition. In Tajikistan as well as elsewhere in Central Asia, religious scholars and authorities simultaneously use a variety of honorific titles common in the Islamic tradition, such as *pir, sheikh, mahdum/mahzum, domullo*, and so forth indicating at times an affiliation to one of the major mystical orders in the region. As for the religious field and Bourdieu's sociology of religion see: P. Bourdieu, *Religion* (Frankfurt: Suhrkamp, 2011).

6   Initially, Nurī and his associates did not give the movement a formal name and simply called it *harakat* (Tajik for movement). In the late 1970s, they adopted the name Revival of Islamic Youth of Tajikistan (*Nahzati Javononi Islomii Tojikistan*). The current designation emerged only during the discussion of the union-wide Islamic Revival Party in 1990. See Q. Sattorī (ed.), *HNIT—Zodai ormoni mardum* (Dushanbe: ShKOS, 2003), 14.

7   See the memoirs of S. Hamad, *Dar payrahai nur* (Dushanbe: Muattar, 2013); S. Husaynī, *Khotiraho az nakhust oshnoiyam ba Harakati Islomii Tojikiston to rasmiyati on* (Dushanbe: Muattar, 2013) and Z. Roziq, *HNIT dar masiri ta'rikh* (Dushanbe: Muattar, 2013). Cf., S. Dudoignon, "Political Parties and Forces in Tajikistan, 1989–1993," in M.-R. Djalili, F. Grare, and S. Akiner (eds), *Tajikistan: The Trials of Independence* (Richmond, UK: Curzon, 1998), 52–85.

cial-political relevance of Islam in Tajik society.[8] While social interventionism was a novelty in the Soviet context, the ideas of a Sunni-Hanafi tradition or normativity were related to one of the key figures of the "Islamic revival" in Central Asia, *domullo* Muhammadjon Hindustonī (1892–1989), who taught many of the proto-IRPT activists in small circles of students—including Nurī. Until the early 1980s the IRPT resembled a regional cultural and religious club with vague political ambitions, not a political party. This might be related to the origins of the IRPT in rural Soviet Tajikistan and among *muhoğir* (internal "exiles" of the Soviet resettlement campaigns) from the Qarotegin Valley—social groups, as Stéphane Dudoignon pointedly remarks, that were theoretically less receptive to political Islamism compared with the "classical" social origins of Islamism in the industrial urban centers.[9] Arguably, Soviet Central Asia is a deviation from this paradigm due to the importance of the agro-industrial complex and cotton cultivation, which shaped the social transformation and mobilization since the 1960s and 1970s. Ultimately, the particular background of the IRPT accounts for the lack of versatile Soviet-urban intellectuals in its ranks who could transmit the IRPT to the urban Soviet electorate in Soviet Tajikistan.[10]

Most of the Islamist activists graduated in disciplines such as applied sciences and economics. Nurī studied geodesy (and worked in the Qūrghonteppa land survey department), Saidumar Husaynī holds a degree in economics, Gadoev (aka: Muhammadnazar) graduated in mechanical engineering (therefore his nickname *inzhener*—engineer) and Davlat Usmon has a law degree. Some activists—despite a higher education and professional career options—assumed positions that offered more time for private studies but still provided a moderate income and the important *propiska* (residence permit), such as nightshifts in the central heating facilities or as night guards. Even in rural Tajikistan, Islamic activists found occupational niches providing additional

---

8   "Normative" (or normativity) are understood as constructed in this context.

9   S. Dudoignon and S.A. Qalandar, "They Were All from the Country: The Revival and Politicisation of Islam in the Lower Wakhsh Valley of the Tajik SSR (1947–1997)," in S. Dudoingnon and C. Noack (eds), *Allah's Kolkhozes: Migration, De-Stalinisation, Privatisation, and the New Muslim Congregations in the Soviet Relam (1950s–2000s)* (Berlin: Klaus-Schwarz, 2013), 47–122. See also Dudoignon, *Political Parties*, 67 and P. Mandaville, *Islam and Politics* (New York: Routledge, 2014).

10   In September/October 1991, the IRPT forged an alliance with the secular opposition in Tajikistan, the Democratic Party of Tajikistan and the civil associations Rastokhez and La'li Badakhshon. But the "radical-religious" alliance was short-lived: Internal dissent, personal animosities, the deepening political polarization, and eventually the outbreak of violence in May 1992 fragmented the opposition.

spare time to continue their private religious studies, such as gathering mulberry leaves, breeding silkworms, or beekeepers. At the same time, the activists emphasize their rigid self-discipline, strict regulation of daily life, abstinence from alcohol and cigarettes, and eschew extramarital relationships.[11] The activists around Nurī thus located themselves outside the mainstream milieus in the later Soviet Union, projecting an alternative lifestyle to the system's career patterns and social recognition.[12]

Abdulloh Nurī emphasizes five central elements in the movement's origin and agenda. First, he depicts the population of the Qarotegin Valley and Vakhyo as particularly pious and devout Muslims deeply rooted in the culture of the mountain valleys and therefore particularly receptive for Islamic activism. Second, the Qarotegin/Vakhyo population values the traditional Islamic education and therefore the region has produced many important religious scholars (like Nurī himself). Third, horticulture and the local work ethic have made local communities prosperous, and therefore they were able to send their sons and daughters to the centers of the Islamic civilization to acquire a higher Islamic education. Fourth, due to the entrenchment of Islam in the local culture of Qarotegin and Vakhyo, the movement emerged within an authentic local context and was not influenced by foreign movements.[13] Fifth, the movement is firmly located within the larger Sunni-Hanafi tradition and as a continuation of the regional *jadidī* movement in the late nineteenth–early twentieth century.[14] However, the reference to the *jadidī* movement remains vague, and Nurī never explicates what the *jadidī* movement in his imagination stands for. Apparently, Nurī considered the *jadidī* movement as an "authentic" Central Asian phenomenon embarking on an indigenous modernization project that was interrupted by 70 years of Soviet rule.[15] Furthermore, the movement nourished a strong anticolonial sentiment and Hojī Akbar Tūrajonzoda (the former *qozikalon* of Soviet Tajikistan) observes that the political

---

11   Conversation with a former member of the IRPT (Dushanbe, September 2008) and Husaynī, *Khotiraho,* 19–33.

12   Cf. A. Yurchak, *Everything was Forever, Until It Was No More: The Last Soviet Generation* (Princeton, NJ: Princeton University Press, 2006).

13   The government frequently portrayed (and stilly portrays) Islamic activism as "foreign" and "alien" to the tolerant, peaceful, and quietist local (authentic Tajik) Islam. See below and Sattorī, *HNIT,* 16.

14   For the *jadidī* movement, see K. Adeeb, *The Politics of Muslim Cultural Reform: Jadidism in Central Asia* (Berkeley: University of California Press).

15   Muhammadsharif Himmatzoda, Nurī's closest associate, elaborates on the *jadidī* heritage as well and depicts the IRPT as the direct successor of the *jadidī* movement after an enforced hiatus of 50 years Soviet rule. See Sattorī, *HNIT,* 17 and 47.

nomenklatura of Soviet Tajikistan feared the IRPT and the "awakening of Islam" (*bidorii islom*) initiated by the IRPT since this posed "a serious threat to their own colonizing project" (*iste'morgarona*).[16] Hojī Qalandar Sadriddin, another founding member of the IRPT, mentions three central concerns of their circle: (1) to reintroduce Islamic culture and teach Islam to the people; (2) to fight against unlawful "novelties (*bid'at*) and superstitions" that had become popular among the common people in Soviet Tajikistan; and (3) eventually to "end the silence of the *ulamo* and to Command Right and Forbid Wrong (*amri ma'rufu nahyi munkar*) in public again"[17] in order to increase Islamic morals (*akhloqi islomī*) among the Muslims of Tajikistan. The movement's agenda and their activism gradually generated tensions with the established religious authorities. Next to the issue of "innovations" and the "correct" religious practice, IRPT members criticized the political quietism and lack of social intervention by the established *ulamo* in Soviet Tajikistan:

> Among the circles of the Sufis (*halqahoi ahli tasavvuf*), the recitation of books was common in which the *pir* of the order (*tariqa*) was reading a book and his students (*muridon*) were contemplating on "Commanding Right and Forbidding Wrong," but never in public meetings.[18]

Zubaydullo Roziq (who joined the movement in 1978) therefore narrates the emerging IRPT also in terms of a generational split: The established—registered as well as unregistered—religious specialists in Tajikistan were largely self-sufficient, conducting general religious services for the population (for remuneration) but did not popularize Islam anymore.[19]

The increasing politicization of Central Asian Muslims in the 1970s and 1980s eventually nurtured dissent among the Islamic activists who refused to constrain themselves to the promotion of quietist normative Sunni-Hanafi Islam as Hindustonī did. The Soviet invasion and prolonged campaign in Afghanistan accelerated the politicization of Uzbek and Tajik Islamists, some of whom had served in the Soviet Army in Afghanistan. Remarkably, the most contentious disputes among the religious activists were not about juris-

---

16   H.A. Tūrağonzoda, *Miyoni obu otash...* (Dushanbe, 1998), 50.

17   Roziq, *HNIT*, 45. See also A. Qayumzod, "Xudo bo most, pirūzī niz," *Čaroği rūz*, no. 45 (1992), 3. The Arabic/Persian term *amri ma'rufu nahyi munkar* (Command Right and Forbid Wrong) refers to a central tenet of the Islamic tradition. Cf. M. Cook, *Commanding Right and Forbidding Wrong in Islamic Thought* (New York: Cambridge University Press, 2000).

18   Roziq, *HNIT*, 49.

19   Ibid., 46–49.

prudence (*fiqh*), theology (*aqida*), or politics and ideology, but about ritual practice, particularly rituals that were silently tolerated by the Soviet authorities, such as funerals (*janoza*)[20] or the popular visit to local shrines (*ziyorat* to a *mazar*), and performed in public.

The funeral ritual became a highly contentious issue since they were conducted in public where the religious specialists could monitor each other. They also often included a variety of local or regional customs such as expressive mourning, the exchange of "gifts," and the expensive community funeral feasts (colloquially often called *osh*, in the religious literature *ta'omi sartakhta*) commemorating the deceased after seven days, 40 days, and/or one year.[21] While the question of ritual normativity was perhaps used as a pretense, the underlying issue was often financial, in particular the financial burden on the deceased's families who were expected to meet certain expectations by the local communities.[22] Roziq reports that with the post-Stalinist revival of religious communities, the "correct" (or normative) practice was increasingly undermined by unacceptable "innovations (*bid'atho*) … local conventions and customs as well as superstitions (*urfu odatho va xurofot*)."[23] Islamic activists around Nurī accused local mullahs of transforming religious rituals into a lucrative business and inventing additional rituals and practices in order to receive additional donations.

Individual religious scholars condemned these practices. For instance *qorī* Odil in Chorkūh ordered his sons in the late 1970s to bury him quietly without a large funeral service. When his father passed away, Abdullo Nurī declined to arrange a *janoza* with the obligatory *osh* expected by the population in the Turkmenistan collective farm.[24] The disputes over the correct religious practice and innovations among the local population, the local mullahs, and adolescent activists triggered fierce debates, and even Zubaydulloh Roziq concedes that some of the activists were too "hot-blooded (*khungarm*) … and

---

20   See Dudoignon and Qalandar, "They Were All from the Country."

21   For an evaluation, see H.A. Tūrajonzoda, *Shariat va jomea* (Dushanbe: Nodir, 2006), 29–38.

22   Still today, a *ğanoza* with complementary *ta'om* is very expensive affair in Central Asia and Tajikistan easily summing up to several thousand USD. The government in Tajikistan tried to regulate the expenses for rituals by a controversial 2007 "Law on Traditions, Festivities, and Ceremonies."

23   Roziq, *HNIT*, 70–71.

24   Roziq (*HNIT*, 74–76) reports that Nurī avoided any *bid'at* during the funeral service of his father, such as the *oshi sartakhta* or the distribution of money to the mourners. However, the "common people" (*ommai mardum*) severely criticized Nurī for burying his father without a "proper" *janoza*. See also Dudoignon and Qalandar, "They Were All from the Country," 91.

outside the limits of etiquette (*odob*) and academic disputation (*munozarai ilmī*)."[25] Their aggressive behavior toward the established religious authorities and their communities significantly damaged the reputation of the IRPT among traditionally minded religious circles.

Defamation and "Othering": The Seal of the Mongols

Analysis of Islam in the USSR, by both Soviet and Western researchers, changed after the Iranian Revolution and the Soviet occupation of Afghanistan. Since the 1980s it has been and dominated by concerns that Islamic extremism would subvert the stability of the USSR (and today's post-Soviet Central Asia), and this concern has become increasingly instrumental for legitimizing a narrow, security-driven and authoritarian approach to Islam. In Soviet Tajikistan, the discussion on the emergence of clandestine Islamist circles and the increasing return to religious practice (often attributed to rural communities) started in the mid-1980s. Soon a hostile discourse unfolded in the media and among the political nomenklatura, depicting any form of public religiosity outside the official institutions as a manifestation of extremism or fundamentalism instigated from abroad. In the mid-1980s the term Wahhabi (*vahhobī*) emerged as a central and influential designation for the forces opposing Soviet modernization and later the secular statehood of independent Tajikistan. Although the term refers to the Saudi Arabian variation of the Hanbali law school in Sunni Islam, the Wahhabiyya, those who employed the term were less concerned about its religious or historical meaning than its potential for defamation. The term was popularized by the Soviet press and used by the KGB and established religious personnel to denounce Islamist activists not registered with the official institutions and who followed "nontraditional" forms of religious practice and thought. The alleged Wahhabis in late-Soviet Central Asia had nothing in common with the Saudi Arabian Wahhabiyya but were labeled Wahhabi due to their noncompliance with the narrowly defined religious normativity of the official institutions (the SADUM).[26] Notably, the introduction of the politicized term Wahhabi in Soviet Central Asia is associated not with a KGB operative but with Hindustonī, who reportedly applied the Wahhabi label the first time for a group of dissident students. Zubaydullo Roziq concedes that "it is a reason for sadness, however, that the term (*vahhobī*) was first used by Mavlavī Qorī

---

25   Roziq, *HNIT*, 75.
26   B.M. Babajanov, A. Muminov, and A. von Kügelgen, *Disputes on Muslim Authority in Central Asia in Twentieth Century* (Almaty: Daik-Press, 2007).

Muhammadjon Hindustonī" in disputes with younger Islamic activists.[27] Hindustonī elaborated on the Wahhabi issue further and composed a short polemic against the Wahhabiyya and its founder Muḥammad b. ʿAbd al-Wahhāb in 1987.[28] However, those Islamic activists disqualified by Hindustonī as Wahhabi understood themselves rather as "renovators (*mujaddidon*)"[29] or "reformers (*islohxohon*)" and certainly not as Wahhabi.

Hindustani's fierce criticism and denunciation of his students as contributed to an increasing polarization between the established religious specialists (born between the 1890s and 1930s) and their younger contenders (born since the late 1940s). The confrontation culminated in a meeting between Hindustonī and his critics in the village of Mirovoy (in the Jilikūl district). A local businessman had invited Hindustonī and a few other established *ulamo*. Activists had waited for the opportunity to confront Hindustonī and to persuade him to retract the Wahhabi accusations against their circle. Reportedly, the atmosphere became increasingly aggressive, and Hindustonī felt pressured by the younger mullahs. He finally gave in and the group dispersed. But a few days later Hindustonī announced that he had felt threatened by the Wahhabi and that his earlier verdict was correct (i.e., that they are actually Wahhabi).

Abdullo Nurī, whose authority partly derives from his intimate affiliation with Hindustonī, tried to mediate and keep the movement aloof from the aggravating conflict.[30] The relation between Hindustonī and his former students, however, became irreconcilable with an open letter by the "reformers/renovators" circulating a few weeks after the meeting, accusing Hindustonī of ignorance (*johil*) in religious affairs, complacency, and portraying him as a puppet of the colonial Soviet regime. They evoke the image of Dukchī-*eshon* (who had led an uprising against the Russian barracks in Andijan in 1898) and his meritorious *jihod* against the Tsar, accusing Hindustonī of collaboration with the colonial system:

> The humiliation of Islam (*horii Islom*) is not important to you. .... You are contemptuous of the time Islam was a free religion and you appraise the rule of the unbelievers (*kufr*). Due to your influence among the common

---

27 Roziq, *HNIT*, 77.

28 For an edition of the letter (in Persian) see: Babajanov, Muminov, and Kügelgen, *Disputes*, 113–116 and, for the Russian translation, 108–112.

29 Within the Islamic tradition, the term *mujaddid* is based on a Prophetic tradition and has been frequently used for various reformers. After Abdullo Nurī's demise in 2006, the IRPT published a memorial volume calling Nurī the *mujaddidi asr*, the "renovator of the age," see M. Kabirī (ed.), *Mujaddidi asr* (Dushanbe: ShKOS HNIT, 2007).

30 For the most vivid narrative see Roziq, *HNIT*, 81–84.

Muslims you profited from the *sadoqat*[31] and you were in the service of a government that was the enemy of God and His religion.[32]

Hindustonī eventually replies to the open letter of the *mujohid* (as he calls him) and reminds his audience that he was three times sentenced to a Gulag: "You address me as ignorant (*johil*), but for more than 20 years I ventured on the journey for knowledge—but where did you study?"[33] Hindustonī expresses his indignation about the unethical and impolite way he was addressed and recalls that the uprising of Dukchī-*eshon* had been suppressed by Tsarist forces with many casualties among the Muslim community in the Fergana Valley. The uprising was not successful and even fostered Russian rule over the region. Muslims should be aware of the Islamic tradition concerning the jihad, which can be the fight against unbelievers in a war, but more importantly, should be understood as the struggle within one's soul, which the Prophet called the "greater (*akbar*) jihad."[34]

The term Wahhabi was eventually plagiarized by the KGB as a "seal" (*tamgho*)[35] for Muslim activists in their defamation campaigns in the public and media and constructed—as Johan Rasanayagam points out—a local Otherness.[36] The label Wahhabi simultaneously entered Western academic circles related to Islam in Central Asia/Tajikistan.[37] For instance, the doyen of Western Soviet "Islamology," Alexandre Benningsen, exploits the Soviet press and in 1988 characterized Nurī as an

ascetic, he knows the Quran by heart and has a solid theological background. Among his followers, he enjoyed the reputation of a saint, but he

---

31   *Sadoqat* is voluntary charity (beyond the *zakot*), in the 1980s, several religious authorities were accused of embezzling *sadoqat*.

32   Quoted in Roziq, *HNIT*, 91. See also A. Rahnamo, *Ulamoi Islomī dar Tojikiston* (Dushanbe: Irfon, 2009), 173–182.

33   Roziq, *HNIT*, 95.

34   Ibid., 85–98.

35   Roziq, *HNIT*, 78. *Tamgho* is originally a Mongol term for the emblem of a particular tribe and seal/stamp, in Farsi *tamḡā* likewise means "stamp" or "stamp-tax" associated with the (non-Islamic) Mongol tax system, cf. B. Fragner "Social and Internal Economic Affairs," in P. Jackson and L. Lockhart (eds), *The Cambridge History of Iran: The Timurid and Safavid Periods* (New York: Cambridge University Press, 1986), 491–567.

36   See J. Rasanayagam, *Islam in Post-Soviet Uzbekistan: The Morality of Experience* (New York: Cambridge University Press, 2010), 122, 144–153.

37   Cf. M. Atkin, *The Subtlest Battle: Islam in Soviet Tajikistan* (Philadelphia, PA: Foreign Policy Research Institute, 1989).

refused to recognize the official Soviet Islamic hierarchy, accusing it of
betraying Islam. Saidov calls himself a "Wahabi." His public preaching
centered on one idea: the creation of the territory of Tadzhikistan of an
independent Islamic republic.[38]

Benningsen's reading of the Soviet press indicates how carelessly the term
Wahhabi has been applied by journalists, the KGB, politicians, diplomats, and
eventually Western academics. A serious Wahhabi would certainly not be
proud of his attention to Sufism (the Wahhabiyya is hostile toward Sufi orders)
or would accept being seen as a "saint" by his followers. Last, but not least, the
entire IRPT leadership carefully avoided any public reference to an "Islamic
state." In the public discussion, the meaning of the term Wahhabi remained
vague, elusive, and a political instrument. Safaralī Kenjaev, an influential conservative politician who adopted an Andropov-style approach to reform in the
perestroika period and became chairman of the Supreme Soviet of Tajikistan
in 1991, insinuates that Wahhabi is in general alien to the Tajik culture and
nation; therefore, a Wahhabi is essentially a foreign "other."[39] In a polemic
against the *qozikalon* Tūrajonzoda and the IRPT, Kenjaev subsumes the
Egyptian Muslim Brotherhood, Hasan al-Banna, Sayyid Qutb, Mawdudi, and
the IRPT as Wahhabi without differentiation demonstrating the ahistorical and
discretionary application of the term.[40] Būrī Karim—a radical reformer, in
many respects Kenjaev's antagonist and former chairman of the state planning
agency Gosplan—categorically rejects the existence of a Wahhabi group in
Tajikistan and concludes that the fight against the Wahhabis is similar to "Don
Quixote's war against wind mills."[41]

The early IRPT was until 1991 a movement that encompassed diverse groups
of Islamist activists adhering to a rather broad religious agenda striving to reestablish their idea of a Sunni-Hanafi normativity among the Muslims in the
Tajik SSR. Nurī and Himmatzoda merged the normative Sunni-Hanafi Islam of
the pre-Soviet Central Asian tradition with the political interventionist teachings of Qutb or Mawdudi and a variation of anticolonial Tajik nationalism. The
first IRPT party program from 1991 was remarkably silent about its religious
agenda:

38   A. Benningsen, "Unrest in the World of Soviet Islam," *Third World Quarterly*, 10, no. 2
      (1988): 778–779.

39   S. Kenjaev, *Tabadduloti Tojikistan* (Dushanbe: Fondi Kenjaev, 1993), 140.

40   Ibid., 259.

41   B. Karim, *Faryodi solho* (Moscow: Transdornauka, 1997), 459.

The IRPT is a social-political entity for the Muslims of the Republic of Tajikistan, based on Islamic principles (*aqidai islomī*) which is based on the belief in the one God and on the prophet Muhammad (s). ... The Islamic Renaissance Party of Tajikistan is a parliamentary party and participates in elections and suggests its own candidates as people's candidates. ... The aims of the IRPT are: Spiritual revitalization (*ehyoi ma'navī*) of the citizens of Tajikistan / economic and political independence of the republic / political and legal awakening (*bedorii siyosī va huquqī*) with the aim to implement the foundations of Islam in the life of Muslims in Tajikistan.[42]

From the perspective of religious practice and agenda, the label Wahhabi is certainly wrong for the leading representatives of the IRPT. Actually, they respected (or even followed) the major Sufi orders in the region and practiced religious rituals not accepted by the Wahhabiyya, such as the *mavlud* (birthday of the Prophet Muhammad), *janozat* (the funeral rites), or the *ziyorat* (visit to a local shrine). The term Wahhabi—in the Russified variation *vovchik*—nonetheless became one of the central markers for Otherness in the early stages of the Civil War in Tajikistan and contributed to the deadly polarization in the Tajik society. The IRPT's role in the Civil War, however, is beyond the limited scope of this chapter.[43]

The conflict between Islamic activists and the established *ulamo* should be seen in the overall context in which political Islamism was negotiated, in particular the latent competition between the lay–religious contenders and the established *ulamo*. Although Nurī and Himmatzoda acquired their symbolic capital to a significant extent by their close affiliation with prominent religious authorities (Nurī was a student of Hindustonī and Himmatzoda affiliated to the imminent Naqshbandī authority *eshoni* Abdurahmonjon), they were never able to transform from political activists to *ulamo* acknowledged for their religious guidance (or the *amri ma'ruf*).[44] The particular origins of the IRPT, its interventionist activism, and its critique of the societal and political quietism

---

42   Cf. the copy of the program in M. Orzu (ed.), *40 soli Nahzat. Khotira, andesha, didgoh* (Dushanbe: Muattar, 2013), 438.

43   See T. Epkenhans, *For the Soul, Blood, Homeland, and Honour: The Origins of the Civil War in Tajikistan* (Lanham: Lexington, 2016).

44   The two ideological key personalities in the IRPT, Abdullo Nurī and Muhammadsharif Himmatzoda, passed away at a relatively early age (both were 59) and left only fragmentary religious treatises. See, for instance, M. Himmatzoda, *Didgoh va masoil* (Dushanbe: Devatich, 2006). Nurī was apparently working on a Quran commentary (*tafsir*) as fragments on his website (www.nuri.tj/kitob/) indicate.

of established *ulamo* are causative for the reservation with which many *ulamo* view the party until today; since the General Peace Accord in 1997 not a single prominent religious authority (registered or independent) has unequivocally expressed his support or sympathies for the IRPT. Admittedly, more than just the IRPT's turbulent past (including the experience of the Civil War) has contributed to the distance between Tajikistan's *ulamo* and the IRPT—the social transformation of the Tajik society since 1997, the consolidation of the religious field including the emergence of a younger generation of religious scholars, and a new assertiveness of lay religious communities as well as shifting government politics regarding Islam have contributed to the divides.[45]

The IRPT and the High Council of *ulamo*

Beginning in 1943, the USSR regulated a state-sanctioned version of Islam with the Spiritual Board of Muslims of Central Asia and Kazakhstan (Russian: *Dukhovnoe upravlenie musul'man Sredney Azii i Kazakhstana*—SADUM). The intricate role of the SADUM—the complicity of Soviet academia, the KGB, and established *ulamo* in defining and categorizing "Islam"—has been aptly addressed by Mark Saroyan, Devin DeWeese, Eren Tasar, Michael Kemper, Stéphane Dudoignon, and Johan Rasanayagam.[46] The SADUM underwent significant changes in the late 1980s when a younger, post-Stalinist generation of religious authorities reorganized the body into a more independent and interventionist institution emphasizing its political and societal relevance. While the *muftī* Muhammad Sodiq Muhammad Yusuf (1952–2015) initiated this change in Soviet Uzbekistan, his associate Hojī Akbar Tūrajonzoda (b. 1954) transformed SADUM's branch in Tajikistan (which was until 1989

---

45   Cf. S. Nozimova and T. Epkenhans, "Negotiating Islam in Emerging Public Spheres in Contemporary Tajikistan," *Asiatische Studien/Études Asiatiques*, 67, no. 3 (2013): 965–90; M. Stephan, "Education, Youth and Islam: The Growing Popularity of Private Religious Lessons in Dushanbe, Tajikistan," *Central Asian Survey*, 29, no. 4 (2010): 469–483 or S. Roche, *Domesticating Youth: Youth Bulges And Its Socio-Political Implications in Tajikistan* (New York: Berghahn Books, 2014).

46   See, for instance, M. Kemper, "Ljucian Klimovič: Der ideologische Bluthund der sowjetischen Islamkunde und Zentralasienliteratur," *Asiatische Studien/Études Asiatiques*, 63, no. 1 (2009), 93–133; M. Saroyan, "Rethinking Islam in the Soviet Union," in S.G. Solomon (ed.), *Beyond Sovietology: Essays in Politics and History* (Armonk, NY: M.E. Sharpe, 1993), 23–52 and the seminal study by E.M. Tasar, "Soviet and Muslim: The Institutionalization of Islam in Central Asia, 1943–1991" (Ph.D. Diss., Harvard University, 2010).

formally subordinated to the SADUM in Tashkent), the *qoziyot*, to an independent institution with significant political leverage in the later perestroika
years.[47] As the *qozikalon*, Tūrajonzoda adopted initially an ambivalent policy
toward the Islamic activists in the IRPT. He pointed out that the Tajik society
was not ready for an Islamic party and even urged the *ulamo* registered with
the *qoziyot* to sign a statement that they were not members of the IRPT and
would not join the party thereafter.[48] At the same time, however, Tūrajonzoda
hired Nurī as the co-editor (next to Tūrajonzoda's brother Mahmudjon) for the
qoziyot's newspaper, *Minbari Islom*, while Muhammadsharif Himmatzoda
wrote the editorial for the first issue.[49] Apparently, Tūrajonzoda intended to
contain the IRPT by including their key representatives in the affairs of the
qoziyot and to utilize the activists' vigor and influence among a younger generation of Muslims. However, the increasing political polarization in Tajikistan
after independence and open hostilities by the former communist nomenklatura against the *qozikalon* made it increasingly difficult for Tūrajonzoda to
maintain the *qoziyot*'s independence, and in spring 1992 he eventually joined
the opposition.[50] In November/December 1992—the Civil War had devastated
the Vakhsh Valley and the 16th Session of Tajikistan's Supreme Soviet had just
elected Emomali Rahmonov to its new chairman adumbrating the defeat of
the opposition—Tūrajonzoda left Tajikistan and went into exile. He even
joined the IRPT as its deputy chairman (next to Himmatzoda) and represented
the party during the peace negotiations. However, his affiliation with the IRPT
had only been a marriage of convenience. In 1999—two years after the General
Peace Accord and his return to Tajikistan—he left the IRPT and became its
most vocal critic throughout the early 2000s.

Immediately after the Rahmonov government was formed in December
1992/January 1993, the *qoziyot* was replaced by a *muftiyot* chaired by Hojī
Fathullokhon Sharifzodai Hisorī, who had a less interventionist agenda and

---

47   Dudoignon, *Political Parties* and T. Epkenhans, "Defining Normative Islam: Some Remarks
      on Contemporary Islamic Thought in Tajikistan—Hoji Akbar Turajonzoda's Sharia and
      Society," *Central Asian Survey*, 30, no. 1 (2011), 81–96. In the 1970s Muhammad Sodiq and
      Tūrajonzoda were classmates in the Miri Arab madrasa in Bukhara and later fellow
      students in Tashkent. Both were among the few religious students who were sent abroad
      for post-graduate studies in the early 1980s, Muhammad Sodiq went to Libya, Tūrağonzoda
      to Jordan.

48   Roziq, *HNIT*, 181–182 and Foreign Broadcast Intelligence Service, *Daily Report: Soviet
      Union*, October 3, 1990, 88.

49   Sattorī, *HNIT*, 19.

50   Tūrajonzoda, *Miyoni*, 23.

had tried to keep the *mufityot* out of the Civil War.[51] Sharifzoda, however, was assassinated in January 1996 and succeeded by *qorī* Amonulloh Neʻmatzoda. Under his long tenure from 1996 to 2010, the *mufityot* was again transformed into the (present) Islamic Center (*Markazi Islomī*) and High Council of Tajikistan's *ulamo* (*Shūroi olii ulamoi Tojikiston*), which exercised limited control over the registered religious institutions and rarely intervened publicly into religious affairs. Instead, the government relied on the Department for Religious Affairs (DRA, in the presidential administration) and the National Security Council (NSC) to regulate and contain religion. Remarkably, two related developments changed the parameters of how religion was perceived and negotiated in Tajikistan during the quiet tenure of Amanullo Neʻmatzoda.

First, for some time the IRPT was able to represent "Islam" in Tajikistan's political public and among the international community. After the 1997 General Peace Accord, the international community (for instance, the United Nations Tajik Office of Peacebuilding and the Organisation for Security and Co-operation in Europe) facilitated dialogue projects with representatives of the "secular" government and the "religious" opposition, in which the IRPT—largely unchallenged—claimed the exclusive representation of and agency for "Islam" in Tajik society.[52] The IRPT's political agenda after 1997 followed the official political discourse of postconflict Tajikistan in which political pluralism, democracy, "peace," and vague Islamic values are conjured but never explicitly defined.[53] Likewise, party representatives never claimed the public "Commanding Right and Forbidding Wrong," as had been demanded by early IRPT activists.

Second, Islam in its many variations and meanings has (re)gained its social relevance in society despite hostile official politics. Independent religious

---

51   Foreign Broadcast Intelligence Service, *Daily Report: Soviet Union*, January 21, 1993, 71–72. Sharifzoda (also Sharifov) was born 1939 into an influential family of Naqshbandī *pir*s and served since the 1980s as a registered *imom-khatib* in Hisor.

52   See, for instance, the documentation on the dialogue project J.-N. Bitter (ed.), *From Confidence Building towards Co-Operative Co-Existence: The Tajik experiment of Islamic-Secular Dialogue* (Baden-Baden: Nomos, 2005) and various similar publications in Russian and German.

53   The collection of articles by Himmatzoda (*Didgoh va masoil*) demonstrates the IRPT's adherence to the discursive conventions of post-conflict Tajikistan: all five chapters deal with general political issues and the how a party with a religious agenda should operate in a secular society and operate within the limits of the constitution and a globalized political context. For the political economy of post-conflict Tajikistan see J. Heathershaw, *Post Conflict Tajikistan: The Politics of Peacebuilding and the Emergence of Legitimate Order* (London: Routledge, 2009).

authorities have become visible public figures "commanding right" while public observance of religious praxis (prayer, mosque attendance, Muslim rites of passage, and so forth) has noticeably increased among a younger generation of Muslims in Tajikistan. Importantly, Tajikistan's *ulamo* have quietly reclaimed the prerogative of interpreting what Islam could mean in Tajik society—albeit without including the IRPT in this project.[54]

Likewise, the Tajik government reconsidered its policy toward Islam. In 2007 the government decided to declare the year 2009 as the "Year of Imomi A'zam," celebrating the founder of the Hanafi school of law (*mazhab*) in Islam (the dominant Sunni *mazhab* in Central Asia) eventually integrating Islam into the official narrative of Tajik history and national identity.[55] While the reconfigurations of official identity politics remain contradictory and ambivalent, the restructuring of the Islamic Center and the High Council of Tajikistan's Ulamo in 2010 after the death of *qorī* Amanullo Ne'matzoda changed the administration of Islam in Tajikistan decisively. To the surprise of many observers, the government arranged the appointment of Saidmukarram Abdulqodirzoda to succeed Ne'matzoda.

Abdulqodirzoda was born 1963 in the Sovietskii district (now Temurmalik) close to Kūlob in southeastern Tajikistan (thus, he has the right regional provenance), into the family *domullo* Abdulqodir (local religious specialists). Abdulqodirzoda completed his graduate studies at the International Islamic University in Islamabad (with a specialization on *tafsir* and *hadith*) in 2000 and continued his postgraduate studies at the same university.[56] In 2003 Abdulqodirzoda returned to Tajikistan and started to teach at Dushanbe's Islamic University Imomi Tirmizī, which is subordinated to the High Council. From 2004 to 2008, he was the vice rector of the university (simultaneously he studied journalism at Tajikistan's State University). In 2008, he shifted to the

---

54   See, for instance, Nozimova and Epkenhans, "Negotiating Islam."

55   During the Civil War, the Rahmonov government reformulated the Soviet historiography of Tajikistan based on the Aryan "ethnogenesis" of the Tajiks and their early statehood in the 10th century CE with the Somonid dynasty. Initially, Zoroastrianism was promoted as the genuine Tajik/Aryan religion, but these efforts were abandoned in the early 2000s. For the secular identity construction see M. Laruelle, "The Return of the Aryan Myth: Tajikistan in Search of a Secularized National Ideology," *Nationalities Papers*, 35, no. 1 (2007): 51–70.

56   In 1991, the *qozikalon* Tūrajonzoda agreed on an exchange program with the International Islamic University in Islamabad (IIU) and over the past decades several Tajik *ulamo* graduated from the IIU, including one of the most popular contemporary religious authorities in Tajikistan, Hojī Mirzo Ibronov, the former *imom-khatib* of the Hiloli Ahmar Friday Mosque in Kūlob.

Department for Religious Affairs in the Presidential Administration until he succeeded Neʿmatzoda as chairman of the High Council in 2010.[57] Abdulqodirzoda's professional pedigree certainly qualified him for the position, and he immediately demonstrated his intention to enforce stricter control over the registered religious institutions and their personnel.

In coordination with the Department for Religious Affairs, the Islamic Center restructured the curriculum of the Islamic University Imomi Tirmizī and imposed stricter control over the 19 religious middle schools (madrasa) in Tajikistan. The Islamic Center promoted a traditional conservative, quietist, and regime-loyal Tajik variation of Islam. Paradoxically, the Islamic Center embraces an idea of Islam that almost resembles a Salafī interpretation, but actually originates in the South Asian Deobandi movement.[58] By embracing a "radical" variant of Islam, the Islamic Center aggressively defines a narrow Islamic normativity that integrates (quietist) Salafī sympathizers but excludes Muslims who follow a broader Islamic tradition or emphasize the political relevance of Islamic thought. The conservative interpretation of Islam by the Islamic Center clearly outpaces popular religious specialists, such as Tūrajonzoda, Hojī Mirzo, and the IRPT in its rigorousness. Furthermore, the Islamic Center has adopted a concerted strategy to (re)capture its dominance within the religious field: Abdulqodizoda confronted and sidelined independent religious authorities (such as the Tūrajon family[59]), and the Islamic Center established a controversial and intimidating examination board for *imom-khatibs* testing their "knowledge" (which—as a matter of course—is defined by the Islamic Center, the DRA, and "experts" on Islam in the Strategic Study Center under the president[60]). Simultaneously, the Islamic Center has started to provide *imom-xatibs* with a monthly income (US$170–300, depending on

---

57 See the short biography on the High Council's website: <http://muftiyat.tj/en/members/ids/3>.

58 The Islamic Center emphasizes the importance of the regional Hanafi tradition and a cursory analysis of the Center's announcements and statements suggests a strong influence of the Deobandi movement (perhaps in continuation to Hindustonī). S. Dudoignon, "From Revival to Mutation: The Religious Personnel of Islam in Tajikistan, from de-Stalinization to Independence (1955–91)," *Central Asian Survey*, 30, no. 1 (2011): 53–80; and Dudoignon and Qalandar, "They Were All from the Country," 86–88.

59 Cf. Nozimova and Epkenhans, "Negotiating Islam."

60 See "V Tadzhikistane nachalas' proverka deiatel'nosti imam-khatibov sobornykh mechetei," *Islam News TJ*, December 14, 2011, <http://islamnews.tj/tajikistan/564-v-tadzhikistane-nachalas-proverka-deyatelnosti-imam-hatibov-sobornyh-mechetey.html>.

their position) and has imposed a uniform dress code.[61] Finally, since 2012 the Islamic Center has issued a list of suitable sermon topics for the important Friday *khutba*, including specifications how long the *khutba* and the "Commanding Right" (*amri ma'ruf*) should take.

The Islamic Center demonstrated its interventionist strategy in the 2015 parliamentary elections. Shortly before election day (March 1), on Friday, February 27, the Islamic Center issued a text for the Friday *khutba* titled "Elections in Islam" (*Intikhobot dar Islom*).[62] The *khutba* underlined that, already in the time of the Prophet Muhammad, elections were an important process and called on the congregation to cast their votes. While this general call for participation might be laudable, the *khutba* eventually revealed its underlying intention: to denigrate the IRPT. The text repeats a well-known slogan from the political confrontations in 1992/97, that "Islam is no (political) party and that if Islam needed a party, the Prophet Muhammad would have established one."[63] Although the *khutba* does not mention the IRPT explicitly, the text refers to "various parties and groups that claim to act in the name of Islam," but these groups have contributed to the conflicts and disunity and they act "against the noble people of Tajikistan, they are against us and you!" (*muqobili movu shumo*).[64] The political discourse in contemporary Tajikistan is rich in insinuations and conspiracy theories; therefore, the audience had no difficulty understanding the subtext of the *khutba*. This equally applies for the final paragraph of the text. Instead of voting for dubious individuals and groups,

We should think who will provide a future for our homeland? Since the future of our homeland, of our children depends on every single of our votes. We should vote for the person, where we can see the results of his activities, we should support the party, that brought peace to the Tajik people, which organized an international symposium for Imomi A'zam (Abu Hanifa) and introduced him to a global audience, and which constructed 4,000 mosques in the Republic.[65]

---

61   See "Tajik Imams get a Makeover," RFE/RL News, January 18, 2014, <http://www.rferl.org/content/tajikistan-imams-makeover/25234064.html>.

62   A copy of the *khutba* text circulated online. See, for instance, <http://www.ozodi.org/content/tjk-officials-recommended-to-imams-to-criticise-islamic-party-in-preelection-cermon-on-fab-27/26870678.html>.

63   Islamic Center, *Intikhobot dar Islam* (Dushanbe, February 27, 2015), 2.

64   Ibid.

65   Ibid., 3.

The rather unsubtle electioneering for President Rahmon and his ruling People's Democratic Party indicates the paradigmatic change in the official perception of the Civil War and the General Peace Accord in 1997. While for several years the IRPT and, in particular, its chairman, Nurī, were allowed a share in the peace process and postconflict rehabilitation, this role is now exclusively reserved for Rahmon himself. A few weeks after the elections, on March 27, the Islamic Center issued an explicit *khutba* calling for a ban on the IRPT. Under the headline "The Unity and Solidarity of the Society in the right Election," the author congratulates the Tajik people for their wise decision to vote for the party that guarantees Tajikistan's future as well as "peace and unity" (*sulhu vahdat*).[66] The outcome of the elections demonstrated that "except for a few divisive (*judoikhohon*) individuals, nobody supports"[67] the IRPT. Notably, the *khutba* refers to Afghanistan, Egypt, Syria, Iraq, and Libya where so-called Islamic parties have destabilized the governments and instigated civil wars, resulting in uncountable civilian deaths and suffering. In particular, the reference to Arab countries after the so-called Arab Spring discredits IRPT chairman Kabirī, who has travelled extensively to the region and expressed his sympathies for political transformation.[68] The *khutba* rhetorically asks whether the events in the Arab world and Ukraine should be understood as a manifestation of democracy. Instead, the Muslims of Tajikistan should understand that President Rahmon is a great blessing (*ne'mati buzrug*) for the country since he established peace and stability in Tajikistan. The repeated references to the political developments in the wider Islamic world indicate how nervous the political elite has been over the Arab Spring.

Eventually, the *khutba* implicitly calls for the suspension of the (albeit virtual) democratic system in Tajikistan. Instead, the people should unite behind Rahmon and his party in order to express their solidarity and unity. The Islamic Center's *khutbas* mark an unprecedented appropriation of religion by Tajikistan's government and the opening salvo in the defamation campaign against the IRPT and its chairman. While there have been defamation campaigns against the IRPT before, the quality and approach have changed

---

66 The second *khutba*, dated March 27, 2015, circulated immediately in the internet. See, for instance, <http://www.ozodi.org/content/deputy-tajik-mofti-about-islamic-revival-party/26923410.html>.

67 Ibid.

68 See the frequent reports in the IRPT's weekly newspaper *Najot*: "Ghanushī: Tunis kishvari dunyavī nest," *Najot*, February 29, 2012, 6; "Az Dushanbe to Baytulmuqaddas," *Najot*, April 4, 2012, 4; K. Misrī, "Ey islamogaroyon, ba mardumi xesh va digaron chī payome doda metavoned?!", *Najot*, January 24, 2013, 13; A. Davlat, "Jahoni Islom," Najot, February 7, 2013, 4.

significantly, indicating a more subtle understanding of how to orchestrate virtual politics in postconflict Tajikistan: The IRPT is no long a mere "radical" or "fundamentalist" Islamic party; now the party is divisive and has a wrong understanding of Islam and of democracy as a political system. The *khutba* furthermore excludes the IRPT and its supporters from the "solidarity" of the "united" and "noble Tajik people" (= us) and constructs them as a diametrically opposed "Other"—narrative strategies that have been employed before and during the Civil War.

The IRPT in Postconflict Tajikistan

The postconflict role of the IRPT has been significantly shaped by Muhiddin Kabirī (b. 1962), who was appointed to the IRPT's Presidium (*Riyosat*) in 1999 and served as Nurī's deputy from 2003 until the latter's death in 2006. As a graduate of the Moscow Diplomatic Academy and an Islamic university in Yemen, Kabirī opened the IRPT to a younger and more urban electorate. Accurately, *The Economist* characterizes Kabiri as "the modern face of the party and the symbol of a new generation."[69] After Nurī passed away, Kabirī won the recognition of the IRPT's Presidium and was eventually elected chairman of the party. However, Kabirī's candidacy was challenged by representatives of the "old guard," who demanded a return to the IRPT's original electorate (conservative rural Tajikistan) and more pronounced Islamist political platform. After losing the vote to Kabirī, veteran IRPT activist Davlat Usmon even resigned his membership in the IRPT, indicating the cleavages within the party.[70] The current charter (*oinnoma*) of the IRPT, which was adopted in September 2003, reflects the development of the IRPT to a conservative party with a vague reference to "Islamic values." The charter states that the IRPT's program is based on the "principles of the Islamic belief" (*dar asosi aqidai islomī*) but continues with very nationalist priorities, demanding

> the protection of the political, economic, and cultural independence of Tajikistan; the protection of the unity (*jakporchagī*) and territorial

---

69   "Allah's Shadow: Is Radical Islam a Threat to Central Asia's Stability?", *The Economist*, May 17, 2003.

70   D. Usmon (b. 1957) had been next to Nurī and Himmatzoda one of the key activists in the early IRPT. In the Government of National Reconciliation (formally in office between May and November 1992), Usmon served as deputy prime minister and, after the General Peace Accord, as minister of economy until 2000.

integrity of Tajikistan; the protection of the consolidation of peace, support for the national unity (*vahdati millī*) and the fraternal co-existence
of the (different) people of Tajikistan; the expansion of the supreme
Islamic values (*arzishhoi voloi islomī*) as well as the national and general
human values among the society of Tajikistan; the resurrection of the
culture and spirituality (*ma'navijot*) of the citizens of Tajikistan based on
the supreme Islamic and national values (*arzishhoi voloi islomī va millī*);
the refutation of regionalism (*mahalgaroī*) and nepotism (*qavmgaroī*) in
the state structures and in the cadre-politics (*sijosati kadrho*); to support
the democratization of the society; the implementation of the objectives
through the participation of party representatives in the legislative
institutions.[71]

This quote from the IRPT's charter demonstrates how much the IRPT's leadership has become a captive of its own postconflict role and discourse as a
nationalist, mildly Islamist opposition party, affirming the terms of the General
Peace Accord and accepting the predominance of the Rahmon government.[72]
The pervasiveness of the postconflict political discourse has resulted in a convergence of the IRPT discourse with the official government one (except for the
explicit reference to Islam).[73]

The official declaration of the year 2009 as the year of "Imomi A'zam," however, indicated a significant change in the political strategy regarding "Islam" in
Tajikistan. Previous commemoration years, including 2006 as the controversial
"Year of Aryan Civilization" (*soli tamadduni orijoī*), reflected the paradigms of
official identity politics, excluding religion from its constituent elements.[74]
However, with the sumptuous celebration of the founder of the Hanafi branch
of Islamic law, the government virtually "poached" in the IRPT's discursive
space and the celebration was one element in the overall struggle for interpretive predominance of what Islam should mean in Tajik society.

---

71   IRPT (Hizbi Nahzati Islomii Tojikiston), *Oinnomai Hizbi nahzati Islomii Tojikiston*
      (Dushanbe 2007). The charter is also online on the IRPT's website: <http://nahzat.tj/13014-
      oinnomai-izbi-nazati-islomii-toikiston.html>.

72   However, several IRPT members received a modest reward for their political restraint,
      mostly in form of business opportunities in an otherwise highly restricted economic
      environment (conversations in Dushanbe, March 2010).

73   See, for instance, the published speeches of President Rahmon(ov): E. Rahmon(ov),
      Istiqloliyati Tojikiston va Ehyoi millat (Dušanbe: Irfon, 2000–2008), 7.

74   Laruelle, "The Return of the Aryan Myth."

Rahmon outlined his interpretation of the significance of Abu Hanifa in a subtle article published in the government mouthpiece *Jumhuriyat*.[75] In it, Rahmon presents Abu Hanifa as a representative of Statism, who considers a strong state as guarantor for peace and stability. Furthermore, Rahmon integrates Abu Hanifa into the Persian literary genre of Mirrors for Princes (usually called *andarz* or *pandu nasihat*) such as the *Qabusnoma* of Kaykavus Ibn Iskander de-Islamizing Abu Hanifa and his heritage. He concedes that the Quran is a source for advice and council (*pandu nasihat*) commanding justice (*insof*), fraternalism (*barodarī*), as well as tolerance (*tahammulpazirī*). However, Rahmon asserts that Abu Hanifa was first and foremost a Tajik merchant (*tojir*) and not merely a religious scholar, thus he was predominately concerned with justice and fairness (*adlu qist*) in commerce (*bazaar*) and less in the political or social system. In Rahmon's version of Abu Hanifa, the founder of the Hanafi law school admonishes his followers to show respect (*ehtirom*) toward the ruler (*podšoh*), to accept one's position in society, and to attend to one's duty, thus legitimizing the existing political and social order. These qualities, Rahmon continues, are needed for the "cultural reconstruction" (*bozsozii farhangi*) of post-Civil War Tajikistan. While Rahmon's interpretation was widely accepted by the Tajik intelligentsia, Muhiddin Kabirī challenges the official interpretation of Abu Hanifa's oeuvre in a commentary for the weekly *Ozodagan*:

> Why do we honor Imomi A'zam only for being a Tajik (*tojik budanash*) and his law school (*mazhab*) only for its opposition against radical currents (*muqobalat bo jarajohoi tundrav*)? Why are we afraid to say that the majority of us are Sunni Muslims of the Hanafi law school and that everyone who respects the Hanafi law school as part of his self-awareness (*khudshinos*) should struggle to comply in his behavior, speech and religious thought with Hanafi law school to the extent possible? Why don't we say that our society should acknowledge the person (of Abu Hanifa) and his law school as they are (*hamon tavre ki hast*) in order to follow them? Why don't we say that the teaching of the Islamic knowledge (*ma'rifati Islom*) is a necessity, because the majority among us are Muslims and every self-aware Muslim has to know the principle

---

75   See "Imomi A'zam va ahloqi umumiinsonī," *Jumhuriyat*, July 9, 2009. The article was reproduced on the *Khovar* homepage, <http://khovar.tj/archive/7549-imomi-azam-va-ahl01178i-umumiinson1250.html>. Already in 2006, an edited volume of Rahmon's speeches was published dealing largely with religious affairs. E. Rahmon(ov), *Dar borai din* (Dushanbe: Sharqi ozod, 2006).

foundations of his religion, just as every Christian or Jew—no one should be afraid or embarrassed to demand this. In case we are confident that the law school of Imomi A'zam is genuine and sincere, and that his thoughts are constituent (*sozgorand*) for our society and that this strengthens our statehood (*davlatdorī*), we need to confirm loudly and with courage.[76]

Kabirī's critique of the de-Islamization of Abu Hanifa/Imomi A'zam by the government went largely unheard; however, his comments indicate the IRPT's concerns regarding the government's official identity politics.

Conclusion

After the General Peace Accord 1997, the IRPT adopted the paradigms of the postconflict political discourse in Tajikistan, conjuring the exigency of "peace" and "stability." While initially the IRPT—and its chairman Nurī—was granted a share in the peace dividend, the government gradually consolidated its position and started to marginalize the IRPT. Since the mid-2000s, and in particular after the death of Nurī in 2006, Rahmon has increasingly presented himself as the exclusive guarantor of peace and stability in Tajikistan as well as the actual "architect of peace,"[77] while the IRPT is presented in official history textbooks as responsible for the outbreak of the Civil War.[78] Simultaneously, the government persecutes IRPT members and severely constricts the party's political activities throughout the country—arguably, the persecution and constant infringements have worn out the party's leadership and consumed its energy more than discussions about the nature of Abu Hanifa's contribution to the official imagination of Tajik identity. However, the IRPT's complex relationship with the *ulamo* and the profound restructuring of the wider religious field in Tajikistan in the past decade has further eroded the party's political and societal relevance. The IRPT never found a successful strategy to respond to the increased assertiveness (and success) of the *ulamo* in "Commanding Right" and its diminished relevance in the larger religious field. Finally, the government's strategy to strengthen the quasi-state-controlled Islamic Center with

---

76   Reprinted in M. Kabirī, *Din va siyosat* (Dushanbe: Muattar, 2010), 12–13.

77   R. Masov, "Emomali Rahmon: "The Architect of Peace"," *Diplomatic World*, no. 36 (2012): 64–68.

78   See R. Nabieva and Z. Foteh, *Ta'rikhi khalqi Tojik. Kitobi darsī baroi sinfi 11* (Dushanbe: Sobiriyon, 2006).

the High Council of *ulamo* and to allow the institution a larger degree of control over religious personnel and institutions has significantly increased the government's "ownership" in the religious sphere and further isolated the IRPT.

Perhaps, the government does indeed plan to ban the IRPT in the near future—the "defeat" in the elections, the belligerent rhetoric by representatives of the government, and the Islamic Center hint at this possibility. However, the government has manipulated and effectively taken over various political parties, orchestrating its version of democracy in recent years and this might be the plan for the IRPT as well.[79] Apparently, Muhiddin Kabirī—as a charismatic, young, and versatile politician—was particularly targeted by defamation campaigns in recent years, and the government might try to arrange Kabirī's removal and the "appointment" of a more compliant and less charismatic successor (such as Nurī's son Muhammad). Although the government has not formally terminated the General Peace Accord of 1997, it has departed from the informal conventions of the postconflict political discourse in Tajikistan and suspended dialogue with the opposition. The recent celebrations on the Day of National Unity, commemorating the General Peace Accord of June 27, 1997, resembled more a monologue in which Rahmon portrays himself as the exclusive guarantor of peace and stability in Tajikistan while he holds the opposition responsible for the outbreak of the Civil War. Uncompromising, he concludes that

> in the course of history, not a single nation and its people have forgiven and will forgive treason against the homeland—mother, government and people. In particular, the noble people of Tajikistan will never forget the perfidious behavior (*raftori khiyonatkorona*) of some groups and individuals who have transformed the homeland of our ancestors into a field of blood and set our country which had only recently gained its independence on fire.[80]

Lacking any subtlety, Rahmon leaves no doubts who these groups and individuals are, underlining the dramatic shift by his government to an increasingly confrontational policy. By excluding the IRPT and conducting a campaign of belligerent defamation against the party, the government has suspended

---

79   Since the mid-1990s, the Democratic Party of Tajikistan and the Agrarian Party were manipulated and split into opposing factions. Except for the CPT, all parties in the current parliament are part of the presidential orchestration of "democracy."

80   "Sukhanronii Emomalī Rahmon, Presidenti Jumhurii Tojikiston, ba munosibati 18-solagii Rūzi Vahdati millī," *Jumhuriyat*, June 27, 2015.

any form of public debate in Tajik society on the legacy of the Civil War, the postconflict transformation, and the contemporary social and political challenges, eventually compromising the very "peace" and "stability" it claims to guarantee.

Acknowledgement

The author would like to thank the two anonymous reviewers for the constructive critique of an earlier draft of this paper. The field research was made possible by a generous grant of the Ministry of Science and Arts, Baden-Württemberg within the project "Men of Disorder" at the University of Freiburg.

CHAPTER 5

Power, "Original" Islam, and the Reactivation of a Religious Utopia in Kara-Suu, Kyrgyzstan

Aurélie Biard

Already facing reduced standards of living, growing inequalities that are perceived in communal and ethnic terms,[1] political instability, and the
criminalization of the political sector, the Kyrgyzstani population is going
through a brutal identity crisis. Different elite networks are struggling for control of the economic and political space. Kyrgyz politics functions according to
a patronage system that is regional or lineage-based. These networks are mal-
leable and easily adapted to current economic conditions. When Kyrgyzstan
achieved independence in 1991, lineal affiliations were updated via networks of
economic and political clientelism, especially during elections. The oligarchs
running the country introduced closed patronage systems that have influenced the views of the population, who perceive the state and central power as
widely corrupt[2] This occurred under President Askar Akayev's government
during the first "privatization" phase in the early 1990s, under President

---

1   For more than 20 years, minorities have perceived themselves as deprived as a result of the
    monopolization of wealth by a specific ethnic or regional group. Hence, in the 2000s, the
    Uzbeks of south Kyrgyzstan, which is administrated by Kyrgyz functionaries even in districts
    with an Uzbek majority, constituted the first demographic kernel of the Hizb ut-Tahrir, an
    internationalist Islamist party of Palestinian origin. Due to its disregard for borders, the Tahrir
    for a time became the party of Uzbek minorities across Central Asia, before more recently
    broadening its base among students and low-level public functionaries throughout the entire
    region. Tahrir is now widespread among the Kyrgyz, the Kazakhs, and certain Tajik groups.
2   Neither the "revolution" of 2005 nor that of 2010 sounded the death knell of the processes of
    monopolizing wealth and stratification of mafias (linked mostly to the drug trade from
    Afghanistan, the jet fuel concession at the U.S. transit Center at the Manas airport before its
    closure in 2014, the looting of mineral resources, and human trafficking—especially prostitu-
    tion) that have further impoverished an already weak population and increased resentment
    toward the politico-economic elites and their illegally procured wealth. In the whole region,
    flagrant corruption, the collapse of social services, the desire for a more equitable social dis-
    tribution, and glaring injustices perpetrated by the security services are all pushing sections
    of citizens to see Islam not only as a moral refuge, but also as an alternative ideology. The ills
    of the regimes are therefore increasingly explained as being due to their secular nature. The
    attacks of September 11, 2001 as well as the Western military presence in Central Asia, which

Kurmanbek Bakiev's government following the Tulip Revolution of March 2005, then again under Roza Otunbaeva's interim government after the "revolution" of April 2010, and most recently under President Almazbek Atambayev's government.

This chapter focuses on the politicization of Islam in this context of political "disenchantment"[3] and economic slump through case studies of the main theologians of the Fergana Valley, both of them Kyrgyzstani Uzbeks and based in the city of Kara-Suu,[4]—Shaykh Alauddin Mansur, imam of the Imam al-Bukhari mosque, and Muhammadrafiq Kamalov, also widely known as Rafiq Qori Kamoluddin, the late imam of the al-Sarakhsi mosque. If both advocated for the implementation of "authentic" Islam at the local level among Muslim communities, Shaykh Alauddin Mansur appears to adopt a quietist stance over politics whereas Muhammadrafiq Kamalov held a discourse of political opposition to "impious" regimes in the name of "original" Islam. Kamalov's son, Rashod, succeeded him as the imam-*khatib* in the same mosque shortly after his father's death in a security raid in 2006; that is, about a year after Kurmanbek Bakiev's accession to power.

These two mosques, among the most important in the Fergana Valley, are both situated in the small town of Kara-Suu (*Qorasuv* in Uzbek). Straddling the Uzbek-Kyrgyz border, Kara-Suu is about 15 kilometres (9 miles) northwest of Osh. The city's bazaar was the first in the region to funnel Chinese products to the rest of Central Asia. Kara-Suu has only 20,000 inhabitants, but its diversity (60 percent Uzbek and 30 percent Kyrgyz) resembles a compact global society, within which the various social milieus communicate and interact with one another. The richness of (urban) sociabilities in Kara-suu, as well as, more broadly, in the Fergana Valley, greatly facilitates social and religious communication.[5]

Kara-Suu is regarded as the Central Asian "capital" of Hizb-ut Tahrir al-Islamiyya ("the party of liberation"), a banned internationalist Islamist party of Palestinian origin, long based in London, with a transnational, neo-fundamentalist rhetoric.[6] Hizb ut-Tahrir has become the *bête noire* of the post-Soviet

---

enabled the established powers to ramp up pressure on their opponents, have engendered growing hostility toward the West, even in the supposedly secular Kyrgyzstan.

3   P. Michel, *Politique et religion : la grande mutation* (Paris: Albin Michel, 1994).

4   The city is concentrated with places of symbolic power, including the geography of the bazaar, many mosques, and tensions between Uzbek and Kyrgyz border guards.

5   It is not an isolated element; it is a milieu in which people meet each other often, where even rivals share a certain number of norms and ideas. There are relations of tension between different religious and/or social actors but also exchanges (of ideas).

6   E. Karagiannis, *Political Islam in Central Asia: The Challenge of Hizb ut-Tahrir* (New York: Routledge, 2010).

governments. The party is relatively popular in Kara-Suu thanks to its condemnation of national borders that have reduced cross-borders commercial flows. Behind Hizb ut-Tahrir's ideological discourse of wanting to establish an Islamic caliphate in Central Asia that would erase national borders, there is actually a discourse about criticizing the confiscation of the wealth generated by privatization which is to the economic advantage of one given ethnic or regional group. According to the Hizb ut-Tahrir, if a caliphate were to be established, then wealth would be redistributed by an Islamic government irrespective of individual and patronal interests. This underlying discourse is inherited from anti-establishment Central Asian Islam during the late 1980s.

This chapter first analyzes the trajectories of the two main advocates of re-Islamization in the Kyrgyz portion of the Fergana Valley, namely Shaykh Alauddin Mansur and Rashod Kamalov, and highlights their contrasting attitudes vis-à-vis the established regimes. It shows how religious debates and postures concerning their relationships with secular power inscribe themselves in patronage and personal clientelist networks as well as power relationships that penetrate the entire society.[7] This makes it possible for certain actors, in the framework of local rivalries, to adopt the practice of informing on one's adversaries by using some of the negative labels borrowed from official state rhetoric. Whatever real beliefs and practices, labels such as "Wahhabi," "extremists," or "Islamic terrorists" discredit opponents, depict them as a threat to the regime, and thus attract the attention of law-enforcement agencies. Finally, this chapter focuses on the reactivation of a religious utopia that challenges the existing secular political and financial order through a local rhetoric of establishing an idealized caliphate, conveying a message not only of social justice but also of economic transparency and free trade.

The material presented here was collected in Kara-Suu in early 2010, before President Bakiev was removed from power and fled the country. This material does not claim to represent the Uzbek community as a whole, whether in Kara-Suu or the Fergana Valley in general. Rather, it is a snapshot of a particular—but important—time because of the strategic position and influence exerted by some of the considered actors, namely Shaykh Alauddin Mansur and Muhammadrafiq Kamalov and his son Rashod, in reshaping the religious landscape and forms of communal identity. The aim is to highlight the diversity of motivations behind the simplistic dichotomy, instrumentalized by the Kyrgyz authorities, of "good" ("moderate" and supposedly adapted to a reified

7   See J. Rasanayagam, "I'm Not a Wahhabi: State Power and Muslim Orthodoxy in Uzbekistan," in C. Hann (ed.), *The Postsocialist Religious Question: Faith and Power in Central Asia and East-Central Europe* (Munich: LIT Verlag, 2006), 99–124.

"Kyrgyzness") and "bad" ("extremist") Islam, the latter being necessarily the one of the Uzbek minority,[8] depicted as a fifth column that undermines the very foundations of the Kyrgyz nation.[9] In so doing, I hope to contribute to our analyzis on the relations among Islam, politics, and ethnicity in Central Asia.

Alauddin Mansur, Rashod Kamalov, and Re-Islamization

Scholars tend to divide Islamic leaders in post-Soviet Central Asia into two categories: Islamists in the 1990s and Salafists (or at least Salafi-inspired) since 2000. The objective of the second-generation appears to be more societal than political. They do not seek to impose an Islamic state from the top-down, but rather to transform post-Soviet Muslims into "good" Muslims.[10]

---

8   See R. Tromble, "Securitising Islam, securitising ethnicity: the discourse of Uzbek radicalism in Kyrgyzstan," *East European Politics*, 30, no. 4 (2014): 526–547.

9   By inviting Islam to constitute one of the foundations of the "national revival" and of a reified "kyrgyzness" (*kïrgïzchilik*), the authorities constrain it to a folklorization designed to avoid any politicization that would undermine the state in its very structures. The authorities thus promote a form of apolitical conservatism that seeks a mere retraditionalization of society, with the so-called terrorist threat making it possible to quash even moderate opposition. In all the post-Soviet states of the region, the authorities aim to separate out a "good" national and traditionalist Islam from the internationalist Salafist movements or the politicized Islamist currents. Nevertheless, Kyrgyzstan, being the most democratic state in Central Asia, is the only state in the region to have accepted the arrival of foreign Islamic and proselytizing Christian movements without repressive measures, even as they bring money, publications, and new ways of thinking. This has increased the globalization of religion in the country, which is thought of as a unique place for debate in the post-Soviet space.

10   For actors and movements in the Salafi spirit, it is about establishing "authentic" Islam at the local level (namely by preaching, among other means). As its etymology indicates, Salafism claims to offer a return to the sources of "original" Islam. As its ultimate guide, Salafism looks to how early Muslims—pious ancestors (*salaf al-salih*) is the specific term—understood and applied Islam in seventh-century Arabia. According to Salafist Muslims, the *sunna* of the Prophet Muhammad—the compilation of his words, actions, and attitudes—not individual judgment must be used to interpret the Quran. The sum of these *hadiths* (accounts or "sayings") forms the tradition of the Prophet—the *sunna* or path he traced for future generations. A complex and evolving movement, Salafism covers a wide range of ideological positions, from "Quietist" Salafism (socially conservative and "politically soft" according to Samir Amghar, and for which action is based on religious education) to revolutionary Salafism (which advocates direct actions with implicit support for the Third World). Salafism is marked by a desire to purge religion of local

Some Central Asian supporters of Salafism appear to be core actors in the current re-Islamization. Kara-Suu is a textbook example of this spread of Salafi Islam at the local and regional level. Two Salafi-inspired Kyrgyzstani Uzbek theologians, Rashod Kamalov and Shaykh Alauddin Mansur, head the two most important mosques in the Fergana Valley. They are also provincial notables with links to patronage networks and the business community: Mansur owns a business in Kara-Suu's bazaar and trades with Dubai, whereas Rashod owns several stores, restaurants, and buildings, including a hotel and even a private hospital.[11] Rashod Kamalov claims to have studied theology for a dozen years at the University of Medina in Saudi Arabia,[12] while Shaykh Alauddin Mansur is only reported to have studied there.[13] Shaykh Alauddin Mansur received religious training in the Uzbek Fergana with Mulla Hakimjan-Qori Morghiloni (Hakîm Qârî Marghilânî),[14] who was a disciple of Dâmlâ Hindustânî (1892–1989) and who distanced himself from the latter in matters of pietism. In Mulla Hakimjan-Qori Morghiloni's *hujra* ("cell": a metonymical term designating a clandestine madrasa), students (*shakirt*) are said to have been influenced by the works of Mawdûdî, Hasan al-Bannâ, and Sayyid Qutb.[15] This training made them sympathetic to a Salafist approach to issues of dogma and jurisprudence.

---

particularities and "innovations" that altered "original" Islam over the centuries. Salafists themselves often see this quest for "original" Islam as the distinguishing feature of their movement. This war against "superstition" also represents an attempt to reaffirm doctrinal unity. By refusing imitation (*taqlîd*) schools of thought, Salafism pushes for a tightening of sources of Islamic jurisprudence around the Quran and *Sunna*, as recorded in the hadiths. See S. Amghar, *Le salafisme d'aujourd'hui. Mouvements sectaires en Occident* (Paris: Michalon Editions, 2011).

11   Rashod is a businessman who appears to have inherited from his father's fortune that was made under the Akayev's regime. See A. Tynchtykbekova, "Imam mecheti 'As-Sarakhsiya' goroda Kara-Suu oshskoi oblasti nameren sozdat' khalifat v iuzhnykh regionakh Kyrgyzstana," *TsentrAziya*, July 17, 2014, <http://www.centrasia.ru/newsA.php?st=1405 618200>.

12   This was confirmed to me through my interviews with him.

13   This information has not been confirmed by Shaykh Aluddin Mansur himself, only by one of my informants.

14   Interview with Moldo Sabyr, imam of the Uchkun mosque in Bishkek, July 21, 2010.

15   See Kariagannis, *Political Islam in Central Asia*; B. Babadjanov and M. Kamilov, "Muhammadjan Hindustani (1892–1989) and the Beginning of the 'Great Schism' among the Muslims of Uzbekistan," in S.A. Dudoignon and K. Hisao (eds), *Islam in Politics in Russia and Central Asia: Early Eighteenth-Late Twentieth Centuries* (New York: Routledge, 2001), 195–219.

Rashod and Shaykh Mansur advocate for a "return" to the Islam of the *salaf*, especially for dealing with the economic, political, and social crises[16] facing post-Soviet Kyrgyzstan and the broader region.[17] Both call for the re-Islamization of the country and emphasize a "return to authentic Islam," stripped of all the religious innovations that have been added to the original faith. However, they disagree on the question of political engagement. According to the Quietist Salafism that Shaykh Mansur seems to support, the priority should be the purification of religious beliefs and dogma, not questions about the authorities and politics.[18] However, Rashod defends a version of Islam similar to that of the Muslim Brotherhood. Like his father, he appears content to take part in oppositional political discourse (limited to anti-regime sermons) in the name of an "authentic" Islam; which, he argues, is against the impious regimes of Kyrgyzstan and Uzbekistan and their "unjust" political order. He has stated a preference—but taken no concrete action whatsoever— for the creation of an Islamic state (*dawla Islamiyya*).

There are many links, at least in Kara-Suu, between this protesting strand of Salafism, embodied by Rashod Kamalov, and Hizb ut-Tahrir al-Islamiyya. A favorite theme of Hizb ut-Tahrir is the immediate establishment of the caliphate, or khilafat (a theme already present in Mawdûdî), in place of the Islamists' smaller Islamic State. Hizb ut-Tahrir considers the Islamists to be circumscribed by the limits of the nation-state and states that the caliphate is central to the reconstruction of the *umma*. Beyond this statement of principle, Hizb ut-Tahrir also acts as a driver of re-Islamization from below through its system of Islamic mutual aid (charitable actions, help to the most destitute, zero-interest loans, free schooling in its clandestine Quranic schools).[19] It is common knowledge that Rashod, like his father, lets members of this party worship at his mosque, even though the party is banned throughout Central

---

16   For Salafi theologians, the *Salaf* are distinguished by their exemplary piety and military achievements, once controlling a vast empire from Spain to India. Theologians and clerics traditionally establish a causal relationship between the faith of the *Salaf* and their political and military successes. Thus, when Muslim societies are faced with a crisis, whether economic, political, or social, some theologians advocate a return to the Islam of the *Salaf*.

17   This was reported during informal discussions, in the case of Shaykh Mansur, with whom I was not able to speak, with some of my informants, including *shakirt* (students) of Shaykh Mansur.

18   Alauddin Mansur's most popular work is the translation of Quran into Uzbek in 1992. Mansur is the director of the Center for the Study of the Holy Quran in Kara-Suu. From 1996 to 1997, he hosted a Friday show called "At Alauddin Mansur's" on the OshTV channel.

19   Karagiannis, *Political Islam in Central Asia*.

Asia. Rashod also has personal ties with the leading Hizb ut-Tahrir members in Kara-Suu.[20]

In contrast, Shaykh Alauddin Mansour demonstrates his loyalty to the Kyrgyz political authorities by not allowing Hizb ut-Tahrir members to pray at his mosque and by openly criticizing the banned group. Mansour's cooperation may have been rewarded with state protection of his business interests. He is also known to have openly backed Askar Akayev's presidential campaign in the early 2000s. Akayev let Uzbek leaders and residents invest the burgeoning private economy, which rallied numerous Uzbek to Akayev's side, whereas his successor, Kurmanbek Bakiev, based his legitimacy on a more pronounced Kyrgyz nationalism, challenging the de facto autonomy acquired by the Uzbek minority in the local management of economic affairs.[21]

As for Rashod Kamalov, some political figures have actively pursued his influence and support. Rashod has given his followers voting recommendations during elections, endorsements that can be decisive in local races. For example, Rashod asked worshippers at his mosque to give their support to Tursunbaï Bakir uluu, a former ombudsman and presidential candidate[22] and to Melisbek Myrzakmatov, a young businessman and former member of parliament who was appointed mayor of Osh in January 2009 by Bakiev's team. Myrzakmatov used his position as mayor to implement a punitive anti-Uzbek policy, aspects of which found expression in the post-2010 reconstruction plans for the town of Osh—re-opening the gaping wound formed by the age-old dispute over land distribution and control of the main urban economic niches such as the bazaar.[23] Myrzakmatov and Rashod may have had been business

---

20   According to one of my informants, who was a childhood friend of Rashod's father, some of these relationships date back to his childhood.

21   Competition for control of economic resources was heightening during the Bakiyev's regime: the Uzbeks traditionally dominate the bazaars and the urban economy, the Kyrgyz the rural economy and the administration, whereas the shadow sectors are divided between both communities, with a growing preponderance of Kyrgyz circles, which were directly supported by the Bakiev family, in particular the brother of the president, Zhanysh, and Kurmanbek's son Maksim.

22   Tursunbaï Bakir uulu currently serves as a member of the Kyrgyz parliament. He was born in Kara-Suu in 1958 and is a great defender of Hizb ut-Tahrir.

23   See M. Laruelle, "The Paradigm of Nationalism in Kyrgyzstan. Evolving Narrative, the Sovereignty Issue, and Political Agenda," *Communist and Post-Communist Studies,* 45, no. 12 (2012): 39–49.

partners.[24] According to Rashod, they have been close friends since 2001, with Rashod helping him win his seat in parliament and, later, city hall:

> I helped him become a Deputy. He is very nationalist. I did not feel it at the time. During the great meetings, before the elections, I was telling people to vote for him. I was telling them that he had a good personality, he will do a good job for people once elected, that there were a lot of things in his program good for the people. Then after he won, he called him a "Sarte" and rejected me. It was dangerous for him to be my friend, this is one of the reasons of the behaviour he adopted towards me afterwards.[25]

The open support Shaykh Alauddin Mansur gave to Akayev during his presidential campaign had been a central point of tension between Mansur and Rashod's father, who condemned Mansur's behavior as not conforming with Islamic doctrine. The public support for a secular political leader granted by a theologian made the competition for religious authority and local and regional influence between the two imams even more vivid.

Local Power Struggles and Negative Labels

The negative labels that government authorities, whether in Kyrgyzstan or Central Asia in general, have applied to all Islamic practices of which they are suspicious, have been adopted within local debates and power struggles to define "real" or "true" Islam. These terms are used among *emic* representations (i.e., those based on the concepts specific to the social actors under study), and their use corresponds to strategic ends.

This accusation of "Wahhabism" and/or "extremism" can then become an ideological weapon used in power struggles at the local level, as it is the case in Kara-Suu. Members of the Kamalov family, known as "reformist" theologians of the Fergana Valley (notably Rashod and Sadykzhan Kamalov, brother of Muhammadrafiq, first mufti of Kyrgyzstan and director of Kyrgyzstan's International Islamic Center) were considered the main detractors of the former Mufti Murataly Zhumanov (who died in 2010 at the age of 37 years), whom they accused of incompetence and corruption, notably regarding the

---

24 Myrzakmatov even borrowed money from Rashod, according to the latter, in 2004 and never paid him back.
25 Interview with Ravhod Kamalov (in Uzbek), Kara-Suu, August 21, 2010.

organization linked to the *hajj* (pilgrimage). Muhammadrafiq Kamalov had been described by Kyrgyz and Uzbek authorities as a "terrorist" and a member of the Islamic Movement of Uzbekistan (IMU). Muhammadrafiq Kamalov was not the first imam to have been targeted by law-enforcement agencies in the region, but he was the first to have been targeted by both the Kyrgyz and Uzbek security services.

Like Shaykh Alauddin Mansur, Rafiq Qori had a religious training in Mulla Hakimjan-Qori Morghiloni's *hujra* in the Uzbek Fergana. Muhammadrafiq was also linked by matrimonial alliances to two prominent religious figures that became his brothers-in-law: Abduvali Qori Mirzaev[26] from Andijon, who is said to have been abducted by the Uzbek secret services,[27] and Muhammadi Qori, his wife's brother.[28] Muhammadi Qori was sentenced to prison several times and died while serving his last term.[29]

The al-Sarakhsi mosque in Kara-Suu is one of the biggest in the region, attended by 5,000–6,000 people during Friday prayers. Kamalov was well known for allowing members of Hizb ut-Tahrir to pray at there, despite being critical of the group's ideology. He believed that members of Hizb ut-Tahrir "went away from the true path, from the 'true' Islam." Worshippers usually came from nearby villages and some 20 percent from bordering Uzbekistan. He was also the author of many popular religious books.[30] In addition to his acknowledged expertise in religion, his rigorous criticisms of the Kyrgyz and Uzbek governments and of the region's socioeconomic problems earned him significant popularity among disaffected people.

According to one of my informants, a Kyrgyzstani Uzbek activist and human rights lawyer who defended many suspected members of Hizb ut-Tahrir, Shaykh Alauddin Mansur founded the Kara-Suu branch of Hizb ut-Tahrir and indoctrinated a certain number of students (*shakirt*) in his *hujra* (cell or a clandestine madrasa) to Hizb ut-Tahrir's ideology, before betraying the party by

26   Abduvali Qori married Rafiq Qori's sister, Sharipakhan.

27   Abduvali Qori Mirzaev has been missing since 1995; he disappeared after clearing passport control at Tashkent's international airport. Mirzaev's relatives have alleged he was detained by the Uzbek security service, secretly tried, and possibly executed.

28   N. Bekmurzaev, "Independent Islam in Central Asia: Reasons behind Independent Islamic Leaders' Resistance towards the State Control of Religion in Kyrgyzstan," (thesis, OSCE Academy, Bishkek, September 2014).

29   Bekmurzaev, "Independent Islam in Central Asia." See also M.B. Olcott, "The Roots of Radical Islam in Central Asia," *Carnegie Endowment for International Peace*, January 2007, <http://carnegieendowment.org/files/olcottroots.pdf>.

30   R. Qori's works include the five-volume *Iymon Risololari* and the two-volume *Din Nasihatdir*.

publicly criticizing its ideology, possibly because he "feared the repression performed by the Uzbek authorities."[31] This informant highlights the rivalry that, according to him, existed between these two imams, whose respective mosques are situated extremely close to one another.

> I am sure that Shaykh Mansur killed (Rashod Kamalov's) father. There was some rivalry between the two of them. More people frequented the mosque of Muhammadrafiq. Shaykh Mansur said that Kamalov's mosque was a *Wahhabî* mosque, a Hizb ut-Tahrir one. He wrote a letter that he did not sign, but some policemen told me that Shaykh Mansur handed it to them in person, a letter in which he explains that Hizb ut-Tahrir is a dangerous party, that these *Wahhabî* are terrorists, that they are dangerous for society. They are worse than AIDS and cancer put together, and they must be made to flee as quickly as possible. Even if one member of your family is a member of the Hizb ut-Tahrir, he or she must be denounced to the authorities. He distributed this letter to the police and among the local population. People distanced themselves increasingly from Shaykh Mansur since they began to see his true face. Indeed, he has been invited to participate at the *Kurultaï* (major meetings) of the *aksakal* ("white beards") organized by Bakiev at Bishkek.[32]

Rashod succeeded his father as imam-*khatib* of the al-Sarakhsi mosque. After studying in Saudi Arabia, he claimed that he attempted, like his father before him, to "show the true Islam to the population, which is very often ignorant; some *kafir* (non-Muslims) know more about Islam than the majority of the villagers." According to Rashod, his father was killed because he spoke out against political leaders:

> My father showed up the faults and failings of secular power and said that it was necessary to live according to the rules of Islam. And also that one must not live according to the rule of the ideology of democracy. He showed this to the politicians. It is the dictatorship that killed him. In a word, the police, the hospitals, the schools, and the universities follow the president (Bakiev) and my father did not. For this he was killed. People who criticize power, who are not satisfied with the state budgets

---

31   Interview with this informer (in Russian, Uzbek and Kyrgyz), Kara-Suu, March 13, 2010. These same students reportedly have remained faithful to this teaching.
32   Shaykh Mansur openly campaigned for Askar Akayev in the 2000 presidential election.

we have, with the economic situation, people who describe reality, are accused of being terrorists, extremists, *Wahhabî*.

(...)

We do not have the right to criticize the president and this is increasingly the case. With you (in Europe), the politicians do not say: "The president is right, the people are wrong." You analyze the situation and you decide if the president is right or wrong. Presently, with us, people who say that the state (whether it is a matter of Muslims, journalists, representatives of rights, politicians, etc.) is not right, all these persons become number one enemies of the state. Each person has the right to judge the system; we should feel free in society. A human being is not a slave.[33]

Rashod Kamalov insists that he is under constant surveillance from the authorities:

They ask people who know me well questions, people who come to the mosque very often—What are his programs, his ideas, and so on." And then SNB agents sometimes call me to interrogate me. They raise questions such as: "Are there are terrorists, extremists, who come to the mosque to pray? Do people criticize the state in your mosque?" I often see people in suits on beside my house, and I am sure that every Friday there are people who monitor me in my mosque, I am certain of it.[34]

Rashod has been detained by the authorities in Kyrgyzstan several times, sparking large protests in Kara-Suu organized by his followers.[35] Since February 2015, he has been detained on suspicion of belonging to Hizb ut-Tahrir.[36]

    The strategy of Hizb ut-Tahrir, which includes a profound yet gradual Islamization of the population (despite its official rhetoric calling for the immediate proclamation of the caliphate), focuses on the real problem of Islamists in Kyrgyzstan and Central Asia more broadly—local people lack interest in political Islam or the idea of the caliphate. Mobilization around the

---

33   Interview with Ravhod Kamalov (in Uzbek), Kara-Suu, March 14, 2010.

34   Ibid.

35   In early 2011, Rashod was arrested on fraud and embezzlement charges. A court ruled that he was innocent and released him after one month.

36   The press officer for the Interior Ministry branch in Osh, Zhenish Ashirbaev, said Rashod was calling for the creation of a caliphate and calling for people to go to Syria to take part in fighting there.

concept of a global caliphate and unified Muslim nation often comes from a long-term ideal that has been consciously or unconsciously rejected.

The rhetoric of the establishment of a regional caliphate in Central Asia can, nevertheless, turn out to be an attractive option for those who want to denounce an unjust political order. Furthermore, the bazaar world in Kara-Suu can be receptive to the message of economic transparency, free trade, and loosening of the borders, all of which are similar to the message of Hizb ut-Tahrir in Central Asia.

The Reactivation of a Religious Utopia

Challenging an "Unfair" Political Order

Militants join Hizb ut-Tahrir mainly to fight against authoritarian ruling regimes, whether in Kyrgyzstan (especially under Bakiev) or Uzbekistan, the deteriorating economic situation, and judicial injustice meted out against those considered "too religious," "Wahhabi," "fundamentalist," and so on. It is precisely this opposition to a political order that is perceived and resented as unjust that forms the basis of the activism of "A," one of the main leaders of Hizb ut-Tahrir in the Fergana Valley. "A" is a Kyrgyzstani Uzbek who served a four-year jail sentence. Since his release, the local authorities have cut off his electricity to harass him. They arrested his disabled younger brother during a raid in March 2010 and imprisoned him in an SNB (ex-KGB) cell in Osh. "A" points to events like one that occurred in Nookat,[37] in the Fergana Valley, as the reason why he joined the party.

On October 1, 2008, during the festival to break the Ramadan fast, local Muslims were preparing to distribute free meat, pilaf, and other food items to believers inside the Nookat stadium. The local authorities (*akim*) stopped this at the last minute, which resulted in a protest (throwing stones, etc.) and a police crackdown on suspected party members, most of whom were of Uzbek origin. The police conducted about 300 arrests in the days following this incident, and many of those who got out paid bribes for their release. Thirty-two defendants—25 Uzbeks and seven Kyrgyz—were tortured during their detention and made to draw up lists of 20 people each of supposed Hizb ut-Tahrir "religious extremists." Some of the accused were not even present at time, and

---

37   See A. Khamidov, "The lessons of the 'Nookat events': central government, local officials and religious protests in Kyrgyzstan," *Central Asian Survey*, 32, no. 2 (2013): 148–160.

yet they were sentenced to prison for 15–20 years.[38] "A" made reference, in his own case,[39] to the 1999 bombings in Tashkent, which he says President Islam Karimov actually commissioned.

> On February 28, 1999, Karimov organized bombings in Tashkent. He accused Hizb ut-Tahrir of being responsible for the attacks, for doing that. An intelligent, well-trained man seeks truth and justice. I read the version of this incident in the Uzbek press. To do the analysis, I researched members of Hizb ut-Tahrir. After having met members of Hizb ut-Tahrir, I could analyze the situation and find the truth. After these explosions, Tajikistan, Kyrgyzstan, Russia, Ukraine, etc. considered Hizb ut-Tahrir to be dangerous. I think that these events, it was a publicity stunt. While Karimov was being interviewed, the explosion happened. I have a psychologist friend and he explained to me that after this stuff, one suffers shock from fear that lasts about three seconds. When told the news, Karimov had no shock. He remained motionless. It is impossible.
>
> We already talked about the events of Nookat. Many people talk about this. In the entire world, there are many members of Hizb ut-Tahrir. Can you name a terrorist, extremist act committed by Hizb ut-Tahrir? We are Muslims, we have two holidays, *Orozo aït* and *Kurban aït*. We want to celebrate these two holidays, we want to have fun in the parks, with our wives and our children. Do we not have the right to do this?
>
> For Nookat, it is the authorities who organized everything. The stadium was closed while the people obtained the permission of the *akim*, they had put water inside the stadium, there was police everywhere and around the *hokimyyat* (city hall), they had placed cameras.
>
> The current repression, it is the system of democracy that comes from Europe, the United States. It is an imported system for the Muslims of Kyrgyzstan.
>
> In 2006, on September 25, I was sentenced to four years in prison. ... Even today, I do not have electricity; that is (what) democracy (has brought me). I went to the police to explain to them why I do not have electricity. They said: "You, you are like this. You are a special case." I have three children, my parents, my wife. Even my lawyer was killed, he was beaten to death in the street in Osh. No one knows who did this. Last year, I got out of prison. There was a new trial and I left. I had been convicted

---

38   The detainees have since been pardoned by the new authorities in Bishkek, who came to power after the so-called revolution of 2010 that removed Bakiev from office.

39   Interview with "A," Kara-Suu, March 10, 2010.

on six counts, for possession of a weapon, for attempted murder, for inter-ethnic hatred. All of this, it is *haram* (forbidden) by God. I am Muslim. If I had done all this, I would be guilty before God. My main purpose is to be thankful to God and to go to Paradise. In the prisons, the prisoners made souvenirs, in the form of weapons, swords, knives. They give these gifts to SNB agents. One found these gifts as if at my home. As the proverb says, "He who wants to be rid of his dog accuses it of being rabid." I am not a dog, I am a Muslim. I want to live according to my religion.

Akayev and Bakiyev were democrats. I do not want to say that one was better than the other. It will be a good situation when we live according to the laws of Islam. We must recognize that it is worse under Bakiev than under the Akayev regime. But one cannot say that Akayev was better; he was a thief.[40]

According to "B," another member of Hizb ut-Tahrir, also a Kyrgyzstani Uzbek, the Nookat events and increased repression by Kyrgyz authorities following Bakiev's rise to power only reinforced the desirability of an Islamic alternative, including Hizb ut-Tahrir:

I think that it is very good that the authorities exert pressure on religion. This brings benefits. There are leaders who appear, there is more education on Islam. They are preparing themselves to be real leaders. The more the authorities exert pressure, the more they prepare themselves to be real leaders. They also are becoming more intellectual. Socialism, capitalism, etc., these are created systems, invented by men. The rules of Islam are better adapted to everyday life. The Prophet Muhammad also was subjected to attacks that made him stronger. The boxer is good not when he trains, but in the ring. After the Nookat events, we had disputes with the government, this was our victory. We became well-known after Nookat. There are always victims; it is better. The members of Hizb ut-Tahrir for Nookat took care of administrative affairs, administrative organization. The people assembled themselves. It will be the people who take power. Then the people will give us power. It will be a peaceful revolution. We can reestablish the Caliphate in Kyrgyzstan in only 38 hours. But we do not need this. Ten thousand people made the revolution of March 24 (2005). For us, 1,500 people, this would be enough. That is enough. Kyrgyzstan, it is too small. For Uzbekistan, it is the same thing. To

40 Interview with "A," Kara-Suu, March 10, 2010.

the contrary, where the authorities are stronger, it is easier. Under Akayev, the authorities were not as strong as they are now. At that time, we needed 50 hours to invade Kyrgyzstan. The anger of the people was less.[41]

One can only wonder about the actual desire of an underground party like Hizb ut-Tahrir to impose a theocratic regime and establish a caliphate in a regional supra-state framework. Hizb ut-Tahrir has never clearly defined the relative modalities for the establishment of such a caliphate. Very active online, it campaigns primarily against "bad Muslims" (i.e., all others except themselves) and refuses to compromise with the *kufr* (impure) world. Hizb ut-Tahrir's vision of the caliphate has no concrete proposal or strategic analysis. The only strategy is the "return to Islam" of every Muslim; in other words, joining the movement in order to form an active minority that will impact the future through its activism (the comparison with revolutionary movements is explicit). The proclamation of the caliphate must be done here and now, and the rest will follow. In this sense, it is close of the approach of the pious *Tablighi Jama'at* (in Urdu) movement (*Jama'at at-Tabligh* in Arabic)[42]: that the individual return of Muslims to "true" authentic Islam will settle the question of the state and Islamic society.

Order and Economic Transparency
The idea of the caliphate may be attractive because of its denunciation of the elites in power and thus the contemporary political and economic order. It is associated with a popular message advocating order and economic trans-

---

41   Interview with "B," Kara-Suu, March 7, 2010.
42   It is a 'preaching group' founded in India in the late 1920s that has branched out to more than ninety countries worldwide. This movement is banned in Central Asia except in Kyrgyzstan. The transnational dimension and neo-fundamentalist discourse of these movements have not prevented them from having a community dimension: Hizb ut-Tahrir among Uzbek minorities of Central Asia and Tabligh within the eponymous Kyrgyz population. The modalities of interaction between the members of the Hizb ut-Tahrir and Tablighi missionaries are most often conflictual in nature. It is for instance prohibited for the Tablighis, or *davachi* in Kyrgyz – who, as a group, are supposed to carry the good word from village to village and town to town – to get involved in religious controversies or to discuss politics, and notably the links between religion and the state (*dîn wa dawla*). The Tablighis thus engage in verbal disagreements (which most often take place in the mosques during heated discussions between believers after Friday prayers) against the members of Hizb ut-Tahrir, whom they accuse of sowing discord (*fitna*) among the Muslim communities of Kyrgyzstan by their wanting to establish a regional Islamic caliphate in Central Asia.

parency. This especially is the case in the towns in the northern and eastern portions of the Fergana Valley (Andijon, Namangan, and Kokand in Uzbekistan; Osh, Kara-Suu, and others in Kyrgyzstan), which are marked by high unemployment and few economic opportunities. This rhetoric seems primarily to appeal to those whose economic survival is linked to the bazaars. Faced with government surcharges[43]and centralizing economic policies—and, in the case of Uzbekistan, very protectionist policies—traders, merchants, and other economic actors are particularly receptive to the rhetoric of those who support a regional caliphate in Central Asia. They are indeed the only ones defending free trade and present themselves, as Stéphane A. Dudoignon has written, "as the sole representatives of an authentic Islamic economy, characterized by reasonable and fixed taxation for all: the *zakât* of a fortieth of revenue and the *'ushr* corresponding to a maximum of ten percent of profits to benefit the needy."[44]

The example of Kara-Suu and its bazaar perfectly illustrates this phenomenon. Growing international markets on Kyrgyzstani territory, namely oriented around Chinese products, alarmed Uzbekistan, which tried to strengthen its border. The rhetoric of Hizb ut-Tahrir, which condemns the new border restrictions and promotes free trade and an "authentic" Islamic tax, is more favorable to professional circles linked to the bazaars—and can thus be a model for the very people who claim to be overtly hostile toward Hizb ut-Tahrir.

This is particularly true of Shamshuddin, an Uzbek Kyrgyzstani from Kara-Suu, who is both a *domlo* (professor) of Arabic and of the Quran and a trader in the city's grand bazaar.[45] The little business he owns in the bazaar suffers, according to him, from surtaxes and corruption practices. In order to sustain his family, he has to work as a mullah-healer and built for himself a clientele from Osh and Jalalabad *oblast'*.[46] Shamshuddin is a student of Shaykh Mansur,

---

43   See on bazaar politics R.A. Spector, "Securing Property in Contemporary Kyrgyzstan," *Post-Soviet Affairs*, 24, no. 2 (2008): 149-176 and G.B. Özcan, *Building States and Markets. Entreprise Development in Central Asia* (New York: Palgrave-Macmillan, 2010).

44   S.A. Dudoignon, "Islam d'Europe ? Islam d'Asie ? En Eurasie centrale (Russie, Caucase, Asie centrale)," in A. Feillard (ed.), *L'Islam en Asie du Caucase à la Chine* (Paris, Les Études de la documentation Française, 2001), 69.

45   "My courses," Shamshuddin made clear, "are on the Quran, and depend on age, there are evening courses, one after school, they also involve pronunciation in Arab, the translation of Arab into Uzbek. In these courses we do not talk about sects, we do not discuss politics, the Hizb ut-Tahrir, or the '*Wahhabî*'."

46   Shamshuddin treats the physical illnesses and psychological complaints, which, he says, are due to the bad economic situation, by *dem-saluu* ("the action of breathing on the patient after having recited the Quran before them"). Shamshuddin details: "there are

whom he consults on occasion to shed light on theological issues. He became pious in Uzbekistan, where he lived until the age of 25 with the father of his childhood friend who was a Mullah, and then with a *ustat* (master) in Andijon, an *ustat* whose name he has always refused to divulge. According to Shamshuddin,

> There are some very bad elements, namely the Hizb ut-Tahrir, the *dava-chi*, which destroy the reputation of Islam. Thanks to science, to education, it is possible to destroy these things. They are ignorance related. ... The town of Kara-Suu is divided into two. The members of the Hizb ut-Tahrir go to the mosque of Rashod, the others to Shaykh Mansur. It's all the same to me to which mosque I go for the *juma-namaz* (the Friday prayer). It depends on where I am at the time. Rashod's father was a good man and well-educated. Shaykh Mansur said that the Hizb ut-Tahrir is against the government and its policies. He criticizes them a lot. ... Shaykh Mansur is an *alim*. Mansur is among the best, the most honorable.

In the course of our exchanges, this *domlo,* who did his utmost to show me the "true Islam" (*taza*), also came out in favor of establishing a regional Islamic caliphate in Central Asia.

> It is necessary to find someone who will say to Bakiev: "Listen, Kurmanbek, you can be very wealthy, so very wealthy, you can have all the money of Russia, but you will not take it with you under the earth." You should fear God, you must think of your people, of your country. They are all corrupt. Each person must reflect upon that, the idea is to think of others. ... The *shahid* is the one who dies during the jihad. There is a second sort of *sha-hid*: if I say something to Bakiev, if I say to him, "do not do that," and he orders to killme. In this case, I will become *shahid*. It is only God who knows who will become *shahid*. Perhaps there is a *shadid* among the dep-uties. Where are we going like this? It's all over for us. The government

---

physically and psychologically ill people. This is due to the economic situation. People live in poverty, in misery. They are being eaten from the inside. It is stressful. (...) I see and treat many sick people. That is my daily reality. During Soviet times, people were more morally resistant. There were few drunkards, few drug addicts, and even no prostitution. Now this has become worse. It is the mass of democracy, which cannot bring anything good to humanity. We have to live according to the rules of pure Islam." Interview with Shamshuddin (in Uzbek and Kyrgyz), Kara-Suu, March, 17 2010.

borrows heaps of money; we owe a lot of money. Future generations will suffer a lot. ... A deputy ought to have the fear of God in him. Even during the electoral campaigns, a deputy will distribute food free of charge so that people vote for him: people are culpable for accepting that.

They distribute things. They buy people and people are corrupt. They do not know what they do; they do not think of the future. It is henceforth difficult to find a "pure" Muslim. In Europe, there will perhaps be someone who will come here to make people understand what must be done. ... I wish to have someone educated, someone who comes among us, and explains the pure Islam to us. It is not Islam that is culpable; it's the people. ... We must reestablish the caliphate. God will give us a Caliph, who will lead the Muslim world. We are looking for him. He will perhaps be a Catholic who will convert to Islam or an African. There have been four Caliphs. The heads of the Arab countries at the present time (the Caliphs, the heads of state) have sold their *Iman* (faith) for money. They are not worthy of being heads of state. We must not wait to reestablish it. We must act now. It is not necessary to reflect upon that. If we create a powerful caliphate, the current system will disappear, there will be no borders, no poor people, if the caliphate extended as far as Sicily, if everyone gave the *zakât* (legal alms), the poor would disappear. No one would think about nuclear weapons. Islam is for peace.

In the course of our exchanges, as trust became more developed, this *domlo* confided in me that:

The people who are against the president are considered as *Wahhabî*, and those who criticize the president, the people, and the government are accused of being *Wahhabî*. But one needs not fear Wahhabism; it is a very pure movement. Some persons say that the Hizb ut-Tahrir is an extremist group, but the Baptist Christians, the *davat* (preaching) of the Baptists, what is that? An intelligent man, a man of science would never say that. It is necessary to make an analysis of Hizb ut-Tahrir, if some things are incorrect, this must be stated. They also have advantages. If one still has bad views of Hizb ut-Tahrir, anarchy or even a dictatorship will be the result. The government does not want to have an Islam expert since it wants a secular state. Power cannot exist without religion. The people who live in the state are religious. If the state is without religion, the people must also be without religion. In Europe, there are Christian parties, in Switzerland, in Germany, in England; in Sweden, the links between the government and religion are very developed. It is necessary to know one thing: everyone must fear God. If we fear God, the Last Judgment, we will continue to survive. If we do not fear God, the government will lie to the people, and the people will lie to the government.[47]

This *domlo* introduced me to his childhood friend, whose father had introduced him to Islam. This friend, who has become a prosperous trader (he made his fortune not so much from the local bazaar but by selling perfume in Arabian Gulf countries), is also a former *shakirt* of Shaykh Mansur. He loudly proclaims his disgust of the elites in power, whether of those in Uzbekistan or in Kyrgyzstan (and notably of the children of the Uzbek and Kyrgyz leaders, namely Gulnara Karimova and Maksim Bakiev). He also states his dislike of democracy (a system within which "thieves are not punished by having their hands cut off, and this ought to be the case"), and of depraved Western mores, and claims "to be ready to die for the pure ideology of the Hizb ut-Tahrir, a number of whose members are prison, solely because they defend this pure ideology."

Conclusion

Some local religious and economic actors in Kyrgyzstan have invoked Islam to legitimize utopian political ideologies that would usher in a new, socially just social order by implementing "original" Islam; that is, through purifying social values and creating exemplary, "authentic" Muslims. This reformulation of Islam sees religion as a mechanism to reinvent and rebuild the social and political system, given globalization and the exhaustion of major political ideologies of the twentieth century (socialism, nationalism, Third World solidarity).

In Kyrgyzstan, it has been the weakness of the state and its absence from everyday life that has provided fertile ground to politicized religious movements.[48] The highly protectionist economic policies of neighboring republics such as Uzbekistan further reactivate, at the local level (namely in towns within a few kilometers of the Uzbek border), the utopia of an "authentically" Islamic political-economic order that would create both Islamic justice and free trade. This local rhetoric of an idealized caliphate that would erase borders and establish Islamic taxation, proposed mainly by Hizb-ut Tahrir, can

---

47   Interview with Shamshuddin (in Uzbek and Kyrgyz), Kara-Suu, March 19, 2010.
48   E. McGlinchey, "Islamic Revivalism and State Failure in Kyrgyzstan," *Problems of Post-Communism,* 56, no. 3 (May/June 2009): 16–28.

attract petty traders from the bazaar world who consider themselves shut out of the wealth generated by privatization.

However, the "losers" of economic privatization are hardly the only ones to hold a discourse of political opposition in the name of an "authentic" Islam. Rashod Kamalov, a prosperous and well-established imam whose father benefited from the economic transition, has also stated a preference for a social and political order informed by Islam. The relationships to Islam and to secular power of some of these "winners" of privatization, like Rashod and Shaykh Alauddin Mansur, cannot be reduced to the affirmation of doctrinal statements: it has rather to do with patronage cooptation and local power struggles.

There are numerous social pockets where the idea of a nonviolent Islamic solution can mature, whether in Uzbek or Kyrgyz communities. Merchants and traders face the surtax on the bazaars and are exposed to corruption and competition from the security services,[49] minor urban elites are moving down the social ladder as they lack professional opportunities and find themselves shocked by growing wealth disparities, younger generations educated abroad cannot find their place in society.

---

49   A. Il'khamov, "Akramiia: ekstremistskoe dvizhenie ili predtecha islamskoi sotsial'noi demokratii?", in S. Abashin and V. Bushkov (eds), *Rasy i narody: Volume 32* (Moscow: Nauka, 2006), 116–156.

CHAPTER 6

Islamic Finance and the State in Central Asia

Alexander Wolters

Introduction[1]

Islamic finance and banking has been developing steadily since the early 1970s. This growth has been concentrated in the Arab states and in Muslim southeast Asia, particularly in Malaysia. Global financial centers like London proved exceptional to this rule and serve as organizational hubs to channel and direct Islamic financial resources.[2] Since the dawn of the global financial crisis, however, interest in Islamic financial products has risen because they have performed much better than conventional products. Islamic banking is duly making its way into non-traditional markets and may now exceed US$2 trillion in assets.[3]

The states of post-Soviet Central Asia have been left out of this emerging picture of global Islamic financial flows. In fact, most countries in the region have experienced only meager growth in Islamic investment in their respective capital markets. And despite repeated proclamations to begin introducing Islamic banks and to benefit from this vibrant economy, the results are

---

1 I would like to thank two anonymous reviewers for their suggestions and comments as well as the *KomPost Research Network* (sub-project D2), sponsored by the German Federal Ministry of Education and Research, for providing the funding for field research. Material for this article includes data gathered during two field trips to the region in September/October 2012 and February/March 2013. An earlier version of this article appeared in the Research Paper Series of the PFH Private Hochschule Göttingen, see A. Wolters, "Islamic Finance in the States of Central Asia: Strategies, Institutions, First Experiences," *Research Paper Series No. 1* (2013), PFH Göttingen.

2 R. Baba "Islamic Financial Centers," in M.K. Hassan and M.K. Lewis (eds), *Handbook of Islamic Banking* (Cheltenham, UK: Edward Elgar, 2007): 384–400. Offshore financial marketplaces are gaining momentum, see "Offshore Financial Centers. Attractive for Islamic Finance," *MIFC Insight Report*, August 13, 2015, <http://www.mifc.com/index.php?ch=28&pg=72&ac=138&bb=uploadpdf>.

3 See "Islamic Finance: Developments in Non-traditional Markets," *MIFC Insight Report*, January 15, 2016, <http://www.mifc.com/index.php?ch=28&pg=72&ac=160&bb=uploadpdf>; for a discussion of recent estimates, see "The Size of the Islamic Finance Market," *IslamicFinance.com*, December 27, 2014, <https://www.islamicfinance.com/2014/12/size-islamic-finance-market-vs-conventional-finance/>.

© KONINKLIJKE BRILL NV, LEIDEN, 2018 | DOI 10.1163/9789004357242_008

disillusioning. Out of five republics, only the National Bank in Kyrgyzstan has issued a license to a local institute to open an Islamic bank, the *EkoIslamikBank*. The other states have been hesitant or delayed in their attempts to provide for the necessary legal changes, or they rely on external initiative and funding.

This state of affairs is perplexing. Considering their much-referenced Muslim heritage, the increasing re-engagement with all parts of the global *Ummah*, and the assumed executive powers of decision-makers in the countries of Central Asia, not to mention the acute needs for fresh capital, the swift introduction of basic principles of Islamic banking across the region seems logical, but that has not happened. What explains this irritating outcome?

To investigate the possible reasons behind such low performance, this chapter focuses on the dynamic relation between political crisis and Islamic finance in the Central Asian republics. When facing global financial shocks, states open up to new and unconventional investment opportunities; in times of political crisis, however, concerns for state security and the need for what is perceived as *social tranquility*[4] quickly undermine such efforts. In their move against possible sources of instability, the states in Central Asia seem to repress all kinds of irritating social innovation. Kazakhstan and Tajikistan were eager to connect with available streams of Islamic investment capital in the early stages of the financial crisis in 2007 or 2008; yet they found it difficult to continue when the political regimes came under threat a few years later. In addition to detailing the nascent evolution of Islamic banking and finance in the region, the chapter thus aims to contribute to an emerging body of literature about the potentials and limitations of Islamic economics in Central Asia.

After a short review of the literature, the text uses case studies that contrast the respective initiatives to introduce Islamic banking in the Central Asian republics with political developments in the region since 2007. Ratings from Freedom House's *Nations in Transit* reports are used to evaluate overall political performance of the Central Asian states throughout the period.

The State and Islamic Finance in Central Asia

In comparison with the many debates about the fate of the state in Central Asia and its relation to economic transformation and development, the role of Islamic finance has been scarcely examined. This can be partly explained with

4 For the use of the term see, for example, "Doverie k vlasti snizhaetsia - Gul'mira Ileuova," *Radio Tochka*, November 28, 2015, <https://radiotochka.kz/18833-doverie-k-vlasti-snizhaetsya-gul mira-ileuova.html>.

the lack of proper material. There were simply not many stories that could have been told about Islamic finance in Central Asia until quite recently.[5] Since 2011 more attention has been paid to the first pioneering projects. Most of this work attempts to examine state capacity to facilitate the establishment of Islamic financial institutes in the respective countries and discusses policy propositions.[6] More recent studies examine the chances of implementing the Islamic leasing instrument *Ijarah* in Uzbekistan or discuss the prospects of *Halal* banking in the wider region.[7] Such contributions reiterate stereotypical images about the prospective markets in Central Asia in order to promote Islamic banking. The line of argument followed here usually includes classifying titular nations as Muslims and therefore potential consumers in Central Asia,[8] as well as identifying impediments in form of the legacy of Soviet secularism among the population, and hence the need to further promote principles of Islamic banking.[9] Instead of questioning the common sense assumptions about the legacy of Soviet secularism or the dynamics of Islamic "re-awakening," these studies tend to use them as explanations.

---

5 A first short article by G.F. Gresh is the exception, see "The Rise of Islamic Banking and Finance in Central Asia," *The Fletcher School Online Journal for Issues Related to Southwest Asia and Islamic Civilization* (Fall 2007).

6 See, for example, B. De Cordier, "The development space(s) of Non-OECD aid donors in Southern Eurasia: A look at the Islamic Development Bank," *Central Asia Economic Paper No. 3* (September 2012); F. Aliyev, "The Politics of Islamic Finance in Central Asia and South Caucasus," *Voices From Central Asia*, 2 (2012); A. Wolters, "Zwischen Scharia und der Suche nach frischem Kapital. Über die Einführung des islamischen Bankwesens in Kasachstan und Kirgistan," *Zentralasienanalysen*, 63 (2013): 2–5; Khaki and Malik's study on Islamic finance in Central Asia borrows in large part – and in unauthorized form – from my own research paper, published in 2013, compare G.N. Khaki and B.A. Malik, "Islamic Banking and Finance in Post-Soviet Central Asia with Special Reference to Kazakhstan," *Journal of Islamic Banking and Finance*, 1, no. 1 (2013): 11–22, and Wolters, "Islamic Finance."

7 A. Asadov and K. Gazikhanov, "Ijarah's Prospects in Central Asia: An Example of Uzbekistan," *Journal of Islamic Economics, Banking and Finance*, 11, no. 2 (2015): 63–85; B.A. Malik, "Halal Banking in post-Soviet Central Asia: Antecedents and Consequences," *Marketing and Branding Research*, 2 (2015): 28–43; G.N. Khaki and B.A. Malik, "Emergence of PLS Industry in Post-Soviet Central Asia: An Empirical Study of Kazakhstan," *Journal of Islamic Economics, Banking, and Finance*, 11, no. 1 (2015): 140–156.

8 Asadov and Gazikhanov, "Ijarah's Prospects in Central Asia," 65; Malik, "Halal Banking," 36.

9 Asadov and Gazikhanov, "Ijarah's Prospects in Central Asia," 73, 80; Malik, "Halal Banking," 33, 36–37.

One exception to this argument is Hoggarth's suggestion that Islamic banking has been used as an instrument for post-colonial nation-branding.[10] She argues that Islamic finance serves Central Asian states, particularly Kazakhstan, in their attempts to formulate an independent foreign economic policy. As such they strive to become part of what she labels a "form of post-colonial capitalism."[11] Kazakhstan is leading this process and intends to utilize Islamic finance to build an alternative to Western, Russian, and Chinese development models.

Studies of the Islamic revival in Central Asia have largely ignored the arrival of Islamic finance. Botoeva's comparison of the establishment of Islamic finance principles in Kyrgyzstan and Kazakhstan offers a first insight into the complex processes of adoption and rejection, of adaptation and contestation of the accompanying norms and values.[12] The advent of Islamic finance, she argues, is neither determined by pure economic rationality, nor can it be reduced to the rising piety among Central Asian Muslims. Botoevas study thus questions both the ready-made assumptions about the natural affinity of Muslim Central Asia for Islamic finance, as well as the quick reference to market logic to explain its development in the region. Her argument adds to Hoggarth's critique about the assumption of Islamic finance as an elite strategy to pacify an Islamized population. In fact, both argue that the development and success of Islamic finance in Central Asia depends on complex adaptation strategies, whether for individual businesses (Botoeva) or national politics (Hoggarth).

The following case studies provide evidence to support this line of critique and also to move beyond it in some respect. Efforts to establish Islamic finance principles are conditioned by the experience of political crisis in the states of Central Asia. The first initiatives to promote Islamic banking, for example in Kazakhstan and Kyrgyzstan, followed a widely accepted belief about the economic nature of the global financial meltdown. Subsequent attempts to deepen the engagement, however, had to maneuver between economic rationalities and changing perceptions of the unfolding political crisis. Thus, individual or national strategies to adopt Islamic finance principles, either out

10   D. Hoggarth, "The rise of Islamic finance: post-colonial market-building in central Asia and Russia," *International Affairs*, 92, no. 1 (2016): 115–136.
11   Ibid., 135.
12   A. Botoeva, "Let's Bank the Muslim Way? Explaining the Establishment of Islamic Banks in the Peripheral Economies of Kazakhstan and Kyrgyzstan," paper presented at SASE *Mini-Conference on Rethinking Islamic Finance: Markets, Firms and Institutions*, University of Milan (June 29, 2013).

of personal needs or for ideological projects, are limited by the crisis management strategies of the political regimes.

Islamic Principles for Business and Finance

Debates about the normative foundations of Islamic finance have become
more intense and diversified following the impressive growth rates of this
industry. The more Islamic finance enters new markets, and designs and offers
new products, the more religious experts and practitioners question the Shari'a
compliance of the business and subject it to their critical inquiry.[13] Scholars
like Choudhury seek to build up theological grounds for a Quranic-based world
order to eventually realize a financial system fully rooted in the real economy.[14]
This contrasts with practitioners such as Yerlan Baidaulet, the head of the
Association of Islamic Bankers in Kazakhstan, who envision the establishment
of Islamic finance as a further branch of modern ethical banking.[15]

Aside from such disputes, the principles of Islamic finance are rather clear.
They rest upon a systemic body of rules for economic engagement in compliance with the Shari'a, and they aim to help develop *asabiyya*, or social cohesion,
in society.[16] For example, *Zakat*, one of the five pillars of Islam, functions as a
special tax on wealth to provide for the poor. More specific conditions for
Islamic finance are the exclusion of excessive risk or uncertainty and related
speculative action, usually referred to as *gharar*, and, most famously, the exclusion of interest.[17] *Riba* or usury leads to excess compensation without due

13   See, for example, M. Asutay, "Conceptualisation of the second best solution in overcoming
       the social failure of Islamic banking and finance: Examining the overpowering of
       homoislamicus by homoeconomicus," *IIUM Journal of Economics and Management*, 15,
       no. 2 (2007): 167–195; U. Derigs and S. Marzban, "Review and analysis of current Shariah-
       compliant equity screening practices," *International Journal of Islamic and Middle Eastern
       Finance and Management*, 1, no. 4, 285–303; for a discussion from a practitioner's point of
       view, see J. Foster, "How Sharia-compliant is Islamic banking?", *BBC News*, December 11,
       2009, <http://news.bbc.co.uk/2/hi/business/8401421.stm>.
14   M.A. Choudhury, "Development of Islamic economic and social thought," in M.K. Hassan
       and M.K. Lewis (eds), *Handbook of Islamic Banking* (Cheltenham, UK: Edward Elgar,
       2007), 21–37.
15   Interview with Yerlan Baidaulet, Astana, Kazakhstan, October 2012.
16   M.U. Chapra, *Morality and Justice in Islamic Economics and Finance* (Cheltenham, UK:
       Edward Elgar, 2014).
17   See S.R. Hakim, "Islamic Money Market Instruments," in Hassan and Lewis, *Handbook of
       Islamic Banking*, 161–171; a narrow definition uses the term *usury* as specific financial

consideration and must be forbidden in accordance with Shari'a law. To counter the negative effects of financial arrangements, Islamic economics instead proposes to balance out the risk to loose and the chance to profit in doing business (Profit-Loss-Sharing). Further principles resemble the criteria developed in conventional ethical banking, for example the ban on investments into gambling or pornography, as well as other activities that are *haram*, i.e., sinful and therefore prohibited.[18]

There are many instruments to allow for the sharing of profits and losses in Islamic finance, and many more are being designed and tested every year, leading to the above-mentioned debates about Shari'a compliance.[19] A *mudarabah*, for example, is a profit- and loss-sharing agreement in which the bank provides financial capital and the partner provides knowledge and skills. The *murabaha*, which comprises more than two-thirds of the market, is a form of a fiduciary sale where the bank obtains a certain good and sells it to the buyer, the bank's client, with a profit. In such transactions Islamic law demands that all information about costs in the transaction be honestly declared and that it be rooted in real commodity trade, not only financial transactions. The bank does actually buy the good, for example a house, and sells it further to the buyer with the added margin. Other commonly known instruments of Islamic finance are *musharakah*, a joint venture in which parties agree in advance on profit sharing, based on shares of investment; the Islamic bond *sukuk*; the above-mentioned Islamic lease arrangement called *ijarah*; and *bai salam*, a financing instrument for a deferred commodity exchange.[20] In general, all instruments in Islamic finance and banking aim to compensate for the time value of money in transactions without resorting to interest, as well as to guarantee that any transaction be rooted in the real economy.[21]

---

interest to designate the prohibition of interest, whereas *riba* more generally refers to addition or excess.

18 For an introduction into the principles of Islamic finance and banking, see T.S. Saher and M.K. Hassan, "A Comparative Literature Survey of Islamic Finance and Banking," *Financial Markets, Institutions, and Instruments*, 10, no. 4 (2001): 155–199.

19 For introductions, see Saher and Hassan, "A Comparative Literature Survey of Islamic Finance and Banking"; Hakim, "Islamic Money Market Instruments"; and *Glossary of Financial Terms*, Institute of Islamic Banking and Insurance, <http://www.islamic-banking.com/glossary_of_key_terms.aspx>.

20 It is such sale- and buy-back instruments or deferred sales that are often criticized for non-compliance with Shari'a law, since many experts believe they disguise a transaction that basically runs on interest.

21 Choudhury explicates: "(In Islam) in the endogenous interrelationships between money and the real economy, the quantity of money is determined and valued in terms of the

Any effort to establish Islamic banking in Central Asia must master the chal-lenge of adhering to Islamic principles in financial investments. Even if Kazakhstan and its neighbors are considered fertile ground for future success-ful Islamic business, the institutionalization of corresponding norms and supervisory practices, for example the establishment of Shari'a councils, must be resolved before such initiatives can bear fruit. At the same time, a broader debate about Islamic economics and the underlying philosophical system still has yet to take off in the region.

Kazakhstan: Future Hub for Islamic Finance in the Former Soviet Union?

Based on the number of international conferences and forums dedicated to Islamic finance and business that it has hosted, Kazakhstan has indisputably become the regional leader in promoting Islamic ideas of banking and doing business in the region. The Seventh World Islamic Economic Forum, held in June 2011, the Second Islamic Finance Forum in September 2011, or the Fourth Kazakhstan Islamic Finance Conference in September 2014, as well as such specialized events like the Kazakhstan International Halal Expo 2012, held in October 2012, and the 12th Islamic Financial Services Board Summit, held in May 2015 in Almaty, underline Kazakhstan's leading role in regional efforts to introduce Islamic finance and banking. Officially the Kazakhstani government has declared its ambition to develop the country into a regional center for Islamic finance in the former Soviet Union. To this end a special roadmap was adopted in 2012 that lists the steps necessary to reach this goal.[22] Financial planners like Baidaulet or Zhaslan Madiyev, the deputy head of the Development Bank of Kazakhstan (DBK), confirm Kazakhstan's potential and have lobbied for the development of Islamic financing in the republic.[23] Before

---

value of spending in shari'a goods and services in exchange. Money cannot have an exchange value of its own, which otherwise would result in a price for money as the rate of interest. Money does not have a market and hence no conceptions of demand and supply linked to such endogenous money in Islam." (Choudhury, "Development of Islamic economic and social thought," 2007, 34.)

22 The roadmap lists eight chapters with specific tasks to realize the goal to become the major hub for Islamic finance by 2020, see "Dorozhnaia karta razvitiia islamskogo finansirovaniia do 2020 goda," *Edilet*, 2012, <http://adilet.zan.kz/rus/docs/P1200000371#z9>.

23 See, for example, "Kazakhstan nachal vnedryat' islamskiy banking," *Deutsche Welle*, May 4, 2012, <http://www.dw.com/ru/kazaxstan-nachal-vnedryat'-islamskij-banking/a-15925120>.

the roadmap was adopted, Ernst & Young favorably assessed the Kazakhstani market opportunities:

> The Government's commitment to make Kazakhstan an Islamic finance centre, coupled with the country's current leadership in the (Commonwealth of Independent States) CIS in making legislative changes to allow the operation of Islamic finance institutions, should give Kazakhstan a unique competitive advantage in attracting Islamic finance investments and help the country achieve its goal of becoming a leading financial centre for the region.[24]

Kazakhstan began to put more efforts into the development of Islamic finance with the onset of the global financial crisis in 2007. Before then, initiatives were limited to two smaller projects in the 1990s. While still a part of the Soviet Union, the Council of Ministers of the Kazakh SSR passed a resolution to found the Al'baraka Kazakhstan Bank as an international project in cooperation with Saudi Arabian partners.[25] Al'baraka Kazakhstan Bank opened on January 1, 1991, and survived the difficult years of the dismantling of the Soviet economy only to be renamed Kaspi Bank and restructured into a conventional commercial financial institute in 1997. A similar fate, according to one observer, was suffered by an initiative from *Lariba*, a riba-free US-based bank that tried to enter the Kazakhstan market in the 1990s.[26]

The Islamic Development Bank (IDB) provided invaluable advice and support for the first Islamic finance initiatives in Kazakhstan. The country had joined the international agency in 1995, and in 1997 Almaty was selected to host one of the bank's four regional offices. Since operations commenced, the IDB has spent more than US$1.2 billion in the republic, which puts it ahead of its Central Asian neighbors in terms of received funding.[27] The IDB observes the standards set for all international development banks, in particular close cooperation with state structures, which has resulted in a predominance of

---

24   "Challenges and opportunities for Islamic finance in Kazakhstan," *Ernst & Young* (2011), <http://documents.mx/documents/islamic-finance-in-kazakhstan-ey.html>.

25   "Postanovlenie Soveta Ministrov Kazakhskoy SSR," *RGP Respublikanskii tsentr pravovoy informatsii Ministerstva Iustitsii Respubliki Kazakhstan*, no. 472, November 30, 1990.

26   Interview with representative of Kazakhstan Development Bank, Astana, Kazakhstan, October 2012.

27   De Cordier, "The development space(s) of Non-OECD aid donors in Southern Eurasia"; also see "IDB investments to Kazakhstan stand at US$500 million," *Tengrinews*, January 16, 2014, <http://en.tengrinews.kz/finance/IDB-investments-to-Kazakhstan-stand-at-500-million-25314/>.

funding and loans to state-organized infrastructural projects.[28] Despite its focus on development aid projects, the IDB emerged as a promoter for Islamic banking when it supported the first attempts to launch legislative reforms.

Several respondents cited the years 2007 and 2008 as a critical period for Islamic finance in Kazakhstan.[29] The global economic crisis caused four major banking institutes in the republic to run into default by 2010.[30] The core of the crisis was made up of accumulated debts of Western states and nonperforming loans in banks in the Western hemisphere. For Islamic finance strategists in the republic, this moment provided an opening to propose ideas to diversify accesses to global capital flows. With advice from the IDB and support from the department for Islamic banking in the commercial Kazakh BTA bank, specialists formed discussion groups to design a project to establish Islamic finance institutes in Kazakhstan.[31] The state lent support as well, with a working group for Islamic finance formed within the presidential administration. Additional advice was also sought from external experts, attracting international business consultants like Ernst & Young Bahrain. These early efforts resulted in a first conference of interested parties in May 2007 in Almaty. Funded by the Abu Dhabi Islamic Bank, representatives of the Ministry of Industry and Trade of Kazakhstan joined with lobby organizations and consultancies in Islamic finance under the auspices of BTA Bank and the Islamic Development Bank, with further participants from various countries in the Muslim World.[32] The agenda for the conference reveals the early conditions for reforms: inquiries about the general nature of Islamic finance abounded, followed by questions about possibilities to adjust legislation and allow Islamic businesses to enter the republic's market.[33]

---

28   IDB assets stem from member states contributions of the IDB group. In its activities the IDB follows Islamic principles, yet it also collaborates with non-Islamic financial institutions to implement projects, see "About IDB," *Islamic Development Bank*, 2015, <http://www.isdb.org/irj/portal/anonymous?NavigationTarget=navurl://24deod5f10da90 6da85e96ac356b7afo>.

29   Interview with representative of ATF Bank, October 2012; and interview with representative of Amanie Advisors CIS, October 2012.

30   See, for example, "Kazakhstan Turns to Sukuk After Eurobond Offering Dropped: Islamic Finance," *Bloomberg*, July 29, 2010, <http://www.bloomberg.com/news/2010–07–29/ka zakhstan-turns-to-sukuk-after-eurobond-offering-dropped-islamic-finance.html>.

31   Interview with representative of Amanie Advisors CIS, October 2012.

32   "Financial Market Participants Will Discuss Islamic Banking Prospects," *BTA Bank* 2007, <http://bta.kz/en/press/news/2007/05/07/238/>.

33   Ibid.

These first initiatives were successful and resulted in a further push for new legislation. In 2008 a draft law was discussed in parliament and in February 2009 the law "On Making Changes and Amendments to Certain Legal Acts of the Republic of Kazakhstan Concerning Organization and Activity of Islamic Banks and Organization of Islamic Financing" was adopted.[34] Since 2009, Kazakhstan has continued to prepare the legal framework for Islamic financial operations in the country. In resolutions both the National Bank of Kazakhstan and the Agency of the Republic of Kazakhstan on Regulation and Supervision of Financial Market and Financial Organizations have formulated new rules for Islamic bookkeeping procedures and for issuing Islamic financial securities, the latter providing legal ground for Islamic social finance companies. The new laws further specified regulations and supported the launch of Islamic financial products, in particular by equalizing the taxation of Islamic with conventional financial products.[35] The roadmap mentioned above served to pool the efforts for further reforms. Adopted in 2012, the roadmap recalls the original stimulus, the economic crisis in 2007, when it stipulates the need for the "Completion of earmarked negotiations and meetings with banks, funds, and companies in countries of Southeast Asia and the Middle East with the goal to attract investments to Kazakhstan (funding of investment projects, finalizing of contracts)."[36]

While legislative developments came rather quickly, the establishment of actual operating Islamic finance institutes in Kazakhstan has been much

---

34 "O vnesenii izmenenii i dopolnenii v nekotorye zakonodatel'nye akty Respubliki Kazakhstan po voprosam organizatsii i deiatel'nosti islamskikh bankov i organizatsii islamskogo finansirovaniia," *Respublika Kazakhstan*, no. 133–134, February 12, 2009; the law itself contains changes and amendments to a number of laws, for example the Civil Code or the Tax Code. It does not introduce terms of Islamic finance instruments like *mudarabah* or *ijarah*, but it tries to distinguish conventional from Islamic banking. An Islamic bank must fulfill special terms to conform with Shari'a law and establish an *Islamic Bank Council*; it also must have the words '*Islamic Bank*' in its name. Furthermore a commercial bank is not allowed to open an Islamic branch, but any Islamic institute must be independent from conventional banking, see "Introduction of Islamic Finance in Kazakhstan," *Banking and Finance - Legal Alert*, Baker & McKenzie, May 29, 2009, <http:// www.legal500.com/assets/images/stories/legal_alert_islamic_ banking_090609_fin_eng. pdf>.

35 For an overview over legislative efforts, see "Islamic Finance in Kazakhstan: New Amendments," *Islamic Finance Almaty – Legal Alert*, Baker & McKenzie, May 12, 2015, <http:// www.bakermckenzie.com/files/Publication/09c10614–0267–40a4-bb58-e8599622299e/ Presentation/PublicationAttachment/5e8972d1-b9b4–474f-986a-efa70e702740/al_ almaty_newamendments_may15.pdf>.

36 *Dorozhnaia karta razvitiia islamskogo finansirovaniia do 2020 goda.*

slower. Consultants and lobby groups like Fattah Finance, a financial broker for Islamic investment and securities, and the Association for the Development of Islamic Finances (ARIF) appeared soon after the first discussion rounds were held. But out of the seven members that ARIF listed in 2012, only one was an actual Islamic bank, the Islamic Bank Al-Hilal, which until recently had been the only Islamic banking institute operating in Kazakhstan. Al-Hilal was founded in 2009 based on an agreement between the governments of the Republic of Kazakhstan and the United Arab Emirates. In line with this agreement, the mother Al-Hilal Bank in Abu Dhabi owns 100 percent of the JSC Islamic Bank Al Hilal headquartered in Almaty, with branches in Astana and Shymkent. Al-Hilal Bank in Abu Dhabi, in turn, is fully owned by the UAE government. It has turned into a major player in the UAE financial market, with only 3 percent of its assets in corporate financing and 97 percent of its activities in the retail market, where it is known for its innovative approach to private customers. In contrast, Islamic Bank Al-Hilal in Kazakhstan operates solely in corporate financing, servicing state holdings and investing in infrastructure projects. Furthermore, with assets slightly more than 13 billion tenge (US\$ 70 million) in 2014 the bank plays an insignificant role in the financial market in the republic, ranked only 31st out of 35 Kazakh banks in 2015 in terms of total assets.[37]

Another member of ARIF and newcomer to the Islamic finance market in Kazakhstan is the insurance company Takaful. Established in 2010 Takaful aims to develop takaful, the Islamic principle of community insurance, where policyholders insure each other by sharing losses and profits. Following the lead of Al-Hilal, Takaful established a Supervisory Board for Principles of Islamic Finances.[38] Other players in the Islamic finance sector in Kazakhstan, like Istisnaa Corporation Inc. or Fattah Education Inc., are lobby groups that do not offer any actual financial services. The last big innovation in the market

---

[37]   Assets decreased from 16 to 13 billion tenge in 2014, see "Financial Statements for the year ended 31 December 2014," 'Al Hilal' Islamic Bank' JSC, March 16, 2015, <http://www.alhilalbank.kz/upload/iblock/a64/a64b5f77bd084ef10a499b551d7a6bd4.pdf>; for ranking in 2015, see "Renking bankov Kazakhstana 2015," Forbes Kazakhstan, December 3, 2015, <http://forbes.kz/leader/renking_bankov_kazahstana_2015_2016>. In terms of Islamic finance instruments, the bank employs ijara leasing and commodity murabaha agreements. It is supervised in its activities by the Islamic Finance Principles Board, which yearly issues a fatwa on the bank's performances, see "Islamic Finance Principles Board Report - Al Hilal Islamic Bank. For the Financial Year Ended on 31 December 2011," 'Al Hilal' Islamic Bank' JSC, May 16, 2012, <http://www.alhilalbank.kz/upload/fatwa%20of%20Shariah%20board%20ofs.pdf>.

[38]   See "OVS Khalalnoe Strakhovanie TAKAFUL," <http://www.takaful.kz/>.

has been the launch of the *sukuk* commodity *murabahah*, an Islamic bond, with a value of US$75 million by the Development Bank of Kazakhstan (DBK) in mid- 2012, in cooperation with the Malaysian Central Bank.[39]

Since 2012 the Islamic financial market has been dormant. Despite promises of new legislation, new initiatives, and new financial institutions, the results have been meager, at best. As of mid-2016 Al-Hilal Bank still had not opened its retail business, while promises for a second Islamic Bank, Zaman Bank, have not materialized.[40] Takaful had not been able to launch products on the market, while lobby groups like Istisnaa Corp. seem to have stopped their activities altogether.[41] A November 2015 conference to create an Islamic micro-finance body merely continues the series of workshops and working groups that try to promote but not achieve the development of Islamic finance in the republic.[42] DBK needs support of the Malaysian government before it can issue further sukuk bonds, while no sovereign sukuk bond still has been released anywhere in Central Asia.

A closer look at the time line of promises and early initiatives reveals the year 2011 as the turning point. For politics in Kazakhstan, 2011 proved to be difficult and loaded with crises, starting with early elections for the presidency—which incumbent Nursultan Nazarbayev won with 95.5 percent of the vote—and finishing with the Zhanaozen events in December, in which labor protests were dispersed violently and 15 workers shot dead. Freedom House, in fact, increased the democracy scores from 6.45 to 6.54 (1 = full democracy), highlighting deteriorating trends for the Civil Society and Local Democratic

---

39   For detailed information about the circumstances of the *sukuk*, including the partnership with Malysian investors and Malaysian jurisdiction, see Wolters, "Islamic finance."

40   For Al-Hilal Bank, see "Al Hilal Bank Awaits New Legislation for Islamic Finance," *The Astana Times*, September 26, 2014, <http://astanatimes.com/2014/09/al-hilal-bank-awaits-new-legislation-islamic-finance/>; for plans to establish Islamic Bank Zaman Bank see "The Islamic Corporation for the Development of the Private Sector goes into a strategic alliance with Zaman Bank of Kazakhstan," *Zaman Bank*, May 23, 2013, <http://zamanbank.kz/en/islamskaya-korporatsiya-po-razvitiyu-chastnogo-sektora-vstupaet-v-strategicheskij-soyuz-s-kazahstanskim-zaman-bankom/>; "Kazakhstan and Central Asia. Accelerated Rise," *IFN Analysis* 12, no. 35, IFN Islamic Finance News, September 1, 2015; <http://www.islamicfinancenews.com/ifn-country-analysis-kazakhstan>; as of January 2016 no Islamic financial operations are being offered by Zaman Bank.

41   For a comparison of a list of activities by Istinaa Corporation, see "O nas," <http://www.istisna.kz/rus/?page_id=2>; the last activity reported took place in 2012.

42   See conference agenda, "Islamic Social Financing: Micro-Finance and Micro-Takaful," <http://www.adfimi.org/userfiles/files/kazakhstan_flyer_03.pdf>.

Governance categories.[43] Furthermore, the emergence and alleged attacks of a hitherto unknown group of Islamic radicals, *Jund al-Kilafah*, in 2011 gave rise to further restrictions on the media sphere, particularly for online media.[44] Overall, the political crisis that unfolded in 2011 seems to have reshuffled governance priorities and diverted attention from innovative economic and financial practices.[45] Still, plans formulated in 2011 were carried out in 2012, most noticeably the adoption of the roadmap, but no further steps were undertaken.[46] Since then, experts have cast doubt on the prospects of Islamic banking in the republic.[47] Summarizing the first cycle of economic and political crisis, expert Mingisheva shares her irritation:

> The government of the Republic of Kazakhstan began to attract Islamic finance in the period of the early financial crisis with the expansion of the investment base and the orientation towards the countries of the Organization of Islamic States. A faster growth of Islamic finance is still possible in Kazakhstan, but in recent times we can observe a certain deceleration concerning the development of Islamic banking in the country.[48]

---

43   See "Kazakhstan," in *Nations in Transit 2012* (New York: Freedom House, 2012), <https://freedomhouse.org/report/nations-transit/2012/kazakhstan>. Freedom House uses a rating scale of 1 to 7, with 1 representing the highest level of democratic progress and 7 the lowest.

44   Ibid.; the drop in ratings for the year 2009 is for the most part connected to the scandalous trial of human rights activist Evgeniy Zhovtis, see "Kazakhstan," in *Nations in Transit 2010* (New York: Freedom House, 2010), <https://freedomhouse.org/report/nations-transit/2010/kazakhstan>.

45   In interviews with the author, members of *Amani Advisors CIS* mentioned the lack of support for their initial plans to spread ideas about Islamic economics in Kazakhstan for the mentioned period, Astana/Almaty, Kazakhstan, October 2012. See also for an assessment of rising political sensitivities, "Islamic finance treads fine political line in Kazakhstan," NBC News, July 2, 2012, <http://www.msnbc.msn.com/id/48040915/ns/world_news-mideast_n_africa/t/islamic-finance-treads-fine-political-line-kazakhstan/#.UMCt7flyhRg>.

46   See *IFN Analysis, 12*, no. 35, September 1, 2015. The exception is the launch of the sukuk in 2015 by the DBK.

47   See, for example, "Kazakhstan poka ne ochen' uspeshen v razvitii islamskogo finansirovaniia," *Liter*, November 17, 2015, <http://liter.kz/mobile/ru/articles/show/14121-kazahstan_poka_ne_ochen_uspeshen_v_razvitii_islamskogo_finansirovaniya>.

48   See "Formirovanie islamskogo bankinga v Kazakhstane: nekotorye aspekty i perspektivy (chast' 2)," *nmingisheva.ru*, August 5, 2015, <http://nmingisheva.ru/islamskii-financy/136-

Periodical announcements of early elections, for example to the parliament in Kazakhstan, announced in January 2016, add to the gloomy picture of further delay in necessary reforms. Legislation still is not ready to allow for retail businesses in the financial sphere, and project initiatives put on hold once again. In general, Islamic finance tends to suffer from its secondary position among policy priorities in Kazakhstan; it quickly falls victim to abrupt changes or, even worse, is increasingly met with suspicion as the mounting discourse of danger alerts against expressions of Islamic piety.

Kyrgyzstan: Ever-Emerging Market for Islamic Retail Banking

Over the last two decades, Kyrgyzstan has pursued a different development path than its neighbors. The often-chaotic events—including two violent overthrows of government in six years, swift changes from open to closed political regimes, and endless demonstrations and strikes—affected many spheres of economic activity in the republic, including Islamic finance.[49]

Kyrgyzstan's introduction to Islamic finance occurred in 1993, when it became the first Central Asian state to join the IDB, following the liberal agenda of then-president Askar Akayev.[50] The IDB invested very little in the country, and in mid-2012 Kyrgyzstan ranked lowest among the Central Asian states in terms of IDB funding, with only US$159 million.[51] However, IDB engagement began to grow after the change of government from Akayev to Kurmanbek Bakiev in 2006, with most funding going into infrastructural projects, especially transportation. That year the IDB signed a memorandum with the Kyrgyz government to establish an Islamic bank in the republic. Then-head of the IDB branch in Kyrgyzstan, Shamil Murtazaliev, laid out several steps for transforming Bishkek into an Islamic financial hub in Central Asia. The first initiative aimed at transforming EkoBank, a commercial bank owned by Murtazaliev, into the first Islamic bank on Kyrgyz soil. More importantly, the memorandum paved the way for new legislation that created one of the most advanced legal systems for regulating Islamic financing business in the region.[52]

---

formirovanie-islamskogo-bankinga-v-kazakhstane-nekotorye-aspekty-i-perspektivy-chast-2.html>.

49 For regime dynamics in Kyrgyzstan, see A. Wolters, *Die Politik der Peripherie: Protest und Öffentlichkeit in der Republik Kyrgyzstan* (Bielefeld: Transcript-Verlag, 2015).

50 Gresh, "The Rise of Islamic Banking and Finance in Central Asia."

51 DeCordier, "The development space(s) of Non-OECD aid donors in Southern Eurasia."

52 Aliyev, "The Politics of Islamic Finance in Central Asia and South Caucasus"; "Informatsiia po islamskim printsipam finansirovaniia i bankovskogo dela," *National Bank of Kyrgyzstan*

Following the memorandum, President Bakiev signed a decree in July 2006 "On the Pilot Project of Introduction of Islamic Financing Principles in the Kyrgyz Republic." This decree enabled the National Bank of Kyrgyzstan (NBK) to move forward with formulating new rules for Islamic financial institutes. Already in October 2006 the NBK adopted a statute for Islamic finance principles, stating in detail conditions for Islamic banking instruments like *mudarabah, ijara, murabaha,* and others. Finally, in December 2006 the NBK was authorized to issue licenses to Islamic financial institutes operating in Kyrgyzstan. The NBK's leading role was further consolidated with two laws adopted by parliament in March 2009, which made changes to the law "On the National Bank of the Kyrgyz Republic" and to the law "On Banks and Bank Operations in the Kyrgyz Republic."[53] Now the NBK was empowered to supervise financial operations in line with the principles for Islamic banking. In addition, the bank had been authorized to formulate normative regulations to further organize the market for Islamic finance in the republic. In September 2009 the government began to prepare the market for the introduction of Islamic securities in the form of *sukuk* and *takaful.*[54] Such groundbreaking work showed its effects, when the government concluded talks with IDB consultants and investors from Malaysia to set up an Islamic insurance company in Kyrgyzstan in 2012.[55] To open up Islamic finance for the fast growing microfinance sector in the republic, the NBK adopted further resolutions to allow agencies to offer micro-credit lines in form of *mudarabah, ijara,* and others.

The EkoBank pilot project was very successful, with branches established in all major cities across the country and gaining market shares. In July 2010 the bank was renamed EkoIslamikBank. In May 2015, the yearly audit revealed assets of more than 3.3 billion som (appr. US$54 million), yet also reported a net loss of almost 10 million som (appr. US$164,000).[56] Such annual loss not-

(2012); "Kyrgyzstan: Islamic Banking Offers Alternative to the 'European System'," *Eurasianet*, June 14, 2011, <http://www.eurasianet.org/node/63675>.

53   "Zakon Kyrgyzskoy Respubliki O Natsional'nom banke Kyrgyzskoy Respubliki," *National Bank Law*, no. 59, July 29, 1997 and no. 60, July 29, 1997.

54   "Pravitel'stvo Kyrgyzstana utverdilo polozheniia ob organizatsii islamskogo strakhovaniyia i tsennykh bumagakh, vypuskaemykh po islamskim printsipam finansirovaniia," *Easttime*, September 16, 2009, <http://www.easttime.ru/news/1/4/1626.html>.

55   "Novosti islamskikh finansov (30.03.2012 g. – 30.04.2012 g.)," *Korporatsiia 'Istisnaia Corporation,'* April 30, 2012; "V Kyrgyzstane aktivno razvivaetsia sektor islamskogo bankinga," *Info Islam*, April 7, 2012, <http://www.infoislam.ru/publ/novosti/mir/v_kyrgyzstane_ aktivno_razvivaetsja_ sektor_islamskogo_bankinga/3–1-0–15382>.

56   See audit report of EkoIslamikBank, "Otchet o finansovom sostoianii po bukhgalterskomu balansu na 31 maya 2015 goda (vklyuchitel'no)," <http://ecoislamicbank.kg/uploads/files/fin_otchot/fr-ecoislamicbank31052015.pdf>.

withstanding, EkoIslamikBank's development is a success story. The bank managed to retain its many depositors who had been clients of the branch of the Russian institute that formed the base for the future EkoIslamikBank. At the same time, it expanded its client base of clientele; and in 2010 alone it registered 2,274 new customers. Based on deposits, EkoIslamikBank ranked eighth, out of 24 institutions, with a 4 percent market share in 2014.[57]

EkoIslamikBank not only engages into Islamic banking operations, it also spreads knowledge about Islamic finance. Its Barakat educational center trains future staff and facilitates cooperation among institutions. In December 2009, for example, representatives from financial institutions and supervisory bodies in Tajikistan visited Barakat to receive training in principles of Islamic finance.[58] In addition to EkoIslamikBank, a small corporate investment firm, called Muslim, started operating in March 2012 in Bishkek, and two micro-credit institutions in Kyrgyzstan announced plans to introduce products in compliance with Shari'a law, Kompanion invest and Kausar, targeting the south and the north of the country, respectively.[59] More firms entered the market in 2011.[60]

Kyrgyzstan has proven to be a promising market for Islamic financial products, with a 5 percent market share in the retail sector in 2012. Predictions that market share would reach 10–12 percent in 2015 did not materialize, however, despite further external assistance such as the agreement between IDB and the Kyrgyz government to support the "further development of Islamic financial services in the country."[61] Initiatives to further adapt the legal framework came to a halt in the aftermath of the government collapse in April 2010, while most

57   "Renking bankov Kyrgyzstana po depozitnoi baze za 2014 god," *Vechernii Bishkek*, March 23, 2015, <http://www.vb.kg/doc/307128_renking_bankov_kyrgyzstana_po_depozitnoy_baze_za_2014_god.html>.

58   "Kyrgyzstan prevrashchaetsia v pionera obrazovatel'nykh tekhnologii v islamskom bankinge," *Business Akipress*, December 21, 2009, <http://www.barakat.kg/novosti-centra/kyrgyzstan-prevrashhaetsja-v-pionera-obrazovatelnyh-tehnologij-v-islamskom-bankinge.html>.

59   "Kyrgyzstan: Islamic Banking Offers Alternative to the 'European System'"; Interview with representative of National Bank of Kyrgyzstan, Bishkek, Kyrgyzstan, October 2012.

60   "Natsional'nyi bank Kyrgyzstana prinial normativno-pravovoi akt v otnoshenii islamskikh mikrofinansovykh organizatsii," *Muslimeco*, December 26, 2011, <http://www.muslimeco.ru/onews/405/>.

61   "Islamic Development Bank to provide technical assistance worth US$193,000 to Kyrgyzstan in introduction of Islamic banking," *Akipress*, July 4, 2012, <http://www.akipress.com/_en_news.php?id=125671>.

Islamic-finance businesses experienced stagnation by the year 2015.[62] Of the three micro-financing institutes that offered Shari'a-compliant products, Ijarah Leasing and Ak-Karzhy started operating only in 2014, while Kompanion Invest seems to be the only company that actually grew in 2015.[63] The Barakat center appears to have run out of interested clients, EkoIslamikBank is experiencing losses, and no other Islamic banking institute is interested in entering the republic.

Kyrgyzstan is the undisputed regional leader in terms of experience in actual Islamic retail banking, servicing private customers and thus moving beyond corporate funding and state orchestrated investments. However, political crises, including the April 2010 revolution, ethnic violence that summer in Osh, as well as elections in December 2010 and October 2015, Bishkek's and counter-terrorist operation, and the hunt for the Islamic extremists who broke out of prison in fall 2015 slowed down initiatives to stimulate the growth of Islamic finance in the republic.[64] Respondents blamed the 2010 slowdown on the dismantling of government structures and legal initiatives, therefore the rising discourse of danger accompanying the events around Islamic extremists in 2015 likely contributed to the further discrediting of Islamic economic practices.[65]

---

62   Interview with representative of National Bank of Kyrgyzstan, Bishkek, Kyrgyzstan, October 2012.

63   "Islamskoe mikrofinansirovanie v Kyrgyzstane na primere uspeshnoi kompanii," *Muslimeco*, January 2, 2016, <http://muslimeco.ru/opubl/462/>; "IJARA COMPANY KYRGYZ-STAN predlagaet uslugi finansovogo lizinga po islamskim printsipam," *Torgovo-promy-shlennaia palata Kyrgyzskoi Respubliki*, <http://www.cci.kg/kommercheskie-predlozhe-nija/kommercheskie-predlozhenija-chlenov-tpp-kr/ijara-company-kyrgyzstan-predlagaet-uslugi-finansovogo-lizinga-po-islamskim-principam.html>.

64   See for anti-terror operation, "Kyrgyzstan: Authorities Present Their Case for Claimed IS Cell," *Eurasianet*, July 21, 2015, <http://www.eurasianet.org/node/74326>; and for prison hunt, "Kyrgyzstan: Prison Break Culminates in Bloody Showdown," *Eurasianet*, October 22, 2015, <http://www.eurasianet.org/node/75676>. It must be added here that the contrast with Freedom House scores does not yield much results. The dismantling of the Bakiyev regime widened the freedoms in many spheres, from *Electoral Processes* to *Civil Society* and *Independent Media*, decreasing scores from 6.21 for the year 2009 to 6.11 for 2010 and 6.00 for 2011.

65   Interview with representative of National Bank of Kyrgyzstan, Bishkek, Kyrgyzstan, October 2012.

Tajikistan: A Market Failing on its Promises for Islamic Finance

Tajikistan seems an attractive place for Islamic finance, considering the significant role Islam occupies in the society. A short summary of macro indicators substantiates this claim: In contrast to Kazakhstan or Kyrgyzstan, only a small percentage of non-Muslim minorities live in the country; until it was banned in August 2015 the Islamic Renaissance Party (IRP) was the only Islamic party legally operating in Central Asia, granting Islam political relevance in public discourse. Furthermore, Tajikistan has strong linguistic connections to Iran and seeks to broaden its relations with Pakistan. Islamic finance principles officially occupy a central place in the doctrines of both states.[66]

However, despite such favorable circumstances, Islamic finance has been very poorly developed in Tajikistan. The republic joined the IDB in 1996, after the civil war, and has received financial support to invest in infrastructural projects, especially power generation and transportation.[67] The cooperation between Tajikistan and the IDB increased in November 2011, when both sides signed an agreement on technical assistance, which foresaw the introduction of Islamic banking in the republic. The aim was to open the first institution by 2013.[68] By 2012 discussions to change legislation accordingly had led to the formation of a working group, consisting of specialists from the National Bank of Tajikistan (NBT) and representatives of Zaid Ibrahim & Co., a Malaysian consulting company and the biggest law firm in the Kingdom.[69] With Tajikistan's political leadership expressing its sincere interest in establishing Islamic finance in the republic, observers expected the first Islamic bank to emerge the following year, mostly like as a branch of an established bank in Tajikistan.[70]

---

66   Iran possesses the largest Islamic finance assets in the world, estimated at appr. US$250 billion; in Pakistan Islamic finance has been fixed as a state policy in the constitution.

67   According to some figures, US$212 million were allocated to projects in the republic by 2012; other estimates add up to US$500 million, see DeCordier, "The development space(s) of Non-OECD aid donors in Southern Eurasia"; "IDB, Tajikistan sign agreement on Islamic banking," *Trend*, November 17, 2011, <http://en.trend.az/regions/casia/tajikistan/1958198.html>.

68   "IDB, Tajikistan sign agreement on Islamic banking," ibid.

69   "Zaid Ibrahim & Co podgotovit dlia Tadzhikistana zakonodatel'stvo ob islamskom bankinge," *News.tj*, November 1, 2012, <http://news.tj/ru/news/zaid-ibrahim-co-podgotovit-dlya-tadzhikistana-zakonodatelstvo-ob-islamskom-bankinge>.

70   "Tadzhikistan gotovitsia k islamskomu bankingu," *Deutsche Welle*, November 13, 2012, <http://www.dw.de/tadzhikistan-gotovitsya-k-islamskomu-bankingu/a-16375122>.

Other players launched efforts to spread Islamic finance instruments as well. The German Society for International Cooperation (GIZ), a prominent development agency, organized special trainings and seminars with interested parties, including staff from the NBT, members of the Association of Micro-Finance Institutes of Tajikistan, and representatives from governmental bodies.[71] According to specialists in the field, some selected forms of Islamic finance were being practiced in Tajikistan as early as 2012. For example, depositing with micro-crediting institutes has been tested in Tajikistan since 2011.[72] Investing into micro-financing seemed plausible, considering the high number of micro-financing agencies operating in the republic. A report from 2010 counts 116 such agencies, dealing with deposits, loan organizing, and loan funding.[73]

Yet by late 2015, no single plan to introduce Islamic finance into Tajikistan had actually materialized. The years 2012 and 2013 turned out to be times of stagnation,[74] and while initiatives resumed in 2014, no concrete projects have emerged. Still in May 2014 the Tajik parliament finally adopted a "Law on Islamic Banking Activities" in Tajikistan. Investors from Qatar promised to fund the opening of an Islamic financial institute, while one of the leading conventional financial institutions in the country, Tojiksodirokbonk, announced plans to transform one of its subsidiaries, the Bonki Rushdi Tojikiston (BRT), into an Islamic bank by mid-2015. Neither the Katar plans nor the transformation of BRT have led to any tangible results.[75]

---

71   "MFO RT realizuet islamskie finansovye produkty," *Khovar*, October 13, 2010, <http://khovar.tj/rus/archive/24818-mfo-rt-realizuet-islamskie-finansovye-produkty.html>; "Razvitie islamskikh printsipov finansirovaniia v Tadzhikistane," *Khovar*, June 5, 2012, <http://khovar.tj/rus/economic/33244-razvitie-islamskih-principov-finansirovaniya-v-tadzhikistane.html>.

72   Interview with representative of Tajik branch of development agency, Dushanbe, Tajikistan, March 2013.

73   "Dawn in Tajikistan," *IslamicFinanceNews – Country Report*, March 17, 2010, <http://www.islamicfinancenews.com/authors/muath-mubarak-0>.

74   A project by the IDB and the *Agroinvestbank* in Tajikistan in 2011 to start operating Islamic banking instruments did not materialize, see "Pochemu v Tadzhikistane ne razvivaetsia islamskii banking?", *Asia Plus*, July 14, 201, <http://news.tj/ru/newspaper/article/pochemu-v-tadzhikistane-ne-razvivaetsya-islamskii-banking>.

75   "Katar sozdast v Tadzhikistane pervyi islamskii bank," *Radio Ozodi*, September 22, 2014, <http://rus.ozodi.org/content/article/26599500.html>; "'Tochiksodirotbonk' vnedriaet islamskii banking," *Radio Ozodi*, December 23, 2014, <http://rus.ozodi.org/content/article/26757999.html>; and still in May 2015 plans were designed, see "V Tadzhikistane poiavitsia pervyi islamskii bank," *Slon*, May 20, 2015, <https://slon.ru/posts/51732>.

Correlating these developments with Freedom House scores reveals a sudden deterioration in 2011. Before then, Tajikistan had scored 6.14 for three consecutive years, suggesting a degree of political stability. In 2011 however, its score rose to 6.18, not least due to tightening control over alleged Islamic extremism, and since then the situation in Tajikistan, according to Freedom House *Nations in Transit* reports, has worsened every year.[76] Developments in 2015, such as banning the Islamic Renaissance Party, new restrictions on religious practices, as well as parliamentary elections, have all brought efforts to promote Islamic finance principles in the republic to a standstill.[77]

Uzbekistan and Turkmenistan: Closed Politics and Fear

Neither Uzbekistan nor Turkmenistan has substantial experience with Islamic finance. The authoritarian nature of the political regimes, with long-serving Islam Karimov as president in Uzbekistan and Gurbanguly Berdymukhammedov in Turkmenistan, make any independent business operation, including Islamic banking, a challenging endeavor.[78] Furthermore, in the case of Uzbekistan, anything carrying the term "Islamic" is subject to special state scrutiny, especially after the bloody events of Andijan in May 2005.[79] This context has led to a situation, where, as one observer notes, the most promising market in Central Asia for Islamic finance has seen the lowest level of activism for the establishment of Islamic institutes and financial agencies.[80]

---

76   See "Tajikistan," in *Nations in Transit, 2012* (New York: Freedom House, 2012), <https://freedomhouse.org/report/nations-transit/2012/tajikistan>; the score for the year 2015 is 6.54.

77   For a critical assessment of the role of the "discourse of danger" and its public instrumentalization, see John Heathershaw and Sophie Roche, "A Recipe for Radicalisation: The Campaign against Islam in Tajikistan," *Open Democracy*, January 17, 2011, <http://www.opendemocracy.net/print/57613>; for the ban see, "Tajikistan Bans Islamic Opposition Party," *Eurasianet*, August 28, 2015, <http://www.eurasianet.org/node/74856>; for new restrictions, "As Tajikistan Limits Islam, Does It Risk Destabilization?", *Radio Free Europe*, December 1, 2015, <http://www.rferl.org/content/tajikistan-islam-destabilization-rahmon-secular-/27400692.html>; and for elections, "Tajikistan's Ruling Party Wins Election Decried As 'Farce'," *Radio Free Europe*, March 2, 2015, <http://www.rferl.org/content/tajik-elections-rahmon-party-victory/26877105.html>.

78   In Freedom House's Nations in Transit ratings both Uzbekistan and Turkmenistan are at the bottom of the list, with scores as high as 6.93 since 2010 and 2008, respectively.

79   T. Epkenhans, "'Islam' in the Security Discourse of the Post-Soviet Republics of Central Asia," *OSCE Yearbook 2010* (Baden-Baden: Nomos Publishers, 2011), 91-105.

80   Aliyev, "The Politics of Islamic Finance in Central Asia and South Caucasus."

Like their Central Asian neighbors, both Uzbekistan and Turkmenistan were introduced to Islamic finance via the IDB. The bank developed relations with both countries and managed to negotiate and agree on country development programs throughout the last decade. Historically, Turkmenistan was the second country in Central Asia to join the IDB group in 1994, whereas Uzbekistan was the last when it entered the institution in 2003. To both countries the IDB has channeled funds worth more than US$1 billion.[81] For the most part, such funding went into the transportation sector and energy. In the case of Uzbekistan, projects worth US$655 million were being planned for the period 2011–2013, and by mid-2015, Tashkent had received more than US$1.2 billion of funding.[82] Typical examples of this cooperation are the financing for the construction of the major canals in the Khorezm region or further investments into the modernization of hydroelectric power stations.[83]

The IDB's cooperation with Uzbekistan also entails investments into the small and medium business sector. To this end, the IDB, via its Islamic Corporation for Development of the Private Sector, signed a memorandum of understanding with Uzbekistan on the further support to small and medium-sized enterprises in the republic.[84] The IDB regularly lends funds on the base of Islamic principles and does so alongside donors that operate with conventional financial instruments. The IDB has been channeling money into small and medium businesses through agencies such as Taiba Leasing, Ipak Yuli Bank, and Uzbek Leasing International while still complying with Shari'a law.[85] Further plans to establish a domestic Islamic financial institution have never been formulated and, with the exception of Taiba Leasing, none of the crediting institutions mentioned above has sustained its activities.[86] Starting in

---

81   To compare data, see DeCordier, "The development space(s) of Non-OECD aid donors in Southern Eurasia" and data from the MFA of Uzbekistan, "Islamskii bank razvitiia (IBR)," <http://www.mfer.uz/ru/international-cooperation/international-organizations/949/>.

82   "Islamskii bank razvitiia dal Uzbekistanu US$57 mln na modernizatsiiu kanalizatsii," *Regnum*, March 14, 2015, <http://regnum.ru/news/economy/1905209.html>.

83   See MFA data, ibid.

84   "Islamskii kapital dlia uzbekskogo chastnogo sektora," *Gazeta.uz*, Novvember 6, 2008, <http://www.gazeta.uz/2008/11/06/nbu/>.

85   See Aliyev (2012); "Islamic Corporation for Development of Private Sector provides US$11 mln to Uzbek banks," *Trend*, April 6, 2012, <http://en.trend.az/capital/business/2011143.html>; Asadov and Gazikhanov, "Ijarah's Prospects in Central Asia."

86   At least at the beginning of 2016, neither *Ipak Yuli Bank* nor *Uzbek Leasing International* or *Uzpromstroybank*, another IDB partner, use Islamic financial instruments for their operations according to their websites.

2013, the IDB's activities in Uzbekistan have been re-oriented toward funding state-supervised development projects.

There is almost no foundation for Islamic financial practices in Turkmenistan. No legal reform was pursued, nor did the annual meeting of the IDB group in Ashgabat in 2009 translate into more than a single investment project.[87] The IDB agreed to fund the construction of the railway line from Bereket (Tukmenistan) to Gorgan (Iran), as part of the wider North–South transport corridor that aims to connect the Russian railway system with the railway network of the Persian Gulf states.[88] Further development projects, however, largely failed to materialize. There was one loan of US$121 million to reconstruct the water supply system in the Western region of Balkan.[89] For the future, the IDB plans major investments into eight selected infrastructural projects.[90]

It is difficult to compare the developments in Uzbekistan and Turkmenistan with the dynamics in the neighboring countries. A slight similarity to the development dynamics in Kazakhstan or Tajikistan appears in Uzbekistan's commitment to Islamic finance. Early initiatives to involve more lines of Islamic crediting and leasing ran out by 2013, and since then only state-sponsored development projects are allowed to receive funding from the IDB. In Turkmenistan all efforts fall victim to the single-market structure of the economy in combination with the purely ceremonial status of political decision-making under President Berdymukhammedov.

The Dynamics of Islamic Finance Development in Central Asia

The evolution of Islamic finance in Central Asia shows a slight convergence of early efforts around the time of the global financial crisis in 2007, at least in the

---

87   "V Ashkhabade otkryvaetsia 34-e zasedanie Soveta Islamskogo banka razvitiia," *Turkmeninform*, June 2, 2009, <http://halalpages.ru/rcief/files/print.php?id=859>.

88   "Islamskii bank razvitiia profinansiruet stroitel'stvo zheleznoi dorogi Turkmenistan-Iran," *Bibo.kz*, June 5, 2009, <http://internet.bibo.kz/288292-islamskijj-bank-razvitija-profinansiruet.html>.

89   "Islamskii bank razvitiia vydelil Turkmenii bolee 121 mln doll na realizatsiiu proektov vodosnabzheniia," *Eurasian Development Bank*, June 25, 2011, <http://www.eabr.org/e/press_center/news-region/index.php?id_4=2181&subject_id_4=119&page_4=1&from_4=288>.

90   "Turkmenistan i Islamskii bank razvitiia podgotoviat programmu sotrudnichestva na 2016–2018 gody," *Turkmenistan.ru*, June 20, 2015, <http://www.turkmenistan.ru/ru/articles/40898.html>.

cases of Kazakhstan, Kyrgyzstan, and, partly, Tajikistan. Further developments stopped or slowed down markedly in periods of political crisis: in Kazakhstan and Tajikistan in the year 2011 and in Kyrgyzstan in 2010 and 2015. Uzbekistan and Turkmenistan, for the most part, only superficially attempted to introduce Islamic finance and banking in their respective domestic markets. One could further speculate about whether the repercussions of the Arab Spring influenced the simultaneous reshuffling of policy priorities in Kazakhstan and Tajikistan, for example, yet evidence to substantiate such a claim is scarce.[91]

As of mid-2016, the Central Asian countries have yet to grant Islamic finance the importance and corresponding institutional settings that exist in the Muslim nations of the Arab peninsula, Iran, Pakistan, or Malaysia. Still, subtle differences exist between the states and their respective attitudes toward Islamic finance and banking. In Kazakhstan much—if not all—depends on state coordination of efforts to advance Islamic finance. The young history of Islamic finance in Kazakhstan consists of lobbyists, who concentrate their work on legislative reform and who reach out to political decision-makers, and of private banks that wait for approval from the presidential administration. The state, in turn, invites experts from abroad and supervises pilot projects that carry the label Islamic, thereby fully controlling the development of Islamic banking. The result is a stark contrast between the number of state organs involved in the process of establishing Islamic finance and the complete absence of a developed retail market for Islamic finance.

In Kyrgyzstan the central state has taken an attitude of benevolent—yet negligible—support. Outsourcing coordination and supervision to the NBK, Kyrgyzstan has used its fragmented political and administrative system to its own benefit, at least regarding the development of Islamic finance. Constant government changes as well as the menace of Islamic extremism, however, pose challenges to any major initiative that would rest on sustained state support.

Tajikistan has taken yet another approach toward Islamic finance. Against supposedly advantageous conditions for Islamic banking, neither the state nor corporate interests have led the initiative. In fact, the few legislative changes and pilot projects that have occurred have been largely due to the efforts of the

---

91   For a first assessment of the influence of the Arab Spring on the Central Asian security discourse, see A. Schmitz and A. Wolters, "Political Protest in Central Asia: Potentials and Dynamics," *SWP Research Paper 7* (April 2012). On the impact of the rise of ISIS in Syria on security discourses in Central Asia, see, "Shadow Boxing With the Islamic State in Central Asia," *Foreign Policy*, February 6, 2015, <http://foreignpolicy.com/2015/02/06/shadow-boxing-with-the-islamic-state-in-central-asia-isis-terrorism/>; and "Central Asia and the ISIS Phantom," *The Diplomat*, October 2, 2015, <http://thediplomat.com/2015/10/central-asia-and-the-isis-phantom/>.

IDB and development agencies. With a rather centralized political system not unlike the one in Kazakhstan, yet without the economic power, the state in Tajikistan seems hesitant to allow for more experiments. And such hesitation apparently turns into strong suspicion with every new initiative to restrict religious practices in all possible forms.

Uzbekistan and Turkmenistan have taken a different tack. Both countries have allowed high-level contacts between state and the IDB. Such contacts show the respective states' commitment to international cooperation, in general, and the intention to benefit from new relations with Islamic investors, in particular. Taking the considerable resources at the disposal of both states into consideration, the continued lack of lasting reforms and of a favorable institutional setting with supervisory bodies leaves the impression that rigid authoritarianism inhibits any meaningful change. What is permissible are top-level decisions regarding investment into the development of state-owned infrastructure.

Conclusion

The case studies examined here reveal a correlation between the phases of development of Islamic finance in Central Asia, and political crises in these countries. They thus support claims made by Hoggarth and Botoeva, for example, that Islamic finance and its introduction to Central Asia depend neither on economic rationale nor on a naturally given cultural predisposition alone.[92] Quite contrary to the beliefs of many practitioners and lobbyists, the success of Islamic finance is conditioned by a situational context that limits the political scope for reforms and the social space for economic initiative. And where Hoggarth examines the post-colonial direction of Kazakhstani efforts to loosen its dependence on Western, Russian, and Chinese capital, and where Botoeva investigates local contexts for the incorporation of Islamic values in business practices, this study also puts their conclusions into a new perspective. It is not long-term strategies to shake off the yoke of alien capitalism, but the level of irritability of the political regime and an ensuing crisis that determine the frame for initiatives to introduce innovative finance and banking principles into the respective domestic markets. The same holds true for individual attempts to adopt and appropriate principles of Shari'a in financial transactions. That is, when a political crisis translates into new rounds of restrictions and repressions, it limits the room to maneuver and experiment with the dynamically developing global market of Islamic finance.

---

92   Hoggarth, "The rise of Islamic finance"; Botoeva, "Let's Bank the Muslim Way?"

PART 3

Islam in Evolving Societies and Identities

∵

CHAPTER 7

Visual Culture and Islam in Kazakhstan: The Case of Asyl Arna's Social Media

Wendell Schwab

Visual content is integral to social media. Posts may simply be a photograph or image, such as Instagram, or may consist of an image accompanied by text, which may or may not be read. Corporations, celebrities' public relations teams, governments, and other powerful organizations use images on social media to create cultural models, norms, and experiences. Revlon creates understandings of beauty in its daily posts of women wearing lipstick. University marketing teams use Facebook accounts to post images of football players mingling with fans at charity events in the offseason, and they create hashtags so fans can post their own pictures with players. Evangelical churches show images of parents interacting with their children in order to model proper Biblical parenting styles. Organizations in Central Asia similarly use social media to create cultural norms and models. This chapter examines how images on the social media pages of Asyl Arna, Kazakhstan's Islamic television network and dominant Islamic media company, create a way of understanding and engaging in contemporary Islamic life in Kazakhstan. The images on Asyl Arna's social media promote Islam as an achievable part of a middle-class life-style that can provide simple rules for a pious, economically successful life and a connection to the numinous through the Qur'an.

Asyl Arna's Social Media

Asyl Arna, founded in 2007 by Mukhammedzhan Tazabek, is the most popular Islamic television channel in Kazakhstan and the dominant Islamic media company in Kazakhstan. Asyl Arna's social media pages, and the television network in general, are associated with "the piety movement" in Kazakhstan, which focuses on spreading a scripturalist form of Islam in Kazakhstan.[1] This

---

1 For previous work on the piety movement, see W. Schwab, "Establishing an Islamic Niche in Kazakhstan: Musylman Publishing House and Its Publications," *Central Asian Survey*, 30, no. 2 (2011): 227–242; W. Schwab, "Traditions and Texts: How Two Young Women Learned to Interpret the Qur'an and Hadiths in Kazakhstan," *Contemporary Islam*, 6, no. 2 (2012): 173–197;

movement is a loose confederation of imams and bureaucrats associated with the Kazakhstani Muftiyat and its mosques throughout Kazakhstan; media companies such as Asyl Arna and Islamic publishers; and individual Muslims who do not make a living through explicitly Islamic work. These different people and organizations have a particular division of labor. The Kazakhstani Muftiyat administers mosques, sends out topics for Friday sermons, certifies imams, and issues fatwas. Media companies produce television programs, websites, magazines, and books on Islam. Individual Muslims use the products produced by media companies and the spaces administered by the Muftiyat to participate in an Islamic community and develop their own piety.

Asyl Arna and the Kazakhstani Muftiyat work with the Kazakhstani government, as made explicit on July 2, 2015, when the Ministry of Culture and Sports, Asyl Arna, and the Kazakhstani Muftiyat signed a cooperation agreement. This agreement was not surprising, as it has long been clear that the Kazakhstani Muftiyat and Asyl Arna are connected to the Kazakhstani government. However, it gives three powerful organizations a common mission: to "protect inter-ethnic peace" and "inter-religious harmony." Asyl Arna's specific role in this enterprise is to show the meaning of religion, tradition, and the Hanafi school of jurisprudence via media programs, including its website and social media feeds.[2]

Asyl Arna maintains nearly identical social media pages on vKontakte (hereafter, vK), with over 244,000 followers, on Facebook, with over 31,000 followers, Instagram, with over 216,000 followers, and on a Twitter feed, with over 10,000 followers.[3] These numbers have grown considerably in the last two years. In early 2014, Asyl Arna had approximately 30,000 followers on vK. Its influence in social media far exceeds that of the Kazakhstani Muftiyat (approximately 19,000 followers on vK) and individual mosques, such as the Khazret Sultan mosque in Astana (about 15,000 followers on vK).[4] Asyl Arna's social

---

W. Schwab, "How to Pray in Kazakhstan: The Fortress of the Muslim and Its Readers," *Anthropology of East Europe Review*, 32, no. 1 (2014): 22–42; and W. Schwab, "Islam, Fun, and Social Capital in Kazakhstan," *Central Asian Affairs*, 2, no. 1 (2015): 51–70. For Geertz's work on scripturalist Islam, see C. Geertz, *Islam Observed: Religious Development in Morocco and Indonesia* (Chicago: University of Chicago Press, 1968).

2 "Kelisim Muraty - Asyl Dindi Ulyqtau," *e-islam*, July 21, 2015, <http://e-islam.kz/qazaqstandagy-islam/item/6676-kelisim-m-raty-asyl-dindi-lyktau>.

3 These sites can be found at <http://vk.com/asyl_arna>, <http://www.facebook.com/asylarna>, <http://www.instagram.com/asylarna/>, and <http://twitter.com/asylarna>. The numbers cited are accurate as of May 3, 2016.

4 See <http://vk.com/muftyatkz and http://vk.com/muslimkz1>.

media feeds are filled with pictures and other images. By its own count, Asyl Arna published over 1,000 images in 2015, along with over 300 articles.[5] And, while articles linked in social media feeds may or may not be read, images are at least scanned and seen. In short, Asyl Arna's social media feeds are popular, and on these feeds, images are the most common way to construct ideas, represent the world, and make arguments.

Picturing an Achievable Piety

Lists are ubiquitous on the internet. There are lists of the hottest celebrities over 50, and lists of the best trees to plant in New Mexico. There are even lists summarizing academic work about why the human species likes lists.[6] However, the meaning of the genre of the list depends on context. Just as an eye closing could be a twitch or a wink or a mocking imitation of a wink depending on context,[7] a list could be derisible clickbait or a set of sacred instructions.

Lists feature prominently in the visual culture of Asyl Arna's social media. The popularity of Asyl Arna on social media such as vK and Facebook, and of Tazabek on Twitter,[8] where he reposts much of Asyl Arna's social media content, has made lists a noticeable feature of the visual culture of the piety movement in Kazakhstan. Two aspects of the post-Soviet Kazakhstani context produce a particular reading of the genre of the Islamic list. The first part of this context is the perceived loss of Islamic knowledge due to Soviet repression of Islam. Bruce Privratsky has argued that Kazakhs generally profess ignorance of many Islamic concepts.[9] Schwab has argued that leaders of the piety movement in Kazakhstan, such as Kazakhstani Islamic publishers, see their audience

---

5   A. Arna's vK page, <http://vk.com/asyl_arna?w=wall-51948252_75156>, posted January 5, 2016.

6   C. Hammond, "Nine Psychological Reasons We Love Lists," *BBC*, April 13, 2015, <http://www.bbc.com/future/story/20150410-9-reasons-we-love-lists>.

7   C. Geertz, "Thick Description: Toward an Interpretive Theory of Culture," *The Interpretation of Cultures: Selected Essays* (New York: Basic Books, 1973), 3–30.

8   By one measure, Tazabek has the eighth most influential Twitter feed in Kazakhstan, and is the fifth most influential personal user of Twitter in Kazakhstan, "Reting—Klout," *Kaznet*, <http://kaznet.me/rating/>.

9   B. Privratsky, *Muslim Turkistan: Kazak Religion and Collective Memory* (London: Routledge, 2001), 7, 91.

as uninformed due to the anti-religious policies of the Soviet Union.[10] Tazabek, the director of Asyl Arna, related similar thoughts in a 2014 interview:

> Our purpose is not, in a single day, to turn everyone into a person who preaches well, wears a headscarf, prays five times a day, and gives charity. The Kazakh nation's ancient traditions and beliefs and way of life collapsed completely during the 70–80 year period of atheism.[11]

Tazabek and Asyl Arna use lists to simplify information for Kazakh Muslims perceived to be unfamiliar with Islamic practices and beliefs due to the repression of the Soviet era.

Simplifying moral injunctions or ritual practice is not new or unique to the post-Soviet context. Take, for example, the simplified Islamic instructions found in early twentieth century Islamic literature in Afghanistan. Shahrani describes how children learned from the "Four Books," which first present short poems on opposing virtues such as arrogance and humility, and then present short, formulaic instructions on prayer and ritual ablutions.[12] Similarly, a hadith on women's comportment was structured as a list of behaviors long before Asyl Arna published it.[13] Lists are pedagogical tools with a long history, both inside and outside of Islamic cultures. What is distinct about lists in Asyl Arna's social media is, in part, their connection with the perception of recent loss due to the historical Soviet experience. The emotions that Asyl Arna hopes to stir in visitors to its social media pages are joy in the simplicity of Islam and pride in their reclamation of Islam. A list is a simple start to recovering from the "collapse" of Kazakhs' traditional beliefs and way of life.

The second part of the post-Soviet context that produces a particular reading of Islamic lists is the understanding that there are simply too many media distractions in twenty-first century Kazakhstani life. Asyl Arna hopes to help their social media audience understand Islam, even while they are struggling with information overload. In an article on Asyl Arna on the role of media in

10   W. Schwab, "Establishing an Islamic Niche in Kazakhstan: Musylman Publishing House and Its Publications," *Central Asian Survey*, 30, no. 2 (2011): 227–242.

11   A. Bitore, "Mukhammedzhan Tazabek: Qazir—Alasapyran Uaqyt. Arkim Zhasyna Zharaspaityn Zhuk Koterip Zhur," *Zhaqsy*, June 27, 2014, <http://jaqsy.kz/article/view?id=383>.

12   M.N. Shahrani, "Local Knowledge of Islam and Social Discourse in Afghanistan and Turkistan in the Modern Period," in R.L. Canfield (ed.), *Turko-Persia in Historical-Perspective* (Cambridge: Cambridge University Press, 1991), 161–188.

13   A. Arna's vK page, <http://vk.com/wall-51948252?day=21042014&z=photo-51948252_329 804490%2Falbum-51948252_00%2Frev>, posted April 21, 2014.

Islam in Central Asia, Tazabek argues that there is too much media for contemporary Muslims to digest.

> Today's readers, listeners, and viewers are too free, too rich in terms of media, and too demanding. For example, today a common person tries to keep up with and take in the same amount of media in one month that a person living in the seventeenth century did in their whole life.[14]

Asyl Arna also posts images and texts showing the dangerous distractions of the internet and other media. One post shows a mother serving dinner to her husband and their four children. The children ignore the food in front of them and play with their tablets or phones, while the parents frown.[15] The accompanying text argues that good Muslims should pay attention to their companions. Media distractions can detract from a good Muslim life.

Tazabek and Asyl Arna view their audience's media use in much the same way that Ben Highmore, following Walter Benjamin's much earlier work, sees twenty-first century media practices, which he describes in terms of "distraction."[16] This term is meant to cut two ways. First, consumers of media are often distracted by other media: viewers blog or read comments while watching a favorite television show; people do chores while the radio plays in the background; web surfers have multiple browser tabs open while listening to music on their tablet. Followers of Asyl Arna's social media pages may be listening to ethno-pop on their computer while seeing an Asyl Arna post on the characteristics of religious hypocrites below a friend's photo at Qapshaghai beach. A list can be quickly scanned before moving on to comment on a friend's new sunglasses. Second, media is absorbing, pulling us away from the rest of the world. A man interested in curtailing his drinking may see a quick list of alcohol's evils in his vK newsfeed, click on it, and then peruse Asyl Arna's other posts for a lengthy period of time, becoming distracted from the world, entranced by images of piety and texts relating these images to Islamic scripture.[17]

---

14   M. Tazabek, "Islamdy Nasikhattauda BAQ-tyng Roli Qandai?", *Turkistan*, May 5, 2014. <http://archive.turkystan.kz/kz/articles/view/49130>.

15   A. Arna's vK page, <http://vk.com/asyl_arna?w=wall-51948252_80059>, posted February 21, 2016.

16   W. Benjamin, *Theory of Distraction. Selected Writings: Volume 3, 1935–1938* (Cambridge, MA: Harvard University Press, 2006), 358–364; B. Highmore, *Ordinary Lives: Studies in the Everyday* (London: Routledge, 2010).

17   For an empirical discussion of this type of distracted and distracting reading, see T. Hillesund, "Digital Reading Spaces: How Expert Readers Handle Books, the Web and

Asyl Arna's employees act on their belief that visitors to their social media pages are distracted and disconnected from Islam, and want their visitors to takeaway simple actions that can make a difference in their lives and perhaps become distracted from non-Islamic life for a bit. One post argues that if you want to pray, you only need to remember, "Daily prayers are made up of *only* four movements" (see Figure 7.1).[18]

A reader does not need to understand the history of daily prayers, variations of them, or their scriptural support; a reader can simply memorize four movements. The message of repeated lists is this: if a Muslim can, for example, remember the four movements of daily prayers, the six evils that drinking brings,[19] the five habits of a Muslim on Friday (see Figure 7.2),[20] the four promises God has made to Muslims,[21] the five things a Muslim should know the value of,[22] the four questions a Muslim will be asked on Judgment Day,[23] or the five qualities of the Day of Arafah,[24] then they will be able to function as a

Electronic Paper," *First Monday*, 15, no. 4 (2010), <http://uncommonculture.org/ojs/index.php/fm/article/view/2762/2504>.

18 Emphasis added. A. Arna's vK page, <http://vk.com/asyl_arna?z=photo-51948252_3698 02318%2Falbum-51948252_00%2Frev>, posted May 21, 2015. Also posted on January 4, 2016: <http://vk.com/asyl_arna?z=photo-51948252_398504792%2Falbum-51948252_00%2 Frev>.

19 A. Arna's vK page, <http://vk.com/wall-51948252?day=02052014&z=photo-51948252_33073 3099%2Falbum-51948252_00%2Frev>, posted May 2, 2014. Also posted on December 30, 2015: <http://vk.com/wall-51948252?day=02052014&z=photo-51948252_330733099%2Fal bum-51948252_00%2Frev>.

20 A. Arna's vK page, <http://vk.com/wall-51948252?day=23052014&z=photo-51948252_33253 8268%2Falbum-51948252_00%2Frev>, posted May 23, 2014. Also posted on October 16, 2014: <http://vk.com/wall-51948252?day=16102014&z=photo-51948252_344977967%2Fal bum-51948252_00%2Frev>. Also posted June 19, 2015: <http://vk.com/wall-51948252? day=19062015&z=photo-51948252_373133148%2Falbum-51948252_00%2Frev>. Also post-ed on February 11, 2016: <http://vk.com/asyl_arna?z=photo-51948252_404338356%2Fal bum-51948252_00%2Frev>. Also posted on April 8, 2016: <http://vk.com/asyl_arna? z=photo-51948252_412552169%2Falbum-51948252_00%2Frev>.

21 A. Arna's vK page, <http://vk.com/wall-51948252?day=10042014&z=photo206952853_3255 54919%2Fwall-51948252_1521>, posted April 10, 2014.

22 A. Arna's vK page, <http://vk.com/asyl_arna?z=photo-51948252_412168368%2Falbum-51948252_00%2Frev>, posted April 5, 2016.

23 A. Arna's vK page, <http://vk.com/asyl_arna?z=photo-51948252_412017267%2Falbum-51948252_00%2Frev>, posted April 4, 2016.

24 A. Arna's vK page, <http://vk.com/wall-51948252?day=03102014&z=photo-51948252_343 637206%2Falbum-51948252_00%2Frev>, posted October 2, 2014. Also posted on Sep-tember 20, 2015: <http://vk.com/asyl_arna?z=photo-51948252_384182400%2Falbum-51948252_00%2Frev>.

FIGURE 7.1
The text reads: "Daily prayers are made up of only four movements. 1. standing straight; 2. bending; 3. touching the head to the floor; and 4. kneeling. These four actions—that a four-year-old could do—are difficult only if you don't have motivation. M. Tazabek"

Muslim. More generally, the repeated device of a list suggests that there are simple Islamic steps to take for any problem, even if a particular list does not apply to a particular Muslim. The genius of Islam represented in these lists is not in long philosophical arguments or the touch of the divine, but in its simple instructions for everyday piety.

This simplicity, however, also creates anxiety. If prayer is only four simple actions that a four year-old child could do, and Muslims don't pray, what kind of excuse do they have? Repeated images of lists of pious practices and beliefs address a general sense of loss of Islamic culture and knowledge, but they also create a paradoxical sense of confidence and doubt: confidence in one's ability to act on a simple list and perform piety adequately; doubt in one's knowledge outside of lists and other simplified instructions. I experienced this paradoxical sensibility when discussing Islam with young Kazakh Muslims, who felt perfectly ready to instruct me on Islamic practices and beliefs that they had learned from social media and short pamphlets, but who also felt that they were inadequately knowledgeable about Islam in general. One young man spoke to me about the benefits of ritual prayer (*namaz*)—one becomes closer to God, more relaxed, more physically fit—for hours in a cafe in Almaty. He continued to repeat these points with increasing passion, as he hoped to help me see the benefits and genius of Islam. When I asked about something other than prayer, he argued that he knew nothing about Islam because he had only read lists and short articles on internet sites. He felt he knew enough to get by, so to speak, but would never have "deep knowledge" because of Kazakhs' Soviet

FIGURE 7.2
The text reads: "Friday's
Etiquette. Whoever...
1. performs the major ablutions,
2. goes to Friday prayers,
3. recites the salutation during
prayers, 4. listens to the sermon
until the end, and 5. prays with
the imam, will have his minor
sins committed between two
Friday forgiven"

experience. Reading lists informed him and gave him great joy and pride in reclaiming "lost" knowledge, but it also reminded him of his perceived ignorance. In the end, the mood created by lists is one of possibility (of knowledge and a pious life) and of anxiety (of failing short of the demands of Islam).

The Aesthetics of Authority

The visual importance of lists in Asyl Arna's social media and their attendant sensibility raises the question: if readers are not experts and need lists to make Islam a part of their lives, who are the experts who can make the lists? Asyl Arna presents two sets of experts in its images: (1) the head mufti, Yerzhan Mayamerov, and other imams and Muftiyat administrators, and (2) Asyl Arna's workers, particularly Asyl Arna's founder, Mukhammedzhan Tazabek. In this section, I will concentrate on the head mufti and Tazabek as representative of these two sets of experts.

The head mufti is always dressed in white robes with gold embellishment and a particular hat.[25] The white color of the head mufti's robes identifies him

---

25   Imams and other members of the Kazakhstani Muftiyat must dress in white. See Spiritual Administration of the Muslims of Kazakhstan, "Din Qyzmetkerline Zhanga Shapan Ulgisi Bekiteldi," *Muftyat.kz*, May 6, 2015, <http://old.muftyat.kz/kz/news/view?id=4466>. The head mufti has argued that imams' clothing models and creates the virtues of cleanliness

as pure and clean (*taza*), two ways Islam is also described in Kazakh. The robe links him to an idealized past when Central Asians , especially Islamic leaders, wore robes, and it also models cleanliness and modesty.[26] The gold embellishment is particularly Kazakh, marking him as an ethnically Kazakh leader. More generally, his clothing sets him apart from other Kazakhs, who do not dress in white robes and stylized hats. His clothing produces an image of a man who is not like other Kazakhs: he is more pure, more Islamic, and more traditional.

The head mufti is most often shown in an office, presumably his own (see Figure 7.3). This image appears in many posts, including congratulatory remarks on the first day of school,[27] the Night of Power,[28] and Kazakhstani Independence Day.[29] The connection of Islam and Kazakhstan through the figure of the mufti is also seen in the image itself. The twin pillars of this image are the head mufti and the flag of Kazakhstan. There are other identifiable objects in the photo—a vintage phone, a portable stereo, books—but the head mufti is the focus of the picture, with the sky blue and gold flag of Kazakhstan supplying a color contrast to the other elements of the photo: the white walls, the Mufti's white robes, the white pages of the books, and the white lamp. The merging of Islamic authority and the Kazakhstani government creates a fuzzy fusion: the head mufti is the highest Islamic authority because he is approved by the Kazakhstani government, but Kazakhstan also becomes an Islamic country because it has an officially appointed mufti. These images are part of a larger enterprise to define a scripturalist Islam specifically for Kazakhstan. He is positioned in front of an open book, which is placed atop several other books. Another open book sits to the side of him, while a newspaper is on his

---

and modesty. See "Ne odezhda i dlina volos opredeliaiut veru cheloveka," *Tengrinew*s, September 15, 2015, <http://tengrinews.kz/conference/106/>.

26   Privratsky provides a longer explanation of the connection of white to purity and Islam, such as "pure blessings" (*aq bata*) and "pure intentions" (*aq niet*). B. Privratsky, *Muslim Turkistan: Kazak Religion and Collective Memory* (London: Routledge, 2001), 125. I want to thank Ulan Bigozhin for drawing my attention to this reference.

27   A. Arna's vK page, <http://vk.com/wall-51948252?q=%D0%BC%D2%AF%D1%84%D1%82%D0%B8&z=photo-51948252_381801265%2Falbum-51948252_00%2Frev>, posted September 2, 2015.

28   A. Arna's vK page, <http://vk.com/wall-51948252?q=%D0%BC%D2%AF%D1%84%D1%82%D0%B8&z=photo-51948252_337673365%2Falbum-51948252_00%2Frev>, posted July 23, 2014.

29   A. Arna's vK page, <http://vk.com/wall-51948252?q=%D0%BC%D2%AF%D1%84%D1%82%D0%B8&z=photo-51948252_350585760%2Falbum-51948252_00%2Frev>, posted December 14, 2014. For a different official photo of the Mufti with similar elements, see A. Arna's vK page, <http://vk.com/asyl_arna?z=photo-51948252_395698956%2Falbum-51948252_00%2Frev>, posted December 15, 2015.

FIGURE 7.3   *Yerzhan Mayamerov, the head mufti of Kazakhstan*

left. The work that the head mufti performs in his office is knowing Islam through textual sources. He reads, collates, and interprets texts in order to produce an official, correct interpretation of Islam for Kazakhstan.

Other aspects of the visual culture of Asyl Arna reinforce the connection between the Muftiate, Islamic authority, and texts, particularly, the Qur'an. For example, the program *Opinion and Understanding* (*Pikir men Paiym*) contrasts the "opinions" of people on the street with the "understanding" of experts, such as doctors, journalists, and imams. In this program, which is often advertised on Asyl Arna's social media and posted on Asyl Arna's YouTube channel, imams are often shown near books or reading books. On the "An Alcohol-Free Feast is not a Feast" ("Araqsyz Toi—Toi Emes") episode of this program, the head imam of the Al-Hamid mosque in Almaty is shown seated at a desk in a mosque, dressed in a white robe with a white turban. The mosque's brown wooden minbar is behind him, and a patterned green carpet covers the floor. In front of him are five books that are oriented toward the imam, that is, upside-down to the viewer. These books include a Kazakh-language translation of the Qur'an.[30] While he is speaking, the program cuts from the imam's

30   A. Arna's YouTube page, "Araqsyz Toi—Toi Emes," December 3, 2015, <http://www.youtube.com/watch?v=7WKYDGQLJ0Y&t=5m30s>.

face to focus on the books and then cuts again to a different camera angle so that the translation of the Qur'an is facing the viewer, and its title is clearly readable. The setting and juxtaposition of the imam and the Qur'an shows that, in contrast to the opinions of common Kazakhs, the understanding and authority of the imam comes from his position at a mosque and his knowledge of the Qur'an and the Islamic textual tradition.

In contrast, Tazabek is often pictured in a suit or collared shirt in a living room.[31] For example, in Figure 7.4, Tazabek sits on a leather couch. Armoires and china cabinets are visible behind him. He models how middle- or upper-class Kazakhs decorate their home, how they should sit, and the types of discussions about Islam they should have. He dresses in a coat without a tie. In contrast to the head mufti, who draws his authority from his association with the Kazakhstani government and visual representations of his scholarliness, Tazabek draws his authority from a liminal position between Islamic authorities, such as the muftiate, and the perceived audience: middle-class Kazakhstanis, or aspiring middle-class Kazakhstanis. The text accompanying this image is a two-paragraph exposition of proper spousal roles according to Tazabek: wives should attempt to make their husbands happy, and husbands must provide for their family members. The text and the image combine to bring Tazabek into domestic life. If the head mufti is a man who studies and knows Islam in the form of texts, Tazabek is a man who can come into your living room and explain how Islam can fit into your everyday life.

The rise of the lay Muslim intellectual has been a trend throughout the Islamic world in the twentieth and twenty-first centuries, including Central Asia.[32] Management gurus in Indonesia combine Islamic ethics and business

---

31   A. Arna's vK page, <<http://vk.com/wall-51948252?owners_only=1&q=%D0%A2%D0%B 0%D0%B7%D0%B0%D0%B1%D0%B5%D0%BA&z=photo-51948252_3719 54964%2Falbum-51948252_00%2Frev>, posted June 8, 2015. For other examples, see A. Arna's vK page, <http://vk.com/wall-51948252?owners_only=1&q=%D0%A2%D0%B0%D0%B0%D0%B0%D0%B7%D0%B0%D0%B1%D0%B5%D0%BA&z=photo206952853_369429545%2Fw all-51948252_36720>, posted June 18, 2015; A. Arna's vK page, <http://vk.com/wall-519 48252?owners_only=1&q=%D0%A2%D0%B0%D0%B7%D0%B0%D0%B1%D0%B5%D 0%BA&z=photo-51948252_371614130%2Falbum-51948252_00%2Frev>, posted June 5, 2015>; A. Arna's vK page, <http://vk.com/asyl_arna?z=photo-51948252_405950555%2Fal bum-51948252_00%2Frev>, posted February 22, 2016.

32   The most comparable case of an Islamic celebrity in Central Asia who does not have a formal Islamic education is that of Hayrollo Hamidov in Uzbekistan. Hamidov is a journalist who combined writing on soccer, Islam, marriage, poetry, and more on the Uzbek-language Internet before he fell afoul of the Uzbekistani authorities. See N. Tucker, "Domestic Shapers of Eurasia's Islamic Futures: Sheikh, Scholar, Society, and the State," in

FIGURE 7.4 *Mukhammedzhan Tazabek, founder of Asyl Arna*

practices in self-help seminars.[33] Lay preachers in Egypt, such as Amr Khaled and Moez Masoud, have become extremely popular with middle-class viewers, eclipsing the popularity of more classically trained preachers and scholars by focusing on personal narratives rather than textual knowledge. Yasmin Moll argues that Khaled, much like Tazabek, "has authority not because he is different from the audience he preaches to, but because he is one of them."[34]

Tazabek's image, and his authority as someone who can explain Islam to the masses, is connected to lists and pithy statements in Asyl Arna's media. Rather than fatwas or learned treatises, Tazabek's name is attached to images that focus on his words, such as "For the prayers coming out of a person's mouth to be accepted (by God), the food entering that person's mouth must be

Thomas W. Simons, Jr. (ed.), *Islam in Eurasia: A Policy Volume* (Cambridge, MA: Davis Center for Russian and Eurasian Studies), 43–76; and N. Tucker, "Hayrullo Hamidov and Uzbekistan's Culture Wars: How Soccer, Poetry, and Pop-Religion Are 'A Danger to Society'," *Uzbekistan Initiative Papers No. 6*, February 2014. For a contrasting examination of the website of well-known, formally trained, Islamic scholars, see S. Nozimova and T. Epkenhans, "Negotiating Islam in Emerging Public Spheres in Contemporary Tajikistan," *Asiatische Studien*, 67, no. 3 (2013): 965–990.

33   D. Rudnyckyj, "Market Islam in Indonesia," *Journal of the Royal Anthropological Institute*, 15 (2009): 183–201.

34   Y. Moll, "Islamic Televangelism: Religion, Media and Visuality in Contemporary Egypt," *Arab Media & Society*, 10 (2010): 13.

righteous,"[35] or the phrase found in Figure 7.1. The name and the image of Tazabek stand for easy-to-relate-to advice.

The dual Islamic authorities constructed on Asyl Arna's social media help the organization to reach different audiences or to address different feelings of the same audience. Someone interested in scholarly texts is shown that the muftiate can provide scholarship and that their mosque is an appropriate place to engage in their search for more knowledge. Someone interested in "living room Islam" or inspiration knows that Asyl Arna can provide everyday advice or short inspirational sayings. Of course, a person may be interested in both of these things at different points of their day or year or life. To connect this point to my point about the achievable piety constructed by the visual repetition of lists: Asyl Arna provides authorities for Kazakhstanis who are distracted but want to engage with Asyl Arna's relatable advice quickly, and also to those who want to become absorbed in the more learned style of the muftiate and Islamic print media.

The Qur'an: Everyday Machine and Connection to the Numinous

Asyl Arna visually depicts the Qur'an in several ways. It can be a mundane object, a machine built to sustain morality in humans, or a supernatural connection to God. My argument is that it is this very combination of the mundane, the mechanical, and the magical that makes imagining the Qur'an central to Muslims' everyday morality and their connection to God.

The images presenting the Qur'an as a machine or analogous to a machine may be unexpected and contrast with the images of the Qur'an as divine light that I will discuss later, but they serve to place the Qur'an in an everyday context. For example, the image in Figure 7.5, taken from a July 8, 2014, post, constructs an analogy between washing a t-shirt with a washing machine and washing a heart with the Qur'an.[36] The analogy is plain: just a washing machine cleans a shirt, reading or reciting the Qur'an cleans the heart or soul.

---

35   A. Arna's vK page, <http://vk.com/wall-51948252?owners_only=1&q=%D1%82%D0%B0 %D0%B7%D0%B0%D0%B1%D0%B5%D0%BA&z=photo-51948252_3777 19204%2Falbum-51948252_00%2Frev>, posted July 29, 2015. For other examples, see A. Arna's vK page, <http://vk.com/asyl_arna?z=photo-51948252_402899259%2Falbum-51948 252_00%2Frev>, posted February 2, 2016; and A. Arna's vK page, <http://vk.com/asyl_ arna?z=photo-51948252_400786223%2Falbum-51948252_00%2Frev>, posted January 19, 2016.

36   A. Arna's vK page, <http://vk.com/wall-51948252?day=08072014&z=photo-51948252_33650 4018%2Falbum-51948252_00%2Frev>, posted July 8, 2014. It was also posted on January 4,

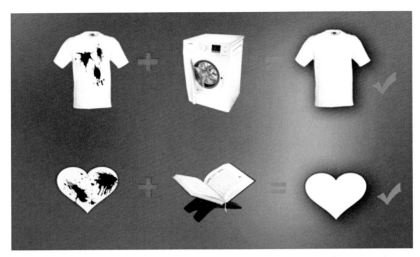

FIGURE 7.5 *Just a washing machine cleans a shirt, reading or reciting the Qur'an cleans*
the heart or soul

   This image builds on a larger cultural understanding: the act of reciting or listening to the Qur'an physically brings a Muslim into contact with God's speech, which can directly affect a human's heart, body, or soul. For example, the Qur'an's words on kindness are the most perfect words on kindness, and listening to them can make a person kinder through their semantic and sonic qualities. Members of the piety movement in Kazakhstan argue that the Qur'an, in Arabic, is inherently different from other speech in its ability to reform human hearts and souls, whether the Qur'an is recited or heard. One woman stated, "If one person is reading supplications in an ordinary language and one person is reading supplications in Arabic, and you listen to those people's supplications, you will know which one is closer to your soul."[37] This image, however, presents a stronger analogy than this interlocutor. It is not simply that the words of the Qur'an are closer to a human soul due to their connection to the divine. Creating a parallel between the Qur'an and a washing machine makes the assertion that the Qur'an is a straightforward tool to be used to reform, or cleanse, one's heart, and the process is relatively automatic.

_____

         2015:   <http://vk.com/wall-51948252?day=04012015&z=photo-51948252_352700841%2Fal
         bum-51948252_00%2Frev>.
37   W. Schwab, "How to Pray in Kazakhstan: The Fortress of the Muslim and Its Readers,"
         Anthropology of East Europe Review, 32, no. 1 (2014): 31.

This is a visual representation of the inherent accessibility of the Qur'an to all Muslims.

A second mechanical representation of the Qur'an presents the Qur'an as a medical device[38] (see Figure 7.6). An image from a February 14, 2016, post overlays the text "The Qur'an is my soul's nourishment" (*quran mening rukhymnyng nari*) on a dark image of a goateed young man holding a Qur'an; a tube connects the Qur'an to an oxygen mask strapped on the young man's face. The young man's legs are not shown, but he appears to be wearing a South Asian-style *kemeez*. Rather than presenting the Qur'an as a sin-cleansing machine, here the Qur'an is necessary for the soul: it is the oxygen of religious life. The text accompanying this image is a poem reinforcing this message, arguing that the Qur'an can answer your questions about the meaning of life, how to find the path to Heaven, and more. This is the pictorial depiction of what Geertz calls scripturalism: the placement of texts at the center of daily life and the elevation, in practice, of the Qur'an and hadiths to a position of highest authority. (In theory, the Qur'an and hadiths have often been the highest authorities, at least for Muslim scholars; however, in practice, the example of elders, those connected to the Prophet by blood, or masters of Sufi techniques, have often been more authoritative than consulting the Qur'an or hadiths.[39]) The Qur'an is oxygen for the soul, and thus there can be no substitute for a constant interaction with the Qur'an. It must be at the center of everyday life and of Muslims' understanding of Islam.

Placing the Qur'an at the center of daily life is reiterated by Asyl Arna and the broader piety movement in Kazakhstan. Elites in the piety movement see sports, for example, through the lens of scripture: archery is a good sport because of its scriptural support, as are wrestling and javelin throwing.[40] Some members of the piety movement go farther than Asyl Arna's representatives or the official Muftiyat Hanafi orientation, and declare that "if it is not in the Qur'an or the hadiths, you don't need it. The Qur'an, the hadiths, that's enough."[41] For Kazakhs not influenced by the piety movement, however, other sources of authority are also, or even more, important than the Qur'an and

---

38   A. Arna's vK page, <http://vk.com/asyl_arna?z=photo-51948252_404714197%2Falbum-51948252_00%2Frev>, posted February 14, 2016.

39   D. Deweese, "Authority," in J.J. Elias (ed.), *Key Themes for the Study of Islam* (Oxford: Oneworld Publications, 2010), 26–52.

40   W. Schwab, "Islam, Fun, and Social Capital in Kazakhstan," *Central Asian Affairs*, 2, no. 1 (2015): 51–70.

41   W. Schwab and U. Bigozhin, "Shrines and Neopatrimonialism in Kazakhstan," in M. Laruelle (ed.), *Kazakhstan in the Making: Legitimacy, Symbols, and Social Changes* (Lanham, MD: Rowman and Littlefield, 2016), 89–110.

FIGURE 7.6
*"The Qur'an is my soul's nourish-
ment"*

hadiths. These sources of authority include such things as the moral habits of
elders, dream omens from ancestors, or descent from saints. For many
Kazakhstani Muslims, the Qur'an is a gift to the Muslim community, and some
members of the community must know, recite, or otherwise interact with the
Qur'an, but it is not an individual obligation to interact with the Qur'an on a
daily basis. Asyl Arna, conversely, constructs an image of the Qur'an as indis-
pensable, not only to the Islamic community, but to each individual Muslim's
everyday life. (Asyl Arna constructs and uses other sources of authority, as seen
in the middle-class authority of Tazabek, but rhetorically, the Qur'an and
hadiths are all-important.)

The Qur'an, however, is not only shown to be the main tool to cleanse the
heart and sustain moral life. It is also the connection between God and this
world, and mysteriously divine or supernatural. Muslims do not experience
reading or hearing the Qur'an with the same emotion produced by using a
washing machine. It is meant to be wondrous and divine, and Asyl Arna also
produces images of the Qur'an using the global visual conventions to show its
magic.

For example, the image shown in Figure 7.7, from a July 29, 2013, post, borrows from Hollywood imagery of the supernatural. On the left-hand side of the
frame, a Qur'an rests on a Qur'an stand, and emanates what viewers of Disney
cartoons can recognize as pixie dust.[42] The Qur'an illuminates this image, and

---

42   A. Arna's vK page, <http://vk.com/wall-51948252?day=29072013&z=photo-51948252_308
        890703%2Falbum-51948252_00%2Frev>, posted July 29, 2013.

the background progressively darkens as the eye travels from the Qur'an. Showing the Qur'an as emitting Disney-esque pixie dust brings it into a global semiotic network juxtaposing the magical with the mundane. This represents a notion of the supernatural that is influenced by—but in opposition to— Hollywood representations of the supernatural. Asyl Arna's social media producers are well-aware of the fact that much of humanity does not believe the Qur'an has special powers. Soviet atheists, Western scientists, and members of other religions fail to see the wonder of the Qur'an, viewing it as a work of literature or superstition. Shifting pixie-dust from the make-believe to the real world glorifies the enchanted and the miraculous in the world. Asyl Arna's implicit argument here is that while many people see magic as something that happens in movies or fantasy literature, real magic happens in the Qur'an. There is something greater, more mysterious, and more powerful than common matter and speech, and that something is the Qur'an. The image of a Qur'an emitting pixie dust or divine light is repeatedly evoked; Asyl Arna posted the same image with additional text on July 18, 2014, and July 15, 2015.[43]

This visual repertoire draws from images across the globe that are easily accessed through the internet. The images in Figures 7.6, 7.7, and 7.8, for instance, are found on many Islamic websites.[44] On an everyday production level, Asyl Arna's workers may choose international images in order to connect Kazakhstani Muslims to a global Islamic visual culture; they also might simply find these images after a quick Google search while trying to meet a deadline. In either case, the effect is the same: Kazakhstani Muslims see the same images of the Qur'an as Muslims elsewhere in the world. The work of creating Islamic visual culture, and visual culture itself, becomes somewhat delocalized.[45]

Other images combine similar elements that emphasize the magical nature of the Qur'an. A May 27, 2014, post shows an image that combines three elements on a blue background: a Qur'an on a Qur'an stand, blue pixie dust

---

43   A. Arna's vk page, <http://vk.com/wall-51948252?day=18072014&z=photo-51948252_33728 1826%2Falbum-51948252_00%2Frev>, posted July 18, 2014. See also A. Arna's vK page, <http://vk.com/asyl_arna?z=photo-51948252_375857211%2Falbum-51948252_00%2Frev>, posted July 13, 2015.

44   For the image shown in Figure 7.7, see al-Morohen's Contest Flickr page, <http://www. flickr.com/photos/almorohenphoto/6106136015/>, August 8, 2010. For the image shown in Figure 7.8, see "Does Qur'an Contradict Science," *Quran and Modern Science*, June 2010, <http://quran-modern-science.blogspot.com/2010/06/does-quran-contradict-science. html>, or <http://www.whyislamtrue.com/panel/imgUrun/19032015214744.jpg>.

45   For more on the delocalization of Islamic authority and culture, see N. Echchaibi, "From Audio Tapes to Video Blogs: The Delocalisation of Authority in Islam," *Nations and Nationalism*, 17, no. 1 (2011): 25–44.

FIGURE 7.7 *Magical fairy dust emanates from a Qur'an*

emanating upward from the Qur'an, and text. The background is blue, and again darkens away from the Qur'an and its illuminating emanation. The text also recalls the touch of the divine or miraculous in the world: "Read the Qur'an! Truthfully, on the Day of Judgment, it (the Qur'an) will be an intercessor for those who have read it." In this image, the Qur'an is presented as an agent rather than an object: it will intercede for Muslims on the Day of Judgment. A June 22, 2015, post shows an almost psychedelic or science fictional image of the Qur'an. (Figure 7.8) In this image, a Qur'an on a Qur'an stand sits on top of a blue planet—the Earth?—and emanates light upward toward the text, "If you are searching for a path to God..." ("Allagha zhaqyndaudyng zholyn izdesengiz...").[46] Stars shine in the black background at the top of the image, while parabolas of light streak upward on the left side of the image. Clouds appear behind these parabolas. Here, the Qur'an is again light-giving, but it also is the road to God, traveling through the literal heavens. This post bludgeons the viewer with the heavenly, supernatural, mysterious nature of the Qur'an, and its ability to connect humans to God.

This image also draws on a well-established Islamic understanding of the Qur'an as God's light (*nur*) in the world.[47] The Qur'an presents itself as a light

---

46   A. Arna's vK page, <http://vk.com/asyl_arna?z=photo-51948252_373488500%2Falbum-51948252_00%2Frev>, posted June 22, 2015.

47   J. Elias, "Light," in J.D. McAuliffe (ed.), *Encyclopaedia of the Qur'an* (Washington, D.C.: Brill Online, 2016).

FIGURE 7.8   *The text reads: "If you are searching for a path to God…"*

for the world; Nisa 174 reads, "O mankind, there has come to you a conclusive proof from your Lord, and We have sent down to you a clear light," while Ma'idah 15–16 reads, "O People of the Scripture, there has come to you Our Messenger making clear to you much of what you used to conceal of the Scripture and overlooking much. There has come to you from Allah a light and a clear Book."[48] Light has significant conceptual meaning in the larger Islamic tradition. Religious knowledge in general is conceived as light, God emanates physical and metaphorical light, and the Prophet is conceived as primordial light.[49] These divine and scriptural lights can even be internalized, as Muslims who have memorized the Qur'an will emanate light on the Day of Judgment.[50] Muslim artists often portray the revelation of the Qur'an during Night of Destiny, or the Qur'an more generally, with similar iconography, such as a beam of light connecting sky and earth.[51] Asyl Arna continues this tradition and adds contemporary elements, such as pixie dust or science fictional parab-

---

48   M. Mir, "Names of the Qur'an," in *Encyclopaedia of the Qur'an.*

49   W. Hartner and T. Boer, "Nur," in P. Bearman, T. Bianquis, C.E. Bosworth, E. van Donzel, and W.P. Heinrichs (eds), *Encyclopaedia of Islam*, 2nd ed. (Washington, D.C.: Brill Online, 2016).

50   W. Saleh, "Word," in J.J. Elias (ed.), *Key Themes for the Study of Islam* (Oxford: Oneworld Publications, 2010), 370.

51   K. George, *Picturing Islam: Art and Ethics in a Muslim Lifeworld* (Oxford: Wiley-Blackwell, 2011), 91. George also details the controversy surrounding the use of the Qur'an in art in Indonesia. There has not been any controversy around Asyl Arna's depiction of the Qur'an, possibly due to a new understanding of the importance of visual culture to proselytizing (*daghuat*, Arabic: *da'wah*).

olas and planets, in order to place the Qur'an as a bridge between man and God and as providing a touch of magic in everyday life.[52]

The image of a July 29, 2013, post has a different type of sensibility, one that is less sensational but still connects the viewer with the divine light of the Qur'an and God, and is perhaps more obviously connected with historical Islamic concepts of the Qur'an.[53] In this image, a Qur'an rests on a Qur'an stand in the left of the frame, while another Arabic-language book, possibly a Qur'an, rests on a rug on the right side of the frame. The background of the image is composed of the aforementioned rug. A lamp sits in the center of the image, behind the books. The lamp is an older railroad-style lantern, burning kerosene or oil, rather than an electric lightbulb. The Qur'an in the picture is in Arabic, bringing the reader to the original language of revelation. The emotional experience of this image is nostalgic, connecting viewers' experience of the light of the Qur'an to past Muslims' experience. The Qur'an is not simply a magic book that flies through the heavens or emits pixie dust. It has also brought the divine to Earth and illuminated the path to God for hundreds of years.

More mundane images of the Qur'an serve to make it clear that Muslims should interact with the Qur'an in everyday life. For example, one post relates that the Qur'an was translated into Ingush for the first time and simply shows the new translation on a wooden surface, presumably a table.[54] Nothing more miraculous than human intellectual labor is depicted here. Another image depicts a finger tracing lines in a book.[55] The book is identifiable as the Qur'an from its adornment and Arabic text, but it does not emit pixie dust or light. It is recognizable as something that a vKontakte user might encounter, particularly if they following the textual encouragement to memorize parts of the Qur'an. This image provides a bridge from the supernatural and divine aspects of the Qur'an to the everyday Qur'an that a Muslim might encounter when first memorizing the Qur'an and learning to feel its divine power. It does not always

---

52   For more instances of glowing or illuminating Qur'an, see, for example, some of the daily
      updates for the 30-part "Facts about the Qur'an" series of posts during Ramadan in 2015:
      <http://vk.com/asyl_arna?z=photo-51948252_374575520%2Falbum-51948252_00%2Frev>
      and   <http://vk.com/asyl_arna?z=photo-51948252_375228505%2Falbum-51948252_00%2
      Frev>.

53   A. Arna's vK page, <http://vk.com/wall-51948252?day=29072013&z=photo-51948252_3088
      68208%2Falbum-51948252_00%2Frev>, posted July 29, 2013.

54   A. Arna's vK page, <http://vk.com/wall-51948252?day=26062014&z=photo-51948252_3355
      31800%2Falbum-51948252_00%2Frev>, posted June 26, 2014.

55   A. Arna's vK page, <http://vk.com/asyl_arna?z=photo-51948252_381075851%2Falbum-
      51948252_00%2Frev>, posted August 27, 2015.

sparkle. It gets translated and put on tables and ignored for part of the day. But if one is correctly attuned to the Qur'an, then one can appreciate the miraculous and the divine at particular times. The Qur'an is at once a mundane guide to life and prayer and also a magical connection to God and miraculous events.

Middle-class Lifestyles and Anxieties

According to James Laidlaw, "Religion is not all there ever is to ethics."[56] Laidlaw's statement concerns the contradictions and negotiations between Jains' ideals of asceticism and their everyday concerns of wealth and prosperity. Similar issues exist in the visual culture of Asyl Arna's social media. On the one hand, Asyl Arna downplays the importance of worldly wealth by posting pictures of impoverished children meant to symbolize childlike innocence, and images of money with text reminding viewers that peace is more important than money. On the other hand, many images portray middle-class or wealthy lifestyles, and Asyl Arna explicitly states that piety is the path to the middle class.

Asyl Arna encourages readers to be happy with the material goods that God has provided for them.[57] Smiling children, often with stereotypical African or South Asian phenotypes, are often shown in posts with texts exhorting viewers to consider what is most important in life: God, Islam, and morality. For example, Figure 7.9 is part of a two-paragraph post titled: "Be pleased with what God Almighty has given, and you will be the wealthiest person!" The image shows a smiling African child against an unfocused background. The child holds a mobile phone made from clay. In its context, this image models what true happiness looks like: a person who makes the best of what God has provided.

This emphasis on spiritual well-being intensified after the tenge devaluation in late August 2015. One simple image from an August 20, 2015, post shows five Euro notes ascending in value from left to right (see Figure 7.10). The notes are rolled into cylinders. The focus is on the €50 note, although this seems to be coincidental. The text at the bottom of the image reminds the viewer that "peace is more precious than money, brother!"[58]

---

56   J. Laidlaw, *Riches and Renunciation: Religion, Economy, and Society among the Jains* (Oxford: Clarendon Press, 1995), 12.

57   A. Arna's vK page, <http://vk.com/photo206952853_314887347>, posted November 28, 2013.

58   A. Arna's vK page, <http://vk.com/asyl_arna?z=photo-51948252_380253243%2Falbum-51948252_00%2Frev>, posted August 20, 2015.

FIGURE 7.9   *True happiness is a person who makes the best of what God has provided*

Another post from August 20th related the following fairy tale.

> One man went to complain about sky-high prices to a man recognized by
> the people as wise. (The wise man) said, "even if one grain of barley was
> one dinar, this would not worry me. Because I have made a habit of serv-
> ing God as He commanded. And He has made a promise to provide."[59]

This fairy tale was accompanied by two images: one of gold coins on a scale,
the other of hands scooping some sort of grain. The gold coins are presented
without a social context, just as the Euros in Figure 7.10 are presented without
a human element. The background of the image is also gold, and creates a
sense of impersonal wealth, or a platonic ideal of currency. The hands scooping grain are closed tightly, supporting the grain and ensuring that none falls.
The hands connect people to simple material needs. People need food, they
touch food, they take care of food. Wealth sits on its own. The connection of
food with humanity and the loneliness of wealth constructs a picture that
wealth cannot fulfill human needs. Only God can do that. Comments on this
post praised its wisdom and chided Kazakhstanis who had become "too
attached to this world."

59   A. Arna's vK page, <http://vk.com/asyl_arna?w=wall-51948252_54253>, posted August 20,
      2015.

FIGURE 7.10   *"Peace is more precious than money, brother!"*

However, Asyl Arna also depicts a middle-class lifestyle as a result of proper Islamic behavior. One post shows an image of a fist clutching money with the caption, "How can one (morally) save and earn money?"[60] (See Figure 7.11.) The fist clutches green money, presumably dollars, linking the morally acceptable ways to earn money to success not just in Kazakhstan, but in the larger world. Live right and you can be successful enough to have dollar holdings if the tenge loses its value. Another image consists of cursive text against a blurred background; the text reads, "Marriage is the road from poverty." The post links to an article arguing that God has made marriage an Islamic duty and will enrich those who follow His commands.[61] These two images make a combined visual and textual argument that Islam is the path to the middle class.

Other images of pious husbands and wives show well-dressed people in identifiably middle- or upper-class settings. For example, in the image accom-

---

60   A. Arna's vK page, <http://vk.com/asyl_arna?z=photo-51948252_409254341%2Falbum-51948252_00%2Frev>, posted March 16, 2016. The linked article gives tips such as "keep an account book" and "don't go out to lunch."

61   A. Arna's vK page, <http://vk.com/asyl_arna?z=photo-51948252_376872076%2Falbum-51948252_00%2Frev>, posted July 22, 2015. It was also posted on September 28, 2015: <http://vk.com/asyl_arna?z=photo-51948252_385083925%2Falbum-51948252_00%2Frev>

FIGURE 7.11 *"How can one (morally) save and earn money?"*

panying a March 19, 2015, post, a husband and wife walk through the grass at a park with trees out of focus in the background[62] (see Figure 7.12.)

The park is empty except for the couple, who face away from the camera. The man wears a black suit, while the woman wears a turquoise headscarf, matching skirt, and a white blouse. The husband leads the wife by the hand; behind her back, she holds a sign that reads, "He is the one who surprises me :)" This is plainly a happy scene, as indicated by the emoticon. Below this sign of marital bliss is the text, "Living a blessed life—it is not merely happy moments. It is loving, trusting, protecting, and respecting one another for God." In this image, the absence of many features of contemporary urban life in Kazakhstan is noticeable. Skyscrapers and tall Soviet apartment buildings are absent. The air is clean. Buses and minibuses are not idling nearby. Garbage is not visible. Spouses are not worried about finding work. Extended family members are not living on pull-out mattresses in the family room. In other words, this couple is not finding love in the microraion. This image provides an ethical example. Happy marriages, nice clothes, and dates in uncrowded green parks are the result of keeping God at the center of a marriage.

---

62   A. Arna's vK page, <http://vk.com/wall-51948252?day=17092014&z=photo-51948252_34 2277788%2Falbum-51948252_00%2Frev>, posted September 17, 2014. It was also posted on March 19, 2015: <http://vk.com/asyl_arna?z=photo-51948252_360667990%2Falbum-51948252_00%2Frev>.

FIGURE 7.12 *"Living a blessed life—it is not merely happy moments. It is loving, trusting, protecting, and respecting one another for God"*

Asyl Arna's depiction of gender and family furthers this class-based depiction of Islamic piety. The ideal role for a woman is made explicit in Figure 7.13.[63] A mother is seated next to her daughter at a table. One assumes they are in conversation, although their faces are not depicted, maintaining Asyl Arna's construction of female modesty. The caption reads: "There is not a rule for women that says 'do not work, do not make money.' But, we would not lose anything if we taught our daughters, before anything else, 'you are the mother of the future.'" The sensibility here is not thought to be a restrictive one. Women should have the option of working. But in an ideal world, husbands would

---

63   A. Arna's vK page, <http://vk.com/asyl_arna?z=photo-51948252_358144815%2Falbum-51948252_00%2Frev>, published February 24, 2015. It was also republished February 17, 2016: <http://vk.com/asyl_arna?z=photo-51948252_405215981%2Falbum-51948252_00%2Frev>.

FIGURE 7.13
"There is not a rule for women that says 'do not work, do not make money.' But, we would not lose anything if we taught our daughters, before anything else, 'you are the mother of the future'"

make enough money that their wives could stay at home, raise children in wholesome environments, and devote time to making their husbands happy by cooking and beautifying themselves. Asyl Arna's construction of a woman's ideal role and her relationship to her husband assumes privacy, leisure time, access to uncrowded parks, vacations, and other middle-class consumerist and public goods.[64]

Where then, should a husband work in this ideal marriage? Figure 7.14 models the types of desk jobs that Asyl Arna sees its audience as having or wanting. This image is the illustration that accompanies a link to a somewhat convoluted article on Asyl Arna's website. The article is supposedly written by a man,

---

64   For a more detailed look at a Central Asian woman's struggle with fashion, Islam, and living a good life, including "well-paid work, good husbands, kind mothers-in-law, and nice homes," see J. McBrien, "Mukadas's Struggle: Veils and Modernity in Kyrgyzstan," *Journal of the Royal Anthropological Institute*, 15, no. 1 (2009): 127–144. For more detail on the dreams of Kyrgyzstani women, including what Kyrgyz women hope for and their Islamic interpretations of dreams, see M. Louw, "Dreaming up Futures: Dream Omens and Magic in Bishkek," *History and Anthropology*, 21, no. 3 (2010): 277–292. For an examination of the "re-traditionalization" of gender roles in Central Asia, which is actually using the authority of "tradition" to advocate for new economic gender roles in a new type of economy, see M. Commercio, "The Politics and Economics of 'Retraditionalization' in Kyrgyzstan and Tajikistan," *Post-Soviet Affairs*, 31, no. 6 (2015): 529–556.

FIGURE 7.14 *"A Director's Regre"*

now 20 years out of school, who visits his former school director in a nursing home. The school director was placed in the nursing home because his children did not want to take care of him. The situation is particularly sad because the school director realizes that he treated his parents in the same way.[65] The drawing shows a man sitting at a desk, staring at a computer. A coffee cup sits to his right. Underneath the desk is a briefcase. A mustached man, presumably a younger version of the director, although this is not at all clear, scowls over the office worker. The text above these two figures reads, "A director's regret."

The strange juxtaposition between the story and the image, however, should not detract from Asyl Arna's creation of a typical work scene. The article is not directly in the post, and followers of Asyl Arna on vK may only see the drawing. Other illustrations more directly related to the story could have been chosen, such as a man in a nursing home. However, a decision was made to show a male office worker at his desk deferring to a supervisor, something that Asyl Arna sees as either reflecting its audience members' experiences or as a model of what work should be like. Geertz would tell us that this image functions both ways.[66] In the context of Asyl Arna's visual culture, a viewer can imagine the harassed office worker going home to his waiting wife and children, like those found in Figure 13.

There is a seemingly contradictory but actually complementary argument on Asyl Arna's social media pages. First, Islam is the path to the middle class;

65   A. Arna's vK page, <http://vk.com/asyl_arna?z=photo-51948252_402960848%2Falbum-51948252_00%2Frev>, posted February 2, 2016.

66   C. Geertz, "Religion as a Cultural System," *The Interpretation of Cultures* (New York: Basic Books, 1973), 87–125.

second, wealth and consumerism are less important than piety. This argument creates a hope for a "normal" life, as one interlocutor put it to me in a Skype conversation, one in which being a pious Muslim and middle-class come naturally and are not such hard work.[67] Or, put differently, a life in which doing the right thing pays off in economic security and a happy domestic life run in accordance with scripturalist Islamic norms. One example of this "normal" life can be found in the background of photos of Tazabek, such as Figure 7.4. In this image, Tazabek wears a tailored jacket and clean white shirt while he sits on a shiny, expensive leather couch with a china cabinet visible behind him. This is the model of "everyday" Islamic life. A second example of this middle-class life can be found Asyl Arna's June 2015 advertisement for curtains, chests, and cribs of "national design."[68] In this set of images, sumptuous pillows lay on a bed and an artisanal wooden crib has a baby monitor attached to it. A third example is an advertisement for "national clothing," which shows children in white suits and dresses embroidered with gold designs similar to those found on the head mufti's robes.[69] A good Muslim can afford, and should buy, consumer goods referencing the same kind of "traditional" and Islamic aesthetics as the head mufti. A modern Muslim life—a "normal" life—includes disposable income to be spent appropriately.

But with this hope for a "normal" life comes anxieties: what if a Kazakhstani Muslim cannot find a middle-class job or the Kazakhstani economy falls into a recession? Asyl Arna's images of happy but impoverished children and statements that money is less important than piety create a fallback position if a Muslim does not find economic success. The same interlocutor told me, in a separate Skype conversation, that he did not worry about the tenge devaluation, because Kazakhs will do what they have always done: make do with what God has given.[70] When times are good, Asyl Arna's readers can model their dreams on depictions of a middle-class Islamic lifestyle; when times are bad, they can take comfort in the fact that real wealth is found in piety.

---

67 For a description of the middle-class "Astana Dream," see K. Osmonova, "Experiencing Liminality: Housing, Renting, and Informal Tenants in Astana," *Central Asian Survey*, 35, no. 2 (2016): 237–256.

68 A. Arna's vK page, <http://vk.com/asyl_arna?z=photo-51948252_373160114%2Falbum-51948252_00%2Frev>, posted June 19, 2015.

69 A. Arna's Instragram account, <http://www.instagram.com/p/BDISLAiiqUw/>, posted March 19, 2016.

70 My interlocutor's specific quote was, "Eh, I lived through the 1990s. God gives and He takes away. Everything will be fine."

Conclusion

I want to use the ways the Asyl Arna discusses its 2015 logo to summarize the hopes and dreams and anxieties modeled in Asyl Arna's visual culture.[71] (See Figure 15 for the new logo.)

> Asyl Arna! A new face for a new season! A new logo! A dome, Kazakh ornamentation, a new moon, and the first letter of Asyl Arna, these all come together in a unified image. Our educational purpose, which offers appropriate guidance to the demands of our time, is to elevate the unity of religion and tradition as well as the harmony of Islam and the nation, and to reveal their beauty year after year. It is to instill our great moral qualities, and direct them to the protection of the nation, in the consciousness of the new generation and to ensure the foundation of our independence is strong. We will make the everlasting example of Muhammad (p.b.u.h.), our great teacher, the cornerstone of our lives in accordance with the laws of a secular society. Tell us, what do you think of our new logo?

This logo, as made clear in the equation in the image and the accompanying text, combines stylized simplifications of a mosque's dome, a Kazakh pattern for rugs and felted goods, the Islamic crescent moon, and the company's initials. What does Asyl Arna stand for? Islam and Kazakhstan, most obviously, but also marketing and media consumption. The presence of a logo and the accompanying branding emphasizes integrating Islam with consumer capitalism. Asyl Arna addresses the concerns of busy middle-class Kazakhs, and middle-class hopefuls, such as their hopes for material wealth and desire for piety and a touch of the numinous in their busy, media-saturated lives. Seeing a glimpse of Asyl Arna's visual culture in a Twitter feed on a smartphone creates hope and joy at the possibilities of an achievable piety, interactions with the divine, and a moral road to a middle-class life. Seeing Asyl Arna's images in a vK feed also creates doubt and uncertainty regarding the possibility of deep knowledge and one's own ritual observances and fears of not reaching or staying in a middle-class life. The overall enterprise of Asyl Arna, the dreams it reflects and creates, is to produce a prosperous, middle-class society in which men work, women raise pious and devout children, Russians and Kazakhs and Ingush and Uyghurs get along in a society led by Kazakhs, and there is no social

---

71   A. Arna's vK page, <http://vk.com/wall-51948252?day=17092015&z=photo-51948252_383 718071%2Falbum-51948252_00%2Frev>, posted September 17, 2015.

FIGURE 7.15
Asyl Arna's new logo

upheaval. Many Kazakhs, including those who are not as observant or pious as they might like to be, find this picture attractive. They see neighboring countries as less wealthy or chaotic. They are not looking for Sharia law or democratic political change.[72] They are looking for a new "normal." The visual culture of Asyl Arna delivers a picture of what a middle-class Islamic life might look like.

---

72   For a complementary examination of how Kyrgyzstani Muslims view democracy, and their hopes for political and economic change, including change based on Islamic law, see D. Montgomery, "Islam beyond Democracy and State in Kyrgyzstan," in M. Laruelle and J. Engvall (eds), *Kyrgyzstan beyond "Democracy Island" and "Failing State": Social and Political Changes in a Post-Soviet Society* (Lanham, MD: Lexington Books, 2015), 229–242.

CHAPTER 8

Playing Cosmopolitan: Muslim Self-fashioning, Migration, and (Be-)Longing in the Tajik Dubai Business Sector

Manja Stephan-Emmrich[1]

In September 2012, I joined a women's gathering hosted by Fatima, the wife of a "Dubai *biznesmen*." Fatima, in her early 30s, regularly spends the summer with her family in their two-story house in the southern outskirts of Tajikistan's capital city, Dushanbe. The rest of the year the family lives in the Dubai emirate. Fatima's husband, Ahmad, is involved in the fur coat business and simultaneously runs a small cargo company exporting kitchenware, home accessories, and roof tiles from Dubai to Dushanbe. When the two businesses began to flourish in 2008, Ahmad bought an apartment in Dubai, and since then the family regularly commutes between Dubai and Dushanbe. The day before the family returned to the emirate, Fatima invited me for what she called *osh-i Arab*, i.e., a modification of *osh-i palav*. While the former is a traditional Tajik rice meal mixed with carrots, lamb meat and a high portion of cotton oil, Fatima reduced the high fat-level and added various "Arab" spices she had bought in Dubai.

When I arrived, other guests were already chatting in the guestroom. Two of the women, dressed like Fatima in clothing appropriate for the Gulf (a black *abaya*, combined with a black hijab and gloves), were introduced as Fatima's Dubai friends (*dugonahoyam az Dubai*); that is, the wives of her husband's business associates. With their "Arab style" (*arabskii stil'*) clothing, they stood

1   This work is part of the research project "Translocal Goods: Education, Work, and Commodities between Tajikistan, Kyrgyzstan, Russia, China, and the Arab Emirates," which since May 2013 has been supported by VolkswagenStiftung (the Volkswagen Foundation) under grant number Az. 86870 (<https://www.iaaw.hu-berlin.de/de/querschnitt/islam/forschung/netz>). I am grateful for the fruitful discussion of an earlier version of this article during the conference "Religion Branding? Central Asia's Integration into the International Scene through Religion," organized by the Central Asia Program at the George Washington University in 2016. Finally, I especially want to thank Marlene Laruelle and Sebastien Peyrouse for generously supporting the writing process and the two anonymous reviewers for their valuable comments, which helped to improve the argument.

© KONINKLIJKE BRILL NV, LEIDEN, 2018 | DOI 10.1163/9789004357242_010

FIGURE 8.1
Famous Tajik pop singer Farzona

FIGURE 8.2
A tradeswomen dressed up in fashionable
„Dubai style" clothing (photos by Abdullah
Mirzoev, 2013)

in contrast to the other local women, who were dressed in multicolored, flowery dresses. The table was set with Arab bread, Iranian sweets, and dried dates from Dubai, served in chrome and gold-plated crockery—the latest trend in tableware as seen in Dubai's shopping malls. Later, when Fatima served the main dish, she explained to her guests: "Anytime I feel homesick for Dubai, I cook *osh-i Arab.*" She then described the health-promoting effects of low-fat Arab food, which helps her to concentrate on the Quran recitations (*tajvid*) she regularly performs when in Dubai. After a bit of silence, one of Fatima's friends joked: "Oh look, we are Tajik women dressing like Arabs do, eating Arab food, feeling homesick for Dubai but always missing our families when we are there (in Dubai). Our husbands do business with Iranians and Arabs, our friends are Arabs, Afghans and Africans." Fatima added: "We are international (*zanhoi bainalmillaty*)!."

Being Muslim in Dubai

This chapter is based on ethnographic fieldwork conducted in different places in the United Arab Emirates and Tajikistan between 2010 and 2014. It takes the growing economic and cultural links between Tajikistan and the Gulf as a point of departure and explores how migration, business, and transnational

Islam intersect in the Tajik business sector in Dubai. Focusing on young, educated, male Tajik migrants,[2] who successfully participate in Dubai's vibrant transregional trading and Russian tourist business, the chapter illuminates how well-educated, multilingual Tajik migrants in the Gulf create, shape, and draw on a sense of cosmopolitanism to convert their vulnerable and uncertain status as "Tajik migrants" into that of independent and successful "Muslim businessmen." Following recent studies on migrants' transnational religious strategies, I use the term "playing cosmopolitan"[3] to depict the various ways in which Tajiks in Dubai mobilize religion in order to stake their claim to Dubai's spatial image and reality as a "Muslim place" and thus make their existential experiences as "migrants" meaningful. The Tajiks I met in Dubai created and drew on the cosmopolitan dimension of their Muslim identity to successfully integrate into the Iranian, Afghan, and Arab commercial networks that dominate Dubai's formal and informal business sectors. Doing so, they become active agents in globalizing Central Asia "from below,"[4] while simultaneously contributing to the political imaginaries of—and the lived realities in—the United Arab Emirates.

However, cosmopolitanism is not exclusively discussed as an economic strategy here. Statements such as Fatima's "we are international" point to spatialized identity politics that bear an obvious tension between "the desire to identify with a transnational *Ummah* and the irrepressible trend towards the vernacularization of Islam."[5] When playing cosmopolitan, Tajik migrants in Dubai engage in transnational Muslim politics;[6] i.e., politics that go beyond the limits for constructing Muslim and other identity at home. They thus do not only contest the limited definitions of identity set by the postcolonial secular nation state, Muslim society, and religious institutions at home. When constructing a self-identity as cosmopolitan Dubai businessmen, Tajik migrants also challenge the negative image of provincialism as the "backward," "unskilled," and "foreign Muslim" Other they have to cope with when facing racial discrimination and structural exploitation in Russia. Finally, the provincialism of rural migrants in Tajikistan's capital city feeds an urban anxiety

2 Although Tajik men and women are likewise involved in the Dubai business, this article exclusively focuses on Tajik business*men* and their wives.

3 S. Sadouni, "Playing Global: The Religious Adaptations of Indian and Somali Muslims to Racial Hierarchies and Discrimination in South Africa," *Global Networks*, 14, no. 3 (2014): 383–400.

4 M. Laruelle and S. Peyrouse, *Globalizing Central Asia: Geopolitics and the Challenges of Economic Development* (Armonk, NY: M.E. Sharpe, 2013).

5 C. Jaffrelot, "Transnational Learning Networks Amongst Asian Muslims: An Introduction," *Modern Asian Studies*, 48, no. 2 (2014): 338.

6 P. Mandaville, *Transnational Muslim Politics: Reimagining the Umma* (London: Routledge, 2003).

among a new globally aspiring middle-class that travels with the well-educated urban sophisticated migrants to Dubai.

This chapter draws on a cosmopolitan perspective to investigate the complex realities of globalization across national boundaries. Following Vora and Koch, who argue that "migration patterns and migrant experiences in the Gulf cannot be bound by territorial status but rather implicate global patterns,"[7] I explore how Tajik migrants' transnational religious strategies relate to the opportunities and constraints of Dubai's business sectors, while they simultaneously respond to migration regimes set by an aggressive nationalism combined with xenophobia in Russia and a Muslim-unfriendly and corruption-promoting secularism in Tajikistan.

According to Beck, Tajik migrants' try to re-fashion their work experiences abroad as part of the "cosmopolitanization of reality." That is, a process that is not intentional but the result of "the dynamics of global risk, of mobility and migration and from cultural consumption."[8] When Fatima publicly displays her family's progressive life in Dubai among her friends at home, she links two different kinds of cosmopolitanism. One is the spatial product of the emirate's political project of branding "Dubai"—a project that constructs Dubai as a modern, global, futuristic metropolis. Tajik migrants do not only consume Dubai's cosmopolitan image. They mediate it materially, display it bodily, and thereby contribute to a global consumerism that services the political idea of the *Arabian Gulf*. The second form of cosmopolitanism is a lived reality grounded in Tajik migrants' daily encounters with the cultural diversity and transregional past of the *Persian Gulf*. It materializes in an urban environment, which mixes the economic life and culture of Indian Ocean mercantilism with that of Afghan trading worlds[9] under the umbrella of a "distinctive Indo-Persian Islamic sense of community."[10]

Cosmopolitanism, as used in this chapter, consequently refers to the product of a particular social context rather than to the adoption of a distant normative European model.[11] This framing is in line with recent works on

7   N. Vora and N. Koch, "Everyday Inclusions: Rethinking Ethnocracy, *Kafala*, and Belonging in the Arabian Peninsula," *Studies in Ethnicity and Nationalism*, 15, no. 3 (2015): 541.

8   U. Beck, "Mobility and the Cosmopolitan Perspective," in W. Cancler, V. Kaufmann, and S. Kesselring (eds), *Tracing Mobilities: Towards a Cosmopolitan Perspective* (Burlington, VT: Ashgate 2008), 26.

9   M. Marsden, *Trading Worlds: Afghan Merchants: Across Modern Frontiers* (London: Hurst, 2016).

10   M. Marsden, "Crossing Eurasia: Trans-Regional Afghan Trading Networks in China and Beyond," *Central Asian Survey*, 35, no. 1 (2016): 12.

11   B. Grant, "Cosmopolitan Baku," *Ethos: Journal of Anthropology*, 75, no. 2 (2010): 125.

migration that point to the social contextuality and vernacular rootedness of "migrant cosmopolitanism" or "cosmopolitanism from below," and that emphasize the desire of not-so-economically privileged actors to find, or at least imagine, a place in the world of global economy.[12] But the chapter goes a step further. I argue that when Tajik migrants play cosmopolitan, they simultaneously refer to the complexity of belonging and longing, shaped by the possibilities that Dubai's economic fields, urban environments, and political realities offer them, and the limitations they face and try to overcome. Doing so, Tajik migrants in Dubai produce a sense of cosmopolitanism and therewith situate themselves and make a place in the world through referring, re-evaluating, and re-making specific histories of global engagement.[13]

Situated at the intersection of Central Asian and Gulf studies, the chapter aims at providing a more nuanced picture of how transnational Islamic practices are shaped, reflected, and re-evaluated by Tajiks outside the territorial borders of their country. Although not all Tajik migrants in the Gulf engage in transnational religious self-fashioning; those engaged in transnational Dubai business lifestyles like Ahmad and Fatima engage in materially mediating both the idea of Dubai as a "Muslim place" and the image of the Gulf as a site of a "pure" and "authentic" Islam. In that sense, the chapter challenges prevailing political representations of cross-border Muslim travel and the "Islamization" of selves and lifestyles in Tajikistan's public sphere as a security issue beyond state control and regulation. By contrasting the cosmopolitanism Tajiks migrants in Dubai engage in with the lasting normative effects of what has been constructed as negative cosmopolitanism during the Soviet era, the chapter also aims at deconstructing the "myth" of radicalized Tajik youth who through traveling to the Middle East adopt a "foreign" and "dangerous" Arab or Salafi-inspired Islam.[14]

---

12   P. Werbner (ed.), *Anthropology and the New Cosmopolitanism: Rooted, Feminist, and Vernacular Perspectives* (New York: Berg, 2008); U. Beck, "The Cosmopolitan Society and Its Enemies," *Theory, Culture, and Society,* 19, no. 1–2 (2002): 17–44; L. Landau and I. Freemantle, "Tactical Cosmopolitanism and Idioms of Belonging: Insertion and Self-Exclusion in Johannesburg," *Journal of Ethnic and Migration Studies,* 36, no. 3 (2010): 375–390.

13   F. Osella and C. Osella, "'I am Gulf': The Production of Cosmopolitanism in Kozhikode, Kerala, India," in E. Simpson and K. Kresse (eds), *Struggling with History: Islam and Cosmopolitanism in the Western Indian Ocean* (London: Hurst, 2007), 2.

14   J. Heathershaw and D. Montgomery, "The Myth of Post-Soviet Muslim Radicalization in the Central Asian Republics," *Russia and Eurasia Programme Research Paper.* London: Royal Institute of International Affairs, 2014.

Possibilities and Constraints in the Tajik Dubai Business

Many actors have influenced the evolution of the Tajik Dubai business. They can be grouped into three categories:

- Pioneers: post-Soviet Tajikistan's old and new political elite (most of them influential warlords from the pro-government and opposition parties in the civil war);
- Entrepreneurs: young, well-educated, university-trained male urbanites from middle-class families; and
- Uneducated followers: close-knit work migrants from Russia and rural youngsters from villages and remote areas.

In the mid-1990s, Tajikistan's then-political elite discovered Dubai as an attractive tourist destination and a potential trading hub. Due to historical and cultural relations[15] and military connections in neighboring Afghanistan, cross-border trade began to flourish between the United Arab Emirates and Tajikistan—primarily in luxury cars, smartphones, flat-panel televisions, and modern kitchen appliances, but also in Dubai's well-established Afghan diaspora community. Facilitating social mobility and wealth, the established commercial ties with the Gulf region induced many Tajiks to follow suit, fueling a Dubai boom that reached its apex in 2010.

Well-educated, young Tajik men with degrees in international relations, economics, or journalism from one of the country's national universities or Turkish highschools were particularly attracted to Dubai. Many of them had pursued additional study at an Islamic university in the Middle East, preferably at Cairo's Al-Azhar or a university in the Hejaz. By drawing on their multiple language skills in Farsi, English, Russian, and Arabic, and capitalizing on their secular and religious knowledge, this group of people successfully utilized their foreign contacts to integrate into established Iranian, Afghan, and Arab commercial networks in Dubai. These "innovative small-scale entrepreneurs" significantly contribute to Tajikistan's "bottom-up" integration into the Gulf's

---

15   Tajiks and Afghans share a long history of cohabitation, kinship relations, and exchange. Even during the Soviet era, many Tajik families continued to maintain close relationships with kin across the Tajikistan–Afghanistan border. After the breakdown of the Soviet Union and the succeeding civil war in 1992, several thousand Tajiks fled to neighboring Afghanistan. Because of the shared Persian language and the shared Persian Islamic tradition, Tajiks feel a strong cultural bond with Sunni Muslim Iranians, with Baluch people in Iran, and with the Dari-speaking Tajik population of Afghanistan.

global economy through establishing private enterprise and thereby "embracing the risk of failure."[16] Combining their university degrees with an advanced Islamic knowledge, many of them become successful street brokers (*kamak*), economic middlemen like Ahmad, whereas others such as Farrukh, whose story will follow later, manage to pursue a career in the prestigious real estate sector, combining high earnings with social mobility and spiritual well-being. Like Ahmad and Fatima, many Tajik migrants in Dubai started to invest in a transnational business that link Tajikistan's markets with a globalizing Islamic consumer culture.[17] Once businesses are firmly established, many Tajiks working in Dubai give relatives back in Tajikistan positions as purchasing agents or local partners, thereby consolidating the transnational structure of their economic enterprise. This eventually allows some of them to reside with their families in the Arab Emirates, like Fatima's husband Ahmed does, while simultaneously remaining bound to their birthplace and cultivating forms of multiple belonging.

Dubai's appeal as a business- and Muslim-friendly urban site has also attracted Tajik migrants based in Russia, who, like "Iskandar," left their jobs in Moscow seeking better safety and respect as Muslims:

> Of course, Moscow is a better place (than Dubai) to earn good money. But you are not safe (there). The streets are full of criminals and drunken guys. They attack you ... But I even didn't trust the police. They don't protect you but take your money! ... I wanted to return home (from Russia to Tajikistan)), but as a Gharmi[18] you cannot live a good life. If you have a good business, they[19] come and destroy everything. They even find you in Russia. That's why I came to Dubai. I don't have rights here and cannot move up in my job. ... But I am safe, autonomous (*ozod*), and I am respected as a Muslim. You know, Dubai is a real Muslim place (*mamlakati Musulmonho*).

16 U. Röschenthaler and D. Schulz, "Introduction. Forging Fortunes: New Perspectives on Entrepreneurial Activities in Africa," in U. Röschenthaler and D. Schulz (eds), *Cultural Entrepreneurship in Africa* (New York, London: Routledge, 2016), 1.

17 M. Stephan-Emmrich and A. Mirzoev, "The Manufacturing of Islamic Lifestyles in Tajikistan through the Prism of Dushanbe's Bazaars," *Central Asian Survey*, 35, no. 2 (2016): 157–177.

18 Gharm is a city and region in the Rasht Valley, i.e., an area in the northern part of Central Tajikistan that was a hotbed of the opposition forces during the Civil War of 1992–1997.

19 Here, he refers to the powerful position of the Rahmon clan and the despotic regime they established in the non-state and informal economy sector in Tajikistan.

Like Iskandar, many Tajiks have tried to find their niche in the booming Dubai business in order to escape the religious discrimination and structural exploitation that Muslim migrants from Central Asia have to endure at their workplaces and in daily life in Russia as the "black" (*chernye*) and "backward" (*churka*, i.e., "tree stub") other.[20]

The majority of Tajiks in the United Arab Emirates work in the Russian tourism sector where they concentrate in offering tour guide service and selling fur coats together with other migrants from Central Asia, the Caucasus, and Sub-Saharan Africa. The fur coat market began to flourish in Dubai's old city center around the Creek side, in Dubai Deira, when Russia's urban middle class discovered the United Arab Emirates as a luxury holiday site and a place for conspicuous consumption from the mid-1990s.[21] Subsequently, many Tajiks, with their Russian language skills and cultural experience as part of the Soviet empire (*shakhrvandhoi shuravy*), became involved in the fur coat business. They became traders purchasing fur coats in China, vendors selling Chinese fur coats in Dubai Deira as fakes of high-quality Greek products, or they started working as a *kamak*, i.e., a street broker who directs Russian tourists to fur shops and gets a commission when they purchase something. However, it was the kamak business that evolved as a lucrative economic sector in Dubai because it enabled Tajik migrants to make a considerable amount of money within one holiday season.

Nevertheless, Dubai is a volatile and precarious sector shaped by Tajiks' limited access to the emirate's sponsorship system (*kafala*) that monitors migrant workers' visa and legal status. Only a small group of Tajik migrants may enter the formal job sector, while the majority integrates in the ethnicity-based networks of the kamak business. As a street broker, a kamak only needs a tourist visa, which allows short-term stays but not work permission. Like other migrant workers in Dubai, Tajiks are perpetual visitors,[22] and, since long-term residency is hard to get, they are pushed toward business activities in the gray zone between formal and informal, documented and undocumented work. This situation makes them more vulnerable to arrest and deportation by the local

20   M. Reeves, "Clean Fake: Authenticating Documents and Persons in Migrant Moscow," *American Ethnologist*, 40, no. 3 (2013): 508–524.
21   After Saudi Arabian and British tourists, the ex-Soviet Russian-speaking states provide the third-biggest group of tourists in Dubai. For instance, in 2007 about 300,000 Russian tourists visited Dubai. See <https://thearabianpost.com/TAP/2015/09/dubai-hopes-to-see-return-of-russians.html> and <http://gulfnews.com/news/uae/society/dubai-s-fur-business-feeling-the-heat-1.1484942>.
22   S. Nagy, "Making Room for Migrants, Making Sense of Difference: Spatial and Ideological Expressions of Social Diversity in Urban Qatar," *Urban Studies*, 43, no. 1 (2006): 119–137.

police. But at the same time, business networks in Dubai offer many possibilities for advancement, as well as facilitating alternative forms of citizenship
and "belonging despite exclusion."[23]

We Do Business; We Aren't Migrants!

Although Tajiks are newcomers in Dubai's business sector, some of these
"small-scale entrepreneurs" became very successful. Due to their knowledge,
cultural competences, and social contacts, they easily navigated the commercial activities within and across the Iranian and Afghan diaspora in the Gulf.
None of my interlocutors belonging to this group perceived themselves as
"migrants" (*migranty*); instead, they insisted that they were "doing *biznes*" or
"being *biznesmen*."

Besides, Tajik migrants in Dubai are highly aware of the critical discourse on
migrants' vulnerable status in the Gulf. However, since the majority of them
work in the informal sector and do not have an Arab sponsor (*kafeel*), structural exploitation is something they associate foremost with migrants working
in Russia. When constructing a self-identity as businessmen, my interlocutors
often stressed the level of autonomy (*ozody*) they experience and can cultivate
when working, for example, as kamak. Even Tajiks with a legitimate employment contract and a long-term residence permit like "Kamal," whose story will
be introduced later, try to run a parallel business as middlemen or kamak to
limit dependency on their employers.

Fashioning their informal work as a proper Muslim business, Tajiks also
seek to differentiate themselves from other Asian migrant workers in Dubai
who predominate in low-skilled, poorly paid jobs in construction or in the
home care and hotel service sector. Besides, Asian migrants are perceived as
non-Muslims and do not fit into the Tajiks' idea of Dubai as a Muslim place.

In many conversations I had with Tajik migrants in Dubai, the meaning of
the term "Dubai businessmen" was closely associated with the idea of kamak
work as an honorable profession. This work identity relies on multilingualism,
a university education, cleverness, ingenuity, as well as the ability to "speak in
a cultivated way (*gapi mulloim, gapi bomadaniyat*)" and "to look always clean
and freshly dressed." When returning to Dushanbe, many Tajik kamak can capitalize on their professional reputation and accumulated wealth and enjoy a
high social status. Once, when joining a wedding celebration in Dushanbe's
southern outskirts, I observed how a young man introduced by the host as a

---

23   Vora and Koch, "Everyday Inclusions," 542.

FIGURE 8.3 *On Dubai Deira's vibrant Al-Nasser Square: Muslims performing the Friday prayer*
             nearby the Red Mosque (photo by Stephan-Emmrich, December 2013)

close relative and a *Dubai buzinesmen* was invited to take a seat at the most
honorable place in the guestroom (*bolo*), a place usually reserved for elderly
people.

In sum, the volatility of the Tajik Dubai business combined with the emirate's limited possibilities for legal work and regime of deportation[24] turn
Dubai into a transitory place comparable to the working and living conditions
faced in Russia or Tajikistan. As a consequence, Tajiks involved in the Dubai
business are pushed to be constantly mobile, to combine different modes of
travel and pursue precarious livelihoods. Precariousness here is understood as
both a socioeconomic condition and an ontological experience. On the one
hand, there is the Tajik migrants' lived experience of risk, ambient insecurity,
and uncertain futures. On the other hand, the term applies to processes of sub-
jectivization in translocal regimes of migration that rely on self-responsibility,
flexibility, creativity, and opportunism. When claiming to "do business" in
Dubai, Tajiks migrants in Dubai embrace both the negative and positive components of their precarious lives, as well as embracing a certain optimism by
opening up to a possibility for entrepreneurship, social mobility, and a different mode of subjectivity.[25] This subjectivity is closely related to individual

24   A. Gardner, "Why Do They Keep Coming? Labor Migrants in the Gulf States," in M. Kam-
      rava and Z. Babar (eds), *Migrant Labor in the Persian Gulf* (London: Hurst, 2012), 43.
25   V. Tsianos and D. Papadopoulos, "Precarity: A Savage Journey to the Embodied Heart of
      Capitalism," *European Institute for Progressive Cultural Policies,* 10 (2006), <http://eipcp.

projects of inner reform (*isloh*), that conflate religious self-fashioning with the making of an entrepreneurial self. This reformism is shaped in Dubai's various cosmopolitan business spaces.

Dubai Deira: Connecting with Iranian and Afghan Businesses

Tajiks involved in the fur coat business work and live in and around Al-Nasser Square, near the Baniyas Square subway station in Dubai's old city quarter, Deira. By calling Al-Nasser "our square" (*maydoni mo*) or "Tajik square" (*maydoni Tojik*), Tajiks claim belonging to the lived spaces of Dubai's historical city center around the Creek side. Al-Nasser square offers a complex ethnic and cultural composition shaped by past and present processes of trade and migration. The cosmopolitan environment of this part of the city, also called the "migrant quarter," developed out of the transregional and transcultural commercial ties and networks spanning the Indian Ocean, thereby linking both the historical port city and today's global city with the people, places, and commercial goods of Asia, Africa, and Europe. While most of the migrants and long-term residents in Dubai Deira are from South and Southeast Asia, there are also well-established Iranian and Afghan diasporas, whose members, together with migrants from Sub-Saharan Africa, Central Asia, and the Caucasus, shape urban life and dominate Dubai's transregional trade business.[26]

Tajiks adopt this cosmopolitan city space when dwelling in Dubai Deira's cheap, overcrowded and often culturally mixed migrant guesthouses run by members of the old established Afghan and Iranian diaspora. There, they quickly connect with Afghan traders, Baluchi businesspeople from Iran, and Arab migrants from Egypt or Syria. While business relations with the latter groups are based on Arabic language skills and alumni networks in Cairo and elsewhere, Tajik migrants connect with Sunni-Hanafi Iranians (mostly Baluchi) and Afghans on the basis of cultural and religious familiarity. Referring to a "shared cultural tradition" composed of the Persian language and a body of literature deeply inspired by Sufi-Islamic philosophy and ethics, Tajiks prefer

---

net/transversal/1106/tsianospapadopoulos/en>.

26   Y. Elshashtawy, "Transitory Sites: Mapping Dubai's "Forgotten" Urban Spaces," *International Journal of Urban and Regional Research*, 32, no. 4 (2008): 978; N. Vora, *Impossible Citizens. Dibai's Indian Diaspora* (Durham and London: Duke University Press, 2013); M. Pelican, "Urban Lifeworlds of Cameroonian Migrants in Dubai," *Urban Anthropology*, 43, no. 1–3 (2014), 255–309; L. Kathiravelu, *Migrant Dubai. Low Wage Workers and the Construction of a Global City* (New York: Palgrave Macmillan, 2016).

to stay with Dari-speaking Afghans or Sunni-Hanafi Iranians simply because they are perceived as culturally "closer" (*nazdik*) than Uzbeks or Kyrgyz from Central Asia—or even Uzbeks from Tajikistan. Members of the latter group are not considered "trusted familiars,"[27] and Tajiks would not consider them "our brothers" (*barodari mo*) or as belonging to the same "people" (*milat*). When dwelling in migrant guesthouses, Tajiks become acquainted with different cosmopolitan traditions formed in and through historical trade-related networks and transregional mobilities. Moving in this Persian world of Muslim business contacts, Tajik migrants like Kamal successfully pursue economic, social, and spiritual careers in Dubai.[28]

"Kamal" has worked and lived in Dubai since 2009. Like the majority of his countrymen he began his urban career as a kamak in al-Nasser Square before he, backed by an Afghan roommate, invested in the second-hand car business with some Afghans and an Iranian Baluchi. Thanks to his multiple business trips to Iran, Kamal established connections with the Iranian diaspora in Dubai[29] and eventually became the manager of a fur coat salon in Deira, owned by a Dubai-based Iranian entrepreneur.

Kamal calls the showroom of the fur salon where he works "my office" (*ofisi man*). Here, he regularly meets his Tajik and Afghan business partners to exchange information over a cup of tea; he confers with the Iranian shop owner or the shops' Arab sponsor (*kafeel*). Kamal also briefs newly arrived kamak workers, and he regularly shares his Islamic knowledge among his co-workers and fellow countrymen as part of his self-image as a religiously trained person who "knows Islam." He uses his office to store and manage the money his kamaks earn, and, when needed, uses their money for his own business purposes until they return home to Tajikistan. Altogether, he is an accepted

---

27   C. Osella and F. Osella, "Migration, Networks and Connectedness across the Indian Ocean," in M. Kamrava and Z. Babar (eds), *Migrant Labor in the Persian Gulf* (London: Hurst, 2012), 128.

28   A. Mirzoev and M. Stephan-Emmrich, "Crossing Economic and Cultural Boundaries: Tajik Middlemen in the Translocal 'Dubai Business' Sector," in M. Stephan-Emmrich and P. Schröder (eds), *Mobilities, Boundaries, and Travelling Ideas: Rethinking Translocality Beyond Central Asia and the Caucasus* (Cambridge: Open Book Publishers, forthcoming).

29   Most Iranians live in the Bastaki area north of the Creek, where they cultivate social (through marriage) and cultural (through Arab language) ties with Emiratis. Thus, Iranians are important gatekeepers to stable employment in the trade, tourism, or real estate business, and they may provide access to the Emirati sponsorship system. See A. Parsa and R. Keivani, "The Hormuz Corridor: Building a Cross-Border Region between Iran and the UAE," in S. Sassen (ed.), *Global Networks, Linked Cities* (New York: Routledge, 2002), 183–207.

religious authority among Tajik kamaks in Dubai; he has advanced proficiency in Arabic and extensive religious knowledge due to his study at Yemen's Al-Iman University; his business is built on trust. Besides his social position as a *shaykh* (an honorific title used by the kamaks working in his shop), Kamal has a sterling reputation as a "big businessmen" because he invests his and the kamak's money in small charity projects to support the Tajik community both in Dubai and at home. Whenever I visited him in his shop, Kamal stressed his international business contacts and his Arabic language proficiency, which has also made him the formal translator between the shop owner and his Arab sponsor. Projecting himself as a cosmopolitan businessman, Kamal has demonstrated his personal capacity to enlarge the scope and scale of his economic activities by bridging ethnic and regional boundaries.

Tajik migrants can elevate their social status through religion as well as through economics, especially when kamak business is put on the same level as trading (*tijorat*) and thus associated with the Prophet Muhammad, who himself was a trader. Once, while sitting with Kamal in his office and debating the properness of the kamak profession, he emotionally called out: "We are Muslims, we do business (*biznes*), we do trading (*tijorat mekunem*). We just follow the example of our prophet!" Consequently, business or trading is often articulated as the most suitable work for a Muslim. This position corresponds to the Salafi views that Tajiks encountered in and around in Dubai's multiple migrant guesthouses or in their workplaces, and they invoke it as a powerful resource to legitimize their involvement in undocumented work. The following story is an example.

The negative image Salafis have in Tajikistan as followers of a "foreign" and "radical" Islam "dangerous" for the social coherence of the Tajik nation was a controversial and often-debated topic among Tajik migrants in Dubai. Kamal, however, had a clear position. He willingly sweet-talked them for the sake of his business and his own profits (even though he knows that the kamak working with him do not have a work permit):

> I met a lot of them (Salafis, *salafih*) when I studied in Yemen ... (Salafis) from many nations. (In Dubai) we do business together. They are all good people, pious Muslims (*dindor*). They are big businessmen doing good (*kori nek*) for society. ... They do trading like our prophet did. ... Like me, many Tajiks come to Dubai. We want to do proper work (*kori sof/pok*). We are Muslims (and) tired of feeding our president's family.[30] ... Bribes here, bribes there (*porakhur*). As long as they (his kamak) do not cheat, are

---

30   A common term to refer to the political elite, i.e., the Rahmon clan.

righteous (*insofkor*), and work hard (*kori mehnaty kunand*), they do nothing wrong and they will get what God provides them (*risq*). They just do business, they serve their families, their community.

Kamal advocates a Salafi position by using key terms (*insofkor* or *kori mehnaty*) from Persian philosophy and the Sufi-influenced local Muslim tradition, which previously determined the concepts of morality and civility (*odobu akhloq*) in Tajikistan.[31] Moreover, he propagates a positive image of Salafis because their value-driven interpretation of the Muslim trade business confirms his pious endeavors. Their interpretation justifies Kamal performing the *hijra*, i.e. the religiously motivated emigration from his birthplace to Dubai, in order to flee the secular environment shaping Tajikistan's public sphere. For Kamal, secularism is a regime that forces Muslims to do forbidden work (*kori harom*), i.e., to serve a corrupt and nepotistic regime, and that stigmatizes and criminalizes educated Muslim travelers like him for his "Salafi" sympathies.

When stating, "We are international!" Tajiks migrants in Dubai like Kamal articulate a sense of cosmopolitanism that links business strategies with a certain openness to religious diversity. As the African historian Lecocq has argued in his work on Tuareg mobility and urban cosmopolitanism, "The essential element shaping the participation of groups and individuals in pattern of globalization and the creation of cosmopolitanism is not to be found (merely) in forms of mobility, but in the shape, constitution, and potential of human networks."[32] Leaving one's own ethnicity or kin-based networks and moving abroad, "where the network is thin, and dependency unequally balanced between those who move and those who are already there,"[33] Tajik migrants in Dubai can become economically active and successful outside kin- or ethnicity-based institutionalized Tajik migrant networks abroad. Kamal with his ability to cross-over, translates cultural and economic contexts into a reform-driven Muslim identity that simultaneously embraces an ethnic or culture-based Tajikness and a rather global oriented self-identity as proper Muslim and successful businessmen.

---

31   M. Stephan, *Das Bedürfnis nach Ausgewogenheit Moralerziehung, Islam und Muslimsein in Tadschikistan zwischen Säkularisierung und religiöser Rückbesinnung* (Würzburg: Ergon Verlag, 2010).

32   B. Lecocq, "Tuareg City Blues: Cultural Capital in a Global Cosmopole," in A. Fischer and I. Kohl (eds), *The Tuareg Society Within a Globalized World: Saharian Life in Transition* (London: Tauris Academic Studies, 2010), 43–44.

33   Ibid., 49–50.

However, and as the following story of Farrukh shows, Tajik migrants play cosmopolitan in very different, sometimes contrasting and competing ways. Doing so, a cosmopolitan Muslim identity also can become a marker of socio-economic distinction within the Tajik migrant community in Dubai itself; particularly when Tajiks are able to join Arab-dominated business fields.

Sheikh Zayed Road: Adopting the World of "Corporate Dubai"

Encompassing sites such as the Dubai Marina, Downtown Dubai, and the shopping malls and tourist attractions along Shaikh Zayed Road, "new Dubai" is the spatial representation of the city's highly touted global cosmopolitan future. In what Ahmad Kanna has termed the "city as corporation,"[34] global business meets luxury and exclusive tourism, and heritage-for-consumption development projects try to "sell Arabia" and display an invented Emirati national history that mixes and exclusive Arab-ness with a modern Muslim identity. Devoid of cultural hybridity and Western modernity, the image of an "authentic" Arabian Gulf aims to serve the consumer aspirations and well-being of high-spending tourists and international business executives.[35]

The material representations and ideological underpinnings of Dubai's urban planning directly reflect the local demography. Only 10 percent of Dubai's population is Emirati; the rest are foreign residents (European businesspeople, Asian and African entrepreneurs, migrant workers, and diaspora families). Moreover, the government is complicit in promoting an elitist and exclusive Emirati nationalism displayed in the spectacular architecture of "new Dubai." A sharp demarcation is created that disregards Tajik and other migrant workers and their cultural lifestyles. Even more, the cosmopolitanism of the "foreign Other," contributing to the multicultural life and transregional commercial networks in "old Dubai," is interpreted negatively as something that dilutes the purity of Emirati culture and Muslimness. Urban planning by the Emirati state therefore legitimizes migrants' and other foreigners' exclusion from political and social citizenship.[36]

Nevertheless, like many other foreigners in the emirate, Tajik migrants consume the global cosmopolitanism of "new Dubai" in materialistic ways. Thus, they claim belonging to the city and actively contribute to "the naturalization

---

34   A. Kanna, *Dubai, the City as Corporation* (Minneapolis: University of Minnesota Press, 2011).

35   Vora, *Impossible Citizens*, 47–49.

36   Ibid., 36.

of racial, national, and other categories that circumscribe Gulf geographies and forms of belonging."[37] They visit Dubai's tourist sites with their families or co-workers on weekends and holidays; they have dinner in Arab restaurants; and they guide Russian tourists on their sightseeing tours through "new Dubai." When the wives of Tajik migrants like Fatima buy fashionable *abaya* and hijab or stylish home decorations in Dubai's many shopping malls, they also consume the publicly advertised Arab elitism.

However, their face-to-face encounters with "real" Emiratis in Dubai are very limited (even the police conducting street raids are non-Emirati Arabs). Still, Tajiks both in Dubai and Tajikistan try, or at least aspire, to create connections with Arabs, either through business or marriage, in order to upgrade their social status back home in Tajikistan. Meanwhile, the perception that Emiratis are unreachable has created ambivalent feelings toward Arabs in general. Tajiks discuss the corrupt practices of local policemen, the ill-mannered behavior of Arab kids, and the lack of urban taste (*odob-u akhloq*) among Arabs whom Tajiks met during their student days in Cairo or when visiting the Hejaz while performing the Hajj pilgrimage to Mecca. The topics of these discussions stand in sharp contrast to Emiratis' posh lifestyle and the Tajiks' assumption that Arabs have a high level of religious knowledge because of their proximity to the holy sites in Mecca and Medina, to the truth of the Quran due to their language proficiency, and to the proximity to the Prophet Muhammad's family. This assumption feeds into an idealized view of Arabs as proper Muslims and promotes the association of Dubai's hyper-modernity with an Arab Islam. Accordingly, through consumption, Tajik migrants long to become part of a new global, post-Western Muslim modernity, which combines autocratic Islamic governance with neoliberal economy.[38]

Arab-led companies and enterprises in Dubai's Islamic economy push this narrative as they help propagate the image of a rising global, and rather elitist, Muslim entrepreneurialism associated with the corporate spirit in the "new Dubai" area.[39] Entering Arabs' business worlds through formal work contracts marks a successful career in the Dubai business. Besides, many of the young, well-educated, and urban sophisticated Tajiks in Dubai absorb the spirit of global Muslim entrepreneurialism cultivated in some Arab companies in order to distance themselves from the poorly trained rural newcomers.

---

37   Vora and Koch, "Everyday Inclusions," 547.

38   Kathiravelu, *Migrant Dubai*, 39.

39   "Chat with Dr. Sayd Farook," *Gulf Elite*, <http://gulfelitemag.com/chat-with-dr-sayd-farook-islamic-economy-entrepreneurship-and-the-dubai-startup-ecosystem/>.

Drawing on theological discourses circulating in the corporate environment of Dubai's Islamic economy, some of the Tajik employees I met articulated a sense of cosmopolitan Muslim elitism. They attempted to distance themselves from their countrymen by labeling them as "migrants" and constructing them as the Tajik Muslim "other." One of these people is "Farrukh," a young Tajik men in his early twenties whom I accidentally met in a Pakistani restaurant in Dubai Deira. With help from his older brother, who is has been working in a Dubai-based charity company since 2005, Farrukh got a two-year job contract in a real estate company near Sheikh Zayed Road; everyone else in this office is Arab. During our discussion, he insisted on not being called Tajik and pressed me to speak only in English. "I am Muslim," he often stressed during our business lunches, articulating his desire to belong to a new, global, and elite class of Muslim professionals. In this way, he distinguishes himself from the Tajik kamak business, which, unlike many other Tajik migrants, was not his route for entering Dubai's business scene:

> My company works for international clients. I only speak English and started to learn Arabic as well. ... Because in my office we are only Arabs. I don't come here (to Al-Nasser Square), only sometimes for lunch. My workplace is close to Sheikh Zayed Road. This is my world ... I don't mingle with Tajik migrants (*migranty*) here. They do kamak work, which is *haram*. They get commission from the fur coat sales. According to the Sharia (*shariyat*), this counts as *riba* (usury). For Muslims it is not permitted to engage in such kind of work. But the majority of Tajiks doesn't know Islam very well. ...Also, many (Tajiks) don't have a work permit. They work illegally (*ghayriqonuny*). I don't like that.

By referring to a prominent legal debate on Islamic economy (particularly Islamic banking), Farrukh demonstrates his savoir faire in global Islamic discourses and thereby emphasizes his superior position and the successful urban career he made as a Tajik in the Dubai business sector. Furthermore, by pointing to the undocumented status of most Tajiks in the emirate, he plays with the negative image that the informal economy had during Soviet times, and, according to the normative Soviet discourse, associates kamak work with cheating, impurity, disorder, and shame;[40] an image Farrukh wants to over-

---

40   D. Kaneff, "The Shame and Pride of Market Activity: Morality, Identity, and Trading in Postsocialist Rural Bulgaria," in R. Mandel and C. Humphrey (eds), *Markets and Moralities: Ethnographies of Postsocialism* (Oxford: Berg, 2002), 33–52; E. Nasritdinov and K. O'Conner, *Regional Change in Kyrgyzstan: Bazaars, Cross-Border Trade, and Social Networks* (Saar-

come through pious self-fashioning and doing proper work. His background as the son of a diplomat, who belonged to the well-connected urban elite of the late Soviet Union, impacts his current mindset and reveals an urban fear of a provincialism, which travels with the Tajik migrants and jeopardizes the value of the Dubai business as an important marker for social distinction.

Fashioning a piety compatible with reformism and neoliberalism, Dubai's vibrant field of Islamic economy offers Tajik migrants new ways of "being Muslim" and a new self-image belonging to the umma outside nationality, ethnicity, or culturally determined identity frameworks. Simultaneously, the Muslim entrepreneurialism discourse pushed in the Arabian Gulf empowers Tajiks to make sense of their precarious visa status and risky economic undertakings, as well as to legitimize their undocumented and often illicit business practices by attaching a religious meaning to them.

This also becomes obvious when Tajik migrants wear national Gulf dresses (*thawb*) at their workplace. Selective clothing is a strategy to obscure ethnic identity and avoid being recognized by Russian clients as "Tajiks"; it is also a practice of camouflage done to be publicly invisible (also to the local police). Jamal is a kamak I run into nearby Banyas Square in November 2013. Working for a fur salon in Dubai Deira, he usually wears a white thawb at work and explained:

> I don't want to be recognized as a Tajik. Russians don't like us, really. Once, I invited one Russian tourist to visit our (fur coat) shop. But he became very angry and rant, "Hey, get lost damn Tajik. I came (to Dubai) to recover from you guys (Tajik migrants). So, get off my back." Therefore, many of us wear Arab clothing (at work) to hide. I started to wear it after returning from the Hajj. ... In such dress you are invisible for the local police as well. As you know, policemen became very clever and conduct their raids now in plainclothes. So, we cannot escape quickly enough.

Wearing Arab-style clothing can also be an attempt to display a successful spiritual image as a reform-minded Muslim. Performing the Hajj pilgrimage to Mecca is a part of this image, and Tajiks do everything to feel assimilated in Dubai as a "Muslim place." By claiming to belong to the city that way, Jamal seeks to transcend the stigma of being a "Tajik migrant" and the boundaries this stigma produces in both Russia and Dubai. The situation of Tajik migrants

---

brücken: Lambert Academic Publishing, 2010); H. Alff, "Basarökonomie im Wandel: Postsowjetische Perspektiven des Handels in Zentralasien," *Geographische Rundschau*, 65, no. 11 (2013): 20–25; Stephan-Emmrich and Mirzoev, "The Manufacturing of Islamic Lifestyles."

resembles the way young Egyptians aspire to make global modernity their own by migrating to Europe. Anthropologist Samuli Schielke, in his work on migratory expectations in Egypt, links cosmopolitanism with longing and emphasizes that Egyptian youngsters' horizon of possibility is strikingly limited and restricted.[41] Following his notion of cosmopolitanism as "a modality of both action and imagination," I argue that Tajik migrants in Dubai engage in a world evoked by the spatial representations and realities of Dubai's cosmopolitan business spaces, which in reality is full of borders and "inhabited by people who try to cross them."[42]

Re-thinking "Migrant Cosmopolitanism"

Tajik migrants participate in Dubai's various business endeavors through different economic and religious practices. They adapt to and interact with a culturally diverse and dynamic urban Muslim environment and thereby show a competence to maneuver through different systems of meaning. Utilizing different cultural registers to be successful, Tajiks become cosmopolitans in Hannerz's sense.[43] However, when Tajik migrants play cosmopolitan, they do not only celebrate cultural sophistication. They at the same time produce as well as cope with boundaries and exclusions, which draw from a wide range of meaning-producing structures and experiences. While a shared cultural proximity allows Tajik migrants to capitalize on Afghan and Iranian business networks and join processes of cultural and economic globalization, the "corporate" and elitist world of the Arab-dominated global Islamic economy in Dubai is hardly attainable. But Tajik migrants still aspire, imitate, and consume habits, lifestyle products, and discursive references to Arabs' business worlds and thereby articulate belonging to the Gulf outside the structurally limited framework of citizenship. According to Vertovec, the production of new arrangements through cosmopolitan practices does not occur in an "unbridled horizon of cultural appropriation and enactment."[44] Social actors are always

---

41 S. Schielke, "Engaging the World on the Alexandria Waterfront," in K. Graw and S. Schielke (eds), *The Global Horizon: Expectations of Migration in Africa and the Middle East* (Leuven: Leuven University Press, 2012), 175–192; see also Grant, "Cosmopolitan Baku," 134.

42 Schielke, "Engaging the World on the Alexandria Waterfront," 178.

43 U. Hannerz, "Cosmopolitans and Locals in World Culture," in M. Featherstone (ed.), *Global Culture: Nationalism, Globalization, and Modernity* (London: Sage, 1990), 237–251.

44 S. Vertovec, "Cosmopolitanism," in K. Knott and S. McLoughlin (eds), *Diasporas: Concepts, Intersections, Identities* (London: Zed Books, 2010), 66.

"embedded in a constellation of relations and structures"[45] that shape and constrain their actions in multiple ways.

But how does the cosmopolitan attitude Tajiks display materialize, aside from cultivating multilingualism, internationalism, or urban sophisticated-ness? Many Tajik men in Dubai dream of marrying an Arab woman but are unable to due to the high dowry (*mahr*) expectations and their status as for-eign migrant workers. In other words, the Muslim business cosmopolitanism of Tajik migrants in Dubai is not necessarily only a lived experience, but above all an imagination—a longing—that reveals the limitations and constraints placed on them not only in the United Arab Emirates, but also in Russia and even in Tajikistan.[46]

Pointing to the mutual conditionality of longing and belonging inherent in cosmopolitanism, I have also shown how Tajiks, when moving in and across their culturally diverse business networks or when engaging in cosmopolitan Muslim spaces, simultaneously emphasize sameness and cope with difference. Doing so, Tajik migrants in Dubai thus do not preserve but continuously re-evaluate and reformulate identity and therewith become deeply involved in ethics of obligation or local engagement. This goes beyond what Landau and Freemantle have coined "tactical cosmopolitanism," i.e., a strategy used by migrants in South Africa to capitalize on cosmopolitanism's power without becoming bound to its spatial responsibilities.[47] In the context of Tajik migrants' engagement in reform-minded self-making projects linked to Muslim business and entrepreneurialism, such an understanding of vernacular cosmo-politanism runs the risk of narrowing down the complexity of my interlocutors' lives in Dubai to economic benefits only; thereby obscuring the fact that politi-cal, social, and above all spiritual regimes matter and form the context in which my interlocutors act as, dream, and strive to become cosmopolitan.

By adopting religious strategies, Tajiks convert their status as "migrants" into that of "Muslim businessmen." This chapter has critically scrutinized the often one-dimensional and politically charged conceptualization of "foreign migrant workers" in the Gulf, which obscures Tajiks' active involvement and symbolic work in different forms of (non-)religious placemaking. Thus, the chapter has offered a more nuanced picture of everyday life in Dubai that goes beyond the "spectacularity" of the city. It also challenges the narrow understanding of

45   Ibid.
46   Schielke, "Engaging the World on the Alexandria Waterfront."
47   Landau and Freemantle, "Tactical Cosmopolitanism and Idioms of Belonging."

Dubai as merely a "Middle Eastern" city[48] that is part the Arabian Gulf. Instead, it focused on how Dubai is imagined and shaped by Tajiks as a "Muslim place."

With its cosmopolitan gaze, the chapter has offered insight into how Central Asian affairs, such as the excluding cultural politics of urban middle classes, or the moral assessment of corruption in the state-dominated job market, are "carried across" by Tajik migrants to the Gulf and negotiated by them outside their "home" region. Nevertheless, the precarious conditions under which Tajik migrants in Dubai play cosmopolitan indicate the crucial role national regimes and forms of secular and nationalist governance play in determining how migrants negotiate, re-value, and articulate Muslim identity under the global condition. Putting emphasis on the complex links between religion and economy, this chapter has also exemplified the limits of methodological nationalism to understand Islam in Tajikistan and wider Central Asia as a lived reality shaped by translocal, mobile livelihoods. Arguably, Tajiks' engagement in cosmopolitan Muslim contexts can result in a heigthened openness toward religious diversity and a heightened mobility within and across different Islamic traditions. Rather than pushing a much invoked and state-feared "Arabization" that imports a de-culturized, puristic Salafi Islam hostile to local and culturally formed Islamic practices, the existential experiences of Tajiks migrants-as-businessmen in Dubai can contribute to a more diverse and differentiated picture of transnational Islam.

---

48   Vora, *Impossible Citizens*, 3.

CHAPTER 9

Informal Economies in the Post-Soviet Space: Post-Soviet Islam and Its Role in Ordering Entrepreneurship in Central Asia

Rano Turaeva

Post-Soviet Central Asia is still undergoing economic and political crises result-ing from both external global forces as well as internal challenges. With non-performing states, non-functioning economies, and ridiculously low state salaries, all levels of society, economics, and politics has become increasingly informalized. This vacuum within the state legal system has been filled by other forms of regulation, such as religion and other traditional forms of obli-gation, duties, and local arbitration. Informal economies have flourished not only in Central Asia, but all over the post-Soviet space. Economic hardships have provided incentives for creativity and innovation among economic entre-preneurs. Both men and women became mobile entrepreneurs to "find money," as they explain their actions. Economic activities, sometimes combined with formal employment, have been described in terms of survival strategies such as *tirikchilik* ("muddling through").[1]

When I inquired about these activities to four groups of female Turkmen entrepreneurs conducting economic activities (mainly trade) between Tas-hauz, Uzbekistan, and Dubai, they used phrases such as *pul tapish* ("find money" or "earning"), *qiyin bolip qaldi hamma sarson sargardon yolda hatin-laram erkaklaram, arkakla orisda hatinla Dubaida* (It became difficult to earn money, so everyone became mobile and went on the road (said in a negative tone); men went to Russia and women to Dubai).[2]

Entrepreneurs have created a kind of social formation comparable to an economic class since the fall of the Soviet Union. Furthermore, informal econ-omies are particularly well-suited for this type of class, as will be discussed in

---

1   R. Turaeva, "Post-Soviet Uncertainties: Micro-orders of Central Asian Migrants in Russia," *Inner Asia*, 15, no. 2 (2013): 273–292; R. Turaeva, "Mobile Entrepreneurs in Post-Soviet Central Asia: Micro-orders of *Tirikchilik*," *Communist and Post-Communist Studies*, 47, no. 1 (2014): 105–114.

2   Author's interviews with a group of women entrepreneurs from Tashauz, Turkmenistan, and conducted in Urgench, Uzbekistan, in 2008 and 2012.

detail below.[3] Islamic rules and other moral commitments and obligations filled the vacuum created by the dearth of functioning state regulations across Central Asia and Russia. Religious, ethnic, and kinship systems provided the social and economic security that national welfare systems failed to provide after the collapse of the Soviet welfare system. Elders, religious leaders, and other respected figures became the governing body on the ground in the context of withering states.

For migrant workers in Russia or anywhere far from home, Islamic belonging became a stronger marker of identity than ethnicity, and mosque communities have grown in influence. Mosques became places of socializing and meeting where contacts are established and maintained. Entrepreneurs visit mosques to make contacts, arrange deals, and seek justice and punishment for free riders or debtors. As one of my respondents said, "*Vse sdelki osushchesvtliaiutsia v mecheti a gde eshche, v mecheti kogda dvoe zakliuchaiut sdelky mezhdu nimi stoit bog i bog sudia*" (All deals are made in the mosques; where else (should someone do this). In the mosque God stands between the two who are making a deal, and God is the only judge for them).[4] Mosques back in Central Asia have not taken on the important role of regulating informal activities if other safety-net structures, such as family and kinship networks, do this job.[5]

In the context of failed states and flourishing informal economies, uncertainty, increased mobility, and globalization, people became increasingly innovative, and a growing number of mobile entrepreneurs have found their niches within and outside of these processes and structures. Since mobility does not recognize rigid state legal systems and boundaries, mobile entrepreneurs have found alternative ways to regulate and administer their economic activities. Today mobile entrepreneurs are the largest category of people who have formed a distinct new economic class

The chapter is structured as follows. First, I trace the formation of informal economies, including the emergence of entrepreneurs in the early Soviet

---

3   K. Meagher, "Trading on Faith: Religious Movements and Informal Economic Governance in Nigeria," *Journal of Modern African Studies,* 47, no. 3 (2009): 397–423.

4   The respondent is a Moscow-based religious and political leader among Central Asian migrants and widely connected both in Russia and Central Asia. Informal conversations with the author since 2014, both face-to-face and, more recently, via Viber mobile application.

5   Author's interviews with migrants and their families in Uzbekistan, Tajikistan, and Turkmenistan. Interviews and informal conversations were conducted in 2012, 2013, 2014, and 2015 in Uzbekistan; 2015 in Tajikistan; 2012 in Uzbekistan with 8 Turkmen families from Tashauz; and follow-up conversations via Line and Telegram mobile messenger during 2014 and 2015.

period and the establishment of an entrepreneurial class today. Furthermore, I introduce the post-Soviet informal economy followed by sections on entrepreneurship and the role of Islam in regulating informal economies and entrepreneurial activities. Finally, I briefly describe Islam and the religious situation in Uzbekistan to show some examples of the domestic context of Central Asian entrepreneurs.

The data for this chapter is derived from both longitudinal research on migrants and social networks in Uzbekistan in 2005–2006, shorter research stays in 2010–2011, and brief visits (less than six weeks) in the years 2008, 2012, 2013, 2014, and 2015 in Uzbekistan, Kazakhstan, Tajikistan, and Kyrgyzstan. The respondents from Turkmenistan were visiting Uzbekistan when they were interviewed. Similarly, those entrepreneurs who work both in Russia and Kazakhstan were interviewed in Uzbekistan during the above-mentioned times. The data presented in this chapter is not systematic since no systematic research has been conducted on the particular topic to date. The argument of this chapter, therefore, is based on my native knowledge of the region in addition to data collected on other topics such as migration, identity, and inter-ethnic relations. My knowledge on state regulation mainly comes from ethnographic research at *propiska* (registry) offices in Central Asia and Russia, and policy research conducted in 2010 and 2011.[6] The main aim of this chapter to advance some of my initial hypothesis in the field of alternative regulation of informal economies in the post-Soviet space, which so far has not received enough attention.[7]

Informal Economies in Soviet and Post-Soviet Space: Early Entrepreneurs

Informalization processes have become stronger and more widespread. Today we speak of informal economies and/or practices not only in third-world countries or the Global South but also in the North. Space does not permit a full discussion about the accelerated informalization of economies, governance, and politics, but it is worth mentioning that informalization is relevant

---

6   R. Turaeva, *Migration and Identity: The Uzbek Experience* (New York: Routledge, 2016).

7   J. Morris and A. Polese, *The Informal Post-Socialist Economy: Embedded Practices and Livelihoods* (New York: Routledge, 2014); A. Polese, J. Morris, and B. Kovács, "Introduction: The Failure and Future of the Welfare State in Post-Socialism," *Journal of Eurasian Studies*, 6, no. 1 (2015): 1–5.

when one describes economic activities anywhere in the world today.[8] There is, by now, a large body of literature on informal economies. There were always two opposite camps dividing this body of literature, namely positive views and optimistic accounts and negative views with pessimistic accounts, whether on informal economies, states, or social networks.[9] The literature on the informal economy is mainly based on examples from Africa, Latin America, and Europe. However, there are also some works based on the USSR.[10] Informal

8   D. Cassel and U. Cichy "Explaining the Growing Shadow Economy in East and West: A Comparative System Approach," *Comparative Economic Studies*, 28 (1986): 20–41; V. Tanzi, "Underground Economy and Tax Evasion in the United States: Estimates and Implication," *Banca Nazionale del Lavoro Quarterly Review*, 32 (1980): 427–453; J. Roitman, *Fiscal Disobedience: Anthropology of Economic Regulation in Central Africa* (Princeton, NJ: Princeton University Press, 2005); K. Meagher, "Culture Agency and Power: Theoretical Reflections on Informal Economic Networks and Political Process DIIS." *Working Paper No. 2009-27* (Copenhagen: Danish Institute for International Studies, 2009); K. Meagher, "The Politics of Vulnerability: Exit, Voice, and Capture in Three Nigerian Informal Manufacturing Clusters," in L. Ilda (ed.), *Africa's Informal Workers: Collective Agency, Alliances, and Transnational Organizing* (London: Zed Books, 2010), 46–64.

9   Cassel and Cichy, "Explaining the Growing Shadow Economy"; Tanzi, "Underground Economy and Tax Evasion in the United States"; E.V. Tokman (ed.), *Beyond Regulation: The Informal Sector in Latin America* (Boulder, CO: Lynne Rienner, 1992; Roitman, *Fiscal Disobedience*; Meagher, "The Politics of Vulnerability"; J. MacGaffey and R. Bazenguissa-Ganga, *Congo-Paris: Transnational Traders on the Margins of the Law Transnational Traders on the Margins of the Law* (Bloomington: Indiana University Press, 2000); C. Muldrew, *The Economy of Obligation* (London: Macmillan, 1998).

10   A.V. Ledeneva, *Russia's Economy of Favours: Blat, Networking, and Informal Exchange* (New York: Cambridge University Press, 1998); A.V. Ledeneva, *How Russia Really Works: Informal Practices in the 1990s* (Ithaca, NY: Cornell University Press, 2006); A.V. Ledeneva, *Can Russia Modernize? Sistema, Power Networks and Informal Governance* (Cambridge: Cambridge University Press, 2013); M. Markova, "Living Through the Fall of Communism: Life Narratives of the Last Soviet Generation" (Ph.D. Diss., University of Washington, 2010); Morris and Polese, *The Informal Post-Socialist Economy*; Polese, Morris, and Kovács, "Introduction"; J. Round, C.C. Williams, and P. Rodgers, "Everyday Tactics and Spaces of Power: The Role of Informal Economies in Post-Soviet Ukraine," *Social & Cultural Geography*, 9, no. 2 (2008): 171–185; G. Mars and Y. Altman, "The Cultural Bases of Soviet Georgia's Second Economy," *Europe-Asia Studies*, 35, no. 4 (1983): 546–560; J.S. Berliner, "The Informal Organization of the Soviet Firm," *Quarterly Journal of Economics*, 66, no. 3 (1952): 342–365; G. Grossman, "The 'Second Economy' of the USSR," *Problems of Communism*, 26, no. 5 (1977): 25–40; V.G. Treml and M.V. Alexeev, "The Growth of the Second Economy in the Soviet Union and its Impact on the System," in R.W. Campbell (ed.), *The Postcommunist Economic Transformation* (Boulder, CO: Westview Press, 1994), 221–248; C. Humphrey (ed.), *Marx Went Away but Karl Stayed Behind* (Ann Arbor: Michigan University Press, 1998); S. Kotkin, *Magnetic Mountain: Stalinism as a Civilization*

economies during the Soviet era ran parallel to the central state planned economy.[11]

There is scant literature on the informal economy during the Soviet era, but these studies suggest that informal economies functioned in the gray area between legal and illegal.[12] There is some literature on shuttle traders (*chelnoki/chelnochkovii biznes*) in the late Soviet era.[13] Cieślewska describes female shuttle traders who were *chelnoki* during the Soviet period in Kyrgyzstan and who are now trading in the Dordoy bazaar in Kyrgyzstan.[14] Her informants[15] share their history of starting their economic activities during the Soviet era, stories that resemble those I was told in Uzbekistan or in Turkmenistan. I myself knew women *chelnoki* from Khorezm in Uzbekistan who were schoolteachers by day in the late 1980s and who moonlighted selling products imported from China and Italy.

I went to school during the Soviet period and remember very well daily life in a small town in Uzbekistan, a small town in Turkmenistan, as well as some parts of Russia, Ukraine, and the Baltic region. During the Soviet era, small-scale traders found their niche within the centralized Soviet supply system. Specifically, they found their place *pod prilavkom*, which translates as "under the table." They sold quality products supplied under *moskovskoe obespechenie* ("Moscow provision," described below). The term *pod prilavkom* was applied to

(Berkeley: University of California Press, 1995); M. Kaiser, "Die Soziologie in der Republik Usbekistan," *Bielefeld University Working Paper No. 265* (Bielefeld: Bielefeld University, 1997).

11   A. Portes and J. Böröcz, "The Informal Sector under Capitalism and State Socialism: A Preliminary Comparison," *Social Justice*, 15, no. 3–4 (Fall/Winter 1988): 17–28; Morris and Polese, *The Informal Post-Socialist Economy*; Polese, Morris, and Kovács, "Introduction"; Round, Williams, and Rodgers, "Everyday Tactics and Spaces of Power"; Mars and Altman, "The Cultural Bases of Soviet Georgia's Second Economy"; Berliner, "The Informal Organization of the Soviet Firm."

12   Markova, "Living Through the Fall of Communism."

13   I. Mukhina, "New Losses, New Opportunities: (Soviet) Women in the Shuttle Trade, 1987–1998," *Journal of Social History*, 43, no. 2 (2009): 341–359; C. Humphrey, "Traders, 'Disorder,' and Citizenship Regimes in Provincial Russia," in M. Burawoy and K. Verdery (eds), *Uncertain Transition: Ethnographies of Change in the Postsocialist World* (Lanham, MD: Rowman and Littlefield, 1999): 19–52; N. Pohorila and G. Korzhov, "Self-Identification in the Society of Crisis: A Case of Cross-Border Traders," *Naukovi zapiski Kievo-Mogilianskoi akademii*, 19 (2001): 58–64; Markova, "Living Through the Fall of Communism"; A. Cieślewska, "From Shuttle Trader to Businesswomen," in J. Morris and A. Polese (eds), *The Informal Post-Socialist Economy: Embedded Practices and Livelihoods* (New York: Routledge, 2014), 50–121.

14   Cieślewska, "From Shuttle Trader to Businesswomen," 213.

15   Ibid.

the situation where products that usually not available in normal shops were sold door-to-door. Enterpreneurship and informal trade were illegal during the Soviet Union, and therefore the products acquired *pod prilavkom* were sold secretly. The respondents from Kyrgyzstan who were also involved in this trade remembered this profession under the term *fartsovshchik* (shuttle trader).[16] My mother was a frequent client of three female *chelnoki* who procured clothing, shoes, and cosmetics. The prices were, of course, higher than normal prices at that time but could be paid in small installments.

"Moscow provision" (*moskovskoe obespechenie*) refers to special products supplied exclusively to specially designated cities (mainly strategically important places and enterprises all over the Soviet Union).[17] Traders who had access to such special products could resell these items to well-off people who could afford better quality items such as shampoos, shoes, clothing, and so on. My parents used to buy those products; I remember, for example, L'Oreal shampoos, knitted wear and jeans from India, Italian shoes, and some clothing from China. These items were labeled *importnyi*—imported.

In addition to *chelnoki*, these small-scale traders were called *spekulyant* (speculators) during the Soviet period, which had a negative connotation.[18] In the late Soviet period, during *perestroika*, it became very popular for Soviet citizens to go to Poland and return home with items to sell. With this practice, the word or label *spekulyant* transformed into the more respectable *biznesmen*. The former label *spekulyant* was more often applied to women, while *biznesmen* typically referred to men. Eventually, in the post-Soviet era, *biznesmen* began to be applied to both men and women.

Since the collapse of the USSR, informal economic activities have increased dramatically, and employment patterns have drastically changed.[19] Security and survival strategies meant that people had to search for employment outside the collapsing state enterprise system. There was no longer an economic or social incentive to remain in state-provided jobs. As many of my respondents said, "Everybody went into the street—doctors and teachers ... Everybody

---

16   Ibid., 213; Humphrey, "Traders, 'Disorder,' and Citizenship Regimes in Provincial Russia."

17   T. Mostowlansky, "The Road Not Taken: Enabling and Limiting Mobility in the Eastern Pamirs," *Internationales Asien Forum*, 45, no. 1–2 (April 2014): 153–170.

18   See the following authors writing on these terms to compare the same categories throughout the Soviet Union: Mukhina, "New Losses, New Opportunities"; Humphrey, "Traders, 'Disorder,' and Citizenship Regimes in Provincial Russia"; Pohorila and Korzhov, "Self-Identification in the Society of Crisis"; Markova, "Living Through the Fall of Communism"; Cieślewska, "From Shuttle Trader to Businesswomen."

19   J. Nazpary, *Post-Soviet Chaos: Violence and Dispossession in Kazakhstan* (London: Pluto Press, 2002).

is a taxi driver now," meaning that even doctors and teachers have abandoned their professions to do something else for living. In part, their official salaries are so small that even doctors and teachers sought more lucrative activities.[20]

As the following examples demonstrate, the informal economy has become more and more relevant to the point that by now it is the only way to secure sufficient income. These examples are taken from Uzbekistan, but similar employment patterns exist in Tajikistan, Kyrgyzstan, and Turkmenistan.

There are different categories of state and non-state employment that offer varying incentives to job seekers in their employment choices. These employment patterns resemble those in other low-income countries, such as in Latin America or Horn of Africa.[21] There are three categories of occupations people usually define in terms of their prestige, the "real" income from an occupation. The first category is comprised of positions such as police chief, customs officer, and so on. These positions are within the state system of employment, which does not pay well, but they potentially provide a steady source of extra income from payments (basically bribes) made by clients of the relevant offices.

The second—and least desirable—occupational category is called simply *davlat ishinda* (state work). This category has low salaries and little opportunity for additional income. Even so, individuals try to retain state employment status as long as possible by keeping their name on the books as if he or she still works, and the salary is collected by the person who maintains the employment registry. This strategy allows a "ghost employee" to demonstrate continuous employment in their work book[22] and to maintain pension eligibility (although pensions are not higher than average salaries).

---

20   The quotations stem not only from my original research in Uzbekistan (2005–2006, 2010–2011), but also from informal conversations throughout my other stays in the region from people of different backgrounds and genders.

21   T. Raeymaekers, K. Menkhaus, and K. Vlassenroot, "State and Non-State Regulation in African Protracted Crises: Governance without Government?", *Africa Focus*, 21, no. 2 (2008): 7–21; K.T. Hansen and M. Vaa (eds), *Reconsidering Informality: Perspectives from Urban Africa* (Uppsala: North Africa Institute, 2004); W.F. Maloney, "Informality Revisited," *World Bank Economic Review*, 32, no. 7 (2004): 1159–178; M.A. Chen, "Rethinking the Informal Economy: Linkages with the Formal Economy and the Formal Regulatory Environment," in B. Guha-Khasnobis, R. Kanbur, and E. Ostrom (eds), *Linking the Formal and Informal Economy: Concept and Measures* (Oxford: Oxford University Press, 2006), 75–92.

22   *Trudovoi* is the adapted local Uzbek version of *Trudovaia knizhka* (Russian: work book). The work book is a small, brochure-like document where citizens' work places are registered. On each page of the employment record, there are two stamps for the records

The next category is *biznes*, which includes both formal and informal trade and which automatically mean that it brings real money. I will focus on this category in a more detailed manner below. *Biznes* refers to an occupation consisting mainly of trade or other forms of self-employment that are known for bringing real money. This often refers to informal economic activities, where there may not be a clear divide between formal business and informal one. This sphere of economic activities is locally defined under the term of *tirikchilik*, which I have elsewhere described in a more detailed manner.[23]

There are differences in governing patterns and the context of Soviet-style legal system when comparing informal economies in post-Soviet space with those found on the African continent or Latin America. Soviet-style governance outlived in many post-Soviet Republics including Central Asia and Russia. Soviet-style governance structures still shape these economies. There is a whole segment of literature on post-socialist informal economies that considers the peculiarities of the socialist past and how they affect current forms of economic activities.[24]

None of the above-mentioned literature has systematically examined the basis of these "informal" economic activities nor studied the principles used to regulate them. Informal economies involve such practices as oral agreements, enforcement of the rules by various means, reciprocity, exchange, religious beliefs and rules (*islamskie normy*, Islamic norms) as well as the pressure of status maintenance. These have been studied in connection with other topics such as kinship and/or religion. Islamic norms are not static, but produced

of acceptance to the job and another stamp is for the records on the release from the job with the clear indication of dates the person worked at this place and the reasons of his/her release. This official document is necessary for claiming a state pension later. Experts advise to avoid having gaps in employment records.

23 Turaeva, "Post-Soviet Uncertainties"; Turaeva, "Mobile Entrepreneurs in Post-Soviet Central Asia."

24 S. Johnson, D. Kaufmann, and A. Schleifer, "The Unofficial Economy in Transition," *Brookings Institution Papers on Economic Activity No. 2* (Washington, D.C.: Brookings Institution Press, 1997), 159–221; M. Kurkchiyan, "The Transformation of the Second Economy into the Informal Economy," in A. Ledeneva and M. Kurkchiyan (eds), *Economic Crime in Russia* (London: Kluwer Law International, 2000); Ledeneva, *Russia's Economy of Favours*; Morris and Polese, *The Informal Post-Socialist Economy*; Polese, Morris, and Kovács, "Introduction"; Round, Williams, and Rodgers, "Everyday Tactics and Spaces of Power"; Mars and Altman, "The Cultural Bases of Soviet Georgia's Second Economy"; Berliner, "The Informal Organization of the Soviet Firm"; Grossman, "The 'Second Economy' of the USSR"; Treml and Alexeev, "The Growth of the Second Economy in the Soviet Union"; Humphrey, "Traders, 'Disorder,' and Citizenship Regimes in Provincial Russia"; Kotkin, *Magnetic Mountain*.

within disputes and debates over interpretations and understanding of textual rules and other spoken rules of being good Muslims.[25] I will come back to Islamic rules later in this chapter.

Entrepreneurship: Post-Soviet Entrepreneurs

Here I will define entrepreneurs, the category used for jobs or activities that often fall under the *biznes* category described earlier and that uses a broader interpretation of the English-language word "business." But before doing this, I would like to examine the etymology of the word "entrepreneur." The term originates from the French word *entrepreneur*, which refers to someone who undertakes a business venture. The term has been discussed so far within economics and political science, where the latter popularized the term academically.

The literature on entrepreneurship has grown since the term was first used by Cantillon in 1755.[26] The most intensive engagement with the term and its definition began much later. Writing in 1921, Knight drew attention to the negative aspects of this occupation, namely risk and uncertainty.[27] The most influential contribution into the literature on entrepreneurship is by Schumpeter, who highlighted the innovative characteristics of entrepreneurial activities that he called "creative destruction."[28] Since then, the term has travelled beyond economics to the social sciences, along with the literature on informal economies. Most of these studies examine the reasons and factors behind the decision to become an entrepreneur. These are capital, educational background, age, and gender.[29] Decision-making theory concerning the choice to become an entrepreneur in the Western economies does not adequately

---

25   J. Rasanayagam, "Informal Economy, Informal State: The Case of Uzbekistan," *International Journal of Sociology and Social Policy,* 31, no. 11–12 (2011): 681–696.

26   R. Cantillon, *Essai sur La nature du commerce en general* (1755; repr., London: Macmillan, 1982); R. Sobel, "Entrepreneurship," Concise Encyclopedia of Economics, <http://www.econlib.org/library/Enc/Entrepreneurship.html>.

27   F. Knight, *Risk, Uncertainty, and Profit* (1921; repr., Mineola, NY: Dover, 2006).

28   J. Schumpeter, *The Theory of Economic Development* (1912; repr., Cambridge, MA: Harvard University Press, 1934).

29   J.C. McIntosh and S. Islam, "Beyond the Influence of Islam on Female Entrepreneurship in a Conservative Muslim Context," *International Management Review*, 6, no. 1 (2010): 102–111; C. Essers and Y. Benschop, "Muslim Businesswomen Doing Boundary Work: The Negotiation of Islam, Gender, and Ethnicity within Entrepreneurial Contexts," *Human Relations,* 62, no. 3 (2009): 403–423.

apply to the context of developing economies. For instance, in the case of Central Asian entrepreneurs in Russia, Western-based decision-making theories are hardly applicable since individuals often choose to become an entrepreneur not because it offers better economic opportunities but rather because this is often the only choice available amid economic and political crisis. To my knowledge, there has not been much research done on entrepreneurship in Central Asia or Russia. However, some economists recently looked into the economic contribution of entrepreneurs and the positive development of labor markets.[30]

Below I will describe entrepreneurs from Central Asia who operate within and beyond Central Asia. Central Asian entrepreneurs are mobile and transnational in terms of their working modus and their networks. Businessmen—or, rather, entrepreneurs—are both female and male in the Central Asian context, and the term refers to both traders (large or small scale) and other entrepreneurs who earn their money thanks to their mobility, social capital, and access to information. They can be also be organizers of work abroad, middlemen/brokers, service providers, matchmakers, information transmitters, permit or transportation providers, distributors, firm representatives, among many others. These people have wide networks, good contacts, financial or social capital, good status within their kinship and neighbourhood communities, good knowledge or economically relevant information, innovative skills, and charisma. Entrepreneurs use both official and alternative legal systems and straddle the boundaries between the formal and informal economies.

Although I do not like to use such adjectives as "formal" or "informal," I use them for clarification purposes here. I would rather argue that there is no clear boundary between the formal and informal economy. In the context of failed or failing state legal systems, more and more alternative regulation is used by entrepreneurs whose economic activities do not know national boundaries. Today, mobile entrepreneurs cross national boundaries to profit from the differences between those countries. Their economic projects vary in content and in size. For instance, this includes foremen who administer one or several construction teams recruiting at home (Uzbekistan, Tajikistan, or Kyrgyzstan) and bring these teams (from two to several construction workers) to Kazakhstan or Russia (the most popular destinations for construction projects). Another example of entrepreneurs are medical specialists who travel from Central Asia

30   M.A. Carree and R. Thurik, "The Lag Structure of the Impact of Business Ownership on Economic Performance in OECD Countries," *Small Business Economics*, 30 (2008): 101–110; P.A. Geroski, "European Industrial Policy and Industrial Policy in Europe," *Oxford Review of Economic Policy*, 5, no. 2 (1989): 20–36.

to Yemen to work and at the same time secure work for others and provide support for them in Yemen.[31] Some entrepreneurs arrange for Central Asian or even Russian clients to receive medical treatment in Europe; another popular option is going to India for heart surgery. These are only a few activities among very many others that connect different countries and require working with different currencies and using very different channels, both formal and informal.

When one becomes familiar with the variety of cross-border economic activities, it is amazing to see how these activities are managed, regulated, administered, and maintained through a combination of formal and informal means. Entrepreneurs are flexible; quick to change or reorient their activities from one country to another or from one sphere to another, matching and fitting to the context, time, situation, and contacts. The cash flow within these economic activities varies from very little to very large amounts of goods and cash (from a few hundred to a few thousand US dollars each month).

Given the lack of legal mechanisms such as contracts and other systems to sanction violators, there are other means of regulating and administrating the economic activities of mobile entrepreneurs. There are obligations and expectation of moral conduct shared within the trust networks.[32] These include—but are not limited to—trust, loyalty, religious belief, collective identification, kinship obligations, and other duties and responsibilities perceived and followed by mobile entrepreneurs.

Islam and Entrepreneurship: Alternative Economic Order

In most countries, the economic activities of mobile entrepreneurs are not formally regulated. Instead, entrepreneurs have their own systems of governing economic and social lives as well as methods and principles of regulating them.

---

31   The medical connection seems to be widespread, particularly in Uzbekistan where female medical doctors and nurses are required to treat female patients in Yemen. My respondents (two female doctors) did not know the language, and their work has been organized informally and therefore they risked exploitation. Both doctors claimed that knowledge of Russian was enough and that they had a translator. Their employment was administered by local entrepreneurs who had wide networks through local state agencies whose connections have been used for these informal employment arrangements.

32   Turaeva, "Post-Soviet Uncertainties"; Turaeva, "Mobile Entrepreneurs in Post-Soviet Central Asia."

Religion plays a crucial role in how economic flows, human relations, and social security are structured and regulated. Mobile entrepreneurs use various sources of authority to regulate their informal economic lives and maintain their trust networks.[33] These include both Islamic and non-Islamic beliefs and rules, culturally laden moral codes, and other kinship and social rules. For instance, fear of dying in debt is often trusted as an effective motive to not violate agreements.

Debt is a major topic in Central Asia, whether it is the result of any economic activity or just a byproduct of economic necessity. This topic was often brought up in the conversations I had with people of different regional and educational backgrounds. The topic of debt is often embedded in the belief that "God stops looking after people who make debts." This is an important informal mechanism against swindling and fraud. Sometimes my interlocutors would ask if this is really written in Quran or not, as citing God is a very popular way of moralizing and disciplining. When an individual starts questioning if this is true or not, people start offering examples from real lives, which are more convincing for people than the text of the Quran. One hears often that "you see the son of so and so had so many debts and died young, now this burden is on his sons and now you see how this family is left by God."[34] The life stories cited for disciplining reasons are very effective, and then these beliefs become strong enough to become unquestionable divine rule for everybody, rich and poor alike, as many say *baymi kambagalmi hamma hudoni oldinda bir* (whether rich or poor, everyone is equal before God).

Meagher writes about "new forms of economic order in the context of state decline" and offers examples from different countries such as Somalia, the Islamic Hawala networks in Dubai, and "the Islamic trading networks of the Mouride brotherhoods." Meagher notes:

> Studies of Islamic as well as Christian religious networks highlight their role in introducing strict moral norms, a range of efficient commercial institutions, and a tendency to operate across communal and class

---

33   C. Tilly, "Trust and Rule," *Theory and Society*, 33, no. 1 (2004): 1–30; C. Tilly (ed.), *Trust and Rule* (New York: Cambridge University Press, 2005); Turaeva, "Mobile Entrepreneurs in Post-Soviet Central Asia."

34   This belief is a common knowledge in Uzbekistan and Turkmenistan. The other formulations used by my respondents were similar and brought up in the context of discussing debt. The questions on debt emerged from the questions relating to economic activities and their administration both at home and abroad. The informants were both from the field research in 2005–2006, 2012 in Uzbekistan, Turkmen female traders, and Moscow-based entrepreneurs in 2014 and 2015.

boundaries, contributing to processes of accumulation and social cohesion in a context of intense hardship and social disruption.[35]

Muslims living in a non-Muslim context, particularly as hostile an environment as Russia is for Central Asians, tend to gravitate toward Mosque communities more frequently than if they were at home. The Central Asian migrant population in Russia is often tightly affiliated with mosque communities and religious networks unless they are integrated within ethnic communities. Mosques serve as a safe (e.g., protected from police raids) place not only to pray but also to meet, socialize, share, and seek refuge from very limited housing (often a one-room apartment shared by 10–15 persons), unfriendly and violent outside (skinhead street violence and interethnic skirmishes). Imams are religious authorities who offer justice, peace, and a moral framework. The institutional framework offered by mosque communities is crucial for any entrepreneurial activity where an Imam can adjudicate conflicts. Religious networks often also offer financial services and transnational capital mobility. These networks are considered safe, as they are backed by religion and morals. Religious networks also serve as trusted routes for transferring remittances and other investments.[36]

Meagher highlighted the significance "of new religious movements in class formation."[37] Based on examples from Nigeria, Meagher stated that the majority of the working population was employed within the informal economy where entrepreneurs had been making significant contribution to developing new markets and forming a new class.

Similar communities are found in non-Muslim countries with large numbers of Muslim migrants, whether living temporarily or permanently in these countries. There is a longstanding debate on the role of religion in establishing

---

35   Meagher, "The Politics of Vulnerability," 400, 402.
36   F. Vogel and S.L. Hayes (eds), *Islamic Law and Finance: Religion, Risk, and Return* (London: Kluwer Law International, 1998); O. Khlevnyuk and R.W. Davies, "The End of Rationing in the Soviet Union, 1934–1935," *Europe-Asia Studies,* 51, no. 4 (1999): 557–609; R.W. Davies, M. Harrison, and S.G. Wheatcroft (eds), *The Economic Transformation of the Soviet Union, 1913–1945* (New York: Cambridge University Press, 1994); T. Inglis, "Catholic Identity in Contemporary Ireland: Belief and Belonging to Tradition," *Journal of Contemporary Religion,* 22, no. 2 (2007): 205–220; T.W. Laqueur, *Religion and Respectability: Sunday School and Working Class Culture, 1780–1850* (New Haven, CT: Yale University Press, 1976); M. Weber (ed.), *The Protestant Ethic and the Spirit of Capitalism* (New York: Allen and Unwin, 1930).
37   Meagher, "The Politics of Vulnerability," 398.

moral standards and ordering human lives. It traces these processes from medieval times to the current period.[38]

The literature on Islam and entrepreneurship has been approached so far from various angles that shed light on different aspects of the link between economics and religion. There have been negative views on the role of religion and the informalization of economies, some of which focused on witchcraft. Meagher stated that the pessimistic views stressed the "anti-Weberian ethic" of superstition and other backward traits hindering neo-liberal market development and showed that, in fact, religious movements follow a very rational Weberian logic and have contributed to the development of new markets.[39]

Kuran traces the links between Islam and entrepreneurship to the advent of Islam in the seventh century when Islam was spread widely thanks to the mercantilist skills of the early practitioners.[40] He also discusses the *waqf* system of welfare regimes that delivered financial services for local entrepreneurs.[41]

Another group includes research on Islamic or religious influence in entrepreneurial activities in general, which also takes a rational choice approach in their analysis. Some authors even spoke of the "Islamization of capitalism" in the Islamic countries where Islam, economics, and entrepreneurship are closely interrelated.[42]

There is also a critical debate over whether religion influences one's rationality, particularly focusing on the governance preferences in Muslim

---

38 Meagher, "The Politics of Vulnerability"; O. Khlevnyuk and R.W. Davies, "The End of Rationing in the Soviet Union, 1934–1935," *Europe-Asia Studies,* 51, no. 4 (1999): 557–609; R.W. Davies, M. Harrison, and S.G. Wheatcroft (eds), *The Economic Transformation of the Soviet Union, 1913–1945* (New York: Cambridge University Press, 1994); Inglis, "Catholic Identity in Contemporary Ireland"; Laqueur, *Religion and Respectability*; Weber, *The Protestant Ethic and the Spirit of Capitalism.*

39 Meagher, "The Politics of Vulnerability," 401.

40 T. Kuran, "The Scale of Entrepreneurship in Middle Eastern History: Inhibitive Roles of Islamic Institutions," *ERID Working Paper No.10* (Durham, NC: Duke University, 2008).

41 H. Salarzehi, H. Armesh, and D. Nikbin, "Waqf as a Social Entrepreneurship Model in Islam," *International Journal of Business and Management,* 5, no. 7 (2010): 179–185; E.S.M. Nezhad and M. Emami, "Changes in Legislation and Principles of Waqf to the New Creation," *Modares Human Sciences,* 8, no. 3 (2004): 179-185.

42 E.B. Adaş, "The Making of Entrepreneurial Islam and Islamic Spirit of Capitalism," *Journal for Cultural Research,* 10, no. 2 (2006): 113; R.I. Bekkin, "Islamskoe ili musul'manskoe pravo? (K voprosu o pravovykh aspektakh islamskikh finansov)," *Problemy sovremennoi ekonomiki,* 4, no. 48 (2013): 429–430.

countries and whether liberal democratic values do or do not contradict religious norms.[43]

Another body of literature on the Islamic countries and economic transactions under Islamic law deals mainly with banking systems and other Islamic business regulations.[44]

Recently, some research has focused on female entrepreneurship both in the context of migration to the West and within developing economies. Essers and Benschop discussed Moroccan women entrepreneurs in the Netherlands, examining their religious and ethnic identities in relation to their occupation and gender.[45] Wetter and Smallbone studied female entrepreneurship in Uzbekistan from an economic point of view, applying quantitative methods that overlook the depth offered by qualitative studies.[46] Studies on female entrepreneurship in Central Asia still finds itself in its embryonic stage that lacks basic empirical systematic research.

Alternative Economic Orders in Post-Soviet Space: Trust and Gender

If an entrepreneur operates within post-Soviet countries (and not in Dubai or Turkey), then their main complaints concern the obstacles to obtaining local registration and work permits. Local registration (*propiska*) is often informally administered by third parties outside the state registration system. The real *propiska* (in Russia) would cost far more money and cause more headaches (*kalla agriq*), according to my informants. It is easier for them to obtain a

43   J.F. Fletcher and B. Sergeyev, "Islam and Intolerance in Central Asia: The Case of Kyrgyzstan," *Europe-Asia Studies*, 54, no. 2 (2002): 251–275; F.B. Adamson, "Global Liberalism Versus Political Islam: Competing Ideological Frameworks in International Politics," *International Studies Review*, 7, no. 4 (2005): 547–569; K. Collins and E. Owen, "Islamic Religiosity and Regime Preferences: Explaining Support for Democracy and Political Islam in Central Asia and the Caucasus," *Political Research Quarterly*, 65, no. 3 (2012): 499–515.

44   B.S. Chong and M.-H. Liu, "Islamic Banking: Interest-free or Interest-based?", *Pacific-Basin Finance Journal*, 17, no. 1 (2009): 125–144; Vogel and Hayes, *Islamic Law and Finance*; P. Gerrard and J.B. Cunningham, "Islamic Banking: A Study in Singapore," *International Journal of Bank Marketing*, 15, no. 6 (1997): 204–216.

45   Essers and Benschop, "Muslim Businesswomen Doing Boundary Work."

46   F. Wetter and D. Smallbone, "Women's Entrepreneurship from an Institutional Perspective: The Case of Uzbekistan," *International Entrepreneurship Management Journal*, 4 (2008): 505–520.

counterfeit *propiska*. "One saves time and money, of course, one should be careful with the police checks."[47] The same is true for the newly introduced patents for work (basically a work permit) in Russia. The patent office in Moscow produces an incredible amount of documents, part of recent efforts to legalize illegal migrants. The office operates around the clock, running special buses to the office for applicants and even providing preparation services on the buses. Some of the entrepreneurs whom I interviewed and have followed since 2005 file multiple applications at the same time to avoid this whole machinery of document production.[48]

Work permits are obtained in a variety of ways. For example, construction crews destined for Russia or Kazakhstan are typically hired in their home villages and within kinship and friendship networks. Potential workers are recommended to foremen, who personally interview candidates, discuss expectations and payments for services, and arrange for travel, housing, and more in the host country.

Trust and religion play crucial roles in the verbal agreements that replace formal contracts. Informal agreements are theoretically enforced by means of obligations sourced from kinship relations and friendship based on trust or mutual dependencies of various kinds.[49]

There are also informal regulatory principles based on men's pride. In the agreements one can often hear promises such as "I give my word as a man" or "If I do this, (break the terms) then I am not a man"; statements that often carry important meaning among Muslim men. Women entrepreneurs do not make the same promises, and women say they are more successful than men because they are less trusting. On the question of how informal regulation, punishment, and other agreements work, women stated that they do all the business themselves without trusting anyone; in other words, women engage in forms of business that do not involve so much administration and management. They often say, "Let the men do the dirty work" (*qara ishni erkakla atsin*).[50] I cannot say very much about female entrepreneurship due to the lack of systematic data on the topic.[51]

---

47   Informal conversation, Tashkent, 2006.
48   For more on the production of identity cards and other documents for migrants in Russia, see M. Reeves, "Clean Fake: Authenticating Documents and Persons in Migrant Moscow," *American Ethnologist*, 40, no. 3 (2013): 508–524.
49   For more details on the kinds of dependencies among migrants in Tashkent, see Turaeva, *Migration and Identity*.
50   Women traders form Tashauz, Turkmenistan who trade between Dubai and Turkmenistan.
51   There is not so much done on women's entrepreneurship in Central Asia and beyond although this economic field is increasingly feminized by now and more and more

The rules governing the economic and social activities of mobile entrepreneurs are ad hoc and flexible. They can be re-negotiated on the spot and are subject to changing circumstances. These and other strategies are, of course, not as simple as I describe. There are many variables in play in all aspects of the negotiating process, institutionalization of new rules and relations, status maintenance, and formation of trust networks. These include: historical institutional development and the history of state formation in the region; current economic and political developments, as well as other aspects of daily life. These, coupled with the currents of globalization processes shared via communication technologies as well as other traditional means of channelling information and knowledge, establish frames of ordering or re-ordering of what I call the *micro-orders* in which transnational economic entrepreneurs operate and live.[52] The establishment of new institutions and new rules has implications for novel economic developments of the post-Soviet period.

Djelic and Sahlin-Andersen, writing about regulation and re-ordering of transnational space, suggested looking at regulating processes and governance with a new perspective that goes beyond state-centric understandings of rule-making, governance, and regulation of transnational activities.[53] Therefore, I suggest looking at the state legal systems from the opposite side, namely with the eyes of those who can choose whether to follow state laws of not. We should not assume that when a state introduces registration policies, all urban residents are either inside the system or outside. Rather, taking the opposite perspective on the issue, namely, the perspective of the mobile entrepreneurs themselves, provides more productive thinking about how these policies shape the actions of those at whom these policies are directed. Namely, mobile entrepreneurs will negotiate the state legal system in their own terms with their own tools that, in turn, will play a part in the process of forming social norms and rules.

These new institutions serve as frames of reference and sources of basic order for transnational entrepreneurs from Central Asia. In this way, now mobile entrepreneurs relate to the state or redefine the state as just one of many actors encountered in the course of their transnational economic

---

women became mobile and entrepreneurial. For a study of female entrepreneurship and the role of religion and ethnicity in the context of Netherlands about Moroccan and Turkish entrepreneurs, see Essers and Benschop, "Muslim Businesswomen Doing Boundary Work." See also Wetter and Smallbone, "Women's Entrepreneurship from an Institutional Perspective," regarding women entrepreneurs in Uzbekistan.

52   Turaeva, "Post-Soviet Uncertainties."

53   M.-L. Djelic and K. Sahlin-Andersson (eds), *Transnational Governance: Institutional Dynamics of Regulation* (Cambridge: Cambridge University Press, 2006).

activities.[54] Within the debate on transnational governance and rule-making, regulation is conceptualized much wider than in its classical definition, which assumes the centrality of the state.[55] The authors also remind of the de-regulation scholarly discourse that undermines the "new age of legalism"[56] and state that "(w)e witness both the decline of state-centred control and the rise of an 'age of legalism'."[57] Comaroff and Comaroff mention this age as "an Iron Cage of Legality" where law fetishism is over-determined and where "(t)he distillation of postcolonial citizens into legal subjects, and postcolonial politics into lawfare, charts the road from the past to the future, albeit less sharply in some places that in others. Not only are government and public affairs becoming more legalistic, but so are 'communities' within nation-states."[58] Djelic and Sahlin-Andersen define transnational regulation as "a mode of governance in the sense that it structures, guides, and controls human and social interactions beyond, across and within national territories."[59] Such communities are also mosque communities that offer space and opportunities, structures and also authority figures (the Imam) to form an alternative legal order, as I described earlier in this chapter.

The above discussion on regulation, de-regulation, re-regulation, and transnational governance recognizes that the state is not the only governing agency and authority for regulation and that there are other actors and sources for authority to provide order and norms. This conclusion regarding regulation is well supported by the examples from alternative regulation, legal pluralism, and the examples offered here on the regulation of transnational economic activities in the post-Soviet space.[60]

---

54   Djelic and Sahlin-Andersson, *Transnational Governance*.

55   R. Baldwin, S. Collin, and C. Hood (eds), *A Reader on Regulation* (Oxford: Oxford University Press, 1998).

56   P. Schmidt, "Law in the Age of Governance: Regulation, Networks and Lawyers," in J. Jordana and D. Levi-Faur (eds), *The Politics of Regulation: Institutions and Regulatory Reforms for the Age of Governance* (Cheltenham, UK: Edward Elgar, 2004), 273–295.

57   Schmidt, "Law in the Age of Governance."

58   J.L. Comaroff and J. Comaroff, "Introduction," in J.L. Comaroff and J. Comaroff (eds), *Law and Disorder in the Postcolony* (Chicago: University of Chicago Press, 2006), 33.

59   Djelic and Sahlin-Andersson, *Transnational Governance*, 6.

60   K. von Benda-Beckmann, F. von Benda-Beckmann, and J. Eckert, "Rules of Law and Laws of Ruling: Law and Governance between Past and Future," in K. von Benda-Beckmann, F. von Benda-Beckmann, and J. Eckert (eds), *Rules of Law and Laws of Ruling: On the Governance of Law* (Burlington, VT: Ashgate, 2009), 1–30; J. Eckert, "Urban Governance and Emergent Forms of Legal Pluralism in Mumbai," *Journal of Legal Pluralism*, 36, no. 50 (2004): 29–60.

Islam in Uzbekistan

So far, I have discussed the regulating potential of Islam in the economic activities of entrepreneurs from Central Asia who operate between and within Central Asia, Russia, Turkey, Dubai, and China. This is mainly relevant in a non-domestic context since at home other factors contribute to the same processes with the same strength such as kinship and patronage networks.

Now the question arises as to how much of Islam is in Central Asia and what kind of Muslims are there in Central Asia. The fundamental difference between Muslims from Islamic countries and Muslims from post-Soviet countries is of crucial importance in this research and must be considered when looking at how religious networks function in this context. The Islam practiced by Central Asian migrants is far different from that observed by Muslims who follow Islamic scripture. Post-Soviet Islam has a particular character and is distinct from the Islam practiced in other Islamic contexts.[61] Historically, it is important to note that Central Asian Muslims have been exposed to various waves of conquest and rule by Mongols, Timurides, Russians, and others. Moreover, since the Silk Road traversed their territory, local Muslims have for centuries been exposed to peaceful foreign and non-Islamic influences through trade. More than 70 years of atheism, as promoted by the Soviet government, left its mark on religious practice and belief, as can be observed in the day-to-day lives of post-Soviet Muslims in Central Asia.[62] Some authors even speak of a "secular Islam."[63]

---

61   H. Fathi, "Women of Authority in Central Asia Islam as Identity Preserving References and Agents of Community Restructuring in the Post-Soviet Period," in P. Sartori and T. Trevisani (eds), *Patterns of Transformation in and around Uzbekistan* (Reggio Emilia, Italy: Diabasis, 2007), 121–138; J. Rasanayagam, "Informal Economy, Informal State: The Case of Uzbekistan," *International Journal of Sociology and Social Policy*, 31, no. 11–12 (2011): 681–696; I. Hilgers, *Why Do Uzbeks Have to be Muslims? Exploring Religiosity in the Ferghana Valley* (Berlin: Lit Verlag, 2009); M. Pelkmans, "Asymmetries on the 'Religious Market' in Kyrgyzstan," in C. Hann (ed.), *The Postsocialist Religious Question: Faith and Power in Central Asia and East-Central Europe* (Berlin: LIT Verlag, 2006), 29–46; B. Privratsky (ed.), *Muslim Turkistan: Kazak Religion and Collective Memory* (New York: Curzon, 2001), 321.

62   For an extensive historical overview of the establishment of the Soviet "scientific atheism" in Uzbekistan, see M.N. Shahrani, "Islam and the Political Culture of 'Scientific Atheism' in Post-Soviet Central Asia: Future Predicament," *Islamic Studies,* 33, no. 2–3 (1994): 139–159. Also see, Rasanayagam, "Informal Economy, Informal State"; Hilgers, *Why Do Uzbeks Have to be Muslims?*; A. Khalid, "A Secular Islam: Nation, State and Religion in Uzbekistan," *International Journal of Middle East Studies,* 35, no. 4 (2003): 573–598; A. Djumaev, "Islam and Culture in the Context of the Central Asian Civilization," *Studies on Central Asia,* 87, no. 1 (2007): 53–84.

63   Khalid, "A Secular Islam."

After the collapse of the Soviet Union, scholars observed processes of re-traditionalization and a return to Islam. Islam emerged in the intimate lives of Central Asian Muslims.[64] These authors argue for a distinction between Islam as a religion and being Muslim as an identity. They argue that Muslim identity in post-Soviet Uzbekistan is not necessarily based on scriptural Islam but rather on the everyday practice of religious rituals, as well as the knowledge of local mullahs and other sources. These practices distinguish post-Soviet Muslims from other Muslims from Islamic countries who learn Islam from texts and in religious schools. These include men who take part in Friday afternoon prayer but still consume alcohol, pray after meals, funerals, wedding rituals with a private visit of mullah after the marriage party (European style), irregular fasting, alms-giving, and many other elements of rituals and practices mixed with other non-Islamic practices such as shamanism, fortune tellers, and belief in spirits.

The Uzbek government has incorporated the spiritual aspect of Islam into the ideological space of its nationalist agenda.[65] This situation, coupled with state authoritarian rule that often uses pretexts for to prosecute citizens for supposedly extremist religious activities. This has so far been done through creating state discourse about good and bad Islam.[66] This limits the approved practice of Islam to attending recognized mosques; Muslims cannot wear religious clothing or discuss Islam in small gatherings.[67] A very limited religious education of female members of the family at home is tolerated to a certain degree. Although it was documented that illegal religious gatherings of male religious leaders and *ulema*s took place in the Fergana Valley in the early 1970s, we can assume that these circles gained even more prominence after Uzbekistan gained independence.[68] Religious censorship and political repression remain prevalent in all of the Central Asian countries. In this context,

---

64 Fathi, "Women of Authority in Central Asia Islam"; Rasanayagam, "Informal Economy, Informal State"; Hilgers, *Why Do Uzbeks Have to be Muslims?*; Pelkmans, "Asymmetries on the 'Religious Market' in Kyrgyzstan"; Privratsky, *Muslim Turkistan*.

65 S. Akiner, "The Politicization of Islam in Post-Soviet Central Asia," *Religion, State, and Society*, 31, no. 2 (2003): 97–122; Hilgers, *Why Do Uzbeks Have to be Muslims?*; Rasanayagam, "Informal Economy, Informal State."

66 Rasanayagam, "Informal Economy, Informal State."

67 S. Kendzior, "Digital Distrust: Uzbek Cynicism and Solidarity in the Internet Age," *American Ethnologist*, 38, no. 3 (2011): 559–575.

68 A. Abduvakhitov, "Islamic Revivalism in Uzbekistan," in D.F. Eickelman (ed.), *Russian Muslim Frontiers: New Directions in Cross-Cultural Analysis* (Bloomington: Indiana University Press, 1993), 79–97; A. Rashid, *Jihad: The Rise of Militant Islam in Central Asia* (New Haven, CT: Yale University Press, 2002), 140; Akiner, "The Politicization of Islam in Post-Soviet Central Asia."

religion serves more as a source of identity and less as a source for rules and norms. Leaving home means also leaving home-based structures and systems behind.[69] In a new foreign environment with another religion dominant and an often hostile environment, migrants and entrepreneurs find stability, authority and other missing links within mosque communities and religious networks safe from police raids, prejudices and discrimination.

Conclusion

In this chapter, I argued that after the collapse of the Soviet Union a new social and economic status or class emerged, namely, mobile entrepreneurs. I have considered Central Asian entrepreneurs, both men and women, who successfully make their living out of their innovative transnational economic activities. Regarding the earlier discussed development of Islam and Islamic practices on the ground after the collapse of the atheist Soviet regime in Central Asia and beyond, I asked the question of what role religion play in the lives and work of Central Asian entrepreneurs.

Depending on the type of work, the distance from home, and the length of stay in one place, there are a variety of institutional arrangements for regulating informal economic activities of mobile entrepreneurs from Central Asia. In an alien context, religion plays a crucial role in the regulation of these activities and administering sometimes very complex economic projects in multiple destinations. I argued that religion and religious authority serve as an anchor in several regards, in terms of destination, reference point, source of authority and stability in the context of accelerated change and mobility.

I followed Meagher in building up the argument of making of a new class within informal economies, namely entrepreneurs. Her examples from the African continent resemble patterns I observed in Central Asia and beyond. I have also made use of the literature on informal economies, transnational governance, as well as entrepreneurship and religion. I pointed out to the gaps in this literature. For instance, the literature on religion is mainly focused on identity, morality, and only recently the economy; and even then mainly with a focus on Islamic banking. The literature on governance and regulation is unfortunately state-centered, and top-down approaches are more popular. In this piece I tried to bring several strands of literature together to show the links

---

69   S. Abashin, "Gellner, the 'Saints,' and Central Asia: Between Islam and Nationalism," *Inner Asia,* 7, no. 1 (2005): 65–86; C. Sengupta, "Dynamics of Community Environmental Management in Howrah Slums," *Economic and Political Weekly,* 34, no. 21 (1999): 1292–96.

among religion, economics, and alternative legal orders. This is an effort to draw attention to the important role of religion and mosque communities in entrepreneurship and transnational economic networks. More research is needed to fill this gap.

PART 4

Female Attire as a Public Debate

∵

CHAPTER 10

The War of Billboards: Hijab, Secularism, and Public Space in Bishkek

Emil Nasritdinov and Nurgul Esenamanova

Introduction: The War of Billboards

In July 2016, the residents of Bishkek and many other cities and towns across Kyrgyzstan woke up to see billboards with banners depicting three images next to each other. The first image portrayed a group of Kyrgyz women wearing traditional Kyrgyz dresses and *elechek* (a traditional, tall Kyrgyz headdress) (see Figure 1). The second image included a group of women in white Islamic dresses, some with their faces covered, raising their hands in supplication. The third image was very dark: it depicted women in black Islamic garb, all with *niqabs* (Islamic face covers). The sign below asked, "*Kairan elim, kaida baratabyz?*" ("My poor people, where are we going?"). The banners were initiated by the head of an unknown private educational foundation,[1] but were later financially supported by the administration of the president of Kyrgyzstan, Almazbek Atambayev.[2] The images and signs indirectly criticized new trends in the way Kyrgyz women supposedly dress, and the first image was there to show that Kyrgyz women had never covered their faces and never worn black.

The banners immediately sparked controversy in the news and social media with people divided into those who supported the installation and those who opposed it. An online poll administered by Sputnik.kg on August 29, 2016, generated 659 responses. The results are shown in Figure 10.2.

The majority of voters among online readers (69 percent) supported the banners, but almost one-third (28 percent) were critical. The criticism of the banners came mostly from practicing Muslims, both women and men, who

---

1   "Bannery so sloganom 'Kairan elim, kaida baratabyz?' vyvesili po ukazaniiu glavy chastnogo prosvestilel'skogo fonda," *Gezitter.org*, July 14, 2016. <http://www.gezitter.org/society/51841_banneryi_so_sloganom_kayran_elim_kayda_baratabyiz_vyivesili_po_ukazaniyu_glavyi_chastnogo_prosvetitelskogo_fonda/>.

2   "Bannery 'Kairan elim, kaida baratabyz?' nachali v yveshivat' po vsei respublike," *Azzatyk.kg*, July 22, 2016, <http://rus.azattyk.org/a/27872844.html>.

FIGURE 10.1
*Banner on Sovetskaya
Street in Bishkek
critical of Islamic style
clothing for women.
"DUMK: banner 'kairan
elim, kaida baratabyz?'
mozhet navredit'
edinstvu"*

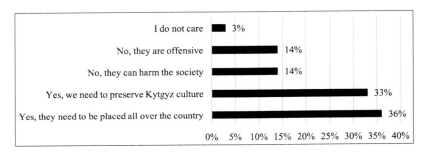

FIGURE 10.2   *Online poll: Do we need banners, "Kairan elim"? "Bannery 'Kairan elim,
kaida baratabyz?' razmeshchaiut po vsemu Kyrgyzstanu," Sputnik.kg,
July 18, 2016, <http://ru.sputnik.kg/Kyrgyzstan/20160718/1027833480.
html>*

perceived this to be an attack on their values and on the sacredness of the hijab
(Islamic veil for women). The Spiritual Board of Muslims in Kyrgyzstan criticized the banners, suggesting that they were a provocation that could harm the
unity of the people.[3] Similarly, Kadyr Malikov, a prominent religious expert,
said that the banners were very dangerous and could lead to the division of
society.[4] One response came from a group called Naasat Media.[5] They produced a video in which several women in hijabs gave their own answers to the
president's "Where are we going?" question. Women stated that they were
going toward morality, purity, honesty, self-respect, and other core Islamic values and that to wear the hijab was their own choice. A more aggressive social

3   "DUMK: banner 'kairan elim, kaida baratabyz?' mozhet navredit' edinstvu," *Sputnik.kg,* July 13,
     2016, <http://ru.sputnik.kg/society/20160713/1027634490.html>.
4   Ibid.
5   Nasaat media, <https://www.facebook.com/NasaatMedia/videos/1748086732096254/>.

FIGURE 10.3
Banners installed in the central parts of Bishkek critical of Western style clothing for women. "Novyi banner peredraznivaet nashumevshee obrashchenie 'Kairan elim'," Limon.kg, July 28, 2016, <http://limon.kg/news:68646?from=kg news&place=newstopic>

reaction resulted in vandalism: some banners were torn;[6] others set on fire.[7] Finally, criticism of banners also came from some civil society activists (not necessarily religious), who perceived them to be an instance of state encroachment on the freedom of religion.

Very soon, there emerged yet another interesting response—in the form of "alternative" banners that depicted women in traditional Kyrgyz dress next to girls in mini-skirts and shorts.[8] The text below was the same: "My poor people, where are we going?" These images were critical of Western-style clothing and implied a similar argument: traditional Kyrgyz women never wore the styles that the majority of young women wear today. Such banners were installed in a few central locations in the city. It was not clear who financed their installation, but they were discussed in the media and social networks just as actively and controversially as the first banners. The game was on, and Bishkek residents anxiously awaited the state's reaction.

The head of the State Committee on Religious Affairs, Orozbek Moldaliev, defended the first banners as neither oppressive nor anti-Islamic.[9] He pointed out that they targeted only women wearing black and reminded the press that Kyrgyz women never wore black except for widows mourning their husbands.

6   "Militsiia ishchet khuliganov, sorvavshikh banner 'Kairan elim, kaida baratabyz'," *Zanoza.kg*, July 14, 2016, <http://zanoza.kg/doc/341553_miliciia_ishet_hyliganov_sorvavshih_banner_kayran_elim_kayda_baratabyz.html>.

7   "Banner 'Kairan elim, kaida baratabyz?' podozhgli v Batkenskoi oblasti," *Sputnik.kg*, July 26, 2016, <http://ru.sputnik.kg/society/20160726/1028159819.html>.

8   "V Bishkeke poiavilsia novyi banner 'Kairan elim, kaida baratabyz'?", *Sputnik.kg*, July 28, 2016, <http://ru.sputnik.kg/society/20160728/1028232189.html>.

9   "Orozbek Moldaliev: V bannerakh 'Kairan elim, kaida baratabyz': nichego provokatsionnogo net," *24.kg*, July 13, 2016, <http://24.kg/obschestvo/34592_orozbek_moldaliev_v_bannerah_kayran_elim_kayda_baratasyin_nichego_provokatsionnogo_net/>.

He also criticized Kadyr Malikov and others who had allegedly misinterpreted the message. The president condemned all these attacks on his banners. In his criticism of the alternative banners, he defended mini-skirts, suggesting that Kyrgyz women had worn them since the 1950s and that women in mini-skirts do not hide bombs under them.[10] This statement made it explicit that the banners were not just about the national identity of Kyrgyz women, but also about fears of terrorism associated with "women in black." Soon, the Mayor's Office of Bishkek gave an order to remove the alternative banners,[11] and the war of billboards ended not long after it started.

This controversial story of billboards is a very powerful illustration of how the religiousness and secularity of urban space in Bishkek today are contested. More and more people have started practicing Islam and the hijab is becoming a regular part of the everyday urban scene across the city. The government's fear of radicalization and its attempts to reclaim secularism often cause the more vocal members of the practicing Muslim community to defend their values and everyday practices. A very complex urban discourse emerges. This chapter explores this discourse and analyzes how the urban space in the capital of Kyrgyzstan is contested and negotiated among religious groups, secular groups, and the government.

Secularism, National Identity, and Extremism

As the focal point of debate on Muslim women, the hijab is subject to many public discourses: on identity, multiculturalism, political Islam, cultural differences, gender roles, power of agency, transnationalism, and globalization, among others.[12] The three main public discourses that we focus on in this chapter are secularism, national identity, and security.

Secularism
The first discourse is on the conceptualization of secularism. The Constitution of the Kyrgyz Republic defines Kyrgyzstan as a secular country. The official

---

10   "Pust' luchshe khodiat v mini-iubkakh, no nikogo ne vzryvaiut—Atambayev," *KyrTAG.kg*, August 1, 2016, <http://kyrtag.kg/society/pust-luchshe-khodyat-v-mini-yubkakh-no-niko go-ne-vzryvayut-Atambayev->.

11   "Novaia versiia bannera 'Kairan elim, kaida bara baratabyz'tasyn' demontirovana," *Knews. kg*, August 28, 2016, <http://knews.kg/2016/07/28/novaya-versiya-bannera-kajran-elim-kajda-baratabyz-demontirovana/>.

12   L. Ryan, "Muslim Women Negotiating Collective Stigmatization: 'We're Just Normal People'," *Sociology*, 45, no. 6 (2011): 1045–1060.

definition of secularism was adopted quite recently—in 2014,[13] and it is fairly neutral: it does not favor either state or religion, as happens in other contexts.[14] Also, because the concept was developed very recently and not widely dis-

---

13   Some main points from the *Concept of the State Policy of the Kyrgyz Republic in the Religious Sphere for 2014–2020*, <http://www.president.kg/files/docs/kontseptsiya_na_rus._prilojenie_k_ukazu_pkr-1.pdf>: The Kyrgyz Republic is a secular state that guarantees its citizens freedom of religion. The religious policy is based on the harmonic coexistence and mutual respect between secular and religious systems of values. The secular principle of state management of the activity of religious organizations means constitutional separation of religion from the state is based on not allowing their interfering in the activity of state institutions. In Kyrgyzstan, nobody can be forced to express or give up their religious views, nobody can be discriminated (against) on the basis of religious belonging or not-belonging. Separation of state from religion happens on following conditions:
      –   The state is officially neutral, does not affiliate itself with any religion, and does not use any religious ideology as obligatory for its citizens;
      –   Religious organizations do not interfere in the activity of state institutions, but can file recommendations, petitions, etc.
      –   Religious organizations do not fulfil any duties of state institutions;
      –   Religious organizations do not participate in the activity of political parties and movements;
      –   The state supports strengthening the relations between confessions and between believing and non-believing citizens;
      –   The state can interfere in the activity of religious organizations only in the cases described by the law;
      –   State control of religious organizations is based on the principle of respect toward religious feelings of believers.
      To protect freedom of religion and individual, public and national interests and to secure stability and safety, the State within the frames of law can:
      –   Act to prevent and solve religious conflicts;
      –   Limit the activity of religious organizations that are dangerous for individuals, society and state;
      –   Control the content of religious education, literature, information in mass-media to prevent spreading of extremist or destructive ideas, religious conflicts, and calls for violence.

14   There are two models of secularism that can be found in other political contexts: French (separatist) and Anglo-Saxon (accommodationist). Both are based on the separation of state from religion, but this separation is interpreted differently. The French model often referred to as laïcité, is based on the protection of state from religion: it bans any form of visual manifestation of religious belonging in the public sphere. The Anglo-Saxon model on the contrary, is based on the protection of religion from the state: this model has much more space for the presence of religion in all spheres of life including public offices and educational institutions. See S. Topal, "Everybody Wants Secularism—But Which One? Contesting Definitions of Secularism in Contemporary Turkey," *International Journal of Politics, Culture, and Society*, 25, no. 1/3 (2012): 1–14; C. Killian, "From a Community of

cussed in public, the common interpretations of secularism in public are quite ambiguous. We can see how people on both sides of the hijab controversy refer to the same constitution and concept of secularism, but interpret it differently. For example, on the controversial question of wearing hijabs in school, a former member of the Kyrgyz parliament, Ainur Altybaeva, said:

> The first article of the Constitution says that Kyrgyzstan is a democratic country where religion is separated from the state. Let anyone believe in what they want to believe. But we should not allow the wearing of religious clothing in state offices and educational establishments because this is also a part of propaganda.[15]

On the contrary, several parliamentarians wrote official letters to the minister of education with the request to protect the rights of girls wearing hijabs in school and to consider their preferences when the new school uniform was designed.[16] They referred to the constitution, which guarantees every person freedom of religion and protection from discrimination on the basis of religion. In their understanding of secularism, the state should not interfere in the religious life of citizens.

In our opinion, local secularism can be better understood from a generational perspective. The majority of state officials today represent the older generation who were brought up in the times of Soviet anti-religious propaganda, and their definition of *svetskost'* (secularism) is more reflective of *sovetskost'*—worldviews based on the visions of Soviet modernity and atheism. Julie McBrien, in her own account of the hijab in Kyrgyzstan, describes how successful the Soviet Union was in objectifying modernity and tradition, in creating the strong secular sphere and shaping "modern" Central Asian subjects.[17]

      Believers to an Islam of the Heart: 'Conspicuous' Symbols, Muslim Practices, and the Privatization of Religion in France," *Sociology of Religion*, 68, no. 3 (2007): 305–320.

15   T. Osmongazieva, "V 'Ar-Namyse' posporili o vynesenii na referendum voprosa o khidzhabe," *Vechernii Bishkek*, September 12, 2014, <http://www.vb.kg/doc/286335_v_ar_namyse_poporili_o_vynesenii_na_referendym_voprosa_o_hidjabe.html>.

16   D. Podol'skaia, "Deputaty parlamenta Kyrgyzstana trebuiut ot ministra obrazovaniia uchest' prava devochek, nosiashchikh khidzhab," *24.kg*, September 15, 2014, <http://arch.24.kg/parlament/186394-deputaty-parlamenta-kyrgyzstana-trebuyut-ot.html>.

17   J. McBrien, "Mukadas's Struggle: Veils and Modernity in Kyrgyzstan," *Journal of the Royal Anthropological Institute*, 15 (2009): 127–144.

Kyrgyz National Identity

The second main public discourse is about Kyrgyz national identity and its protection from various foreign influences. The government of Almazbek Atambayev is promoting a locally appropriate model of Islam that does not contradict local customs and traditions and is modern at the same time. Often the hijab is portrayed by officials as an element of foreign Arabic culture that has nothing to do with traditional Kyrgyz female clothing. Parliament member Mairamkul Tilenchieva stated:

> The hijab was never a part of traditional Kyrgyz clothing for women. Today, the Arab and Pakistani dresses are being imposed on us. We have our own beautiful traditional clothing. We should stick to it.[18]

President Almazbek Atambayev, at a meeting of the Security Council in February 2014, warned that, behind the massive Islamization, is an attempt to make Kyrgyz people lose their national identity and uniqueness:

> To preserve the national heritage and uniqueness, it is important that they would not be replaced by other norms, including the religious ones. If we do not pay attention to that, we will gradually lose our national identity. If someone imposes the so-called Islamic clothing and hijab on us, there will be a time when those who wear traditional or comfortable contemporary clothing will be called unbelievers. In the Holy Quran there is no concept about what clothing is Islamic and what is not. Islam only requires clean and neat dress.[19]

Interestingly, some representatives of the Muslim community also perceive the hijab as a way of protecting Kyrgyz identity because, according to them, Islamic dress and hijabs are much closer to the traditional Kyrgyz dress than contemporary Western-style clothing, such as jeans, mini-skirts, shorts, and t-shirts. Old photographs of Kyrgyz men with long *chapans* (coats) and beards

---

18   A. Kutueba, "Mairamkul' Tilenchieva: khidzhab nikogda ne byl traditsionnoi odezhdoi kyrgyzov," *24.kg*, September 12, 2014, <http://arch.24.kg/parlament/186330-majramkul-tilenchieva-xidzhab-nikogda-ne-byl.html>.

19   Prezident Kyrgyzskoi respubliki, "Gosudarstvennoe regulirovanie v sfere religii budet tol'ko usilivat'sia, no s uchetom osnovopolagaiushchikh printsipov svobody sovesti i prav cheloveka," November 3, 2014, <http://www.president.kg/ru/news/4818_prezident_almaz bek_Atambayev_gosudarstvennoe_regulirovanie_v_sfere_religii_budet_tolko_usili vatsya_no_s_uchetom_osnovopolagayuschih_printsipov_svobodyi_sovesti_i_prav_ cheloveka/>.

and of Kyrgyz women in long dresses, *elechek*, hijab, and *topu*[20] for younger girls are commonly present in numerous Facebook posts as evidence of their similarity to contemporary Islamic clothing. Again, just like with the constitution and secularism, the same theme—national identity—is explored by both sides of the discourse, but interpreted differently.

Security

The third public discourse is about security framed as radicalism, extremism, and terrorism. In the context of terrorist attacks happening across the world, all Central Asian states are quite paranoid about such threats and today work actively to prevent them, although all in their own ways. Due to the global media influence, a woman in a black dress with her face obscured with a burka or niqab is a very powerful and threatening image. Even practicing Muslim respondents in our survey admitted the power of such an image and were critical of women dressing in such way. Both global and governmental security agendas contributed to the stigmatization and "othering" of Muslim women in hijab perhaps more than any other public discourse.

These three discourses on secularism, national identity, and terrorism are common not only for politicians. As Montgomery shows, concepts used by politicians and media in Kyrgyzstan become a part of the everyday language of home and street: people use them while making sense of changes taking place in the society and positioning themselves in relation to these changes.[21] In our next section, we illustrate one such change by describing how the practice of wearing the hijab and its perception by society have evolved in Kyrgyzstan since the early 1990s to the present day. We will do it from the words of Jamal Frontbek kyzy, the leader of Mutakalim, a foundation that works to protect the rights of Muslim women.

History of the Hijab in Bishkek

Jamal Frontbek kyzy was among the first practicing Muslim women to start wearing a hijab in Bishkek. She was a typical Soviet city girl who never wore any Islamic dresses during her school days. After completing high school in the early 1990s, she became interested in religion and entered the Islamic University

---

20   A small round or square hat.
21   D.W. Montgomery, "Towards a Theory of the Rough Ground: Merging the Policy and Ethnographic Frames of Religion in the Kyrgyz Republic," *Religion, State, and Society*, 42, no. 1 (2014): 23–45.

in Bishkek. She described how it was impossible to find any Islamic attire to buy anywhere in the city and how she and her friends used to travel to Jany-Jer—a small village near the city populated by Dargins,[22] where they could buy traditional Dargin shawls and long dresses. These were usually worn by old Dargin ladies and looked very bulky and strange on young city girls. Later, Jamal's sister, unhappy with the way Jamal looked in the Dargin outfit, helped her find a local seamstress and, since then, Jamal and her friends have ordered individual dresses and hijabs.

In the 1990s, to see a woman in a hijab on the street was something very extraordinary, and people looked very puzzled, surprised, and, most of the time very critical of it. Jamal describes how people used to call her *babushka* (granny) because of the hijab.

> People were staring at us as if they were in a zoo. Every second person would come and ask why I wear it. On my way to a bus stop, I would be approached or reprimanded like 20 times. It was difficult, but we perceived this as an opportunity to explain and invite people to Islam. They did not understand. My neighbor used to regularly bother my sister asking her about my hijab, until my sister got tired and said that I wear it because I don't have any hair on my head. Our teachers at the university were of great support in these difficult times, they helped us stay strong and reminded of all the *savabs* (rewards) we will receive in the next world for doing this.

At this time, Jamal and her friends discovered that girls were not allowed to wear hijabs in schools and universities. They thought that something must be done and decided to create an organization that would help Muslim women defend their rights. From 1996 to 1999, they tried to convince the Muftiyat and the State Committee on Religious Affairs that this was necessary, and eventually they succeeded. They next established the Mutakalim. This was the first female Muslim organization in the entire post-Soviet space. They got actively involved with the issues of girls prevented from wearing hijabs to school and university. Whenever they came across such cases, they took matters to the court and they were always successful. In 2008, the minister of education issued an order that banned wearing hijabs in public schools. Mutakalim received a huge number of complaints from children's parents that year. They again took the issue to the courts and organized several rallies in the city

---

22   An ethnic group of Muslims whom Stalin deported to Kyrgyzstan from the Caucasus in
      1930s and 1940s.

FIGURE 10.4   *Members of Mutakalim and sympathizers rally in front of the Ministry of Education against the ban of hijab in schools (Photo by Almaz Isman Kalet). The signs say: "Hijab is the woman's honor" and "Hijab is not an obstacle to studying"*

raising the public awareness of the issue. As a result, the minister was fired and his order was cancelled.

During the late 1990s and early 2000s, things were gradually changing. Islam was becoming both more a prominent and more visible part of urban life. There were more men wearing Islamic clothes and growing beards, and more women wearing long dresses and hijabs. This was also a period of high rates of internal migration from the southern regions of Kyrgyzstan where Islam was historically much more prominent than in the North and where it was more common for women to wear Islamic-style clothing. By the late 2000s, the hijab had become a normal part of the urban scene in Bishkek, and nobody was surprised or puzzled by it anymore.

In 2002, Jamal was invited to attend a United Nations conference in Europe, but when she was at the airport, the customs officers refused to let her go through unless she took off her hijab, because her passport photo showed her without it. She refused and boarded the plane only at the last minute after she threatened to create an international uproar with the help of the UN. Upon her return, she collected 300,000 signatures in support of permission to take passport photos with a hijab on. It then took her several years to have all ministries and governmental bodies somehow involved in this question to give their permission. She was able to get all necessary endorsements except for one from the Ministry of International Affairs, which refused to sign it. In 2007, when Bishkek hosted the Shanghai Cooperation Organization meeting and expected the arrival of several presidents, Jamal and her supporters decided to organize a rally to fight for their cause and blocked the main road from the airport. They started gathering crowds and this had an effect: the ministry got scared and signed the permission. "We were young and fearless," says Jamal.

Today, according to Jamal, hijabs in schools and universities are no longer a big issue. Now Mutakalim, receives only about 15–20 complaints a year on this matter. The main difficulty Muslim women in hijab face today is related to employment. Many state offices and private companies refuse to hire women in hijabs, citing company dress codes. Mutakalim tries to get involved whenever it is possible. There are also many other options nowadays for practicing Muslim women to be employed in Muslim-friendly organizations and businesses.

The major issue for Muslim women in Bishkek today, according to Jamal, is their internal divisions. As Islamic practices become more popular, there are a greater and greater variety of religious influences and, as a result, Muslim society in Bishkek is becoming strongly divided into groups influenced by the Arab, Turkish, Indo-Pakistani, Egyptian, or Iranian forms of Islam. Women representing these groups often dislike each other and lack solidarity. The city is divided and, interestingly, members of these groups have their own unique way of wearing the hijab. A female insider can easily "read the city" and distinguish among all these various groups by the style of their veil. Mutakalim does not follow any specific branch of Islam; they try to help all women who come to their center. All these groups also have their own places to meet, socialize, and obtain religious knowledge. Most of these meetings take place in the private sphere of homes or on the grounds of some religious foundations because in Bishkek, there are only four mosques with rooms for women. Jamal complained that the city infrastructure is still not considerate of Muslim women. For example, her husband and son went to a swimming pool, but she and her daughter cannot because there was no single swimming pool open for women for even a short period of time.

In 2012, Jamal was among those who helped organize the first ever Islamic Fashion Week, where eight designers presented their work. This event attracted a large audience and strong media attention. The show has become a regular event since then. Long gone are the days when Jamal was buying bulky dresses and veils from Dargin ladies. Now, Muslim clothing is not only easily available, it is becoming a part of a growing consumer culture with specific orientation toward Muslim women. There are many shops that sell Islamic-style dresses. Many of these shops are concentrated in one area—around the

FIGURE 10.5   *Islamic Fashion Week in Bishkek. "V Bishkeke vpervye proshel pokaz*
musul'manskoi mody," Limon.kg, November 23, 2012, <http://limon.kg/news:172>

Central Mosque in Bishkek. These shops, the large number of women in hijabs who study at the nearby Islamic University, or come to the female prayer space in the central mosque contribute to the overall feeling of an Islamic oasis in the center of a very busy secular city.

Active Muslim women in hijab also make their presence known in other ways. In November 2013, Mutakalim organized a collective bike ride for women in hijabs. Nearly 200 women rode bikes along one of the main city streets toward the blood collection center where they donated blood that was later sent to Maternity Hospital #4. The aim of this event was to encourage women to participate in sports and to attract attention to the problem of anemia among new mothers. The event also showed the proactive stance of many Muslim women in Bishkek.

As this brief overview shows, the hijab in Bishkek has evolved in complex ways from being something abnormal and extraordinary to something that is common, diverse, and proactive. Members of Mutakalim have played a very dynamic role in reclaiming the urban space: they became effective actors and urban agents capable of mobilizing the sympathetic female Muslim community in support of their common cause and interests. We also see how the forms of hijabs became richer in colors, shapes, and semiotics. In our next

FIGURE 10.6
*Activist Muslim women's
bike ride in Bishkek
(Photo by Ulan
Asanaliev),* "V Bishkeke
proshel veloprobeg
musul'manok protiv
malokroviia," Ozodaron,
November 7, 2013, <http://
catoday.org/centrasia/
kgru/11209-v-bishkeke-
proshel-veloprobeg-
musulmanok-protiv-
malokroviya.html>

section, we want to look at the meanings of the hijab for women in relation to
their religious subjectivities.

The Meaning of Hijab for Practicing Muslim Women

This section is based on the analysis of interviews and focus-group discussions
with practicing Muslim women from research conducted by one of the co-
authors[23] in 2015–2016, which studied the perception and experience of
religious freedom among practicing Muslim women in Bishkek and the Chui
Valley. The research was based on a questionnaire given to 440 practicing
Muslim women, four focus-group discussions, and seven expert interviews.
The main aims of this research were to understand the social stereotypes
regarding Muslim women, impediments to religious freedom, and factors
affecting the fear and mistrust between secular and religious groups.

Muslim female respondents in this survey perceive the hijab in complex
ways. Some describe it as *farz* (obligation), inscribed by Quran for all women.
By wearing the hijab, women fulfill their duties to the Creator[24] and feel the
completeness of their belief.[25] At the same time, respondents said the hijab
gives women freedom and protection in their everyday lives in society.[26] They

---

23   Temporarily removed for reviewers.
24   FGD with women in Bishkek, December 25, 2015.
25   FGD with women in Bishkek, January 9, 2016.
26   FGD with women in Belovodskoe, November 13, 2015.

feel more respectful toward themselves[27] and particularly from men.[28] They also feel that they protect their own and other families by hiding their female beauty and preventing men's interest.[29] It is undoubtedly an important marker of their identity: with the hijab they remind themselves and others about who they are.[30]

Wearing the hijab is described as a sacred practice connected with the search for God. Very few women come to it right away. The traditional scenario mentioned by several respondents includes: first, interest in Islam, then praying one time a day and irregular fasting, followed by praying five times a day and complete fasting, attending Islamic gatherings or classes, and only then putting on the hijab. For some women, putting it on for the first time can be perceived as a part of Islamic fashion. For others, it is a result of their search for the truth. Later, many perceive the hijab as a duty to God.[31] In the final stage, wearing it affects their way of life: it is expected to stop women from un-Islamic behavior and motivate them to be more moral and tolerant.[32] One respondent explained:

> My daughter in school used to attend wrestling. When she entered the Medical Academy, she started wearing the hijab. She says how sometimes she is tempted to use her strong wrestling skills when solving the conflicts, but her hijab stops her.[33]

Women describe the hijab as something that disciplines them and even helps in their studies: "Without the hijab, I was always focused on the way I looked. Now, when my hair is covered, I can concentrate better on my studies."[34] However, some respondents mentioned that many women in hijabs do not understand the essence of religion, that it is to be reached internally with one's heart, not externally with the garment itself. So they do not change and continue behaving improperly, thus discrediting other women in hijab:[35]

---

27   FGD with women in Bishkek, January 9, 2016.
28   FGD with women in Bishkek, January 9, 2016.
29   FGD with women in Bishkek, January 9, 2016.
30   FGD with women in Bishkek, January 9, 2016.
31   FGD with women in Bishkek, November 25, 2015.
32   FGD with women in Bishkek, January 9, 2016.
33   FGD with women in Belovodskoe, November 13, 2015.
34   FGD with women in Belovodskoe, November 13, 2015.
35   FGD with women in Bishkek, December 25, 2015.

We ourselves are guilty of secular extremism. Our rudeness, lack of courtesy, poor education and poor understanding of the meaning of hijab reinforce the negative image of Muslim women.[36]

Some respondents mentioned that the hijab helps them hide certain features of their body they are not happy with: "The hijab is good both for thin and ample-bodied women. For example, my granddaughter is fifteen and she is quite heavy for her age. The Islamic dress helps her hide that and she feels more confident in the streets."[37]

Many secular groups believe that Muslim parents force their children to wear hijab and perceive this as a violation of children's rights.[38] Muslim female respondents reject such claims and suggest that girls who put on hijab under parental pressure usually take it off soon: "My niece put on hijab because her parents insisted. But after marriage she took it off."[39] They suggest that children in Muslim families wear the hijab because their mothers do and because they themselves believe that this is their religious duty.[40] The majority of respondents who have daughters said that for those children who decided to wear the hijab in school it was their own decision. Parents understand that wearing the hijab can create the sense of discomfort due to peer pressure.[41] That is why many Muslim parents do not insist and even, as in the case of one respondent, prohibit their daughters from wearing it in school.[42]

Respondents complained that society often perceives them as uneducated, limited, and suppressed by their husbands because of hijab,[43] and they argue strongly against such stereotypes. One-quarter of survey respondents were, in fact, university students. Women who did not work frequently said that this was their own choice toward fulfilling their family obligation, not their husband's dictate.

Several forms of moral and social discrimination were mentioned. "I trade bread in the market and my neighboring trader wears a hijab. I often hear how people call her a ninja-turtle."[44] According to respondents, this happens

36   FGD with women in Bishkek, January 9, 2016.
37   FGD with women in Kara-Balta, December 12, 2015.
38   Interview with expert.
39   FGD with women in Kara-Balta, December 12, 2015.
40   FGD with women in Belovodskoe, November 13, 2015.
41   FGD with women in Bishkek, December 25, 2015.
42   FGD with women in Bishkek, December 25, 2015.
43   FGD with women in Bishkek, January 9, 2016.
44   FGD with women in Kara-Balta, December 12, 2015.

because the number of women in hijab is still very small,[45] which makes them easily noticeable in a crowd and thus more vulnerable. However, some Muslim respondents suggest that women without a hijab experience more discrimination than they do, while they themselves are more respected.[46]

Women also defend themselves against the accusations of losing national identity:

> We are blamed for copying Arabs. However, we do not blame secular women for not covering their hair and for short haircuts, in which they copy the Europeans. Historically, Kyrgyz women always covered their head. In Kyrgyz tradition, women should never have short hair. In fact, to cut woman's hair short was a way of public punishment and humiliation.[47]

At the same time, many respondents agreed that one of the main reasons for the confrontation with secular groups is the black color of dress and hijab with niqab, which people associate with suicide bombers and ISIS. In Bishkek black is usually worn by women from the Salafi group, while women of other Muslim groups wear it very rarely. Ryan describes how British Muslim women challenge the stigma of posing a security threat by distancing themselves terrorist groups, by trying to show Islam from a good side, by socializing and getting along with non-Muslim communities and by adjusting their clothing style (e.g., wearing jeans and hijab).[48] Similarly, respondents in our survey distance themselves from radical Islam and reflect on their clothing style: "We should not wear black dress and, by that, create fears and reinforce stereotypes."[49] Some respondents, including Jamal Frontbek kyzy, do not favor hiding their faces. They suggest that this makes people afraid, reinforces the negative image of Islam, and attracts unnecessary attention to all Muslim women. Maria Louw, in her study of Muslim revivalism in Kyrgyzstan, proposes that, in the context of radical change, the majority of Kyrgyz Muslims strive for a balance, for a golden mean between blind radical belief and cynical pragmatism.[50]

---

45   FGD with women in Belovodskoe, November 13, 2015.
46   FGD with women in Bishkek, January 9, 2016.
47   FGD with women in Belovodskoe, November 13, 2015.
48   Ryan, "Muslim Women Negotiating Collective Stigmatization."
49   FGD with women in Belovodskoe, November 13, 2015.
50   M. Louw, "Even Honey May Become Bitter When There is Too Much of It: Islam and the Struggle for a Balanced Existence in Post-Soviet Kyrgyzstan," *Central Asian Survey*, 32, no. 4, (2013): 514–526.

Most participants in our survey did not position themselves against the secular residents of Bishkek. As we can see from their statements, the majority are not fanatical in their adherence to the hijab; they do not always contrast it against the secular lifestyle. The relationship is much more complex: they aspire to be a part of society, but not at the cost of their Islamic moral principles, which disapprove of certain Western-like lifestyles.[51] As pointed out by Montgomery, the boundaries between the two communities are very vague, with multiple overlapping fields and crossing paths.[52] Although on a personal level, the decision to veil themselves might be of great individual significance and, thus, seemingly radical for family and friends, on the community level, it is by now a normative practice that places a woman in the specific societal niche and assigns certain social expectations. How women fit into these societal roles is the subject of our next section.

Being a Muslim Woman in Bishkek

The questionnaire survey, from which this chapter draws, was conducted in Bishkek and several other settlements in the Chui Valley. The survey consisted of two parts: revealing the current situation with religious freedom for Muslim women and looking for recommendations to improve the situation. The sample included 440 women who attend various religious classes and gatherings organized by the Mutakalim. Not all respondents were wearing hijabs, but they all were interested in Islam: some were still learning and others had more experience with Islamic religious practices. Some 95 percent of respondents were ethnically Kyrgyz. The majority were young, as can be seen from Table 10.1.

One-third (33 percent) of respondents were unemployed and one-quarter (25 percent) were students. Private businesses (17 percent) and working in a religious organization (8 percent) were the two most feasible options for practicing Muslim women. Another 7 percent worked in the sphere of education and 4 percent for the state.

As for the question of what religious issues are the most important for respondents today, the biggest percentage (37 percent) was that of the hijab in school. Despite the improvements in this sphere and fewer cases of banning it, it was still important for the respondents. Three other issues were almost equally important: mistrust and fear among religious and secular groups (22 percent), discrimination of Muslim women's rights in general (21 percent),

---

51   Ryan, "Muslim Women Negotiating Collective Stigmatization."

52   Montgomery, "Towards a Theory of the Rough Ground."

TABLE 10.1 *Age distribution of survey respondents*

18-25	26-35	36-45	46-55	55+
36%	21%	20%	14%	9%

and disagreements among women belonging to different Islamic groups (20 percent).

In regard to the question of how much they know about the freedom of religion, 17 percent said that they know a lot, 65 percent a little, and 21 percent knew nothing. On a more specific question of how they understand the freedom of religion, the majority (50.1 percent) described it as the freedom of choice in religion and freedom to practice it without discrimination. Other respondents produced more specific visions, such as practicing Islam as it should be practiced (2.5 percent), freedom to dress according to beliefs (0.9 percent), freedom to obtain religious education (0.7 percent), when society is familiar with Islam and does not oppose it (0.7 percent), when the rights of all Muslims are protected (0.7 percent), democracy (0.5 percent), and freedom to call people to Islam (0.2 percent). One-third of respondents (34.7 percent) could not give an answer to this question.

The majority of respondents (55.8 percent) have never experienced pressure or discrimination because of their religious identity; 21.5 percent experience it sometimes; and 22.7 percent experience it frequently. For those who experienced it, most of this pressure was moral or verbal, such as humiliation, sneering, and jeering (92 percent). However, 7 percent of respondents had also experienced physical discrimination. Table 10.2 shows the explanations that respondents offered for they faced discrimination. Misunderstanding and lack of knowledge about religion, and the association of Muslims with extremists and terrorists were the most common answers.

Women who experienced discrimination have in the past taken their complaints to—or said they would consider contacting—the following organizations: religious bodies such as the Muftiyat, Kaziyat, and local imams (33.3 percent), local administrations (28.3 percent), police (24.9 percent), or nongovernmental organizations (8.8 percent).[53] As we can see, the state and civil society sectors are still trusted by practicing respondents. This finding also comes through strongly in their recommendations for future improvement of the situation. As for who should be responsible for the protection of Muslim women's rights, the most important bodies were the Muftiyat (46.9 percent)

---

53   Some 4.5 percent of respondents did not have an answer to this question.

TABLE 10.2 *How respondents explain the social pressure and discrimination against them*

No answer	40.1%
Misunderstanding and lack of knowledge about religion	21.8%
Because of extremist, groups, terrorism and ISIS	15.3%
Lack of secular and religious education	5.0%
Because of ISIS	4.5%
Atheism	3.9%
Black dress and niqab	1.8%
Lack of mutual understanding between secular and religious gorups	1.4%
Growth in the number of religious groups	0.7%
Other	5.5%
Total	100.0%

TABLE 10.3 *How respondents explain the social pressure and discrimination against them*

Muftiyat	43.3%
Central government	20.5%
Police	13.8%
Local administration	10.4%
International organizations	7.1%
Local NGOs	4.9%
Total	100.0%

and the state (44.4 percent). NGOs were also in the list (8.6 percent). Table 10.3 contains the list of organizations respondents were ready to collaborate with in the future:

All major recommendations on how to improve relations between them and the secular world were connected to strengthening the knowledge base: 40 percent of recommendations suggested educating the secular population about religion, 32 percent to educate religious women about secularism, and 27 percent to increase knowledge about tolerance. Survey respondents also saw their own role in this process: particularly in explaining the secular groups the tenets of religion (17.6 percent), organizing religious classes and trainings (14.2 percent), and helping the society unite (9.8 percent). Other visions were more faith-based: to invite them to Islam (5.1 percent) and to uproot atheism (3.7 percent). Respondents also suggested engaging with mass media (2.4 percent), actively protecting the rights of women (1.7 percent), and improving one's own behavior in order to show Islam from a positive side (1.1 percent).

One of the most important and controversial questions about the city space and religion today is that of prayer rooms for women in the mosques. There is a common belief in Kyrgyz society that women should pray at home, while mosques should be exclusively for men. Interestingly, the majority (44 percent) of women support this opinion and did not request designated spaces in the mosques. However, 38 percent of respondents disagree: they want special rooms where they can pray (at least while traveling or during work hours) and where they can socialize.[54] Similarly, 40 percent of respondents (versus 43 percent) believe that it is unfair that there is no female department in the Muftiyat. Often, women cannot go to the Muftiyat with specific questions, because they cannot openly discuss such questions with a male religious scholar or expert. It would be much easier for her to discuss such matters with a female religious practitioner. Thus, 64 percent believe that opening such a department would be beneficial for them.

As the survey results in this section revealed, being a Muslim woman in Bishkek or the Chui Valley is not that difficult, but it is not that easy, either. About 40 percent of women experience discrimination and 7 percent even experience violence. However, what is important is that women do not necessarily see the state as an oppressor, and they are ready to collaborate with it to improve their own position in the society. Having reviewed the history of the hijab in Bishkek, its meanings for practicing Muslim women, and their religious experiences with it, we would like to come back to the analysis of the billboard controversy, from which this whole story started.

Objectification of Female Body and Power of Women's Agency

In the heat of debate provoked by the images depicted on the controversial billboards in Bishkek, one interesting question somehow escaped public attention: Why is it that the president's banners and their alternative visions depict only women and not men? In the public discourse, one hears a great deal of critical comments about men wearing Pakistani-style garments, but somehow images of men do not appear in any platforms. Why has the woman's hijab, not the man's beard, become the main focus of visual contestation?

The answer might be quite simple, yet quite universal. The main controversy, perhaps, centers on the hijab in Bishkek for the same reasons that it

---

54   18 percent did not have a clear opinion on this question.

focuses on it in other urban contexts: it might all be about the traditional male patriarchy and objectification of women. Behind all these debates between secularists and Islamists on the issues of constitution, national identity, and terrorism, lurks the age-old struggle for man's control over the female body.

Ryan refers to Fortier, who describes how women's bodies are used to symbolize the transgression of social boundaries.[55] So, in Bishkek on one side, we have the strong patriarchal figure of President Atambayev who has power and money to project on the whole country his vision of how women should and should not dress, or former prime minister Temir Sariev who openly criticized the hijab. For them, women who wear it transgress the limits of a "normal" secular dress codes and that is what they want to control. On the other hand, we have such public male figures as Tursunbai Bakir uulu, a former member of parliament and social media activist, who strongly propagated Islamic dress code for women and fought the prime minister after his attacks on hijab. For him and other Islamists, it is women in mini-skirts who transgress the boundaries of Islamic norms and must be reprimanded.

The effort to control how women dress is not recent nor is it unique to Kyrgyzstan. Feyzi Baban, discussing the controversies of the hijab ban in Turkey, describes how control of a female body has double symbolism: a woman's body is perceived as the carrier of religion and is an important subject of Turkish modernization.[56] An educated young woman in a hijab is perceived as posing a direct assault on the century-long Turkish modernization effort. In Central Asia, men in power were trying to control the way Central Asian women dress in the pre-Soviet, Soviet, and now in post-Soviet contexts. In fact, as Julie McBrien shows, the Soviets succeeded in eliminating the religious influence in Central Asia only after they unveiled women because, she concurs, the woman embodies the religion.[57] Interestingly though, the act of unveiling also became an act of emancipation, and, during the last 70 years of Soviet rule, Kyrgyz women who even in the pre-Soviet times were quite independent compared with women in more settled Central Asian cultures, became even more empowered.

So, one must consider that it is not a traditional Kyrgyz woman who is veiling herself today, but a post-Soviet modern subject with a strong background

---

55   Ryan, "Muslim Women Negotiating Collective Stigmatization," refers to A.-M. Fortier, "Re-membering places and the performance of belongings," *Theory, Culture and Society*, 16, no. 2 (1999): 41-64

56   F. Baban, "Secular Spaces and Religious Representations: Reading the Headscarf Debate in Turkey as Citizenship Politics," *Citizenship Studies*, 18, no. 6–7 (2014): 644–660.

57   McBrien, "Mukadas's Struggle."

in (for older women) or legacy of (for younger women) Soviet female emancipation. Despite efforts by secularists and Islamists to control her, a Kyrgyz Muslim woman refuses to be objectified by either side. She has her own visions and ways of getting toward her goals. As interviews and focus-group discussions in this research show, very few women start practicing Islam and wearing the hijab under pressure of their fathers, brothers, or husbands. For the majority, it is their own conscious choice, the outcome of an internal search, various life struggles, and influence from their female peers. Farideh Heyat shows that for women in Kyrgyzstan, Islam became a source of moral support in the context of the deep moral crisis produced by the post-Soviet chaos, while the hijab helped them safeguard their female dignity.[58] For a Kyrgyz woman, being veiled became both an act of piety and a "means of realigning cultural landscapes and of creating herself as a modern individual through, within, and in reaction to 'Western,' 'Soviet,' and 'Islamic' normative frameworks."[59]

Similarly, Habiba Fathi, in her study of *otines* (female Islamic teachers) in Central Asia, shows how women refuse to be classified as passive objects, but find themselves at the heart of the social order as honorific figures, guardians of faith, who played important roles in preserving Islamic knowledge during Soviet times, and further expanding and distributing this knowledge in the post-Soviet context.[60] Thus, they re-Islamize Central Asian cities and towns.

The history of the hijab, exemplified in the history of such organizations as Mutakalim, shows that since the early 1990s, activist Muslim women in Bishkek were themselves fighting for their rights: rallying people into the streets, taking government ministries to court, blocking roads, filing petitions, and sponsoring blood drives. This is what makes Kyrgyzstan's veil controversy unique: the proactive position of women and their will and ability to stand up for themselves and choose their own path.

Manja Stephan-Emmrich and Abdullah Mirzoev show that in Dushanbe, the hijab became a cultural strategy that helped women protect their modesty, adapt to urban life, gain access to the economic sector traditionally dominated by men, and develop trust as important economic resources.[61] By "fashionalizing" the hijab and wearing it in many colors and forms, Tajik women were

---

58   F. Heyat, "Re-Islamisation in Kyrgyzstan: Gender, New Poverty, and the Moral Dimension,"
       Central Asian Survey, 23, no. 3–4 (2004): 275–287.

59   McBrien, "Mukadas's Struggle," 140.

60   H. Fathi, "Otines: The Unknown Women Clerics of Central Asian Islam," *Central Asian Survey*, 16, no. 1 (1997): 27–43.

61   M. Stephan-Emmrich and A. Mirzoev, "The Manufacturing of Islamic Lifestyles in Tajikistan through the Prism of Dushanbe's Bazaars," *Central Asian Survey*, 35, no. 2 (2016): 157–177.

also able to connect to the global market for Islamic styles and recreate themselves as followers of "modern Islam." Robin Wright, in his essay titled "Pink Hijab," describes Dalia Ziada, a representative of what he calls the "pink hijab generation" in Egypt—women who are both committed to faith yet resolute about their rights.[62] Ziada is a female Muslim activist fighting for civil rights using methods of civil disobedience. For Ziada and her friends, a colorful hijab is not a symbol of suppression, but "social armor that enables Muslim women to chart their own course, personally or professionally." It is an equalizer that gives women more power in a men's world. It is both a stamp of authenticity and symbolic demand for change.

Yet in analyzing the active role of women's agency, we should not confuse it with feminism. Jamal Frontbek kyzy, in her interview, clearly stated, "I am not a feminist. There is no feminism in Islam. I am simply a human-rights defender for Muslim women." Jamal does not rebel against men per se. Christine Jacobsen, in her study of Norwegian Muslim women, discusses the failures of feminist theories to fully portray the individual religious subjectivities in the female Islamic revivalism.[63] She suggests that it is impossible to understand the hijab through the "rebel" versus "conformist" discourse, which is often employed by feminists in the study of women in Islam. Rather, the hijab is a part of the "technique of self" that manifests and helps women become obedient to God, submit to religious norms, and even reaffirm the unequal Islamic gender constructs. Instead, "liberation," according to Jacobsen, should be read in relation to the language of authenticity and autonomy: for Muslim women in Norway and in Kyrgyzstan today, Islam is their own choice and this is what gives legitimacy to their religious practice as authentic and reflexive.

Conclusion

In our chapter, we have tried to show how urban life in the capital of Kyrgyzstan is very dynamic and complex. The freedom that Kyrgyzstan has and many other neighboring Central Asian capitals lack creates the conditions where all kinds of claims become possible. Religion, as one of the most influential forces affecting the urban community of Bishkek's residents today, also produces its claims for the city. It contests secular, nationalist, security, and other claims. The growing community of practicing Muslims assert their right to be in the

---

62   R. Wright, "The Pink Hijab," *Wilson Quarterly*, 35, no. 3 (2011): 47–51.
63   C. Jacobsen, "Troublesome Threesome: Feminism, Anthropology, and Muslim Women's Piety," *Feminist Review*, 98, no. 1 (2011): 65–82.

FIGURE 10.7   *New banner on Sovetskaya Street with the Kyrgyzstan Olympic team.*
"Bannery s khidzhabami zamenili na foto olimpiiskoi sbornoi
*Kyrgyzstana," Zanoza.kg, July 14, 2016, <http://zanoza.kg/doc/341502_*
bannery_s_hidjabami_zamenili_na_foto_olimpiyskoy_sbornoy_kyr-
gyzstana.html>

city, live according to their religious ideals, and create Islamic urban spaces.
The growing number of mosques, madrasas, halal shops, and the like form part
of a new urban infrastructure.

Such claims do not remain uncontested. Because religious identity has
strong visual manifestations and all residents at some point in their life have to
position themselves in relation to religion, religious claims become the subject
of strong public debate. The Soviet atheist legacy explains why the secular
community does not want to give up its position and stake its own counter-
claims on the urban space. The controversy of billboards is a perfect illustration
of secular–religious urban contestation.

As in many other parts of the world, this contestation overlaps with socially
constructed gender hierarchies. Religious and secular claims over the urban
space turn into male claims over women, with both sides insisting they know
what women should wear. Yet as our research shows, Kyrgyz women in Bishkek
do not need fashion advice. The Islamic revivalist movement among women in
the Kyrgyz capital has, since the 1990s, created a strong momentum that has a
life of its own and is fairly independent. Muslim women wearing the hijab have
become very visible and influential urban actors with their own claims to the
city. At the next level of complexity, Muslim women do not represent one
homogenous group, but a large variety of Islamic influences—all with their
own unique visual appearance and competing claims for the city. The resulting

effect is a great diversity of urban environment that contributes to the cosmopolitan feel of urban experience.

Epilogue

Following the controversy of public debate on the provocative banners, in July, half of them were replaced by new banners showing Kyrgyzstan's Olympic team going to Rio de Janeiro—another source of "national pride" (see Figure 10.7). The team returned home from the 2016 Olympics with only one medal and even that was soon revoked because of doping accusations. Pathetic as it is, perhaps the banner controversy tells us is that it is time for Kyrgyz politicians to stop beating their proud national chests, making populist statements, and instead start addressing serious issues related to corruption, economic stagnation, migration, and numerous others.

CHAPTER 11

Hijab in a Changing Tajik Society[1]

Shahnoza Nozimova

All major religions offer normative prescriptions regarding the body, such as sexuality, hygiene, dress code, and dietary restrictions. Similarly, the political project of modern nation-states has evolved around the conception that the *body* of the citizenry is the source and subject of political authority.[2] Thus, in the contemporary era, the human body serves as a canvas to demarcate the boundaries of the multi-layered identities, power relations, and limitations of the dominant discourses, as well as the desire to be uniquely *oneself*. In this view, the contestation over dress is an inherent and critical component of the political process. Indeed, as pointed out by Fandy, "Political science without clothes" presents an incomplete picture of contestation, where the political power is:

> focused on the manifest, naked, and concentrated formal power of the state and other formal institutions … at the expense of the diffuse, fragmented, and localized disciplinary power and technologies of resistance – the informal politics and economy in which most people function.[3]

In contemporary Tajik society, female dress is often viewed through such a symbolic prism and used as a roadmap to navigate competing identities and systems of hegemony. Thus, for different observers regard certain items and combinations of clothing as embodying the ideas (and ideologies) they seek or avoid.

In official discourse, where combatting alien influences has been identified as the utmost goal, the modern Islamic headscarf has become the nemesis of

---

1   Research for this chapter was supported in part by the Doctoral Fellowship Program, which is funded and administered by the Open Society Foundations (OSF). The opinions expressed herein are my own and do not necessarily express the views of OSF. I am also thankful to two anonymous reviewers for their helpful comments and critique.
2   T.B. Hansen and F. Stepputat, *Sovereign Bodies: Citizens, Migrants, and States in the Postcolonial World* (Princeton, NJ: Princeton University Press, 2005), 9–10.
3   M. Fandy, "Political Science Without Clothes: The Politics of Dress or Contesting the Spatiality of the State in Egypt," *Arab Studies Quarterly*, 20, no. 2 (Spring 1998): 88.

Tajik statehood.[4] Moreover, other specific characteristics of female Islamic practice in Tajikistan, such as the activities of female religious specialists, are receiving greater scrutiny and criticism.[5] Thus, distinct features of female habitus that normally were characterized as belonging to private religious domain and practice, have become a policy and security matter. This phenomenon is unprecedented (certainly, in post-Soviet history), yet unsurprising given, the increasing scale of state activism in the religious field.[6]

This chapter looks at three aspects of the hijab controversy in Tajikistan. First, I trace the politicization of female Islamic attire in contemporary Tajikistan and outline the official discourse (often supported by experts and observers) that views hijab as a token of new forms of religious practice and identity. I also present some general theoretical approaches in the literature on female religious dress. Second, I present a small selection of stories, including those of the women who have adopted hijab and one woman who did not. Finally, I propose an alternative perspective on hijab – a socially acceptable mechanism that reinstates male domination and, by so doing, also reestablishes the individual woman and her family's social status – thus becoming a practice that is often (re)produced and valued by women themselves.

---

4   According to Eshoni Saidjon, *imomkhatib* of the central mosque of Khatlon and deputy chairman of the Council Ulamo, the Islamic *satr* that is worn by women nowadays "is not a Tajik item (*moli tojikon nest*) and is taken from the culture of the other nations, especially Arab, so wearing of it does not correspond to the Tajik women's shame/dignity (*sharmu hayo*)." Moreover, according to Eshoni Saidjon, veiling that covers the face also does not correspond to Tajik state politics (*siyosati davlatdori*). See G. Ganj, "Mulloho guftand, ki zanho digar libosi tang napushand," *Radioi Ozodi*, July 29, 2014, <http://www.ozodi.org/content/tajik-national-dress-propaganda-in-tajikistan-mosque/25473550.html>.

5   Abdujabbor Rahmonzoda, assistant to the president for social development and public relations and a former minister of education, insists that the activities of the female religious specialists should be put stopped (*khotima guzorem*) on the grounds that leaders (*rohbaron va mas'ulon*) of the Islamic Movement of Uzbekistan (IMU) are propagating their ideology through these bibiotuns. See S. Gulkhoja and U. Nazar, "Bibiotunho" ba guruhi "risk" shomil meshavand," *Radioi Ozodi*, September 29, 2015, <http://www.ozodi.org/content/religious-women-prohibited-attending-ceremonies/27277518.html>. Meanwhile, in the northern city of Khujand, a public council of bibiotuns was established in 2011 and is reportedly actively involved in promoting state policies and regulations. "Bibiotun ne ekstremisty, bibiotun - arkhitektory dushi," *Asia-Plus*, October 7, 2015, <http://news.tj/ru/news/bibiotun-ne-ekstremisty-bibiotun-arkhitektory-dushi>.

6   H. Zainiddinov, "The Changing Relationship of the Secularized State to Religion in Tajikistan," *Journal of Church and State*, 55, no. 3 (2013): 456–477.

Hijab as Controversy

The hijab, a female dress style that is also a powerful and instantly recognizable symbol of Islam, remains a hotly contested issue in Tajikistan. *Hijab* is a new phenomenon in Tajikistan and began to be worn in the early 2000s. Often viewed as an expression and measure of a new practice of Islam – different from the traditional practice[7] – hijab quickly became a symbol of new forms of piety and more devout commitment to Islamic modesty and Quranic gender roles.

In this chapter, the term hijab (Taj: *hijob, satr, satri Islomi*) is used in the way the word is used and understood in the context of Tajikistan – a headscarf that conceals a woman's hair and neck (often her chin, too). In part, the peculiarity of the Tajik hijab debate lies in the fact that hijab is understood to be meaningfully different from *ruymol* (*qascha, kosynka*) – a ubiquitous headscarf/kerchief (smaller in size and tied at the nape of the neck, which usually covers only parts of the hair but leaves the neck and chin exposed) that is worn by women across Tajikistan. Certainly, this is a more "lay" understanding of the term, quite different from the traditional interpretation of hijab, which in the Quran "refers to a spatial curtain that divides or provides privacy"[8] and not to any specific item of clothing.

The first problems with hijab in Tajikistan's public sphere began to surface in 2003 with reports that some academic institutions did not allow female students to attend classes while wearing an unusual headscarf.[9] These and similar reports (e.g., passport officials refusing to issue documents to women pictured in hijab) initially were largely dismissed by the general public and politically active segments of the population. Even the leadership of the Islamic Renaissance Party of Tajikistan (IRPT) (at the time still a legal political party and an active member of the country's political processes) did not take a firm position on the matter; the IRPT chairman "believe(d) that these cases of discrimination against believers are not state policy," rather actions taken "at

---

7   For example, Thibault uses the term "born-again" to describe the stricter religious lifestyle and dress styles that some of her interlocutors in Sughd region have adopted. See H. Thibault, "Religious Revival in Tajikistan: The Soviet Legacy Revisited" (Ph.D. Diss., University of Ottawa, 2014), <https://www.ruor.uottawa.ca/bitstream/10393/31787/1/Thibault_Helene_2014_These.pdf>.

8   R.C. Martin (ed.), *Encyclopedia of Islam and the Muslim World* (New York: Macmillan Reference, 2004), 721.

9   I. Rotar, "Tajikistan: Religious Freedom Survey, November 2003," *Forum 18*, November 20, 2003, <http://www.forum18.org/archive.php?article_id=190>.

the whim of the officials."[10] Ever since then the controversy around the hijab has grown in scale and degree. In particular, the Ministry of Education has been at the forefront of the battle against "foreign garb," alien culture and ideology, and, ultimately, so-called non-Tajik Islam.

In 2005 the Ministry of Education banned hijab in secondary schools on the basis that it "is unacceptable in secular schools and violates the Constitution and the new law on education" and issued instructions barring children from going to mosques.[11] Again, the response from IRPT leadership was half-hearted. While recognizing the issue as "flagrant infringement of Muslims' rights," its chairman nevertheless tried to avoid the debate, lamenting that the Council of Ulama (the state-controlled council of religious scholars[12]) did not even respond to this "disgraceful and arbitrary order."[13] The IRPT and its chairman's position on this matter is important to mention, because, as reported in 2006, all of the female members of the party (about 15,000 women at the time) wore hijab.[14]

Yet, the challenges faced by female students wearing hijab were never properly addressed or remedied – for example, hijab-wearing girls faced unnecessary hurdles to receiving school certificates.[15] In 2007, Davlatmoh Ismoilova, a third-year university student, initiated a legal battle to secure her right to wear hijab at the Institute of Languages. Yet, her case against the Ministry of Education was thrown out of court and she lost the suit against the school; as a result, she did not return to finish her degree.[16]

The president of Tajikistan, Emomali Rahmon, has consistently maintained the need to fight foreign influences and since 2000 has used the combination

---

10   Ibid.

11   I. Rotar, "Tajikistan: Mosque Visits and Hijabs Banned for Children," *Forum 18*, October 31, 2005, <http://www.forum18.org/archive.php?article_id=679>.

12   T. Epkenhans, "Regulating Religion in Post-Soviet Central Asia: Some Remarks on Religious Association Law and 'Official' Islamic Institutions in Tajikistan," *Security and Human Rights*, 20, no. 1 (2009): 94–99.

13   Kabiri quoted in Rotar, "Tajikistan: Mosque Visits and Hijabs Banned for Children."

14   R. Mirzobekova, "Khidzhab dlya tadzhichki: moda ili dan' vere?", *Asia-Plus*, November 12, 2006, <http://www.centrasia.ru/newsA.php?st=1165788180>.

15   Igor Rotar, "Tajikistan: New Moves against Muslims in North," *Forum 18*, March 7, 2006, <http://www.forum18.org/archive.php?article_id=739>.

16   "Hijab-Wearing Students Dismissed from Tajik University," *Radio Free Europe/Radio Liberty*, May 26, 2009, <http://www.rferl.org/content/HijabWearing_Students_Dismissed_From_Tajik_University/1739828.html>; F. Najibullah, "Tajikistan: Court Rejects Student Challenge of Head-Scarf Ban," *Radio Free Europe/Radio Liberty*, July 12, 2007, <http://www.rferl.org/content/article/1077592.html>.

of *farhang* and *begona* ("other/foreign" and "culture") in at least 60 distinct speeches. Specific references to clothing and recommendations to express pride in national dresses started appearing in the president's speeches in 2009.[17]

In 2015, the fight against hijab reached new heights, with high-level government officials (from Rahmon to regional governors and city mayors) stepping up the rhetoric against hijab, calling it a cradle for fomenting foreign religious extremism (Taj: *ifrotgaroi*[18]) and a threat to country's peace (*sulh*) and unity (*vahdat*). Both terms, *sulh* and *vahdat* (sometimes: *sulhu subot* – peace and stability), refer to the specific political order that has emerged in the post-Civil War Tajikistan. The following quote from President Rahmon's "Lesson of Peace" speech (delivered on September 1, 2015, in Kulob) conveys the message directly:

> In particular, I want to warn that externalism (*zohirparasti*), worship of the foreign (*begonaparasti*), and superstition (*khurofot*) will bring a horrifying end (*oqibati dahshatnok*) to the society and statehood of the ancient Tajik nation, as these phenomena threaten the country's security and stability, prevent its development, and cause misfortune.[19]

Moving beyond the specific episodes and narratives of politicization, the major point is that in Tajikistan the debate over hijab revolves around the perspective that it is a symbol of a qualitatively different interpretation and practice of Islam. A similar view emerges from scholars – e.g., Thibault presents hijab as an attribute of the "born-again"[20] Muslims in northern Tajikistan. Miles views "an increase in the number of women and girls enacting the

---

17   Press service of President of Republic of Tajikistan, <http://president.tj/, 2005, 2015>.

18   "Qarori Ubaydulloev alayhi 'ifrotgaroi'-i zanon," *Ozodagon*, March 16, 2015, <http://www.ozodagon.com/20691-arori-ubaydulloev-alayi-ifrotgaro-i-zanon.html>.

19   E. Rahmon, "Sukhanroni bakhshida ba Ruzi donish va 70-solagii ta'sisi Donishgohi davlatii Kulob ba nomi Abuaddullohi Rudaki," *president.tj*, September 1, 2015, Kulob, Tajikistan, <http://president.tj/node/9731>.

20   In Thibault's work, the term "born again" refers to "believers who lived a secular life before 'discovering' faith and adopting a lifestyle based on religious principles." In particular, in Thibault's account men contrasted their newly acquired piety "to their previous 'sinner's lifestyle' defined as: "drinking, smoking, and fooling around with women (*ya pil, kuril i gulyal*)." And importantly, for women, the term denotes "the fact that they did not know God and therefore were neither praying nor wearing hijab." See Thibault, "Religious Revival in Tajikistan," 139–140.

Islamic principle of wearing hijab" as an "aspect of Islamic revival in Tajikistan."[21] Among observers and the policy community, this form of Islam was often viewed as political and contentious to the extent that images of women wearing hijab were displayed and viewed as evidence of growing religious radicalism in the Central Asian region. For example, Salhani hopes that Kazakhstan will serve as a moderate path to be emulated by other Muslim states, precisely because it embodies "Islam without a veil" – "the kinder, gentler, and more humane face of Islam."[22]

In comparative perspective, it is crucially important to note that the debate over female Islamic dress is not happening in a vacuum and is not, by any measure, a development unique to Tajikistan or other predominantly Muslim post-communist states and territories.[23] Over the past 15 years, hijab has become a major point of legislative and political contention in contexts where Muslims live as minority groups (namely, Europe, the United States, Canada, and Australia).[24] Female Islamic dress produced an even longer history of controversial debate in other Muslim majority contexts (e.g., in Middle East and South Asia).[25] Moreover, while strong connotations persist, such "veiling" debates are not exclusive to Islam and Muslim communities: in 2010 an Israeli rabbinical court, prompted by the husbands of Jewish women who had decided

21   M. Miles, "Switching to *Satr*: An Ethnography of the Particular in Women's Choices in Head Coverings in Tajikistan," *Central Asian Affairs*, 2, no. 4 (2015): 368.

22   C. Salhani, *Islam Without a Veil: Kazakhstan's Path of Moderation* (Washington, D.C.: Potomac Books, 2011), 166.

23   Human Rights Watch, "You Dress According to Their Rules," New York: Human Rights Watch, 2011, <https://www.hrw.org/report/2011/03/10/you-dress-according-their-rules/enforcement-islamic-dress-code-women-chechnya>; M.E. Commercio, "The Politics and Economics of 'Retraditionalization' in Kyrgyzstan and Tajikistan," *Post-Soviet Affairs*, 31, no. 6 (2015): 529–556.

24   Europe: S. Rosenberger and B. Sauer (eds), *Politics, Religion, and Gender: Framing and Regulating the Veil* (New York: Routledge, 2011); A. Vakulenko, *Islamic Veiling in Legal Discourse* (New York: Routledge, 2012); E. Tarlo, *Visibly Muslim: Fashion, Politics, Faith* (English ed). (New York: Berg, 2010); B. Winter, *Hijab and the Republic: Uncovering the French Headscarf Debate* (Syracuse, NY: Syracuse University Press, 2009); J.R. Bowen, *Why the French Don't Like Headscarves: Islam, the State, and Public Space* (Princeton, NJ: Princeton University Press, 2007). Canada: S.S. Alvi, H. Hoodfar, and S. McDonough, *The Muslim Veil in North America: Issues and Debates* (Toronto, ON: Women's Press, 2003). US: L. Ahmed, *A Quiet Revolution: The Veil's Resurgence, from the Middle East to America* (New Haven, CT: Yale University Press, 2011).

25   Turkey: J. White, *Muslim Nationalism and the New Turks* (rev. ed.) (Princeton, NJ: Princeton University Press, 2014); R. Peres, *The Day Turkey Stood Still: Merve Kavakci's Walk into the Turkish Parliament* (Reading, UK: Garnet, 2012). For Egypt, see Ahmed, *A Quiet Revolution*.

to wear the Jewish *burqa*, declared *burqa* a "sexual fetish" on the basis that covering "too much" (i.e., "exaggerating") could be considered equally as "promiscuous" as covering "too little."[26] The legal context for these debates is especially murky in the former cases, as there are clear references to secularism, freedom of conscience, and human rights in their respective supreme legal codes.

Literature on Religious Dress

The literature on religious dress is vast. Numerous scholars from distinct disciplines have studied the subject. The following literature review presents some of the perspectives that have emerged through a diverse research agenda, studying religious dress of different confessions, as well as in diverse geographic contexts. In this section, I discuss three distinct approaches that have been crucial in developing explanations for the hijab phenomenon in contemporary Tajikistan, which I present in the subsequent sections.

Social Control Approach

From a sociological perspective, dress is a social artifact that contains and reproduces elements and cues of non-verbal communication expressing an individual's disposition to the immediately surrounding social order. Building on theories of leading sociologists, e.g., Douglas, Goffman, Foucault, Bourdieu, and others, Arthur argues that dress "provides a window" through which one can examine the power and limits of social control systems.[27] Her edited collection, *Religion, Dress, and the Body*, engages the social control approach in a variety of conservative religious contexts (Mennonite, Mormon, Amish, Catholic nuns, Afghan Muslims, and Hasidic Jews) in the United States and demonstrates that, for the most part, religious dress is the individual's internalized (yet, outward) manifestation of the particular group's religious doctrine and social hierarchies that reproduce patriarchal domination. Since all of the works in the volume are based on qualitative methods and ethnographic fieldwork, authors provide a wealth of insights on the causal mechanisms of social control. For example, Graybill and Arthur, analyzing women's dress in the Mennonite communities, list personal (self-regulation, self-censorship), infor-

---

26   A. Blomfield, "Israeli Rabbis Clamp down on Burka," *Telegraph*, July 30, 2010, <http://www.telegraph.co.uk/news/worldnews/middleeast/israel/7919501/Israeli-rabbis-clamp-down-on-burka.html>.

27   L.B. Arthur (ed.), *Religion, Dress, and the Body* (New York: Berg, 1999), 1.

mal (peer pressure, gossip), and formal (sanctions of the religious specialists) means of control to ensure conformity and inhibition of deviance.[28]

In Tajikistan, Harris reports similar mechanisms of social control of female dress, body, and overall (sexual) behavior.[29] However, an important qualification needs to be introduced: in *Religion, Dress, and the Body* the individual women are seen as both the subjects and objects of communal control. In Harris' account in Tajikistan it is the men who are the subjects of social control, and while women's behavior is still the object of control, male honor (Taj: *nomus*) is dependent on "control over women and younger family members, and virility."[30] Consequently, how well women in the family perform their gender-assigned roles and duties, measured by conforming to the norms pertaining to submission, virginity, chastity, and fertility, adds up to the social perception of the male, head-of-household's, and subsequently family's, honor.[31]

Personal Security Approach

Another set of literature has emerged from the ethnographic studies carried out in the Middle East and, more recently, in the Europe and North America among Muslim immigrant communities, and focuses on hijab and Islamic dress. Leila Ahmed's aptly (and somewhat presciently) titled book, *A Quiet Revolution*, explores the phenomenon the (re)emergence of veiling in Egypt and United States.

Ahmed begins her (often personal) account of the dramatic story of the veil, which is ultimately located in the political context, by tracing the intellectual and institutional origins of the movement for unveiling in Egypt in the early twentieth century.[32] In this account, sartorial transformations were contemporaneous to the changes in people's lifestyles (e.g., preference for Western furniture), architectural remake of the cities, etc. – processes that were per-

---

28   Arthur, *Religion, Dress, and the Body*, 10.

29   C. Harris, *Control and Subversion: Gender Relations in Tajikistan* (Sterling, VA: Pluto Press, 2004).

30   More on Tajik conception of *nomus*, see S. Roche, *Domesticating Youth: Youth Bulges and Its Socio-Political Implications in Tajikistan* (New York: Berghahn, 2014); also White, *Muslim Nationalism and the New Turks*, for ethno-gendered reading of honor in the Turkish context.

31   In Harris's own account "what counts is *image*." See Harris, *Control and Subversion*, 20.

32   For similar issues in other Muslim contexts, see D. Kandiyoti (ed.), *Women, Islam, and the State* (Philadelphia, PA: Temple University Press, 1991) and L. Abu-Lughod (ed.), *Remaking Women: Feminism and Modernity in the Middle East* (Princeton, NJ: Princeton University Press, 1998).

ceived to be a prerequisite and, ultimately, measures of societal advancement.[33]
By the mid-twentieth century, Ahmed maintains unveiling became a norm of
life, not only for urban middle – and upper – class, but even in the more conservative rural areas.[34] A few decades later, however, women began to don
headscarves again, and this time it was not the headscarves that their mothers
and grandmothers wore before unveiling but the "Muslim Brotherhood" veil
– hijab.

The transformation of the Central Asian social landscape in the first half of
the twentieth century was no less dramatic.[35] Similarly, unveiling was seen as
central to the conception of (Soviet) modernity. Yet, while there are certainly a
number of parallels that we can draw upon between the Tajik and Egyptian (or
Turkish) experiences of unveiling, it is important also to keep in mind the differences. In some sense, Soviet Central Asia never fully unveiled. Yes, the *faranji*
(*burqa*-style attire) was no longer worn, but women did not fully transform
into a bareheaded, European-style proletariat either. National dress and different kerchiefs and headscarves were the new alternatives.[36] And women
remained not too keen on joining the workforce – women composed 39 percent of the total labor market, well below the all-Soviet average of 51 percent.[37]
Similarly, Harris argues that woman's public submission to the male guardian
was a transformed practice of seclusion.

Ahmed's account of the reemergence of hijab in Egypt is based on her reading of various ethnographic studies carried out in the 1970s, 1980s, 1990s and
later.[38] In the early years, some of the common threads that came up in vari-

33   Ahmed, *A Quiet Revolution*, 27–31.
34   Ibid., 20, 43.
35   G.J. Massell, *The Surrogate Proletariat: Moslem Women and Revolutionary Strategies in
       Soviet Central Asia, 1919–1929* (Princeton, NJ: Princeton University Press, 1974); D.T.
       Northrop, *Veiled Empire: Gender and Power in Stalinist Central Asia* (Ithaca, NY: Cornell
       University Press, 2004); M. Kamp, *The New Woman in Uzbekistan: Islam, Modernity, and
       Unveiling under Communism* (Seattle: University of Washington Press, 2006); D. Kandiyoti,
       "The Politics of Gender and the Soviet Paradox: Neither Colonized, Nor Modern?", *Central
       Asian Survey*, 26, no. 4 (2007): 601–623.
36   S. Tadjbakhsh, "Between Lenin and Allah: Women and Ideology in Tajikistan," in
       H.L. Bodman and N. Tohidi (eds), *Women in Muslim Societies: Diversity within Unity*
       (Boulder, CO: Lynne Rienner, 1998), 163–186.
37   Z. Madaminzhanova and I. Mukhtarov, "Cultural Life in the Ferghana Valley under
       Khrushchev and Brezhnev," in S.F. Starr et al. (eds), *Ferghana Valley: The Heart of Central
       Asia* (Armonk, NY: M.E. Sharpe, 2011), 166.
38   F. El Guindi, "Veiling Infitah with Muslim Ethic: Egypt's Contemporary Islamic Movement,"
       Social Problems, 28, no. 4 (1981): 465–485; G. Kepel, *Muslim Extremism in Egypt: The
       Prophet and Pharaoh* (Berkeley: University of California Press, 2003); A.E. MacLeod,

ous women's accounts for donning the veil were personal – responses and solutions to the problems that they were facing in everyday lives.[39] The women are portrayed displaying strong agency in choosing to dress in Islamic styles. In fact, in some scholarly accounts, the phenomenon of *les femmes reli-gieuses* is understood as a women's movement to reclaim – not withdraw from – the public sphere.[40]

Among the accounts of "personal reasons" for veiling, there are some that clearly echo the earlier-presented analytical lens on social control, where women (in Egypt in 1970s and 1980s) reported that it was a religious/pious thing to do, or as mothers and Egyptian women they needed to dress accordingly.[41] For others, it was a concession to their male family members that would allow them to work, study, and more in public.[42] However, while the critique of the social control hypothesis may be the apparent lack of female agency, in the personal accounts the decision to wear a veil is not viewed as utter submission to religion and societal norms of patriarchy; rather, it is a negotiated and conscious choice.

In such accounts the Islamic veil is liberating: by imbuing "women with a kind of moral and religious authority" the Islamic dress styles discouraged harassment in public transportation or places where women studied, worked, and lived.[43] It was argued in the 1980s that hijab allowed Egyptian women to work and "go about their lives" while "affirm(ing) community belonging and respect for community values;" moreover, for the male family members it was a sufficient symbol of the women's "commitment to their families and their roles as wives and mothers."[44]

"Hegemonic Relations and Gender Resistance: The New Veiling as Accommodating Protest in Cairo," *Signs*, 17, no. 3 (1992): 533–557; G.H. Talhami, *The Mobilization of Muslim Women in Egypt* (Gainesville: University Press of Florida, 1996); C. Rosefsky Wickham, *Mobilizing Islam: Religion, Activism and Political Change in Egypt* (New York: Columbia University Press, 2002); J.A. Williams, "Return to the Veil in Egypt," *Middle East Review*, 11, no. 3 (1979): 49–54; S. Zuhur, *Revealing Reveiling: Islamist Gender Ideology in Contemporary Egypt* (Albany: SUNY Press, 1992).

39   Ahmed, *A Quiet Revolution*, 88–89, 123.
40   Ibid., 87, 125.
41   Ibid., 88–90.
42   Ibid., 119–130.
43   Ibid., 87.
44   Ibid., 122.

Strategic Marriage (Economic) Approach

In the recent years the phenomenon of women adopting conservative elements of dress and lifestyle, in a socio-political environment where such behavior does not seem to be sanctioned and/or enforced, has puzzled many scholars. Such behavior is seen as contradicting the commonly accepted (i.e., Western, liberal) narratives of female emancipation,[45] subsequently deemed as suboptimal action that goes against the women's interests as a group. Thus, unsurprisingly, there has been a considerable effort on behalf of behavioral social scientists to explain this apparent paradox and to rationalize women's individual choices that seemed to contradict their group interests.

In one such study, Blaydes and Linzer explore female support for what they identify as "Islamic fundamentalism," operationalized, among other variables, as wearing of Islamic headscarves.[46] The authors offer an interesting theory, arguing: "Financial insecurity is a key determinant of the propensity to adopt fundamentalist beliefs and preferences."[47] Moreover, under the conditions where insecurities persist in terms of succeeding in a job market, women may find marriage as an alternative route to economic stability.[48] Thus, to increase chances of a favorable marriage, women need to find ways to improve their positions in the marriage market and adopting "fundamentalist values" (i.e., conservative dress) might be a decision that is in their best individual economic interests, even if that might go against the interests that women have as a group.

In the course of analysis of the data gathered through fieldwork,[49] (which consisted of interviews and participant observation) in Dushanbe and Khujand, I found that while all three approaches were helpful in explaining the dynamics that govern the lives of my interlocutors, there was also a need to contextualize and refine some of the assumptions. In the following section,

---

45   S. Peshkova, "A Post-Soviet Subject in Uzbekistan: Islam, Rights, Gender, and Other Desires," *Women's Studies*, 42, no. 6 (2013): 667–695.

46   L. Blaydes and D.A. Linzer, "The Political Economy of Women's Support for Fundamentalist Islam," *World Politics*, 60, no. 4 (2008): 580.

47   Ibid.

48   Ibid.

49   My most recent fieldwork in Tajikistan took place in early fall of 2015. Dushanbe and Khujand were chosen as field sites because we can observe a variety of styles of dress and head coverings among women in these urban centers and often women dressed in different styles live in one family/house. Interviews were for the most part conducted in Tajik, although on frequent occasions respondents did use Russian words and phrases. All of the names of the respondents have been changed and I am omitting specific references to residences to protect the identities of my interview subjects.

I present vignettes of women who wear and do not wear hijab, followed by a more nuanced perspective that proposes adopting a contextualized view on hijab.

Hijab as Peace

My conversations with several women who wear hijab/*satr*, both in Dushanbe and Khujand, revealed that they view their attire as fulfilling, not contradicting, both religious and national norms and codes of dress and behavior. Although most talked about initial discomfort associated with the first adoption, it was attributed to the necessary learning curve of placing each needle pin correctly for secure fit of the scarf and overcoming the feeling of unprecedented visibility.

> I was entering Bunafsha's house (*havli* – compound), expecting to see her in some beautiful head covering that I was told she usually wears. Instead, she appeared in her loose, *hijabi*-style dress (with large abstract color patterns of fuchsia pink and black) with long sleeves and black leggings peeking out from under the dress as she walked. Her head was bare and there were two, big patches of baldness on her head. She wasn't always bald, she rushed to tell me as soon as she offered me a seat at her kitchen table. In fact, she used to have a floor-length, bright auburn braid, thick as a trunk of a young tree (she has cut off the braid many years ago and now keeps her hair at shoulder-length). To my question, then what's happened, she had a straightforward answer – she's been wearing hijab for too long. Hair loss is common for hijab-wearing women (*hijobu satrpushon*), "don't you know?" I was asked. "No" I replied.[50]

Indeed, our general (scholarly, too) attempt to put *hijabi* women into some nicely fitting categorical box, which would "rationalize" and explain their choice of practicing some degree of gender seclusion, or the tendency to view them as indicators of some worrisome social (and political) developments, all have left us fixated on the headscarf, often uninterested in getting to know the "head" of the person (woman) underneath it.

The middle-aged women (aged between 35 and 45) that I talked to in Dushanbe and Khujand would insist that it wasn't changes in faith, degrees of religiousness, or practice of religion that has led them to adopt hijab. Most of

---

50   Author's field notes.

them insisted that they were quite religious, devout and practicing Muslims, long before changing their sartorial styles. Instead, each would recall a family scandal preceding the adoption of the new headscarf, saying that they had to do it to prevent their marriages and families from falling apart (often "in the name of children").

For Bunafsha (39 years old) and Nargis (38 years old), the scandals involved their new occupations. They both entered the shuttle-trade business, which required travel outside of Tajikistan and considerable working hours outside of home. Bunafsha's adoption of *satr* was very dramatic – she had to put on hijab a few hours before her third trip to Bishkek. She said, while she wasn't opposed to the idea of hijab, she just wished she was given some time to learn to "manage" (*uhda kardan*) it.

Nargis, on the other hand, was completely opposed to hijab. She says she is "modern" and the idea of hijab did not register with her at all. Nargis has a degree in journalism and had a short-lived TV career that ultimately ended at her husband's insistence. Soon after she started her shuttle-trade business, her husband began arguing with her anew, saying that an honorable (*poriadoch-naia*) woman must first of all think about the honor and status of her husband (*chest' i dostoinstvo muzha*) and that her unchaperoned trips to Turkey and China were casting a shadow on his manhood and family's honor (*chest' sem'i*). In response to these scandals, she took the kids and left her marital home. Nargis stayed at her parents' house for 10 days with her three children (one with a severe disability) and decided that she cannot care for them on her own, so she agreed to put on hijab and returned home. Nargis laughed off the recollection of this traumatic episode by mentioning that hijab came with a good "bonus" – a lump sum of US$1,000 from her husband. "At least I made him pay for it" – she said.

It has been four years for Nargis and three years for Bunafsha since they adopted hijab, and both say that now they cannot imagine (*tasavvur*) themselves without it, even though both mention severe hair loss and recent harassment from the government officials at their workplaces (mostly tax-officers and police that have been frequenting their stores since the most recent anti-hijab campaign took off in the spring of 2015).

It has been a year since Sadbarg (age 42) put on hijab, but she says she still cannot get used to it or start liking it. Swiping through the images on her smartphone that bear evidence of how "contemporary" (*sovremennaia*) she used to be in her over-the-knee length denim skirt and short-sleeve tops, Sadbarg says that her late mother-in-law for many years tried to talk her into (*ugovorit'*) dressing more conservatively (*bama'nitar*). About a year ago, Sadbarg's mother-in-law began insinuating that she had been unfaithful to her husband with a man at her workplace. Sadbarg insisted all of it was fabricated, made up (*vydu-manno*) by her mother-in-law. After numerous rumors and insults, divorce seemed imminent for Sadbarg (in fact, it was actively pushed by her mother-in-law). Yet, fearing for her future and dreading the reputation associated with a divorced woman accused of adultery and the shadow it would cast on the marriage prospects of her teenage daughters, she had to quit her well-paying job and put on hijab to regain her husband's trust.

All three women said that they do not plan on taking off the hijab. They say in our society taking off hijab is viewed very negatively. Moreover, Bunafsha says it is a "big sin" (*gunohi buzurg*) in front of God to put on hijab – to uphold God's order (*farzi khudoro ijro kardan*) – and then to take it off – as if not recognizing the authority of God's words (*gapi khudoro nabardoshtan*). Also, all three dread the prospects of their family scandals resuming anew. *Hamin mo tinj gardemu moro tinj guzoran, ba mo digar hej chiz darkor nest* (All we want is to be peaceful and be left at peace, nothing else) said Sadbarg, referring to recent government intrusions that were creating new difficulties in a lifestyle that she has learned to manage.

Hijab in Tajikistan in a New Perspective

I look at the phenomenon of hijab among women in contemporary Tajikistan through a new lens. I agree that hijab may be an attribute of the women who have found (or adopted) new piety (or new ways of expressing religiosity) and began living and practicing a qualitatively different interpretation of Islam. Yet, nevertheless, we should recognize that not all the women who have adopted hijab are necessarily doing so because of changes in their religiosity or religious practice. In fact, based on my encounters, most women who wear hijab do not view themselves as "born-againers" – even before wearing hijab they have performed Islamic religious obligations and did not consider their past selves any less Muslim or pious. For the women whose vignettes I presented, hijab serves a specific function – to mediate the effects of the socially unacceptable situations, which they have encountered.

With Bunafsha and Nargis, many aspects of their new occupation are socially condemned and viewed as inappropriate for women. They engage in business activities that require considerable outside-of-the-home working hours, where their encounters with people are not gender secluded, unchaperoned foreign travels for many days, and considerable autonomy in financial decision-making: all of these actions challenge socially accepted male-dominated hierarchies. In a society where family honor (and manhood) depends on the man's ability to successfully control female sexuality and autonomy, it is in the woman's best interest to maintain and reestablish male dominance to ensure social status, reputation, and honor of the family and herself.[51]

Evidently, this was even truer in Sadbarg's situation, no matter how humiliating the conditions upon which a woman puts on hijab, she still in many ways acts in her own self-interest, often weighing the risks (for herself and family) of the alternative. Sadbarg says she was horrified by the thought that she could dishonor her old, sickly father and bring the shame of an adulterous divorced daughter upon his house and name. Moreover, she feared that her daughters' prospects for marriage would be irreparably tainted (she also has a younger son, but she never mentioned possible damage to his future). In fact, she said the only way she was able to persuade her husband not to proceed with the divorce was by urging him to think about the future of their daughters.

Thus, in situations where the male-dominated social order is challenged to the extent that other mechanisms to reestablish the system are no longer sufficient (for example, dressing in other non-*hijabi* yet conservative styles – Tajik national dress) there is a need to construct new, socially acceptable mechanisms to manifest and protect female purity (*iffat*) and honor (*nomus*): hijab/ *satr* and (pious) Islamic identity, which hijab relates, can possibly offer both.

An important issue that needs to be addressed here is that while the imperatives of wearing hijab are certainly part of the patriarchal system that by definition provides greater advantages to men, it would be erroneous to conclude that women have accepted hijab from a position of weakness. Instead, often we find women are exactly the ones who mastermind the change to hijab and often men merely serve as mediums to "voice" the need for a new norm of dress. Thus, even if it might appear that women are submitting to a patriarchal social order, framed in the language of religious or national codes of normative behavior, we should nevertheless allow for the possibility that women also use those codes to further their interests.

> Bunafsha left the house to go to the store (where she worked) soon after her mother-in-law, Sanavbar-khola, returned home from a private physiotherapy session. Sanavbar-khola is in her early 70s and only occasionally puts on an elegant scarf that shows her immaculately black-dyed hair gathered in a neat updo. Since she did not wear hijab, I wanted to know how she reacted to her daughter-in-law's satr. She said it pleased her, in fact, she insisted that she was the one initiating the change (not her son, as Bunafsha told me). Sanavbar-khola said she goes to various

51   Harris, *Control and Subversion*.

community and family gatherings (*ma'rakahoi* mahalla/*kheshu tabor*) and has heard scandalous gossip (*gaphoi bema'ni*) about women who engage in the shuttle trade (*biznes*). She said she feared for her son's (and family's) honor and reputation in the community. But ultimately, Sanavbar-khola said, it was the fact that Bunafsha and her son had two teenage daughters (*dukhtarhoi khona*), who needed to be married off soon after they graduate from secondary school, which convinced her to push for her daughter-in-law's adoption of hijab. Sanavbar-khola claimed that a woman wearing hijab (*zani bahijob*) is considered well-behaved and honorable (*baodob, bamai'ni, baoru banomus*),[52] and gossips that tarnish name and reputation (*nomu obru merezonad*) do not spread so easily, so everybody wants to marry her daughters.[53]

In Bunafsha's own perception, too, until recently the only major downside to her hijab was the hair loss (government pressures to stop wearing and selling Islamic style clothes became a "new" problem). Otherwise, she insists her complete comfort with the garb and the sense of newfound freedom it provides. Bunafsha married into a relative's family in her late teens and although she was allowed to continue her education (on part-time, *zaochno* basis) and eventually received a diploma in banking and finance, she had not had any formal or informal employment for close to 15 years since she graduated.

> You know, I was supposed to begin a prestigious internship (*praktika*) at a bank. I had begged, cried, left to my parents' house, all to no avail – I was not allowed to work. The only times I would get out of the house (shared with in-laws) was when I visited my parents every two weeks or we'd go to some family event (*ma'raka*). My husband has a successful business, so I did get most of the things that I asked for: food, clothes, jewelry. ... But when I started doing "biznes" I felt so independent, I started earning my own money, I did not have to ask my husband for money and report in every detail how and why I spent it.

---

52 Stephan similarly observes that hijabs "(a)part from their function as a religious statement ... are an unmistakable attribute of female morality and as such place the sexual reputation (*obru, sharmu hayo*) of the wearer at the center of public attention." See M. Stephan, "Education, Youth, and Islam: The Growing Popularity of Private Religious Lessons in Dushanbe, Tajikistan," *Central Asian Survey*, 29, no. 4 (2010): 478.

53 Author's field notes, 2015.

So, when it came down to the choice, "You either put on a hijab or stop working," Bunafsha's decision, in her own mind, was easily understood and justifiable. Although, she said, her father – an "old-school" man with a government career in Soviet and post-Soviet times – still cannot come to terms with her being "all-wrapped-up" (*pechondagi*). Besides hijab, Bunafsha says there is very little change in the style of her clothing: "I can still wear my European-style skirt suits," provided she puts on a fine-knit top with a mock turtleneck underneath. Also, the seamstresses have come up with new designs that combine Tajik traditional dress with the elements required for *hijabi* dress (long sleeves and closed upper chest), which allows Bunafsha to dress in the new fashionable fabrics each season.

My exchanges with women who did not wear hijab also seemed to support the view that hijab has to be understood contextually. For example, my lengthy conversation with 38-year-old Lola about hijab, its doctrinal basis, and her opposition to this form of dressing was very revealing. Lola has some "expensive" (Turkish-made) skirt suits but mostly wears traditional Tajik dresses, which in 2015 summer season were tailored as form-fitting with a narrow and tight bodice, higher hemline than traditionally (but still well over the knee), with side slits and slim trouser pants made of matching fabric.

> To my question of how was she feeling today, Lola said "Oh, I am so tired," she sounded somewhat irritated. Yet, she said she did not mind talking to me. So, I asked her why she was feeling tired. Lola said, she spent the whole previous day waiting for the marriage negotiators (*khostgorho*), who have previously come to seek her daughter's hand in marriage (Yasmina, Lola's eldest daughter has recently turned 19 and started her second year in university). "Oh, so you wanted to agree to the proposal (*rozigi dodan*)?" – I asked. "No, quite the opposite, I wanted to say no, so that they don't keep coming" – Lola said and continued, "they are from *raion* (rural area), (their) living conditions are poor (*sharoit nest*), and more than anything, all of the women in the family wear hijab! (*hamai zanhoyashon hijobpush!*)" When I asked if that was one of the conditions (wearing hijab) that the marriage negotiators mentioned, she admitted that it was not the case. Yet, Lola maintained that such things are rarely discussed now; it has become part of a new norm (*qoidahoi nav*).[54]

Lola's stand on hijab turned out to be complex: about three years ago her husband has asked her to put on *satr*, she furiously refused and told him that he

---

54   Author's field notes, 2015.

was in no position to dictate the way she should dress. She says her husband was somewhat disappointed and surprised: Lola, as a devout Muslim diligently performs her daily prayers (she started praying five times a day six years ago) and a few years back began taking private Arabic classes from a local university professor and became a disciple of her neighborhood *bibiotun* (female religious specialist). Thus, in her husband's mind, given her serious interest in religious practice and activities, his request to put on hijab did not constitute anything extraordinary. However, Lola was convinced that what is required of pious women ("and men!" – she added, making sure I noted it) according to teachings of Islam is modesty: "Nowhere is it mentioned how many centimeters should your hemline or sleeves (*domanu ostin*) be." She viewed such sartorial norms as necessarily a product of history, culture, geography, climate, etc. Lola has a university degree in exact sciences and although she is "officially listed" as a part-time lab assistant in an educational institution, her main source of income is tailoring and embroidery of traditional dresses. Lola says, part of her not wanting to put on hijab was related to her occupation, too – she saw a conflict in that by putting on hijab either she would be producing clothing items that were not Islamic enough or that she would be presenting herself as more pious than her clients. In Lola's words hijab could jeopardize the independence and self-realization that she was achieving through her home-based work:

> I love what I do! I get to meet and talk to many women, I get to share and participate in their most joyful experiences – weddings and special events (*tuyu ma'raka*), I deal with aesthetically beautiful fabrics, I always have my own money (*puli khudam* (not accountable to her husband or part of family budget)). Thus, I will not risk losing all of these aspects of my nice life for wearing a headscarf, which I am not fully convinced is needed by religion or appropriate in our society.[55]

The very factors that have pushed previously discussed women to adopt the Islamic headscarf were, in fact, working for the opposite outcome in Lola's case. It was particularly the nature of her occupation – being home-based and exclusively gender-secluded that has allowed Lola to refuse to put on the hijab. Evidently, her decision also reflects a great degree of autonomy, in that she has approached the issue from the perspective of measuring her individual benefits, fearing that an Islamic headscarf might push away her usual clientele (mostly young and mid-age women who order custom-tailored traditional

---

55   Author's field notes, 2015.

Tajik dresses from ornate, expensive fabrics with elaborate embroidery and beading), Lola consciously chose to adopt an interpretation of "modest dress" that closely echoes state-sponsored discourse.

The new approach proposes to look at hijab contextually, by carefully examining the limitations and affordabilities it produces for each woman, who chooses to wear or not wear hijab. It is a refined amalgamation of the previously presented approaches in the literature on religious dress and hijab. It agrees with the social control approach in recognition that hijab in the context of Tajikistan reproduces a male-dominated social order; however, it adds a dimension that for some women the decision on hijab can still be a product of her autonomy and agency, no matter how limited under certain circumstances. The personal security approach is the most specific of the approaches presented. However, in the context of Tajikistan we still have to take into account the peculiarities of the activities in which the women might be engaged – if those activities produce substantial female autonomy in non-gender secluded environments, then hijab appears to afford the utmost protection and support for "respected woman" status. And finally, the strategic marriage approach has to be modified to include that insecurities do not always have to be economic, there is also greater social value in marriage itself as a source of respectable social standing – hijab can be used as a tool to enter and preserve familial unions (no matter how economically viable they may be).

In many ways, this perspective of situating hijab in the context of a specific socio-economic order continues in the line of the recent research on Islam and women in Central Asia, for example, Stephan and Commercio.[56] In particular, these studies suggest a relationship between economic uncertainty and an increase in manifest religious behavior, especially among young and urban women. Notably, based on a small survey of female students studying in Islamic and secular universities in Tajikistan and Kyrgyzstan, Commercio presents evidence for increased support of "retraditionalization"[57] among "young, urban, educated women" that should necessarily be placed "in the context of ongoing economic uncertainty." Stephan, in her study of private Islamic education and veiling in Dushanbe, also concludes that "in the context of market transition,

---

56   Stephan, "Education, Youth, and Islam"; Commercio, "The Politics and Economics of 'Retraditionalization' in Kyrgyzstan and Tajikistan."

57   The term is used to denote "a return to traditional values, family life, and religion, which entails, in part, women being moved out of work force." Kligman, cited in Commercio, "The Politics and Economics of 'Retraditionalization' in Kyrgyzstan and Tajikistan," 529–531.

impoverishment and limited career prospects, Islam offers an 'honourable' option for urban youth to increase their social status."[58]

In these studies, "retraditionalization," or the increase in female Islamic practice and attire, is perceived as an alternative to, or a step away from, the workforce. However, cursory observations do not support this perspective: if anything we have witnessed an exponential increase in women wearing hijab and working in private, non-governmental, and informal (e.g., bazaars) labor market sectors of Tajikistan. General labor force data also indicate a stable rate of female labor force participation, as well as a steady share of women in the national labor force (see Figure 1). Moreover, women are increasingly pursuing work options outside of Tajikistan: the share of women labor migrants practically doubled from 6.61 to 13.1 between 2007 and 2009.[59] And recent statistics from the Migration Service of Tajikistan (2012) suggest that women still make up about 14 percent of the nearly 900,000 total labor migrants leaving the country in search of wages in Russia.[60] The impetus for women to join the migrant outflow stems from the evidence that while migrant remittances helped to reduce poverty rates significantly, they have also left individual households substantially dependent on the incomes earned abroad.[61] As securing (construction) jobs in Russia became more difficult for men in the immediate aftermath of the 2008 financial crisis due to both the economic downturn and an increase in the inflow of migrants, their earnings decreased, leading most remittance-dependent households to send female household members, too, to capture employment opportunities in other sectors of the menial and low-skilled labor market of Russia.[62] Thus, the available macroeconomic data suggest that women are more active in the labor market if we combine insights from domestic and migrant female labor force statistics.

The perspective presented herein adds to the existing scholarship by offering a nuanced understanding of the phenomenon of hijab in Tajikistan: it can mediate the effects of an obviously paradoxical situation that most women have encountered. The imperatives of female docility are paramount, yet socio-economic realities push women to seek wage labor both in Tajikistan

---

58   Stephan, "Education, Youth, and Islam," 479.

59   A.M. Danzer and O. Ivaschenko, "Migration Patterns in a Remittances Dependent Economy: Evidence from Tajikistan during the Global Financial Crisis," *Migration Letters*, 7, no. 2 (2010): 190.

60   S. Kurbanov, "Gender Shape of Labor Migration in the Republic of Tajikistan," *Agency on Statistics under the President of the Republic of Tajikistan*, 2013, 2, <http://stat.tj/img/en/ Gender%20aspects%20in%20migration(1).pdf>.

61   Danzer and Ivaschenko, "Migration Patterns in a Remittances Dependent Economy," 190.

62   Ibid., 199.

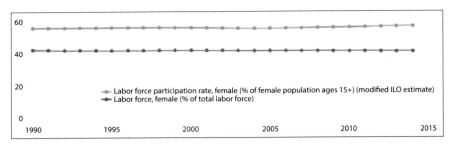

FIGURE 11.1   *Female labor force and participation rate in Tajikistan, 1990–2014*

and abroad. As proposed by the new insights offered in this research, hijab can potentially serve as a mechanism to reconcile the pressures faced by women to seek and remain in non-gender secluded, outside-of-the-home employment (or situations that can be socially perceived as deviant), without jeopardizing the publicly manifested image of domesticity and conformity to a patriarchal value system that are viewed as the basis for an individual woman's and her family's honorable social status.

Concluding Remarks

The centrality of the body in various political and religious projects cannot be overstated. This appears to be especially true in relation to female bodies, dress code, and, as presented in this chapter, head coverings. Indeed, in the discursive field, the competition in the sphere of "control of women and of their appropriate conduct had long been used to demarcate the identity and boundaries of the Muslim community" in different Islamic contexts.[63] Similarly, in the context of Tajikistan it was observed that normative codes regarding role, right, and behavior of women serve as one of the most important factors differentiating between competing religious discourses, and, moreover, control over the female body (sexuality, dress code, female public sphere) might serve as a measure of success in such discursive contestation.[64]

In this manner, the narrative of the foreignness of hijab and *satri Islomi* in Tajikistan fundamentally relies on the assumption that as a new (transplanted) garb it also represents a new system of values and practice of religion. Such narrative also creates seemingly legitimate basis for excluding groups adhering

63   Kandiyoti, *Women, Islam, and the State*, 6.
64   S. Nozimova and T. Epkenhans, "Negotiating Islam in Emerging Public Spheres in Contemporary Tajikistan," *Asiatische Studien/Études Asiatiques*, 67, no. 3 (2013): 984.

to the new norms and values from various public goods (e.g., education, political process, rule of law) by generating, for the most part, false dichotomies of "us" vs. "them." The discourse becomes even more legitimate and consequential when scholarly research appears to support such assumptions by paying attention to those who practice such new forms of piety and noting that they also happen to don hijab. Thus, there appears to be a need for a timely intervention in both scholarly and policy perspectives. We should recognize that hijab, even if transplanted, acquired new meanings and wider audience in Tajik society and began to be used for a specific social function of reestablishing a male-dominated social order, often by women themselves, to maintain, promote and project a respectable social standing for themselves and their families. This characteristic of assimilation might pose even greater challenges for the state and be indicative of the societal pushback that it is due to encounter in its anti-hijab campaign.

CHAPTER 12

Switching to Satr: An Ethnography of the Particular in Women's Choices in Head Coverings in Tajikistan

Marintha Miles

Sitora watched another YouTube video explaining the newest styles of hijab. She already knew how to arrange and pin it in at least five different ways. She frequently went to Korvon, the large bazaar just outside of Dushanbe, to purchase ornate beads, and jewels to add to her hijab and other clothing. Her parents did not approve of hijab and chided her for covering her head, but the Islamic revival moving swiftly through Tajik society caught hold of her as it did a growing number of young people.

Since perestroika and the collapse of the Soviet Union, the people of Central Asia have grappled with national and religious identities. Women's behavior, dress, and roles in both the public and private spheres have become targets of nation building and religious revival. Against the backdrop of a civil war, the secular elite's fears of Islamic revival in Tajikistan have resulted in governmental rhetoric and legislation sharply focused on the dress and behavior of women. A hallmark of the new national identity promoted by the state is a young Tajik woman in national dress. Despite increases in political and social pressure on women to adopt the state vision of the Tajik-Muslim woman, an Islamic awakening informs the construction of an alternative female Muslim identity. This chapter explores the push-and-pull factors women experience amid the Islamic revival as they decide whether to adopt hijab, challenge the imagined national identity, and lean toward one of Muslim piety and find social and political belonging through the enactment of Islamic practice.

I use "Islamic revival" or "Islamic awakening" to mean a societal trend toward greater awareness of Islamic principles and ideas (orthodoxy) and an increase in Islamic practice such as *namaz* (prayers), fasting, and wearing hijab (orthopraxy). It is not meant to mean a structured, formal movement with leadership or hierarchy, but rather an informal surge in the transmission of religious knowledge and enactment of religious practice by an increasing number of people within the population.

My research does not quantify an increase in Islamic orthodoxy or orthopraxy in Tajikistan, and it would be difficult to carry out quantifiable research on this subject without a longitudal study. However, other scholars of Central

Asia have also described an Islamic revival, though not always using this term. For example, Michele E. Commercio describes it as "retraditionalization," and Wendell Schwab as a "piety movement."[1] This chapter focuses on one aspect of the Islamic revival in Tajikistan, an increase in the number of women and girls enacting the Islamic principle of wearing hijab.

Methodology

My fieldwork incorporates discussions and semi-structured interviews in June–September 2013, and June 2014 in Dushanbe and Kulob, Tajikistan. I also carried out Skype interviews with some of the women in July 2014. Follow-up on the lives of some of the women includes events as late as May 2015. This chapter pivots around the decisions of 15 women ages 18–56 from two extended kinship networks, exploring both their practice of wearing hijab and the transmission of religious knowledge that informs their decision whether to wear it. Access to these families was created through networking and months and even years of developing close relationships of trust. Much of my research was carried out through participant observation. I spent days and nights in the homes of different women, preparing and serving meals, interacting with their children, observing and participating in rituals reserved for women such as the *arūstalʙon* (return or welcoming of a recently married female relative) and *gahvoraʙandon* (a celebration of a new mother being welcomed back into full social life after relative isolation for 40 days postpartum), was instructed in the differing styles of hijab, namaz, and observed the transmission of religious knowledge through word of mouth or electronically from online recordings or DVDs. Of all the women in Tajikistan I interacted with who did or did not veil, I chose to focus on two family groups for this study. In one family, all but one woman chose to wear hijab; conversely, in the second family none of the women chose to wear hijab with one exception, providing an interesting juxtaposition.

Anthropologists have long recognized kinship relationships as the foundation of culture.[2] Studying women in their kinship environment provides intimate details of their lives and decision making processes, while the use of

---

1   M.E. Commercio, "The Politics and Economics of 'Retraditionalization' in Kyrgyzstan and Tajikistan," *Post-Soviet Affairs*, 2015; W. Schwab, "Islam, Fun, and Social Capital in Kazakhstan," *Central Asian Affairs*, 2, no. 1 (2015): 51–70.

2   C. Levi-Strauss, *The Elementary Structures of Kinship* (Boston: Beacon Press, 1971); A.R. Radcliffe-Brown, *The Andaman Islanders a Study in Social Anthropology* (1906; repr., London:

surveys that may disconnect respondents from the influence of kinship ties that inform their behavior. I frame the decisions of these women in what Lila Abu-Lughod describes as "ethnography of the particular," agentive acts made in a particular time and place under the influence of several sociocultural factors.[3] I hope that because the two families I discuss are from very different socioeconomic backgrounds and parts of Tajik society, I am able to capture some of the diverse ways women come to decisions about hijab. Ethnographers portray only snapshots of the lives of their research subjects; this privileged information is in some ways always a convenience sample and should be considered such, rather than a rigid characterization of the entire population.[4]

I also incorporate discussions from media and social media in Tajikistan collected from public Facebook postings in Facebook-hosted groups and comments from online media outlets between June 2012 and May 2015. At some points I was a member of some of the groups; other times informants alerted me to discussions regarding hijab that I then copied and pasted into my research collection. The groups I followed include Platforma, Ya Dushanbenets, Ya Dushanbenets 2, Tarbiya Omoni, and Tajik Mama, some of which are cited.

The sermons of influential mullahs in Tajikistan regarding the practice of women veiling (including niqab and hijab) retrieved from public websites and videos uploaded to YouTube are incorporated into the discussion. I also use press reports from Tajikistan's independent and state media agencies, and official government statements on women's dress in my analysis.

Finally, I use hijab and *satr* (the word most commonly used in Tajikistan for hijab) interchangeably throughout the chapter.

Background

The traditional Central Asian practice of women veiling was the antithesis to the Soviet conceptualization of the emancipation of women. On International Women's Day, March 8 1927, a mass unveiling, known as *faranjipartoi* (veil throwing) or *faranjisuzi* (veil burning) to people in Tajikistan and Uzbekistan, forced women to remove the heavy cotton and horsehair *faranji* (Tajiki) or

Forgotten Books, 2012); H.L. Morgan, *Systems of Consanguinity and Affinity of the Human Family* (1870; repr., Charleston, SC: Nabu Press, 2012).

3   L. Abu-Lughod, "Writing Against Culture," in R.G. Fox (ed.), *Recapturing Anthropology: Working in the Present* (Santa Fe, NM: School of American Research Press, 1991), 137-62.

4   M. Duneier, "How Not to Lie with Ethnography," *Sociological Methodology*, 41 (2011): 1–11.

paranja (Russian) (veil covering the body and face) they traditionally wore.[5] Sporadic but ongoing violence followed for the next few years. Soviet Russians killed men who resisted the unveiling of women; and women who unveiled were often killed in villages by male relatives and neighbors.[6] Gregory Massel notes the women who unveiled were no longer considered Muslim by their countrymen. Within society, women were increasingly viewed as either Muslim or communist, but not both.[7]

At the close of 1991, Tajikistan was forced into independent statehood, an unwilling victim of the collapse of the Soviet Union.[8] The bubblings of pre-collapse rifts and the political motivations of the Islamic Renaissance Party of Tajikistan (IRPT) and its allies threw the country into civil war as the Soviet elite struggled to cling to power. After five years of fighting, Moscow brokered a peace deal and left the old regime at the helm. The government of President Emomali Rahmon worked to create an historical narrative and national identity without the appearance of religious elements that could lend support to the defeated IRPT. It focused on maintaining the character of the state and citizens as secular.[9]

---

5   *Hujum* is the word used in most scholarship. It comes from the Arabic word for assault or attack and is used in Uzbek. However, the Tajik word is *faranjipartoi*, best translated as "veil throwing." The other word used in Tajik is *faranjisuzi* (veil burning). Rather than *paranja*, the word *faranji* is used in Tajik. Kamp notes that some women unveiled before sovietization. See M. Kamp, *The New Woman in Uzbekistan: Islam, Modernity, and Unveiling under Communism* (Seattle: University of Washington, Press, 2006).

6   Kamp, *The New Woman in Uzbekistan*, 150–185. Also see, G.J. Massell, *The Surrogate Proletariat: Moslem Women and Revolutionary Strategies in Soviet Central Asia, 1919–1929* (Princeton, NJ: Princeton University Press, 1974); D. Northrop, *Veiled Empire: Gender and Power in Stalinist Central Asia* (Ithaca, N.Y.: Cornell University Press, 2004).

7   Massell, *The Surrogate Proletariat,* 225.

8   A nationalist movement began before independence, attached to a pan-Persian ideology. See G.E. Curtis, *Tajikistan: A Country Study* (Washington D.C.: GPO for the Library of Congress, 1996), <http://countrystudies.us/tajikistan/24.htm>; D. Dagiev, *Regime Change in Central Asia Stateness, Nationalism, and Political Change in Tajikistan and Uzbekistan* (New York: Routledge, 2014).

9   Olivier Roy labels the promoted national identity of Tajikistan *Islamo-nationalism*. This term has also been adopted by other scholars. However, in my opinion this term needs more explanation. The government actively legislates against the practice of Islam and agitates against Islamic practices in other ways. Therefore, when it is claimed that the national identity of Tajikistan (and indeed the government) can be characterized as Islamo-nationalism, it is not clear to me what this means. See O. Roy, *The New Central Asia: Geopolitics and the Birth of Nations*, rev. ed. (New York: New York University Press, 2007).

Anthropologist Gillian Tett observed that while men's religious activities began to increase at the collapse of the Soviet Union in Tajikistan, women's did not. This was simply because women's religious practice in Tajikistan—prayers, recitation of the Quran, and other activities—remained prevalent during the Soviet period.[10] After the civil war ended in 1997, Tajikistan's government sought to reify the state, changing the name of the state religious apparatus from the *Muftiyat* to the *Shuroi ulamo* (religious council). It is hard to say what affinity the public initially had toward the new council, but it quickly lost face and was not considered anything other than anti-Islamic. In 2004 the Council of Ulamo issued a fatwa prohibiting women to pray in mosques. In 2005, the minister of education issued a statement banning hijab in schools, and in 2007 it instituted a mandatory dress code that reinforced the ban.[11] Much like the Soviet hujum (Russian: *khudzhum*), fatwas derived by the state apparatus and legalism sought to cut women out of religious life. Further, the government ban on women visiting mosques reduced women's access to IRPT political rhetoric and the speeches of politically inclined mullahs. It also served to curtail women's ability to pass religious practices onto their children.

While in Tajikistan political Islam—the IRPT—has been undermined by the political elite, a socially driven Islamic revival created the opportunity for political belonging. Although not deliberately political, it includes acts of resistance within the cultural hegemony that create a social climate fertile for political Islamism. Emile Durkheim theorized that beliefs and practice in action unite individuals "into one single moral community."[12] Tajikistan presents an interesting case, then, wherein almost all actors in society accept a Muslim identity, but disagree on what that moral-Muslim community and identity is.

Social Schisms

The discourse of the national identity of the Tajik-Muslim woman is centered on externality versus internality; that is, the performance (actions) versus the

---

10   G. Tett, "'Guardians of the Faith?': Gender and Religion in an (ex) Soviet Tajik village," in
      C.F.El-Solh and J. Mabro (eds), *Muslim Women's Choices: Religious Belief and Social Reality*
      (Providence, R.I. : Berg; (New York): Distributed in North America by New York University
      Press, 1994), 160–190.

11   "Tajikistan International Religious Freedom Report, 2007," U.S. Department of State,
      <http://www.state.gov/j/drl/rls/irf/2007/90235.htm>.

12   E. Durkheim, *Elementary Forms of Religious Life*, trans. K.E. Fields (New York: Free Press,
      1995), 44.

ethical internality of behavior. Facebook and Odnoklassniki (the popular Russian-based social networking site) networks from Central Asia often focus on Islam. The virtues of hijab are frequently extolled and sometimes debated. Translated excerpts from the following discussion in the Facebook group Ya Dushanbinets 2 in August 2014 underscore perceived threats that *satr* (the word for hijab used by both Russian and Tajik speakers in Tajikistan) poses to the secular cultural hegemony.

NATALYA:[13]
Another question that interests me!
I was recently very frightened by the abundance of girls in satr. And obviously very bright makeup and even more "bright" behavior. Moreover, women 40 and older are less likely to (wear) satr. Is this a temporary fashion (trend), or is it forever?

LEAH:
Temporary. Fools.

TANYA:
When I was in Kurgan I did not see any woman in satr and was pleasantly surprised!

FARIDUN:
For some of them it is a fashion, for others—a way of life. Without a sociological survey among them, you cannot exactly understand.

FARANGIS:
It kills me that most of the girls in satr lead a bad lifestyle. They are on social networks, and do not behave properly.[14]

SAODAT:
One said—her husband forced her.

LUDMILA:
It's more for fashion of course!

---

13   All names have been changed. I chose Russian names for posters who had Russian names and Tajik names for posters who had Tajik names.
14   The commenter is a woman in the process of using Facebook, but her comment denotes her differentiation between herself and a young, presumably unmarried woman who is using social media.

LEAH:
Stupid fashion, which is nothing but irritation. Sorry for the harshness, but it's not about being true believers … these "fashionistas" have no idea about the canons of religion.

SHUHRAT:
Crazy. Most of them lead a bad lifestyle … stupid fashion. … It's irritating… It's pleasantly surprising when I haven't seen a woman in satr.

FARIDUN:
Excuse me … we certainly have no right to discuss people this way.

SHUHRAT:
Faridun, why? This discussion is not about a specific person.

FARIDUN:
Well, somehow it is ugly, especially talking about girls.

CHUHRAT:
I think it's both possible and necessary to discuss trends.

LEAH:
I explained my attitude only to those who use religion and satr to cover their own shortcomings and indiscretions. My attitude to a true believer is diametrically different.

FARIDUN:
Girls have the right to their "shortcomings," including discussions of each other.

MUNISA:
But you must admit many of our sisters contradict *Satr avrat* (the hiding of the body)—*Odobi libospushii* (proper cultural dress)

TIMUR:
Looking at the man on the street for a couple of minutes, can we determine for what purpose he uses his clothes, as fashion or to cover up? For example, today I am wearing a T-shirt and jeans, how have I used them? How can you tell if the girl you saw for maybe 15 seconds on the street in satr is a true believer or not?

SUHROB:

I would never suggest in any of the (social media) groups that we should not raise this topic, why?

1. The secular world of fashion changes day-by-day. For secular society it is the norm; the religious world of fashion also evolves, and unfortunately secular society doesn't like this.
2. If secular radicalism grows, religion grows.
3. Satr in Islam is not clothes, but a law of dress. This is *farz* (commandment), is thus obligatory for both men and women.
4. If secular society will accept this as normal as it accepts secular fashion, then believe me, it isn't a problem.

Finally, I agree with Timur. How can you tell if the girl you saw for maybe 15 seconds on the street in satr is a true believer or not?

LEAH:

How can you tell? It's very simple. A girl sits at 11 pm in a restaurant, smoking, drinking alcoholic cocktails, with paint (make-up) like an Apache Indian on the warpath, neighing like a horse (laughing loudly), and drawing attention of all the surrounding men with her behavior. But IN SATR? The discussion is namely about these (type of girls), and namely these are becoming more and more (common). I personally consider that they are simply a disgrace to religion. IMHO.

TIMUR:

Are you suggesting they remove satr and behave this way in European clothes, huh?

LEAH:

Well, at least it will be honest, or correspond to the clothes they are wearing. I believe the girls described completely lack understanding of the requirements for a woman in Islam, and (lack) understanding of the religion in general.

TIMUR:

About bright makeup and challenging behavior, I agree. With or without satr, I think make-up should be for their own husbands. So you believe that drinking, smoking, laughing … is for those who don't cover their heads? Just understand, I think, we've had enough already of judging people by their clothes. Let people dress how they want, do what they want, as long as their freedom restrict and bother others.

LEAH:

To begin with, if a girl is wearing satr, she accepts and complies with Sharia ... no drinking, no smoking—visits to restaurants without being accompanied by her husband (brother, father, son) are FORBIDDEN. ... So if women are not willing to follow all the precepts of Islam, it is not necessary to show off with their headscarves.

In this discussion the power struggle lies in the opportunity to claim the construction of the legitimate Muslim woman. Michel Foucault wrote,

How can one analyze the connection between the ways of distinguishing true and false and ways of governing oneself and others? The search for a new foundation for each of these practices, in itself and relative to the other, the will to discover a different way of governing oneself through a different way of dividing up true and false-this is what I would call "political spirituality."[15]

The victor in these conversations wins the political-spiritual, claiming the true or legitimate identity of the Muslim woman. The victor dictates and sanctions her religious practices, her habitus, and determines who has a right to political belonging within the constructed identity of a Muslim woman.

Regarding the veil, Austrian diplomat and thinker Andreas Stadler mused, "We humans have more potential for hatred when the object our hatred is part of our own identity."[16] Because persons in Tajikistan almost universally consider themselves Muslim, women who do not veil find it more than irritating when other Muslim women do because it threatens their own identity as a Muslim. Benedict Anderson wrote that a nation (and thus national identity) is defined by imagination rather than "hard" structures, "It is imagined because the members of even the smallest nation will never know most of their fellow-members, meet them, or even hear of them, yet in the minds of each lives the image of their communion."[17]

---

15   M. Foucault, "Questions of Method" in G. Burchell, C. Gordon, and P. Miller (eds), *The Foucault Effect: Studies in Governmentality* (Hemel Wheatsheaf: Hemel Hempstead, 1991), 87–104; A. Rizvi, "Foucault, Iran, and Revolution," *Foucauldian Reflections*, October 9, 2004, <http://foucauldians.blogspot.com/2004/10/foucault-iran-and-revolution.html>.

16   A. Stadler, "It's Not About the Veil, It's About Us" (speech, Austrian Cultural Forum, New York, May 2009), <http://www.acfny.org/category/exhibitions/the-veil/its-not-about-the-veil-its-about-us/>.

17   B. Anderson, *Imagined Communities: Reflections on the Origins and Spread of Nationalism* (London: Verso, 1993), 6.

Women and girls who wear hijab challenge the imagined national identity. They are considered too religious, backward, *qişloqī* (villagers—used as a pejorative), and uneducated. Similar to the Soviets before them, for the Tajik elite, hijabi women are seen as the antithesis to modernity. The promotion of this idea is ever present. For example President Rahmon addressed young people at the National Agrarian University to mark the Day of Unity on June 26, 2015, saying, "Explain to all the girls, those who wear hijab at times, first of all this is from lack of education and knowledge. They do not have enough knowledge. They are misguided. They don't even know what they are doing in life."[18] The official website of the IRPT issued an article refuting the illiteracy of hijabi girls and women and insisting that they are not misguided.[19]

The sharp divide in society over hijab is further reflected in social media as in passages from the following edited discussion that took place in March 2013 in the Facebook political group Platforma. The moderators posted a provocative image ostensibly of a mother with her daughter in black burkas standing next to black garbage bags.[20]

SINO:

(Referring to the moderators) Stupid people. Make their faces black. (Pejorative expression). You like to gaze at women's bodies. Just imagine how a strange man (non-family member) will look with lust (intimate desire) at your sisters, mothers, and wives' breasts and naked legs. What do you imagine then, *dayus* (pejorative: signifying weak).

MANUCHEHR:

These *shaitans* (devils) are fighting with their own god, they do not even care about the hijab of Muslim girls.

AZIM:

It's not about how they look. What's important is they have come to this (wearing satr)? If this is their conscious choice founded on religious prin-

---

18   E. Rahmon, "Emomali dubora kofir budani xudro ikror kard," June 26, 2015. Uploaded by Filmi Online, June 28, 2015, <https://www.youtube.com/watch?v=I-4eVcYRJR8&feature=youtu.be>.

19   "Korşinosi toçik: Hiçoв вema'rifatī, gumrohī va вesavodī nest," July 2, 2015, <http://nahzat.tj/14824-korshinosi-toik-iob-bemarifat-gumro-va-besavod-nest.html>.

20   L. Abu-Lughod discusses the use of the same image in her book, *Do Muslim Women Need Saving?* (Cambridge, MA: Harvard University Press, 2013).

ciples, we don't have the right to judge them. But if so they were forced to
(wear satr), then this is something worth considering.

SINO:
On my honor, I am surprised how these people (moderators) have such
enmity toward Muslims, let me see the faces of all moderators in the
grave.

(MP–Moderators Platforma), I don't understand, do you actually stand on
the positions of secular fascism or, decided to tease believers for public-
ity? But my friends, (the) right to believe in his own God is in each of us,
it is guaranteed by the Constitution and the Conscience. Let us respect
the law and each other.

MANUCHEHR:
Umed, You correctly note the behavior of the (MP) moderators of Platforma as fascism. I think MP are not Muslim, and not even Tajik. Who can
offend their own people, but only one who has deeply hostile feelings
toward this people?
You like to have your wives, daughters, sisters, etc. walked naked and half-
naked? Who's stopping you? But you have no right to tell anyone else how
to dress.

PARVIN:
So if she is not in hijab she is naked or half-naked? Interesting logic. In
the days of the Women's Union in Tajikistan they were not in Arab clothing; were they all immoral? European women do not wear Arab dress, are
they also immoral? And those that are in hijab, burkas, and the saints ...
so holy many glow in the dark.

MANUCHEHR:
The discussion is about personal choice. How to dress is every woman's
personal choice. We must learn to respect the choices of others. ... What
you insist on calling "Arab dress" for women, hijab, is considered native
(to Tajikistan) and godly.

UMED:
Manuchehr, my friend, you are too dogmatic. The truth is that a large
number of people, including the very educated, are nervous about the
increase of religious sentiments our society. And due to the fact that their

scientific, or pseudo-scientific European worldview is not satisfied with the explanation of this phenomenon, they are looking for salvation in a position that is actually counterproductive.

If you didn't know, the Soviet Union was dominated the Bolshevik ideology of fascism, and the citizens of the country did not have religious freedom. By the way, some religious fanatics like yourself are against other clothes, for example against the British jacket and tie. You are you are also no different.

RUSTAM:

What makes you think that if a girl does not wear hijab, by default she is *prostitutka* (prostitute) naked, etc.???? Personally, I like it when our girls dress in national Tajik beautiful dresses.

Community Religious Leaders and Transfer of Religious Knowledge

Influential mullahs such as Eshoni Nuriddinjon of the Turajonzoda family, and Hoji Mirzo (Hoji Mirzo Ibronov) deliver sermons disseminated by word of mouth, social media, DVDs, and their own websites regarding the obligation of women to wear satr. Women often seek out distributed sermons like the following by Hoji Mirzo, and are thus persuaded to wear satr:

> A Muslim woman must wear a satr. God tells us this. It means, if our wives, our daughters do not wear satr, then we are the ones to answer for them in front of God. God says, I will ask you about your wife and children, if you passed them God's words. I will ask you. If we passed God's words to our families, good; if not, then we are sinners.[21]

It is notable that while women seek out these sermons themselves, the excerpt is clearly addressed to men. The trend to adopt satr and the prominence of male speech about women's dress has sometimes led outsiders to the belief and portrayal of hijabi women in Tajikistan as creatures without agency subordinate to male domination.[22] Certainly there are cases in which violent beatings by male relatives are associated with a woman's refusal or failure to

---

21   "Hoji Mirzo dar Kazokiston," June 16, 2014, YouTube, <https://www.youtube.com/
      watch?v=sS-oo-BMauY>.

22   L. Hough, "Tajikistan's Competing Social and Political Forces: The Politics of Traditional
      versus Women's Dress," Washington, D.C.: IREX, 2011.

properly wear hijab; however there is also violence, disenfranchisement, refusal of employment, and threats of divorce for wearing hijab.[23] Either way, these discussions decenter the Muslim woman. It is critical that the subjects, the women who wear hijab, are the center of these discussion. The women must speak for of themselves.

Ethnography of the Particular

Zebo was raised in a large family in a village in Khatlon. Her family owned a food-processing firm and sent the children to a private school in a nearby city. Zebo advanced quickly in her studies, won many educational opportunities, and married into an upper class and respected family when she was 24 years old. When Zebo's future husband came to her and asked for her hand in marriage, he asked if she would agree to wear hijab. Zebo already wore rumol (a brightly colored headscarf that does not completely cover the hair), just as her mother and older sister did. She agreed to wear it and believed that it was the will of Allah that women wear hijab. However, after the wedding, she refused. She said, "Probably it is *farz* (obligation or commandment), and I should wear it. But after marriage I told him no. I told him you will look at other women if I cover my hair and don't wear makeup."

Zebo feared her husband would take a second wife. Although according to her religious leanings of orthopraxy she would wear satr, she chose not to in the context of her situation. She viewed a resurgence of polygyny, allowed in Islam, as a threat to her marital relationship. This is compounded by the fact that her father had two wives while she was growing up in the Soviet era, and her mother (the first wife) did not want her own daughters to experience polygyny within their own marriages. Her mother made a point of working very hard to educate her daughters so they would have career options and be able to divorce if their husbands took a second wife. Although she accepted

---

23   One glaring example took place in August 2014 when a mother-in-law took her daughter-in-law to court for wearing hijab—claiming the family was afraid of women who wear hijab and pray, and demanded legal action to force her to discontinue the practice: "Himojati dodras az kelini hiçoвpüş va raddi da'voi xuşdoman," *Ozodagon*, August 2, 2014, <http://www.ozodagon.com/17440-shikoyati-hushdoman-az-boloi-kelini-iobpshash-ba-dodgo.html>; "Zakrytaia po sobstvennomu zhelaniiu," *VIP Zone Online*, June 28, 2014, <http://vipzoneonline.ru/life/468-zakrytaya-po-sobstvennomu-zhelaniyu.html>. In contrast, a woman was killed in June 2015 by her husband for refusing to wear hijab, see *Ozodagon*, July 1, 2015, <http://www.ozodagon.com/22338-atli-amsar-baroi-iob-dar-sud.html>.

orthodox ideas and practices regarding hijab, her decision to not wear it reflects her agency in the particular context of avoiding a polygynous marriage. She considered herself deeply religious, and said that before the birth of her child, she prayed five times a day whenever possible and recited the Quran. She did not do these things as regularly when we spoke about it, the duties of housewife and mother occupying her time.

Zebo's child's nanny attended classes for women on the Quran and Islam at the Embassy of the Islamic Republic of Iran regularly. She then passed on to Zebo and Zebo's sister-in-laws what she learned and gained respect as a knowledgeable woman of Islam in the community. Other women in the community perceived to be knowledgeable about Islam did not necessarily attend classes. A few times I was introduced to a woman who other women called a *bibi khalifa* (woman with great understanding of Islam). I discovered each time she did not have special training, but rather was self-taught by her own reading and seeking out sermons to listen to—and she was bold enough to claim knowledge. This is contrary to suggestions by some scholars that in Tajikistan religious training has created a particularly educated class of women religious teachers and leaders.[24] This is to be expected since any formal training was disrupted by the civil war, law prohibits women's attendance at mosques, and formal structure for women's religious education like that at the embassy is rare.

Unlike most Tajik families, at her marriage Zebo moved from her natal home to a renovated flat in Dushanbe near her husband's family members and was able to continue her studies to meet her career goals. Zebo's husband's oldest sister, Mahina, was married with two children and either wore rumol or no headscarf at all. Shahnoza, Zebo's 24-year-old sister-in-law who lived with her and her husband in Dushanbe, chose to wear rumol and short sleeves except for prayer times, when she wore satr.

However Sitora, the youngest sister-in-law, a 19 year-old university student, wore satr. This created some family tensions. Sitora's parents did not approve of satr and encouraged her not to wear it. She recited namaz five times a day alongside her sister Shahnoza; recited the Quran, listened to Hoji Mirzo, was an excellent university student, and loved to shop. When asked how she decided to wear satr while the rest of her family did not, she replied, "I studied the Quran and understood this was the proper way. At first it was strange. But then the more I wore it, the more I liked it."

---

24   H. Fathi, "Otines: The Unknown Women Clerics of Central Asian Islam," *Central Asian Survey*, 16, no. 1 (1997): 27–43; H. Fathi, "Gender, Islam, and Social Change in Uzbekistan," *Central Asian Survey*, 25, no. 3 (2006): 303–317.

Sitora explained how she also began lowering her hemlines to the ankle (although she admitted this was also a fashion trend) and sleeves dropped past her wrist to the palms of her hands. "I like going out and just going, no one can see … I want to wear niqab, but it is against the law." As mentioned, Sitora frequented bazaars, purchasing shiny and glittering ornamental beads to add to her clothing in elaborate designs. Turkish styles and the Chanel label enthralled her, and she very often added Chanel logos to her hijab.[25] These actions pointed to the influence of fashion and social trends as much as they show a personal devotion to Islam, a phenomenon also noted by Annelies Moors in "Fashionable Muslims."[26]

Sitora married in May 2015 when she was 20. She wore a trendy full white wedding gown with a slender, white, silky hijab. It is traditional in Tajikistan for the bride to order several new dress ensembles for her presentation, where she models the clothing in succession. Sitora adhered to this tradition and had several photographs taken in different traditional or "national" clothing. Instead of hijab, she chose the traditional sheer veil and held it over her head, toka, a traditional square hat, or nothing. In this particular context, her adherence to orthopraxy was not strong enough to subvert familial and social customs, although she continued wearing hijab after the wedding.

Maryam's family background was very different from Zebo and Sitora's. Maryam and her extended family lived in villages outside the city. While the women in Zebo's family were highly educated and, in general, planned on a family and children alongside a career, the women in Maryam's family usually married around 16 or 17 years old. They usually left school between 14 and 16 years of age. Working outside the home was acceptable if necessary, however; it brought stigma upon husbands because they were not the sole breadwinners. Maryam wore rumol before her marriage at 18. She began wearing hijab shortly after her wedding when a neighbor woman explained to her that it was her duty as a Muslim woman. Having a wife in hijab was unexpected by her husband. She said, "He got used to it. I am hidden from the gaze. I like that my husband likes it."

---

25   In a December 18, 2014, email, Chanel responded to my email inquiry about their marketing to Muslim women, and the pirating of their brand in Central Asia. "We are delighted to learn of your interest in our legendary brand. Since Chanel is a privately owned company, we are unable to accommodate your request for any information. We sincerely apologize for any inconvenience that this may cause you."
26   A. Moors, "Fashionable Muslims: Notions of Self, Religion, and Society in San'a," *Fashion Theory*, 11, no. 2–3 (2007): 319–346.

Maryam's aunts, sisters, and cousins shared a similar background and similar attitudes. Mastura, an aunt, said, "My husband didn't like it. But I told him I like to wear it. All the women do this. Then he didn't say anything about it. All of my family does it. All the women wear satr."

Gulchera is 38 years old and began wearing satr when she was 30 years old. She said, "My husband didn't want me to, but I did it anyway. It is an Islamic rule." When asked how she knew it was an Islamic rule, or how did she find out about this she said, "My brother told me." Gulchera explained she wasn't comfortable wearing satr at first, but then got used to it. She added, "Allah will punish us if we don't wear satr ... at first my husband didn't like it, but now he does."

Malika is 27 and the mother of three daughters. She began wearing satr seven years ago, "Satr is written by Allah. I personally have a neighbor. She read all this and explained it to me ... my mother does not wear satr and did not wear rumol. Then two to four years ago my father died, and she started wearing rumol." Malika and other women often note that their mothers, who were raised in the Soviet era, wear rumol and not hijab. However, sometimes young women adopting hijab influences the older generation to follow suit. It this case, it was clarified that her mother began wearing rumol only after her husband died, a Tajik tradition. During the marriage, she did not cover her head.

Shafoat married into the family when she was 17 after a young engagement at just shy of 15. She attended city schools, but her conservative family—and she herself—desired an early marriage. Shafoat did not cover her head until marriage, and did so with a simple traditional headscarf to honor her new in-laws. She lived with her in-laws for a number of years before she and her husband and children moved to their own flat. While all other members of the family wear hijab, she chooses not to. She did not seem bothered by this, and no one pressured her to wear it. She was asked once by her husband why she did not wear it when all other did, and she responded that she had an uncovered head before marriage and covered it now out of respect, and that was enough.

The women in the family all discussed gaining religious knowledge from word-of-mouth, from neighbors or other relatives. One woman reported that she heard from another female relative about hijab and assured me that her relative read Arabic and was very educated in Islam. However, when I talked with the woman herself and other family members, it was clear she did not read Arabic and had very little education because the civil war had erupted when she was a child. She had memorized a few verses of the Quran and said she started wearing hijab when others did. This informal learning and informal authority-granting creates an unordered, rather than hierarchal dispersion of religious knowledge, leading to a horizontally propelled social-Islam.

Zarangez, a 33-year-old woman explained, "I wear it because I like it. (Before) in Tajikistan, the communists would not allow it (hijab), now everyone can, so they do. When *begona* (non-kin) men come into the home, we do this to be hidden from *chashmoni begona* (eyes of non-kin men)." I asked her when she would have her daughter, who was nine years old, cover her head. She said, "She already does. There is a neighbor man who scolds (everyone in the neighborhood) if girls don't cover their heads. So we do." Zarangez said her own husband didn't care either way and doesn't discuss satr at home in regard to herself or their daughter. She said, "My husband didn't like it. He asked me, 'Why are you wearing that?' But I told him I would wear it, all the other women were wearing it."

Most of the women adopting hijab did not grow up in the Soviet era. Zebo was a young teen when the Soviet Union collapsed. The inscribed collective memory of the younger generation of Muslim women in Tajikistan is often one of Soviet suppression of religious piety, and this oppression must be resisted. Zarangez's realization that women wear hijab now because they can now without the oppression of the Soviet government should not be overlooked.

Hijab as Political

Resistance to contemporary power structures is also present within this practice of veiling. In a move hauntingly similar to the Soviet hujum on International Women's Day in 1927, on International Women's Day March 2015, President Rahmon addressed the women of the nation and expounded upon the hazards of clothing "alien" to Tajikistan. He announced that government officials would mandate dress codes for women working in public spaces. The dangers of religious extremism and lightly veiled references to the civil war were cited as justification for the new measures (see Appendix). The state demands that women wear "traditional" or "national" clothing were followed by raids on hijab vendors, women's black apparel, and instructions to the police to curb the "foreign dress" of women. In some cases, women working in bazaars were hauled to local police stations and forced to remove their hijab.[27]

---

[27]   "Militsiia Tadzhikistana boretsia s khidzhabami," *Islam Today*, March 30, 2015, <http://islam-today.ru/novosti/2015/03/30/milicia-tadzikistana-boretsa-s-hidzabami/>; "Pervyi zamministra MVD Tadzhikistana ozabochen tem, chto tadzhikskie zhenshchiny nosiat chuzhuiu odezhdu," *Ozodagon*, March 28, 2015, <http://catoday.org/centrasia/19033-per

Women who wear hijab do not necessarily consciously create an alternate identity outside the national identity of the Tajik Muslim woman, but engage in piety within the framework of a socially propelled Islamic revival. There is no evidence in Tajikistan that the act of wearing hijab leads to dangerous religious extremism, or that women in hijab promote radical Islam, which then threatens the security of Tajikistan or the Rahmon regime. Resistance scholars Stellan Vinthagen and Mona Lilja suggest resistance as "a subaltern response to power; a practice that challenges and which might undermine power." They further posit that resistance does not have to be conscious, but contain the possibility to change the current power structure.[28] In this way wearing hijab can be seen as a resistance, changing the social power structure to one of piety.

The piety of the veil and other modes of conservative female dress in Tajikistan threaten the nationalists' imaginary. In one example, in March 2013 Minister of Education Abdujabbor Rahmonov demanded that women wear high-heeled shoes to the university and colleges and criticized them as unfeminine, sloppy, and having poor posture.[29] The influential mullah Hoji Akbar Turajonzoda responded,

> Usually *zani fosiqa* (a sexually promiscuous woman) wears those types of shoes and they make sounds while walking. Wearing and selling those types of shoes for women is not acceptable. In the surah "an-Nour" (The Light), verse 31, while talking about Muslim women Allah says, "(they) should not knock on the ground with their feet to inform others about the beauties they wear." It means in this verse Allah forbids the sound. ... But if the high-heeled shoes (with condition that the heels are not too high) do not make any sound, and they are not linked with *zanhoi fosiqa*, and are not harmful for women, then there is no fear, *inshallah*, in wearing and selling them. But of course it's better for women not to wear these types of shoes, especially when medicine has proven that wearing high heel shoes is harmful.

vyy-zamministra-mvd-tadzhikistana-ozabochen-tem-chto-tadzhikskie-zhenschiny-nosyat-chuzhuyu-odezhdu.html>; K. Ato and M. Xoliqzod, "Raisi Xuçand: Zanon libosi toçiki pushand, na 'eroni' va 'afghoni'," *Radio Ozodi*, March 27, 2015, <http://www.ozodi.org/content/mayor-of-khujand-city-about-tajik-women-dress/26924034.html>.

28   S. Vinthagen and M. Lilja, "Understanding Resistance: Exploring Definitions, Perspectives, Forms, and Implications. Unpublished paper.

29   "Abdudzhabbor Rakhmonov vnov' v tsentre skandala," *News.tj*, April 4, 2013, <http://news.tj/ru/newspaper/article/abdudzhabbor-rakhmonov-vnov-v-tsentre-skandala>.

For practitioners, wearing the veil transcends fashion and rises to a spiritual plane. At the same time wearing satr creates a parallel cultural hegemony. Thus, the veil, rooted in a belief in Allah and farz, embodies Foucault's idea of the political-spiritual experience.[30] For a woman in Tajikistan the practice of wearing hijab is the visible manifestation of her identity as a Muslim woman; a shift away from the relic of the dual identity of the secular Soviet-Muslim woman, and away from the new state-driven national identity.

Conclusion

In Tajikistan, the practice of veiling has the power to contest social and political power structures, approaching a theory of political spirituality. A woman's desire to wear hijab is contextualized by cultural pressures, fashion trends, historical processes, and current political processes. A socially driven Islamic revival has caused religious knowledge about Islamic practices, namely hijab, to be transferred through informal ways. Women seek religious knowledge and share religious understanding about orthodox practices, like hijab, mostly by word of mouth, neighbor-to-neighbor, and woman-to-woman.

Government structures regard the spread of veiling among women and girls as a threat the current political regime and the imagined collective national identity. Because women and girls who wear hijab challenge the socio-political hegemony, officials link hijabi women and girls to the civil war and extremist organizations. In the early years of the Soviet Union, violence, including the forced unveiling of women in Central Asia, was used in attempts to suppress Islam and create the new Soviet woman. Contemporary rhetoric and legislation mimic Soviet ideology and practice, as elites seek to suppress religious learning and orthopraxy.

My research shows that amid these forces, women's experiences and practice of wearing hijab is imbued with socio-spiritual meaning. Most importantly, women's choice to wear hijab is situational, or particular. Understanding these cultural webs through ethnographic research provides deeper insight into current social and political dynamics in Tajikistan and offers the opportunity to see beyond the veil.

---

30   M. Leezenberg, "Power and Political Spirituality: Michel Foucault on the Islamic Revolution in Iran," in J. Bernauer and J. Carrette (eds), *Michel Foucault and Theology: The Politics of Religious Experience* (Aldershot, UK: Ashgate, 2004), 99–115; J. Afray and K.B. Anderson, "Revisiting Foucault and the Iranian Revolution," *New Politics*, X-1, no. 37 (2014), <http://newpol.org/content/revisiting-foucault-and-the-iranian-revolution>.

Appendix

President Emomali Rahmon's speech
International Women's Day
March 8, 2015

Dear women and mothers!
Recently a trend of worshiping an alien culture and the pull of women and girls of the country toward it (this alien culture), and the propaganda of foreign clothes in some cities and regions of the country has become a disturbing process.

A sense of admiration for the foreign and imitation regarding clothing, behavior, communication among women and girls may have a negative effect on the strength of the foundations of national culture.

According to scientific ethnographic sources, from ancient times our people had beautiful female apparel, our women and girls never wore black clothes. ... However, some Tajik girls and women (now) dress in black...

If some of the women and girls, because of fashion, imitate a similar style of apparel, then they spread similar (styles) clothes among our women and girls with the goal of the promotion of imposing ideas, and they want to form in our country yet another new extremist movement.

According to recent data, some girls and women dressed in black go to the funeral of strangers and try to promote everything foreign to our ancient history and cultural ideas among the women participating at the funeral.

However, the relevant authorities, persons in charge of the social sphere, active women and parents do not to take any measures to prevent this phenomenon, and all of this is also the responsibility of the state.

In this regard, it is necessary that the Ulama Council, Center for Islamic Studies, Committees on Women and the Family, Youth, Sport and Tourism, in the affairs of religion, ordering traditions and national ceremonies on television and radio, together with the heads of regions, cities and regions have taken measures to prevent the spread of foreign culture and apparel, the results will be systematically reported to the Government.

The Tajikmatlubot Union, the chairmen of regions, cities and districts jointly entrusted to develop fashions with fashion models, clothes for people working in the markets, shopping centers, cafeterias, restaurants and other public places and to control the use of such clothing.

The historical experience of the past and present realities of the country, which did not attach great importance to the issue of strengthening the family, show that such indifference is the reason for collision with a sharp spiritual and demographic crisis.

Therefore, we must strive to protect the family as the most important social value, firmly maintain the true face, the true essence and value of the traditional Tajik family, as the sacred and invaluable foundation of our nation.

Acknowledgement

Special thanks to Abdulfattoh Shafiev for his help and guidance with translations.

Bibliography

Abashin, Sergei. "The Logic of Islamic Practice: a Religious Conflict in Central Asia." *Central Asian Survey* 25, no. 3 (2006): 267–286.

Abashin, Sergei. *Sovetskii kishlak: mezhdu kolonializmom and modernizatsiei.* Moscow: Novoe literaturnoe obozrenie, 2015.

Abashin, Sergey. "Gellner, the 'Saints,' and Central Asia: Between Islam and Nationalism." *Inner Asia* 7, no. 1 (2005): 65–86.

Abdakimov, Abdijapar. *Istoriia Kazakhstana*, 4th ed. Almaty: "Kazakhstan," 2003.

Abduvakhitov, Abdujabbar. "Islamic Revivalism in Uzbekistan." In *Russian Muslim Frontiers: New Directions in Cross-Cultural Analysis,* edited by Dale F. Eickelman, 79–97. Bloomington: Indiana University Press, 1993.

Abu-Lughod, Lila, ed. *Remaking Women: Feminism and Modernity in the Middle East.* Princeton, NJ: Princeton University Press, 1998.

Abu-Lughod, Lila. "Writing Against Culture." In *Recapturing Anthropology: Working in the Present*, edited by Richard G. Fox, 137–162. Santa Fe, NM: School of American Research Press, 1991.

Abu-Lughod, Lila. *Do Muslim Women Need Saving?* Cambridge, MA: Harvard University Press, 2013.

Adamson, Fiona B. "Global Liberalism Versus Political Islam: Competing Ideological Frameworks in International Politics." *International Studies Review* 7, no. 4 (2005): 547–569.

Adaş, Emin Baki. "The Making of Entrepreneurial Islam and Islamic Spirit of Capitalism." *Journal for Cultural Research* 10, no. 2 (2006): 113–137.

Adeeb, Khalid. *The Politics of Muslim Cultural Reform: Jadidism in Central Asia.* Berkeley: University of California Press.

Ahmed, Leila. *A Quiet Revolution: The Veil's Resurgence, from the Middle East to America.* New Haven, CT: Yale University Press, 2011.

Akiner, Shirin. "The Politicisation of Islam in Postsoviet Central Asia." *Religion, State, and Society* 3, no. 2 (2003): 97–122.

Alff, Henryk. "Basarökonomie im Wandel: Postsowjetische Perspektiven des Handels in Zentralasien." *Geographische Rundschau* 65, no. 11 (2013): 20–25.

Aliyev, Fuad. "The Politics of Islamic Finance in Central Asia and South Caucasus." *Voices From Central Asia*, no. 2 (July 2012).

Al-Tarablusi, Sayid ibn Muhammad al-Asali al-Shami al-Dimashqi, "Al-Djumal al-Mufida fi Sharh al-Djawhara al-Farida," in *Disputy musul'manskikh religioznykh avtoritetov v Tsentral'noi Azii v XX veke,* edited by Bakhtiyar Babadjanov, Ashirbek Muminov, and Anke von Kugelgen, 62-71. Almaty: Dayk-Press, 2007.

Alvi, Sajida S., Homa Hoodfar, and Sheila McDonough. *The Muslim Veil in North America: Issues and Debates*. Toronto, ON: Women's Press, 2003.

Amghar, Samir. *Le salafisme d'aujourd'hui. Mouvements sectaires en Occident*. Paris: Michalon Editions, 2011.

Anderson, Benedict. *Imagined Communities: Reflections on the Origins and Spread of Nationalism*. London: Verso, 1993.

Arthur, Linda B., ed., *Religion, Dress, and the Body*. New York: Berg, 1999.

Asadov, Alam, and Khurshid Gazikhanov. "Ijarah's Prospects in Central Asia: An Example of Uzbekistan." *Journal of Islamic Economics, Banking and Finance* 11, no. 2 (2015): 63–85.

Asutay, Mehmet. "Conceptualisation of the second best solution in overcoming the social failure of Islamic banking and finance: Examining the overpowering of homoislamicus by homoeconomicus." *IIUM Journal of Economics and Management* 15, no. 2 (2007): 167–195.

Atkin, Muriel. *The Subtlest Battle: Islam in Soviet Tajikistan*. Philadelphia, PA: Foreign Policy Research Institute, 1989.

Baba, Ricardo. "Islamic Financial Centers." In *Handbook of Islamic Banking,* edited by M. Kabir Hassan, and Mervyn K. Lewis, 384–400. Cheltenham, UK: Edward Elgar, 2007.

Babadjanov, Bakhtiyar M. *Kokandskoe Khanstvo: vlast,' politika, religiia*. Tashkent: TIAS, 2010.

Babadjanov, Bakhtiyar, and Muzaffar Kamilov. "Muhammadjan Hindustani (1892–1989) and the Beginning of the 'Great Schism' among the Muslims of Uzbekistan." In *Islam in Politics in Russia and Central Asia: Early Eighteenth-Late Twentieth Centuries,* edited by Stéphane A. Dudoignon and Komatsu Hisao, 195–219. New York: Routledge, 2001.

Babadjanov, Bakhtiyar, Ashikbek Muminov, and Anke von Kugelgen. *Disputy musul'manskikh religioznykh avtoritetov v Tsentral'noi Azii v XX veke*. Almaty: Dayk-Press, 2007.

Babajanov, Bakhtiyar M., Ashirbek K. Muminov, and Anke von Kügelgen, eds. *Disputes on Muslim Authority in Central Asia in Twentieth Century*. Almaty: Daik-Press, 2007.

Baban, Feyzi. "Secular Spaces and Religious Representations: Reading the Headscarf Debate in Turkey as Citizenship Politics." *Citizenship Studies* 18, no. 6–7 (2014): 644–660.

Baldwin, Robert, Scott Collin, and Christopher Hood, eds. *A Reader on Regulation*. Oxford: Oxford University Press, 1998.

Bassin, Mark, Sergey Glebov, and Marlene Laruelle, eds. *Between Europe and Asia: The Origins, Theories, and Legacies of Russian Eurasianism*. Pittsburgh, PA: University of Pittsburgh Press, 2015.

Bassin, Mark. *The Gumilev Mystique: Biopolitics, Eurasianism, and the Construction of Community in Modern Russia*. Ithaca, London: Cornell University Press, 2016.

Beck, Ulrich. "Mobility and the Cosmopolitan Perspective." In *Tracing Mobilities: Towards a Cosmopolitan Perspective,* edited by Weert Cancler, Vincent Kaufmann, and Sven Kesselring, 25—36. Burlington, VT: Ashgate, 2008.

Beck, Ulrich. "The Cosmopolitan Society and its Enemies." *Theory, Culture, and Society* 19, no. 1–2 (2002): 17–44.

Bekkin, Renat I. "Islamskoe ili musul'manskoe pravo? (K voprosu o pravovykh aspektakh islamskikh finansov)." *Problemy sovremennoi ekonomiki* 4, no. 48 (2013): 429–430.

Bekmurzaev, Nurbek. "Independent Islam in Central Asia: Reasons behind Independent Islamic Leaders' Resistance towards the State Control of Religion in Kyrgyzstan." Thesis. Bishkek: OSCE Academy, September 2014.

Benda-Beckmann, Keebet von, Franz von Benda-Beckmann, and Julia Eckert. "Rules of Law and Laws of Ruling: Law and Governance between Past and Future." In *Rules of Law and Laws of Ruling: On the Governance of Law,* edited by Keebet von Benda-Beckmann, Franz von Benda-Beckmann, and Julia Eckert, 1–30. Burlington, VT: Ashgate, 2009.

Benjamin, Walter. "Theory of Distraction." In *Selected Writings: Volume 3, 1935–1938,* edited by Howard Eiland and Michael W. Jennings, 141–143. Cambridge, MA: Harvard University Press, 2006.

Bennigsen, Alexandre, and S. Enders Wimbush. *Muslims of the Soviet Empire.* London: C. Hurst & Co., 1985.

Benningsen, Alexandre. "Unrest in the World of Soviet Islam." *Third World Quarterly* 10, no. 2 (1988): 778–779.

Bergne, Paul. *The Birth of Tajikistan: National Identity and the Origins of the Republic.* London: I.B. Tauris, 2009.

Berliner, Joseph S. "The Informal Organization of the Soviet Firm." *Quarterly Journal of Economics* 66, no. 3 (1952): 342–365.

Bitter, Jean-Nicolas, ed. *From Confidence Building towards Co-Operative Co-Existence: The Tajik Experiment of Islamic-Secular Dialogue.* Baden-Baden: Nomos, 2005.

Blaydes, Lisa, and Drew A. Linzer. "The Political Economy of Women's Support for Fundamentalist Islam." *World Politics* 60, no. 4 (July 2008): 576–609.

Bohr, Annette. "Uzbekistan: Politics and Foreign Policy." London: The Royal Institute of International Affairs, 1998.

Bourdieu, Pierre. *Religion.* Frankfurt: Suhrkamp, 2011.

Bowen, John R. *Why the French Don't Like Headscarves: Islam, the State, and Public Space.* Princeton, NJ: Princeton University Press, 2007.

Bregel, Yuri E. *Historical Atlas of Central Asia.* Leiden: Brill, 2003.

Bromley, Yulian V. *Ocherki teorii etnosa.* Moscow: LKI, 2008.

Brower, Daniel. *Turkestan and the Fate of the Russian Empire.* London: Routledge, 2003.

Brubaker, Rogers, Mara Loveman, and Peter Stamatov. "Ethnicity as Cognition." *Theory and Society* 33, no. 1 (2004): 31–64.

Cantillon, Richard. *Essai sur La nature du commerce en général* (1755; repr.). London: Macmillan, 1982.

Carree, Martin A., and Roy Thurik. "The Lag Structure of the Impact of Business Ownership on Economic Performance in OECD Countries." *Small Business Economics* 30 (2008): 101–110.

Carrere d'Encausse, Helene. *Islam and the Russian Empire: Reform and Revolution in Central Asia*. London: I.B. Tauris, 2009.

Cassel, Dieter and Ulrich Cichy. "Explaining the Growing Shadow Economy in East and West: A Comparative System Approach." *Comparative Economic Studies* 28 (1986): 20–41.

Chapra, Muhammar U. *Morality and Justice in Islamic Economics and Finance*. Cheltenham, UK: Edward Elgar, 2014.

Chen, Martha A. "Rethinking the Informal Economy: Linkages with the Formal Economy and the Formal Regulatory Environment." In *Linking the Formal and Informal Economy: Concept and Measures*, edited by Basudeb Guha-Khasnobis, Ravi Kanbur, and Elinor Ostrom, 75–92. Oxford: Oxford University Press, 2006.

Chong, Beng Soon, and Ming-Hua Liu. "Islamic Banking: Interest-free or Interest-based?" *Pacific-Basin Finance Journal* 17, no. 1 (2009): 125–144.

Choudhury, Masudul Alam. "Development of Islamic economic and social thought." In *Handbook of Islamic Banking,* edited by M. Kabir *Hassan* and Mervyn K. Lewis, 21–37. Cheltenham, UK: Edward Elgar, 2007.

Choueiri, Youssef M. *Islamic Fundamentalism: The Story of Islamist Movements*, 3rd ed. London: Continuum, 2010.

Cieślewska, Anna. "From Shuttle Trader to Businesswomen." In *The Informal Post-Socialist Economy: Embedded Practices and Livelihoods,* edited by Jeremy Morris and Abel Polese, 121–134. New York: Routledge, 2014.

Collins, Kathleen, and Erica Owen. "Islamic Religiosity and Regime Preferences: Explaining Support for Democracy and Political Islam in Central Asia and the Caucasus." *Political Research Quarterly* 65, no. 3 (2012): 499–515.

Collins, Kathleen. *Clan Politics and Regime Transition in Central Asia*. Cambridge: Cambridge University Press, 2006.

Comaroff, John L., and Jean Comaroff. "Introduction." In *Law and Disorder in the Postcolony,* edited by John L. Comaroff and Jean Comaroff, 1–56. Chicago: University of Chicago Press, 2006.

Commercio, Michele E. "The Politics and Economics of 'Retraditionalization' in Kyrgyzstan and Tajikistan." *Post-Soviet Affairs* 31, no. 6 (2015): 529–556.

Cook, Michael. *Commanding Right and Forbidding Wrong in Islamic Thought*. New York: Cambridge University Press, 2000.

Cordier, Bruno de. "The development space(s) of Non-OECD aid donors in Southern Eurasia: A look at the Islamic Development Bank." *Central Asia Economic Paper No. 3* (September 2012).

Cosmo, Nicola Di, ed. *The Cambridge History of Inner Asia: The Chinggisid Age.* Cambridge: Cambridge University Press, 2009.

Crews, Robert D. *For Prophet and Tsar: Islam and Empire in Russia and Central Asia.* Cambridge, MA: Harvard University Press, 2006.

Cummings, Sally. *Understanding Central Asia: Politics and Contested Transformations.* London: Routledge, 2012.

Dadabaev, Timur. "Introduction to Survey Research in Post-Soviet Central Asia." *Asian Research Trends: New Series* 3(2008): 45–69.

Dadabaev, Timur. "Post-Soviet Realities of Society in Uzbekistan." *Central Asian Survey* 23, no. 2 (June 2004): 141-166.

Dadabaev, Timur. "Recollections of Emerging Hybrid Ethnic Identities in Soviet Central Asia: The Case of Uzbekistan." *Nationalities Papers* 41, no. 6 (November 2013): 1026–48.

Dadabaev, Timur. "Religiosity and Soviet 'Modernisation' in Central Asia: Locating Religious Traditions and Rituals in Recollections of Anti-Religious Policies in Uzbekistan." *Religion, State, and Society* 42, no. 4 (December 2014): 328–353.

Dagiev, Dagikhudo. *Regime Change in Central Asia Stateness, Nationalism, and Political Change in Tajikistan and Uzbekistan.* New York: Routledge, 2014.

Danzer, Alexander M., and Oleksiy Ivaschenko. "Migration Patterns in a Remittances Dependent Economy: Evidence from Tajikistan during the Global Financial Crisis." *Migration Letters* 7, no. 2 (2010): 190-202.

Davies, Robert W., Mark Harrison, and Stephen G. Wheatcroft, eds. *The Economic Transformation of the Soviet Union, 1913–1945.* New York: Cambridge University Press, 1994.

Davis, Nancy J., and Robert V. Robinson. "The Egalitarian Face of Islamic Orthodoxy: Support for Islamic Law and Economic Justice in Seven Muslim-Majority Nations." *American Sociological Review* 71, no. 2 (2006): 167–190.

Derigs, Ulrich, and Shehab Marzban. "Review and analysis of current Shariah-compliant equity screening practices." *International Journal of Islamic and Middle Eastern Finance and Management* 1, no. 4 (2008): 285–303.

Devonshire-Ellis, Chris. *The Great Eurasian Game and the String of Pearls.* Hong Kong: Asia Briefing, 2015.

DeWeese, Devin. "Authority." In *Key Themes for the Study of Islam*, edited by Jamal J. Elias, 26–52. Oxford: Oneworld Publications, 2010.

DeWeese, Devin. "Islam and the Legacy of Sovietology: A Review Essay on Yaacov Ro'i's Islam in the Soviet Union," *Journal of Islamic Studies* 13, no. 3 (2002): 298–330.

DeWeese, Devin. *Studies of Sufism in Central Asia.* Farnham, UK: Ashgate, 2012.

Djelic, Marie-Laure, and Kerstin Sahlin-Andersson, eds. *Transnational Governance: Institutional Dynamics of Regulation.* Cambridge: Cambridge University Press, 2006.

Djumaev, Alexandr. "Islam and Culture in the Context of the Central Asian Civilization." *Studies on Central Asia* 87, no. 1 (2007): 53–84.

Dudoignon, Stéphane A. "Islam d'Europe? Islam d'Asie? En Eurasie centrale (Russie, Caucase, Asie centrale)." In *L'Islam en Asie du Caucase à la Chine*, edited by Andrée Feillard, 21–80. Paris: Les Études de la documentation Française, 2001.

Dudoignon, Stéphane A., and Sayyid A. Qalandar. "They Were All from the Country: The Revival and Politicisation of Islam in the Lower Wakhsh Valley of the Tajik SSR (1947–1997)." In *Allah's Kolkhozes: Migration, De-Stalinisation, Privatisation, and the New Muslim Congregations in the Soviet Relam (1950s–2000s)*, edited by Stéphane A. Dudoignon and Christian Noack, 47–122. Berlin: Klaus-Schwarz, 2013.

Dudoignon, Stéphane. "From Revival to Mutation: The Religious Personnel of Islam in Tajikistan, from de-Stalinization to Independence (1955–91)." *Central Asian Survey* 30, no. 1 (2011): 53–80.

Dudoignon, Stéphane. "Political Parties and Forces in Tajikistan, 1989–1993." In *Tajikistan: The Trials of Independence*, edited by Mohammad-Reza Djalili, Frédéric Grare, and Shirin Akiner, 52–85. Richmond, UK: Curzon, 1998.

Duneier, Mitchell. "How Not to Lie with Ethnography." *Sociological Methodology* 41 (2011): 1–11.

Durkheim, Emile. *Elementary Forms of Religious Life*, trans. by Karen E. Fields. New York: Free Press, 1995.

Echchaibi, Nabil. "From Audio Tapes to Video Blogs: The Delocalisation of Authority in Islam." *Nations and Nationalism* 17, no. 1 (2011): 25–44.

Eckert, Julia. "Urban Governance and Emergent Forms of Legal Pluralism in Mumbai." *Journal of Legal Pluralism* 36, no. 50 (2004): 29–60.

Eickelman, Dale F. "Introduction. The Other 'Orientalist' Crisis." In *Russia's Muslim Frontiers: New Directions in Cross-Cultural Analysis,* Dale F. Eickelman, 1–15. Bloomington: Indiana University Press, 1993.

Elena Paskaleva, "Ideology in Brick and Tile: Timurid Architecture of the Twenty-First Century," *Central Asian Survey* 34, no. 4 (December 2015): 418-439.

Elshashtawy, Yasser. "Transitory Sites: Mapping Dubai's 'Forgotten' Urban Spaces." *International Journal of Urban and Regional Research* 32, no. 4 (2008): 968–988.

Epkenhans, Tim. "'Islam' in the Security Discourse of the Post-Soviet Republics of Central Asia." In *Yearbook on the Organization for Security and Co-operation in Europe (OSCE) 2010*, 91-103. Baden-Baden: Nomos Publishers, 2011.

Epkenhans, Tim. "Defining Normative Islam: Some Remarks on Contemporary Islamic Thought in Tajikistan—Hoji Akbar Turajonzoda's Sharia and Society." *Central Asian Survey* 30, no. 1 (2011): 81–96.

Epkenhans, Tim. *For the Soul, Blood, Homeland, and Honour: The Origins of the Civil War in Tajikistan*. Lanham: Lexington, 2016.

Epkenhans, Tim. "Regulating Religion in Post-Soviet Central Asia: Some Remarks on Religious Association Law and 'Official' Islamic Institutions in Tajikistan." *Security and Human Rights* 20, no. 1 (2009): 94–99.

Ertürk, Korkut A., ed. *Rethinking Central Asia: Non-Eurocentric Studies in History, Social Structure, and Identity.* Reading, UK: Ithaca Press, 1999.

Essers, Caroline, and Yvonne Benschop. "Muslim Businesswomen Doing Boundary Work: The Negotiation of Islam, Gender, and Ethnicity within Entrepreneurial Contexts." *Human Relations* 62, no. 3 (2009): 403–423.

Fandy, Mamoun. "Political Science Without Clothes: The Politics of Dress or Contesting the Spatiality of the State in Egypt." *Arab Studies Quarterly* 20, no. 2 (Spring 1998): 87-104.

Fathi, Habiba. "Otines: The Unknown Women Clerics of Central Asian Islam." *Central Asian Survey* 16, no. 1 (1997): 27–43.

Fathi, Habiba. "Women of Authority in Central Asia Islam as Identity Preserving References and Agents of Community Restructuring in the Post-Soviet Period." In *Patterns of Transformation in and around Uzbekistan,* edited by Paolo Sartori and Tommaso Trevisani, 121–138. Reggio Emilia, Italy: Diabasis, 2007.

Fierman, William, ed. *Soviet Central Asia: The Failed Transformation.* Boulder, CO: Westview, 1991.

Finke, Peter. "Central Asian Attitudes towards Afghanistan: Perceptions of the Afghan War in Uzbekistan." In *Ethnicity, Authority, and Power in Central Asia: New Games,* edited by Robert L. Crawfield and Gabriele Rasuly-Paleczek, 61-76. London and New York: Routledge, 2011.

Finke, Peter. *Variations on Uzbek Identity: Strategic Choices, Cognitive Schemas, and Political Constraints in Identification Processes.* Oxford, UK: Berghahn Books, 2014.

Fletcher, Joseph F., and Boris Sergeyev. "Islam and Intolerance in Central Asia: The Case of Kyrgyzstan." *Europe-Asia Studies* 54, no. 2 (2002): 251–275.

Foucault, Michel. "Questions of Method." In *The Foucault Effect: Studies in Governmentality,* edited by G. Burchell, C. Gordon, and P. Miller, 87–104. Hemel Wheatsheaf: Hemel Hempstead, 1991.

Fragner, Bert. "Social and Internal Economic Affairs." In *The Cambridge History of Iran: The Timurid and Safavid Periods,* edited by Peter Jackson and Laurence Lockhart, 491–567. New York: Cambridge University Press, 1986.

Frank, André G. "ReOrient: From Centrality of Central Asia to China's Middle Kingdom." In *Rethinking Central Asia: Non-Eurocentric Studies in History, Social Structure, and Identity,* edited by Korkut A. Ertürk, 11-38. Reading, UK: Ithaca Press, 1999.

Frye, Richard N., ed. *The Cambridge History of Iran, Vol. 4. From the Arab Invasion to the Saljuqs.* Cambridge: Cambridge University Press, 1975.

Gardner, Andrew. "Why Do They Keep Coming? Labor Migrants in the Gulf States." In *Migrant Labor in the Persian Gulf*, edited by Mehran Kamrava and Zahra Babar, 41—58. London: Hurst, 2012.

Geertz, Clifford. "Religion as a Cultural System." In *The Interpretation of Cultures*, 87–125. New York: Basic Books, 1973.

Geertz, Clifford. "Thick Description: Toward an Interpretive Theory of Culture." In *The Interpretation of Cultures: Selected Essays*, 3–30. New York: Basic Books, 1973.

Geertz, Clifford. *Islam Observed: Religious Development in Morocco and Indonesia.* Chicago: University of Chicago Press, 1968.

Geiss, Paul G. *Pre-Tsarist and Tsarist Central Asia: Communal Commitment and Political Order in Change.* London: Routledge, 2003.

George, Kenneth. *Picturing Islam: Art and Ethics in a Muslim Lifeworld.* Oxford: Wiley-Blackwell, 2011.

Geroski, Paul A. "European Industrial Policy and Industrial Policy in Europe." *Oxford Review of Economic Policy* 5, no. 2 (1989): 20–36.

Gerrard, Philip, and J. Barton Cunningham. "Islamic Banking: A Study in Singapore." *International Journal of Bank Marketing* 15, no. 6 (1997): 204–216.

Golden, Peter B. *Central Asia in World History.* Oxford: Oxford University Press, 2011.

Grant, Bruce. "Cosmopolitan Baku." *Ethos: Journal of Anthropology* 75, no. 2 (2010): 123—147.

Gresh, Geoffrey F. "The Rise of Islamic Banking and Finance in Central Asia." *The Fletcher School Online Journal for Issues Related to Southwest Asia and Islamic Civilization* (Fall 2007).

Grossman, Gregory. "The 'Second Economy' of the USSR." *Problems of Communism* 26, no. 5 (1977): 25–40.

Guindi, Fadwa El. "Veiling Infitah with Muslim Ethic: Egypt's Contemporary Islamic Movement." *Social Problems* 28, no. 4 (1981): 465–485.

Gunn, T. Jeremy. "Shaping an Islamic Identity: Religion, Islamism, and the State in Central Asia." *Sociology of Religion* 64, no. 3 (2003): 389–410.

Habiba Fathi, "Gender, Islam, and Social Change in Uzbekistan," *Central Asian Survey*, 25, no. 3 (2006): 303–317.

Hacker, Jacob, and Paul Pierson. *Winner-Take-All Politics: How Washington Made the Rich Richer—and Turned Its Back on the Middle Class.* New York: Simon and Schuster, 2010.

Hakim, Sam R. "Islamic Money Market Instruments." In *Handbook of Islamic Banking,* edited by M. Kabir *Hassan* and Mervyn K. Lewis, 161–171. Cheltenham, UK: Edward Elgar, 2007.

Hamad, Sulton. *Dar payrahai nur.* Dushanbe: Muattar, 2013.

Hann, Chris, and Mathijs Pelkmans. "Realigning Religion and Power in Central Asia: Islam, Nation-State and (Post)Socialism." *Europe-Asia Studies* 61, no. 9 (2009): 1517–1541.

Hannerz, Ulf. "Cosmopolitans and Locals in World Culture." In *Global Culture: Nationalism, Globalization, and Modernity,* edited by Mike Featherstone, 237–252. London: Sage, 1990.

Hansen, Karen T., and Mariken Vaa, eds. *Reconsidering Informality: Perspectives from Urban Africa.* Uppsala: North Africa Institute, 2004.

Hansen, Thomas Blom, and Finn Stepputat. *Sovereign Bodies: Citizens, Migrants, and States in the Postcolonial World.* Princeton, NJ: Princeton University Press, 2005.

Harris, Colette. *Control and Subversion: Gender Relations in Tajikistan.* Sterling, VA: Pluto Press, 2004.

Heathershaw, John, and David Montgomery. *The Myth of Post-Soviet Muslim Radicalization in the Central Asian Republics.* Russia and Eurasia Programme Research Paper. London: Royal Institute of International Affairs, 2014.

Heathershaw, John, and David Montgomery. *The Myth of Post-Soviet Muslim Radicalization in the Central Asian Republics.* London: Chatham House, 2014.

Heathershaw, John. "The Global Performance State." In *Ethnographies of the State in Central Asia: Performing Politics,* edited by Madeleine Reeves, Johan Rasanayagam, and Judith Beyer, 29–54. Bloomington: Indiana University Press, 2013.

Heathershaw, John. *Post Conflict Tajikistan: The Politics of Peacebuilding and the Emergence of Legitimate Order.* London: Routledge, 2009.

Heathershaw, John. *Tajikistan: The Politics of Peacebuilding and the Emergence of Legitimate Order.* London: Routledge, 2009.

Heyat, Farideh. "Re-Islamization in Kyrgyzstan: Gender, New Poverty and the Moral Dimension." *Central Asian Survey* 23, nos. 3–4 (2004): 275–287.

Hierman, Brent. "Central Asian Ethnicity Compared: Evaluating the Contemporary Social Salience of Uzbek Identity in Kyrgyzstan and Tajikistan." *Europe-Asia Studies* 67, no. 4 (June 2015): 519-539.

Highmore, Ben. *Ordinary Lives: Studies in the Everyday.* London: Routledge, 2010.

Hilgers, Irene. *Why Do Uzbeks Have to be Muslims? Exploring Religiosity in the Ferghana Valley.* Berlin: Lit Verlag, 2009.

Hoggarth, Davinia. "The rise of Islamic finance: post-colonial market-building in central Asia and Russia." *International Affairs* 92, no. 1 (2016): 115–136.

Hopkirk, Peter. *The Great Game: The Struggle for Empire in Central Asia.* New York: Kodansha International, 1992.

Hough, Leslie. "Tajikistan's Competing Social and Political Forces: The Politics of Traditional versus Women's Dress." Washington, DC: IREX, 2011.

Humphrey, Caroline, ed. *Marx Went Away but Karl Stayed Behind.* Ann Arbor: Michigan University Press, 1998.

Humphrey, Caroline. "Traders, 'Disorder,' and Citizenship Regimes in Provincial Russia." In *Uncertain Transition: Ethnographies of Change in the Postsocialist World,* edited by

Michael Burawoy and Katherine Verdery, 19–52. Lanham, MD: Rowman and Littlefield, 1999.

Hunter, Shireen T. "Iran, Central Asia, and the Opening of the Islamic Iron Curtain." In *Islam and Central Asia: An Enduring Legacy or an Evolving Threat?,* edited by Roald Sagdeev and Susan Eisenhower, 171–191. Washington, DC: Center for Political and Strategic Studies, 2000.

Husaynī, Saidumar. *Khotiraho az nakhust oshnoiyam ba Harakati Islomii Tojikiston to rasmiyati on.* Dushanbe: Muattar, 2013.

Il'khamov, Alisher. "Akramiia: ekstremistskoe dvizhenie ili predtecha islamskoi sot-sial'noi demokratii?" In *Rasy i narody: Volume 32,* edited by Sergey Abashin and Valentin Bushkov, 116–156. Moscow: Nauka, 2006.

Inglehart, Ronald, and Christian Welzel. *Modernization, Cultural Change, and Democracy: The Human Development Sequence.* New York: Cambridge University Press, 2005.

Inglis, Tom. "Catholic Identity in Contemporary Ireland: Belief and Belonging to Tradition." *Journal of Contemporary Religion* 22, no. 2 (2007): 205–220.

Isaacs, Rico, and Abel Polese. "Between 'Imagined' and 'Real' Nation-Building: Identities and Nationhood in Post-Soviet Central Asia." *Nationalities Papers* 43 no. 3 (May 2015): 371–372.

"Is Radical Islam Inevitable in Central Asia? Priorities for Engagement." *Asia Report* 72, International Crisis Group, December 22, 2003.

Jacobsen, Christine. "Troublesome Threesome: Feminism, Anthropology, and Muslim Women's Piety." *Feminist Review* 98 no. 1 (2011): 65–82.

Jafrelot, Christophe. "Transnational Learning Networks Amongst Asian Muslims: An Introduction." *Modern Asian Studies* 48, no. 2 (2014): 331–339.

Jessa, Pawel. "Aq Jol Soul Healers: Religious Pluralism and a Contemporary Muslim Movement in Kazakhstan." *Central Asian Survey* 25, no. 3 (2006): 359–371.

Johnson, Simon, Danny Kaufmann, and Andrei Schleifer. "The Unofficial Economy in Transition." *Brookings Institution Papers on Economic Activity No. 2.* Washington, D.C.: Brookings Institution Press, 1997.

Junisbai, Azamat. "The Determinants of Economic System Legitimacy in Kazakhstan." *Europe-Asia Studies* 66, no. 8 (2014): 1234–1252.

Junisbai, Azamat. "Understanding Economic Justice Attitudes in Two Countries: Kazakhstan and Kyrgyzstan." *Social Forces* 88, no. 4 (2010): 1677–1702.

Kabirī, Muhiddin, ed., *Mujaddidi asr.* Dushanbe: ShKOS HNIT, 2007.

Kabirī, Muhiddin. *Din va siyosat.* Dushanbe: Muattar, 2010.

Kaiser, Markus. "Die Soziologie in der Republik Usbekistan." *Bielefeld University Working Paper No. 265.* Bielefeld: Bielefeld University, 1997.

Kamp, Marianne. *The New Woman in Uzbekistan: Islam, Modernity, and Unveiling under Communism.* Seattle: University of Washington Press, 2006.

Kandiyoti, Deniz, ed. *Women, Islam, and the State*. Philadelphia, PA: Temple University Press, 1991.

Kandiyoti, Deniz. "The Politics of Gender and the Soviet Paradox: Neither Colonized, Nor Modern?". *Central Asian Survey* 26, no. 4 (2007): 601–623.

Kaneff, Deema. "The Shame and Pride of Market Activity: Morality, Identity, and Trading in Postsocialist Rural Bulgaria." In *Markets and Moralities: Ethnographies of Postsocialism,* edited by Ruth Mandel and Caroline Humphrey, 33–52. Oxford: Berg, 2002.

Kanna, Ahmed. *Dubai, the City as Corporation*. Minneapolis: University of Minnesota Press, 2011.

Karagiannis, Emmanuel. "Political Islam and Social Movement Theory: The Case of Hizb ut-Tahrir in Kyrgyzstan." *Religion, State, and Society* 33, no. 2 (2005): 137–150.

Karagiannis, Emmanuel. *Political Islam in Central Asia: The Challenge of Hizb ut-Tahrir*. New York: Routledge, 2010.

Karim, Būrī. *Faryodi solho*. Moscow: Transdornauka, 1997.

Karim, Mohammad. "Globalization and Post-Soviet Revival of Islam in Central Asia and the Caucasus." *Journal of Muslim Minority Affairs* 25, no. 3 (2010): 439–448.

Karimov, Islam. *Uzbekistan on the Threshold of the Twenty-First Century: Challenges to Stability and Progress*. New York: St. Martin's, 1997.

Karin, Erlan. *The Soldiers of the Caliphate: The Anatomy of a Terrorist Group*. Astana: KazISS, 2016.

Kathiravelu, Laavanya. *Migrant Dubai. Low Wage Workers and the Construction of a Global City*. New York: Palgrave Macmillan, 2016.

Kemper, Michael. "Ljucian Klimovič: Der ideologische Bluthund der sowjetischen Islamkunde und Zentralasienliteratur." *Asiatische Studien/Études Asiatiques* 63, no. 1 (2009), 93–133.

Kendzior, Sarah. "Digital Distrust: Uzbek Cynicism and Solidarity in the Internet Age." *American Ethnologist* 38, no. 3 (2011): 559–575.

Kendzior, Sarah. "Poetry of Witness: Uzbek Identity and the Response to Andijon." *Central Asian Survey* 26, no. 3 (September 2007): 317–334.

Kenjaev, Safaralī. *Tabadduloti Tojikistan*. Dushanbe: Fondi Kenjaev, 1993.

Kepel, Gilles. *Muslim Extremism in Egypt: The Prophet and Pharaoh*. Berkeley: University of California Press, 2003.

Khaki, G.N., and Bilal Ahmad Malik. "Emergence of PLS Industry in Post-Soviet Central Asia: An Empirical Study of Kazakhstan." *Journal of Islamic Economics, Banking, and Finance* 11, no. 1 (2015): 140–156.

Khaki, G.N., and Bilal Ahmad Malik. "Islamic Banking and Finance in Post-Soviet Central Asia with Special Reference to Kazakhstan." *Journal of Islamic Banking and Finance* 1, no. 1 (2013): 11–22.

Khalid, Adeeb. "A Secular Islam: Nation, State and Religion in Uzbekistan." *International Journal of Middle East Studies* 35, no. 4 (2003): 573–598.

Khalid, Adeeb. *Islam after Communism: Religion and Politics in Central Asia.* Berkeley and Los Angeles: University of California Press: 2007.

Khalid, Adeeb. *The Politics of Muslim Cultural Reform: Jadidism in Central Asia.* Berkeley: University of California Press, 1998.

Khamidov, Alisher. "The Lessons of the 'Nookat Events': Central Government, Local Officials and Religious Protests in Kyrgyzstan," *Central Asian Survey* 32, no. 2 (2013): 148–160;

Khlevnyuk, Oleg, and Robert W. Davies. "The End of Rationing in the Soviet Union, 1934–1935." *Europe-Asia Studies* 51, no. 4 (1999): 557–610.

Killian, Caitlin. "From a Community of Believers to an Islam of the Heart: 'Conspicuous' Symbols, Muslim Practices, and the Privatization of Religion in France." *Sociology of Religion* 68, no. 3 (2007): 305–320.

Knight, Frank. *Risk, Uncertainty, and Profit* (1921; repr.). Mineola, NY: Dover, 2006.

Kotkin, Stephen. *Magnetic Mountain: Stalinism as a Civilization.* Berkeley: University of California Press, 1995.

Kugelgen, Anke Von. *Legitimizatsiia sredneaziatskoi dinastii Mangytov v proizvedeniiakh ikh istorikov (XVIII-XIX vv.).* Almaty: Dayk-Press, 2004.

Kuran, Timur. "The Scale of Entrepreneurship in Middle Eastern History: Inhibitive Roles of Islamic Institutions." *ERID Working Paper No. 10.* Durham, NC: Duke University, 2008.

Kurkchiyan, Marina. "The Transformation of the Second Economy into the Informal Economy." In *Economic Crime in Russia,* edited by Alena Ledeneva and Marina Kurkchiyan, 83–98. London: Kluwer Law International, 2000.

Laidlaw, James. *Riches and Renunciation: Religion, Economy, and Society among the Jains.* Oxford: Clarendon Press, 1995.

Landau, Loren B., and Iriann Freemantle. "Tactical Cosmopolitanism and Idioms of Belonging: Insertion and Self-Exclusion in Johannesburg." *Journal of Ethnic and Migration Studies* 36, no. 3 (2010): 375–390.

Laqueur, Thomas W. *Religion and Respectability: Sunday School and Working Class Culture, 1780–1850.* New Haven, CT: Yale University Press, 1976.

Laruelle, Marlene, and Sebastien Peyrouse. *Globalizing Central Asia: Geopolitics and the Challenges of Economic Development.* Armonk, NY: M.E. Sharpe, 2013.

Laruelle, Marlene. "The Paradigm of Nationalism in Kyrgyzstan. Evolving Narrative, the Sovereignty Issue, and Political Agenda." *Communist and Post-Communist Studies* 45, no. 12 (2012): 39–49.

Laruelle, Marlene. "The Return of the Aryan Myth: Tajikistan in Search of a Secularized National Ideology." *Nationalities Papers* 35, no. 1 (2007): 51–70.

Laruelle, Marlene. "us New Silk Road." *Eurasian Geography and Economics* 56, no. 4 (2015): 360–375.

Laruelle, Marlene. *Russian Eurasianism: An Ideology of Empire.* Baltimore, MD: Johns Hopkins University Press, 2008.

Lecocq, Baz. "Tuareg City Blues: Cultural Capital in a Global Cosmopole." In *The Tuareg Society Within a Globalized World: Saharian Life in Transition,* edited by Anja Fischer and Ines Kohl, 41–58. London: Tauris Academic Studies, 2010.

Ledeneva, Alena V. *Can Russia Modernize? Sistema, Power Networks and Informal Governance.* Cambridge: Cambridge University Press, 2013.

Ledeneva, Alena V. *How Russia Really Works: Informal Practices in the 1990s.* Ithaca, NY: Cornell University Press, 2006.

Ledeneva, Alena V. *Russia's Economy of Favours: Blat, Networking, and Informal Exchange.* New York: Cambridge University Press, 1998.

Leezenberg, Michiel. "Power and Political Spirituality: Michel Foucault on the Islamic Revolution in Iran." In *Michel Foucault and Theology: The Politics of Religious Experience,* edited by James Bernauer and Jeremy Carrette, 99–115. Aldershot, UK: Ashgate, 2004.

Levi-Strauss, Claude. *The Elementary Structures of Kinship.* Boston: Beacon Press, 1971.

London, Perry, and Alissa Hirschfeld. "The Psychology of Identity Formation." In *Jewish Identity in America,* edited by David M. Gordis and Yoav Ben-Horin. Los Angeles: Wilstein Institute, 1991.

Louw, Maria Elisabeth. "Dreaming up Futures: Dream Omens and Magic in Bishkek." *History and Anthropology* 21, no. 3 (2010): 277–292.

Louw, Maria Elisabeth. "Even Honey May Become Bitter When There is Too Much of It: Islam and the Struggle for a Balanced Existence in Post-Soviet Kyrgyzstan." *Central Asian Survey* 32, no. 4 (2013): 514–526.

Louw, Maria Elisabeth. *Everyday Islam in Post-Soviet Central Asia.* New York: Routledge, 2007.

Louw, Maria. *Everyday Islam in Post-Soviet Central Asia.* London: Routledge, 2008.

Luong, Pauline Jones. *Institutional Change and Political Continuity in Post-Soviet Central Asia: Power, Perceptions, and Pacts.* New York: Cambridge University Press, 2012.

MacGaffey, Janet, and Rémy Bazenguissa-Ganga. *Congo-Paris: Transnational Traders on the Margins of the Law Transnational Traders on the Margins of the Law.* Bloomington: Indiana University Press, 2000.

MacLeod, Arlene Elowe. "Hegemonic Relations and Gender Resistance: The New Veiling as Accommodating Protest in Cairo." *Signs* 17, no. 3 (1992): 533–557.

Madaminzhanova, Zukhra, and Ildar Mukhtarov. "Cultural Life in the Ferghana Valley under Khrushchev and Brezhnev." In *Ferghana Valley: The Heart of Central Asia,* edited by S. Frederick Starr, et al., 164–177. Armonk, NY: M.E. Sharpe, 2011.

Malashenko, Alexei, and Alexei Starostin. "Islam na sovremennom Urale." Carnegie Center, Moscow,April 2015.

Malik, Bilal Ahmad. "Halal Banking in post-Soviet Central Asia: Antecedents and Consequences." *Marketing and Branding Research* 2 (2015): 28–43.

Maloney, William F. "Informality Revisited." *World Bank Economic Review* 32, no. 7 (2004): 1159–1178.

Mandaville, Peter. *Islam and Politics*. New York: Routledge, 2014.

Mandaville, Peter. *Transnational Muslim Politics: Reimagining the Umma*. London: Routledge, 2003.

Markova, Mariana. "Living Through the Fall of Communism: Life Narratives of the Last Soviet Generation." Ph.D. Dissertation, University of Washington, 2010.

Mars, Gerald, and Yochanan Altman. "The Cultural Bases of Soviet Georgia's Second Economy." *Europe-Asia Studies* 35, no. 4 (1983): 546–560.

Marsden, Magnus. "Crossing Eurasia: Trans-Regional Afghan Trading Networks in China and Beyond." *Central Asian Survey* 35, no. 1 (2016): 1–15.

Marsden, Magnus. *Trading Worlds: Afghan Merchants: Across Modern Frontiers*. London: Hurst, 2016.

Martin, Richard C., ed. *Encyclopedia of Islam and the Muslim World*. New York: Macmillan Reference, 2004.

Martin, Richard C., Mark R. Woodward, and Dwi S.Atmaja. *Defenders of Reason in Islam: Mu'Tazilizm from Medieval School to Modern Symbol*. London: Oneworld Publications, 1997.

Masanov, Nurbulat. "Mifologizatsiia problem etnogeneza kazakhskogo naroda i kazakhskoi nomadnoi kul'tury." In *Nauchnoe znanie i mifotvorchestvo v sovremennoi istoriografii Kazakhstana*, edited by Nurbulat Masanov, Zhulduzbek Abylkhozhin, and Irina Erofeeva, 52–131. Almaty: Dayk-Press, 2007.

Masov, Rahim. "Emomali Rahmon: "The Architect of Peace"." *Diplomatic World*, no. 36 (2012): 64–68.

Massell, Gregory J. *The Surrogate Proletariat: Moslem Women and Revolutionary Strategies in Soviet Central Asia, 1919–1929*. Princeton, NJ: Princeton University Press, 1974.

Mati, Hamamoto. "Tatarskaiia kargala in Russia's Eastern Policies." In *Asiatic Russia: Imperial Power in Regional and International Contexts,* edited by Uyama Tomohiko, 32–51. New York: Routledge, 2012.

McBrien, Julie. "Mukadas's Struggle: Veils and Modernity in Kyrgyzstan." *Journal of the Royal Anthropological Institute* 15, no. 1(2009): 127–144.

McGlinchey, Eric. "Islamic Revivalism and State Failure in Kyrgyzstan." *Problems of Post-Communism* 56, no. 3 (May/June 2009): 16–28.

McIntosh, John C., and Samia Islam. "Beyond the Influence of Islam on Female Entrepreneurship in a Conservative Muslim Context." *International Management Review* 6, no. 1 (2010): 103–110.

McMann, Kelly. *Economic Autonomy and Democracy: Hybrid Regimes in Russia and Kyrgyzstan.* New York: Cambridge University Press, 2006.

Meagher, Kate. "Culture Agency and Power: Theoretical Reflections on Informal Economic Networks and Political Process DIIS." *Working Paper No. 2009-27.* Copenhagen: Danish Institute for International Studies, 2009.

Meagher, Kate. "The Politics of Vulnerability: Exit, Voice, and Capture in Three Nigerian Informal Manufacturing Clusters." In *Africa's Informal Workers: Collective Agency, Alliances, and Transnational Organizing,* edited by Lindell Ilda, 46–64. London: Zed Books, 2010.

Meagher, Kate. "Trading on Faith: Religious Movements and Informal Economic Governance in Nigeria." *Journal of Modern African Studies* 47, no. 3 (2009): 397–423.

Meyer, James. *Turks across Empires: Marketing Muslim Identities in the Russian-Ottoman Borderlands, 1856-1956.* Oxford: Oxford University Press, 2014.

Michel, Patrick. *Politique et religion : la grande mutation.* Paris: Albin Michel, 1994.

Mirzoev, Abdullah, and Manja Stephan-Emmrich. "Crossing Economic and Cultural Boundaries: Tajik Middlemen in the Translocal 'Dubai Business' Sector." In *Mobilities, Boundaries, and Travelling Ideas: Rethinking Translocality Beyond Central Asia and the Caucasus,* edited by Manja Stephan-Emmrich and Philipp Schröder. Cambridge: Open Book Publishers, forthcoming.

Misrī, Kamol. "Ey islamogaroyon, ba mardumi xesh va digaron chī payome doda metavoned?!". *Najot,* January 24, 2013.

Montgomery, David W. "Islam beyond Democracy and State in Kyrgyzstan." In *Kyrgyzstan beyond "Democracy Island" and "Failing State": Social and Political Changes in a Post-Soviet Society,* edited by Marlene Laruelle and Johan Engvall, 229–242. Lanham, MD: Lexington Books, 2015.

Montgomery, David W. "Namaz, Wishing Trees, and Vodka: The Diversity of Everyday Religious Life in Central Asia." In *Everyday Life in Central Asia: Past and Present,* edited by Jeff Sahadeo and Russell Zanca, 355–370. Bloomington: Indiana University Press, 2007.

Montgomery, David W. "Towards a Theory of the Rough Ground: Merging the Policy and Ethnographic Frames of Religion in the Kyrgyz Republic." *Religion, State, and Society* 42, no. 1 (2014): 23–45.

Montgomery, David W. *The Transmission of Religious and Cultural Knowledge and Potentiality in Practice: An Anthropology of Social Navigation in the Kyrgyz Republic.* Ph.D. Dissertation. Boston University. Ann Arbor MI: ProQuest Information and Learning Company, 2007.

Moors, Annalies. "Fashionable Muslims: Notions of Self, Religion, and Society in San'a." *Fashion Theory* 11, no. 2–3 (2007): 319–346.

Morgan, Henry Lewis. *Systems of Consanguinity and Affinity of the Human Family* (1870; repr.). Charleston, SC: Nabu Press, 2012.

Morris, Jeremy, and Abel Polese. *The Informal Post-Socialist Economy: Embedded Practices and Livelihoods*. New York: Routledge, 2014.

Mostowlansky, Till. "The Road Not Taken: Enabling and Limiting Mobility in the Eastern Pamirs." *Internationales Asien Forum* 45, no. 1–2 (April 2014): 153–170.

Muhammad Orzu, ed. *40 soli Nahzat. Khotira, andesha, didgoh*. Dushanbe: Muattar, 2013.

Mukhina, Irina. "New Losses, New Opportunities: (Soviet) Women in the Shuttle Trade, 1987–1998." *Journal of Social History* 43, no. 2 (2009): 341–359.

Muldrew, Craig. *The Economy of Obligation*. London: Macmillan, 1998.

Muminov, Ashirbek. "Fundamentalist Challenges to Local Islamic Traditions in Soviet and Post-Soviet Central Asia." In *Empire, Islam, and Politics in Central Eurasia,* edited by Uyama Tomohiko, 249–261. Sapporo: Hokkaido University, Slavic Research Center, 2007.

Nabieva, Rohat, and Zikriyoev Foteh. *Ta'rikhi khalqi Tojik. Kitobi darsī baroi sinfi 11.* Dushanbe: Sobiriyon, 2006.

Nagy, Sharon. "Making Room for Migrants, Making Sense of Difference: Spatial and Ideological Expressions of Social Diversity in Urban Qatar." *Urban Studies* 43, no. 1 (2006): 119–137.

Nasritdinov, Emil, and Kevin O'Conner. *Regional Change in Kyrgyzstan: Bazaars, Cross-Border Trade and Social Networks*. Saarbrücken: Lambert Academic Publishing, 2010.

Naumkin, Vitaly V. *Radical Islam in Central Asia: Between Pen and Rifle*. Lanham, MD: Rowman & Littlefield, 2005.

Nazpary, Joma. *Post-Soviet Chaos: Violence and Dispossession in Kazakhstan*. London: Pluto Press, 2002.

Nezhad, Enjavi S.M., and M. Emami. "Changes in Legislation and Principles of Waqf to the New Creation." *Modares Human Sciences* 8, no. 3 (2004): 179-185.

Northrop, Douglas T. *Veiled Empire: Gender and Power in Stalinist Central Asia*. Ithaca, NY: Cornell University Press, 2004.

Northrop, Douglas. *Veiled Empire: Gender and Power in Stalinist Central Asia*. Ithaca, N.Y.: Cornell University Press, 2004.

Novikov, Vladimir I., ed. *Russkaia literatura XI–XVII vv*. Moscow: Olimp, 1998.

Nozimova, Shahnoza, and Tim Epkenhans. "Negotiating Islam in Emerging Public Spheres in Contemporary Tajikistan." *Asiatische Studien/Études Asiatiques* 67, no. 3 (2013): 965-990.

Nurulla-Hodjaeva, Nargis. "'Tantsuiushchie' kuptsy vne imperii na shelkovom puti." *Vestnik MGIMO-Universiteta* 1, no. 52 (2017): 119–139.

Olcott, Martha Brill. "The Roots of Radical Islam in Central Asia." Carnegie Endowment for International Peace, January 2007.

Olcott, Martha Brill. "Kazakhstan: Unfulfilled Promise." Carnegie Endowment for Peace, Washington, D.C., 2002.

Omelicheva, Mariya Y. "Islam in Kazakhstan: A Survey of Contemporary Trends and Sources of Securitization." *Central Asian Survey* 30, no. 2 (2011): 243–256.

Omelicheva, Mariya Y. "The Ethnic Dimension of Religious Extremism and Terrorism in Central Asia." *International Political Science Review* 31, no. 2 (2010): 167–186.

Osella, Caroline, and Filippo Osella. "Migration, Networks and Connectedness across the Indian Ocean." In *Migrant Labor in the Persian Gulf,* edited by Mehran Kamrava and Zahra Babar, 105–136. London: Hurst, 2012.

Osella, Filippo, and Caroline Osella. "'I am Gulf': The Production of Cosmopolitanism in Kozhikode, Kerala, India." In *Struggling with History: Islam and Cosmopolitanism in the Western Indian Ocean,* edited by Edward Simpson and Kai Kresse, 323–355. London: Hurst, 2007.

Osmonova, Kishimjan. "Experiencing Liminality: Housing, Renting, and Informal Tenants in Astana." *Central Asian Survey* 35, no. 2 (2016): 237–256.

Özcan, Gül Berna. *Building States and Markets. Entreprise Development in Central Asia.* New York: Palgrave-Macmillan, 2010.

Page, Benjamin, Larry Bartels, and James Seawright. "Democracy and the Policy Preferences of Wealthy Americans." *Perspectives on Politics* 11, no. 1 (2013): 51–73.

Parsa, Ali, and Ramin Keivani. "The Hormuz Corridor: Building a Cross-Border Region between Iran and the UAE." In *Global Networks, Linked Cities,* edited by Saskia Sassen, 183–207. New York: Routledge, 2002.

Pelican, Michaela. "Urban Lifeworlds of Cameroonian Migrants in Dubai." *Urban Anthropology* 43, no. 1–3 (2014): 255–309.

Pelkmans, Mathijs. "Asymmetries on the 'Religious Market' in Kyrgyzstan." In *The Postsocialist Religious Question: Faith and Power in Central Asia and East-Central Europe,* edited by Chris Hann, 29–46. Berlin: LIT Verlag, 2006.

Peres, Richard. *The Day Turkey Stood Still: Merve Kavakci's Walk into the Turkish Parliament.* Reading, UK: Garnet, 2012.

Peshkova, Svetlana. "A Post-Soviet Subject in Uzbekistan: Islam, Rights, Gender, and Other Desires." *Women's Studies* 42, no. 6 (2013): 667–695.

Peyrouse, Sebastien, and Gaël Raballand. "The New Silk Road Initiative's Questionable Economic Rationality." *Eurasian Geography and Economics* 56, no. 4 (2015): 405–420.

Peyrouse, Sebastien. "Islam in Central Asia: National Specificities and Post-Soviet Globalisation." *Religion, State and Society* 35, no. 3 (2007): 245–260.

Peyrouse, Sebastien. *Turkmenistan: Strategies of Power, Dilemmas of Development.* Armonk, NY: M.E. Sharpe, 2012.

Pohorila, N., and G. Korzhov. "Self-Identification in the Society of Crisis: A Case of Cross-Border Traders." *Naukovi zapiski Kievo-Mogilianskoi akademii* 19 (2001): 58–64.

Polese, Abel, Jeremy Morris, and Borbála Kovács. "Introduction: The Failure and Future of the Welfare State in Post-Socialism." *Journal of Eurasian Studies* 6, no. 1 (2015): 1–5.

Portes, Alejandro, and József Böröcz. "The Informal Sector under Capitalism and State Socialism: A Preliminary Comparison." *Social Justice* 15, no. 3–4 (Fall/Winter 1988): 17–28.

Privratsky, Bruce G. *Muslim Turkistan: Kazak Religion and Collective Memory.* London: Routledge, 2001.

Privratsky, Bruce G. *Muslim Turkistan: Kazak Religion and Collective Memory.* Richmond, UK: Curzon Press, 2001.

Privratsky, Bruce, ed. *Muslim Turkistan: Kazak Religion and Collective Memory.* New York: Curzon, 2001.

Pulleyblank, Edwin G. *The Background of the Rebellion of An Lu-Shan.* London: Oxford University Press, 1955.

Qayumzod, Abduqayum. "Xudo bo most, pirūzī niz." *Čaroġi rūz* 45 (1992): 24.

Radcliffe-Brown, Alfred Reginald. *The Andaman Islanders a Study in Social Anthropology* (1906; repr.). London: Forgotten Books, 2012.

Raeymaekers, Timothy, Ken Menkhaus, and Koen Vlassenroot. "State and Non-State Regulation in African Protracted Crises: Governance without Government?", *Africa Focus* 21, no. 2 (2008): 7–21.

Rahmon(ov), Emomalī. *Dar borai din.* Dushanbe: Sharqi ozod, 2006.

Rahmon(ov), Emomalī. *Istiqloliyati Tojikiston va Ehyoi millat.* Dushanbe: Irfon, 2008.

Rahnamo, Abdulloh. *Ulamoi Islomī dar Tojikiston.* Dushanbe: Irfon, 2009.

Rasanayagam, Johan. "I'm Not a Wahhabi: State Power and Muslim Orthodoxy in Uzbekistan." In *The Postsocialist Religious Question: Faith and Power in Central Asia and East-Central Europe,* edited by Chris Hann, 99–124. Munich: LIT Verlag, 2006.

Rasanayagam, Johan. "Informal Economy, Informal State: The Case of Uzbekistan." *International Journal of Sociology and Social Policy* 31, no. 11–12 (2011): 681–696.

Rasanayagam, Johan. *Islam in Post-Soviet Uzbekistan: The Morality of Experience.* New York: Cambridge University Press, 2010.

Rashid, Ahmed. "Islam in Central Asia: Afghanistan and Pakistan." In *Islam and Central Asia: An Enduring Legacy or an Evolving Threat?,* edited by Roald Sagdeev and Susan Eisenhower, 213–236. Washington, D.C.: Center for Political and Strategic Studies, 2000.

Rashid, Ahmed. *Jihad: The Rise of Militant Islam in Central Asia.* New Haven, CT: Yale University Press, 2002.

Reeves, Madeleine. "Clean Fake: Authenticating Documents and Persons in Migrant Moscow." *American Ethnologist* 40, no. 3 (2013): 508–524.

Reeves, Madeleine. "The Time of the Border: Contingency, Conflict, and Popular Statism at the Kyrgyzstan–Uzbekistan Border." In *Ethnographies of the State in Central Asia,* edited by Madeleine Reeves, Johan Rasanayagam, and Judith Beyer, 198–220. Bloomington: Indiana University Press, 2014.

Reeves, Madeleine. *Border Work: Spatial Lives of the State in Rural Central Asia*. Ithaca, NY: Cornell University Press, 2014.

Ro'I, Yaacov, and Alon Wainer. "Muslim Identity and Islamic Practice in Post-Soviet Central Asia." *Central Asian Survey* 28, no. 3 (September 2009): 303–322.

Ro'i, Yaacov. *Islam in the Soviet Union: From the Second World War to Gorbachev*. London: Hurst & Co., 2000.

Roberts, Sean R. "Everyday Negotiations of Islam in Central Asia: Practicing Religion in the Uyghur Neighborhood of Zarya Vostoka in Almaty, Kazakhstan." In *Everyday Life in Central Asia: Past and Present,* edited by Jeff Sahadeo and Russell Zanca, 339–354. Bloomington: Indiana University Press, 2007.

Roche, Sophie. *Domesticating Youth: Youth Bulges And Its Socio-Political Implications in Tajikistan*. New York: Berghahn Books, 2014.

Roitman, Janet. *Fiscal Disobedience: Anthropology of Economic Regulation in Central Africa*. Princeton, NJ: Princeton University Press, 2005.

Röschenthaler, Ute, and Dorothea Schulz. "Introduction. Forging Fortunes: New Perspectives on Entrepreneurial Activities in Africa." In *Cultural Entrepreneurship in Africa,* edited by Ute Röschenthaler and Dorothea Schulz, 1–15. New York, London: Routledge, 2016.

Rosenberger, Sieglinde, and Birgit Sauer, eds. *Politics, Religion, and Gender: Framing and Regulating the Veil*. New York: Routledge, 2011.

Round, John, Colin C. Williams, and Peter Rodgers. "Everyday Tactics and Spaces of Power: The Role of Informal Economies in Post-Soviet Ukraine." *Social & Cultural Geography* 9, no. 2 (2008): 171–185.

Roy, Olivier. *The New Central Asia. Geopolitics and the Birth of Nations*. London and New York: I.B. Tauris, 2007.

Roziq, Zubaydulloh. *HNIT dar masiri ta'rikh*. Dushanbe: Muattar, 2013.

Rudnyckyj, Daromir. "Market Islam in Indonesia." *Journal of the Royal Anthropological Institute*, 15 (2009): 183–201.

Ryan, Louise. "Muslim Women Negotiating Collective Stigmatization: 'We're Just Normal People'." *Sociology* 45, no. 6 (2011): 1045–1060.

Rywkin, Michael. *Moscow's Muslim Challenge*. Armonk, NY: M.E. Sharpe, 1982.

Sadouni, Samadia. "Playing Global: The Religious Adaptations of Indian and Somali Muslims to Racial Hierarchies and Discrimination in South Africa." *Global Networks* 14, no. 3 (2014): 383–400.

Sagdeev, Roald, and Susan Eisenhower, eds. *Islam and Central Asia: An Enduring Legacy or an Evolving Threat?* Washington, D.C.: Center for Political and Strategic Studies, 2000.

Saher, Tarek S., and M. Kabir Hassan. "A Comparative Literature Survey of Islamic Finance and Banking." *Financial Markets, Institutions, and Instruments* 10 no. 4 (2001): 155–199.

Salarzehi, Habibollah, Hamed Armesh, and Davoud Nikbin. "Waqf as a Social Entrepreneurship Model in Islam." *International Journal of Business and Management* 5, no. 7 (2010): 179–185.

Saleh, Walid A. "Word." In *Key Themes for the Study of Islam,* edited by Jamal J. Elias, 356–376. Oxford: Oneworld Publications, 2010.

Salhani, Claude. *Islam Without a Veil: Kazakhstan's Path of Moderation.* Washington, DC: Potomac Books, 2011.

Salmorbekova, Zumrat, and Galina Yemelianova. "Islam and Islamism in the Ferghana valley." In *Radical Islam in the Former Soviet Union,* edited by Galina Yemelianova, 211–243. London: Routledge, 2010.

Saroyan, Mary. "Rethinking Islam in the Soviet Union." In *Beyond Sovietology: Essays in Politics and History,* edited by Susan Gross Solomon, 23–52. Armonk, NY: M.E. Sharpe, 1993.

Satoru, Kimura. "Sunni-Shi'i Relations in the Russian Protectorate of Bukhara, as Perceived by the Local 'Ulama'." In *Asiatic Russia: Imperial Power in Regional and International Contexts,* edited by Uyama Tomohiko, 189–215. New York: Routledge, 2012.

Sattorī, Qiyomiddin, ed. *HNIT—Zodai ormoni mardum.* Dushanbe: ShKOS, 2003.

Schielke, Samuli. "Engaging the World on the Alexandria Waterfront." In *The Global Horizon: Expectations of Migration in Africa and the Middle East,* edited by Knut Graw and Samuli Schielke, 175–192. Leuven: Leuven University Press, 2012.

Schimmelpennick, David. *Russian Orientalism: Asia in the Russian Mind from Peter the Great to the Emigration.* New Haven, CT: Yale University Press, 2010.

Schmidt, Patrick. "Law in the Age of Governance: Regulation, Networks and Lawyers." In *The Politics of Regulation: Institutions and Regulatory Reforms for the Age of Governance,* edited by Jacint Jordana and David Levi-Faur, 273–295. Cheltenham, UK: Edward Elgar, 2004.

Schmidtz, Andrea, and Alexander Wolters. "Political Protest in Central Asia: Potentials and Dynamics." *SWP Research Paper No. 7.* German Institute for International and Security Affairs, Berlin, 2012.

Schumpeter, Joseph. *The Theory of Economic Development* (1912; repr.). Cambridge, MA: Harvard University Press, 1934.

Schwab, Wendell, and Ulan Bigozhin, "Shrines and Neopatrimonialism in Kazakhstan." In *Kazakhstan in the Making: Legitimacy, Symbols, and Social Changes*, edited by M. Laruelle, 89-110. Lanham, MD: Rowman and Littlefield, 2016.

Schwab, Wendell. "Establishing an Islamic Niche in Kazakhstan: Musylman Publishing House and Its Publications." *Central Asian Survey* 30, no. 2 (2011): 227–242.

Schwab, Wendell. "How to Pray in Kazakhstan: The Fortress of the Muslim and Its Readers." *Anthropology of East Europe Review* 32, no. 1 (2014): 22–42.

Schwab, Wendell. "Islam, Fun, and Social Capital in Kazakhstan." *Central Asian Affairs* 2, no.1 (2015): 51–70.

Schwab, Wendell. "Traditions and Texts: How Two Young Women Learned to Interpret the Qur'an and Hadiths in Kazakhstan." *Contemporary Islam* 6, no. 2 (2012): 173–197.

Sengupta, Chandan. "Dynamics of Community Environmental Management in Howrah Slums." *Economic and Political Weekly* 34, no. 21 (1999): 1292–1296.

Sergeev, Evgeny. *The Great Game, 1856–1907: Russo–British Relations in Central and East Asia.* Baltimore, MD: John Hopkins University Press, 2013.

Shahrani, Nazif M. "Islam and the Political Culture of 'Scientific Atheism' in Post-Soviet Central Asia: Future Predicament." *Islamic Studies* 33, no. 2–3 (1994): 139–159.

Shahrani, Nazif M. "Local Knowledge of Islam and Social Discourse in Afghanistan and Turkistan in the Modern Period." In *Turko-Persia in Historical-Perspective,* edited by Robert L. Canfield, 161–188. Cambridge: Cambridge University Press, 1991.

Shlymova, Gulnar E., ed. *Protestantizm: istoriia, napravleniia i kazakhstanskie realii.* Astana: RGU, 2012.

Sinor, Denis. *Inner Asia: History, Civilization, Languages: A Syllabus.* Bloomington: Indiana University Press, 1969.

Smith, Graham, Vivien Law, Andrew Wilson, Annette Bohr, and Edward Allworth. *Nation-Building in the Post-Soviet Borderlands: The Politics of National Identities.* New York: Cambridge University Press, 1998.

Soucek, Svat. *A History of Inner Asia.* Cambridge: Cambridge University Press, 2000.

Spector, Regine A. "Securing Property in Contemporary Kyrgyzstan." *Post-Soviet Affairs* 24, no. 2 (2008): 149-176.

Spehr, Scott, and Nargis Kassanova. "Kazakhstan: Constructing Identity in a Post-Soviet Society." *Asian Ethnicity* 13, no. 2 (2012): 135–151.

Stephan-Emmrich, Manja, and Abdullah Mirzoev. "The Manufacturing of Islamic Lifestyles in Tajikistan through the Prism of Dushanbe's Bazaars." *Central Asian Survey* 35, no. 2 (2016): 157–177.

Stephan, Manja. "Education, Youth and Islam: The Growing Popularity of Private Religious Lessons in Dushanbe, Tajikistan." *Central Asian Survey* 29, no. 4 (2010): 469–483.

Stephan, Manja. *Das Bedürfnis nach Ausgewogenheit Moralerziehung, Islam und Muslimsein in Tadschikistan zwischen Säkularisierung und religiöser Rückbesinnung.* Würzburg: Ergon Verlag, 2010.

Sultanova, Razia. *From Shamanism to Sufism: Women, Islam, and Culture in Central Asia.* London: I.B. Tauris, 2014.

Tadjbakhsh, Shahrbanou. "Between Lenin and Allah: Women and Ideology in Tajikistan." in *Women in Muslim Societies: Diversity within Unity,* edited by Herbert L. Bodman and Nayereh Tohidi, 163–186. Boulder, CO: Lynne Rienner, 1998.

Talhami, Ghada Hashem. *The Mobilization of Muslim Women in Egypt.* Gainesville: University Press of Florida, 1996.

Tanzi, Vito. "Underground Economy and Tax Evasion in the United States: Estimates and Implication." *Banca Nazionale del Lavoro Quarterly Review* 32 (1980): 427–453.

Tarlo, Emma. *Visibly Muslim: Fashion, Politics, Faith.* New York: Berg, 2010.

Tasar, Eren Murat. "Soviet and Muslim: The Institutionalization of Islam in Central Asia, 1943–1991." Ph.D. Dissertation, Harvard University, 2010.

Tazmini, Ghoncheh. "The Islamic Revival in Central Asia: A Potent Force or a Misconception?". *Central Asian Survey* 20, no. 1 (2001): 63–83.

Tett, Gillian. "'Guardians of the Faith?': Gender and Religion in an (ex) Soviet Tajik village." In *Muslim Women's Choices: Religious Belief and Social Reality*, edited by Camillia Fawzi El-Solh and Judy Mabro, 160–190. Providence, R.I.: Berg; (New York): Distributed in North America by New York University Press, 1994.

"The World's Muslims: Unity and Diversity." *Pew Forum on Religion and Public Life.* Washington D.C.: Pew Research Center, September 8, 2012.

Thibault, Helene. "Religious Revival in Tajikistan: The Soviet Legacy Revisited." Ph.D. Dissertation, University of Ottawa, 2014.

Tilly, Charles, ed. *Trust and Rule.* New York: Cambridge University Press, 2005.

Tilly, Charles. "Trust and Rule." *Theory and Society* 33, no. 1 (2004): 1–30.

Tokman, Viktor E., ed. *Beyond Regulation: The Informal Sector in Latin America.* Boulder, CO: Lynne Rienner, 1992.

Tomohiko, Uyama, ed. *Asiatic Russia: Imperial Power in Regional and International Contexts.* New York: Routledge, 2012.

Topal, Semiha. "Everybody Wants Secularism—But Which One? Contesting Definitions of Secularism in Contemporary Turkey." *International Journal of Politics, Culture, and Society* 25, no. 1/3 (2012): 1–14.

Treml, Vladimir G., and Michael V. Alexeev. "The Growth of the Second Economy in the Soviet Union and its Impact on the System." In *The Postcommunist Economic Transformation,* edited by Robert W. Campbell, 221–248. Boulder, CO: Westview Press, 1994.

Tromble, Rebekah. "Securitising Islam, securitising ethnicity: the discourse of Uzbek radicalism in Kyrgyzstan." *East European Politics* 30, no. 4 (2014): 526–547.

Tucker, Noah. "Domestic Shapers of Eurasia's Islamic Futures: Sheikh, Scholar, Society, and the State." In *Islam in Eurasia: A Policy Volume,* edited by Thomas W. Simons, Jr., 43-76. Cambridge, MA: Davis Center for Russian and Eurasian Studies, 2015.

Tucker, Noah. "Hayrullo Hamidov and Uzbekistan's Culture Wars: How Soccer, Poetry, and Pop-Religion Are 'A Danger to Society'," *Uzbekistan Initiative Papers No. 6*, February 2014.

Tucker, Noah. "Public and State Responses to ISIS Messaging: Tajikistan." *Central Asia Program paper No. 11*.George Washington University, Washington, D.C., 2016.

Turaeva, Rano. "Mobile Entrepreneurs in Post-Soviet Central Asia: Micro-orders of *Tirikchilik*." *Communist and Post-Communist Studies* 47, no. 1 (2014): 105–114.

Turaeva, Rano. "Post-Soviet Uncertainties: Micro-orders of Central Asian Migrants in Russia." *Inner Asia* 15, no. 2 (2013): 273–292.

Turaeva, Rano. *Migration and Identity: The Uzbek Experience.* New York: Routledge, 2016.

Tŭrağonzoda, Hojī Akbar. *Miyoni obu otash...* Dushanbe, 1998.

Tŭrajonzoda, Hojī Akbar. *Shariat va jomea.* Dushanbe: Nodir, 2006.

Vakulenko, Anastasia. *Islamic Veiling in Legal Discourse.* New York: Routledge, 2012.

Vertovec, Steven. "Cosmopolitanism." In *Diasporas: Concepts, Intersections, Identities,* edited by Kim Knott and Sean McLoughlin, 63–68. London: Zed Books, 2010.

Vogel, Frank, and Samuel L. Hayes, eds. *Islamic Law and Finance: Religion, Risk, and Return.* London: Kluwer Law International, 1998.

Vora, Neha, and Nathalie Koch, "Everyday Inclusions: Rethinking Ethnocracy, *Kafala*, and Belonging in the Arabian Peninsula." *Studies in Ethnicity and Nationalism* 15, no. 3 (2015): 540–552.

Vora, Neha. *Impossible Citizens. Dibai's Indian Diaspora.* Durham and London: Duke University Press, 2013.

Vulpius, Richard. "The Russian Empire's Civilizing Mission in the Eighteenth Century: A Comparative Perspective." In *Asiatic Russia: Imperial Power in Regional and International Contexts,* edited by Uyama Tomohiko, 13–31. New York: Routledge, 2012.

Weber, Max, ed. *The Protestant Ethic and the Spirit of Capitalism.* New York: Allen and Unwin, 1930.

Werbner, Pnina, ed. *Anthropology and the New Cosmopolitanism: Rooted, Feminist, and Vernacular Perspectives.* New York: Berg, 2008.

Wetter, Frederike, and David Smallbone. "Women's Entrepreneurship from an Institutional Perspective: The Case of Uzbekistan." *International Entrepreneurship Management Journal* 4 (2008): 505–520.

White, Jenny. *Muslim Nationalism and the New Turks.* Princeton, NJ: Princeton University Press, 2014.

Wickham, Carrie Rosefsky. *Mobilizing Islam: Religion, Activism and Political Change in Egypt.* New York: Columbia University Press, 2002.

Williams, John A. "Return to the Veil in Egypt." *Middle East Review* 11, no. 3 (1979): 49–54.

Wilson, Andrew. *Virtual Politics: Faking Democracy in the Post-Soviet World.* New Haven, CT: Yale University Press, 2005.

Winter, Bronwyn. *Hijab and the Republic: Uncovering the French Headscarf Debate.* Syracuse, NY: Syracuse University Press, 2009.

Wolters, Alexander. "Islamic Finance in the States of Central Asia: Strategies, Institutions, First Experiences." *Research Paper Series No. 1*, PFH Göttingen, 2013.

Wolters, Alexander. "Zwischen Scharia und der Suche nach frischem Kapital. Über die Einführung des islamischen Bankwesens in Kasachstan und Kirgistan." *Zentralasienanalysen* 63 (2013): 2–5.

Wolters, Alexander. *Die Politik der Peripherie: Protest und Öffentlichkeit in der Republik Kyrgyzstan.* Bielefeld: Transcript-Verlag, 2015.

Wright, Robin. "The Pink Hijab." *Wilson Quarterly* 35, no. 3 (2011): 47–51.

Yavuz, M. Hakan. "Turkish Identity Politics and Central Asia." In *Islam and Central Asia: An Enduring Legacy or an Evolving Threat?*, edited by Roald Sagdeev and Susan Eisenhower, 193–211. Washington, D.C.: Center for Political and Strategic Studies, 2000.

Yemelianova, Galina M. "Islam and Power." In *Islam in Post-Soviet Russia: Public and Private Faces,* edited by Hilary Pilkington and Galina Yemelianova, 61–116. London, New York: RoutledgeCurzon, 2003.

Yemelianova, Galina M. "Islam, National Identity, and Politics in Contemporary Kazakhstan." *Asian Ethnicity* 15, no. 3 (2016): 286–301.

Yemelianova, Galina M. "The National Identity of the Volga Tatars at the Turn of the 19th Century: Tatarism, Turkism, and Islam." *Central Asian Survey* 16, no. 4 (1997): 543–572.

Yemelianova, Galina M. *Russia and Islam: A Historical Survey.* London: Palgrave, 2002.

Yemelianova, Galina M., ed. *Radical Islam in the Former Soviet Union.* London: Routledge, 2010.

Yurchak, Alexei. *Everything was Forever, Until It Was No More: The Last Soviet Generation.* Princeton, NJ: Princeton University Press, 2006.

Zainiddinov, Hakim. "The Changing Relationship of the Secularized State to Religion in Tajikistan." *Journal of Church and State* 55, no. 3 (2013): 456–477.

Zanca, Russell. "Believing in God at Your Own Risk: Religion and Terrorism in Uzbekistan." *Religion, State, and Society* 33, no. 1 (2005): 71–82.

Ziyaeva, Diora. "Changing Identities among Uzbek Youth: Transition from Regional to Socioeconomic Identities." National Bureau of Asian Research (NBR), Seattle, WA, June 2006.

Zuhur, Sherifa. *Revealing Reveiling: Islamist Gender Ideology in Contemporary Egypt.* Albany: SUNY Press, 1992.

Index

Printed in the United States
By Bookmasters